RADICAL HERMENEUTICS

Repetition, Deconstruction, and the Hermeneutic Project

JOHN D. CAPUTO

INDIANA
UNIVERSITY
PRESS

Bloomington and Indianapolis

Manufactured in the United States of America

Library of Congress Cataloging-in-Publication Data

Radical hermeneutics.
(Studies in phenomenology and existential philosophy)
Bibliography: p.
Includes index.
1. Hermeneutics. 2. Deconstruction. I. Title.
II. Series.
BD241.C34 1987   121'.68   86-46143
ISBN 0-253-34785-8
ISBN 0-253-20442-9 (pbk.)
2 3 4 5 91 90 89 88

To David,
Shining,
Exuberant
First Born

CONTENTS

Contents

Part Three
The Hermeneutic Project

Acknowledgments

I wish to thank the publishers of the following journals for permission to use parts of earlier articles of mine in the present work: Martinus Nijhoff for permission to use parts of "Husserl, Heidegger, and the Question of a Hermeneutic Phenomenology," *Husserl Studies*, 1 (1984), 157–78, and "Hermeneutics as the Recovery of Man," *Man and World*, 15 (1982), 343–67; Wolfe Mays for permission to use parts of "Cold Hermeneutics: Heidegger and Derrida," *Journal of the British Society for Phenomenology*, 17 (1986), 252–74; The Journal of Philosophy, Inc. for permission to use parts of "Telling Left from Right: Hermeneutics, Deconstruction, and the Work of Art," *The Journal of Philosophy*, 83 (1986), 678–85; the University of Chicago for permission to use parts of "From Uselessness to Full Employment: The Economy of Signs in Husserl and Derrida," in *Deconstruction and Philosophy*, ed. John Sallis (Chicago: University of Chicago Press, 1987); and Robert Whittemore for permission to use parts of "'Supposing Truth to be a woman . . .': Heidegger, Nietzsche, Derrida," *Tulane Studies in Philosophy*, 23 (1984), 15–22.

I am very happy to acknowledge the support I received from the American Council of Learned Societies for a fellowship (in 1983–84) and from the National Endowment for the Humanities for a 1985 summer stipend. I am profoundly indebted to Villanova University for its generous support: a 1981 sabbatical, a 1982 summer grant, and supplementary support during the tenure of my ACLS and NEH grants. In particular, Dr. Bernard Downey, dean of the Graduate School, Rev. Lawrence Gallen, O.S.A., vice-president of academic affairs, and Rev. John O'Malley, formerly dean of the College of Arts and Sciences, have been particularly supportive of my work.

I am grateful to Janet Rabinowitch, senior sponsoring editor at Indiana University Press, and to John Sallis, Schmitt Professor of Philosophy at Loyola University of Chicago, for their interest in this work.

My colleagues and graduate students at Villanova, and the members of the Philadelphia Consortium under the leadership of Joseph Margolis, have listened to and criticized many versions of these ideas over the past few years, from which I have profited considerably. Finally, I am deeply grateful to my wife, Kathy, not only for her patience with my work, which has too often taken me away from home, but also for the design and illustration of the jacket of this book.

RADICAL
HERMENEUTICS

INTRODUCTION

Restoring Life to Its Original Difficulty

We have it from Aristotle himself that life is hard. There are many ways to miss the mark of virtue, he said, but only one way to hit it, and so the former is easy but the latter is difficult (*Nic. Ethics* 1106 b 28ff.). "Factical life," the young Heidegger comments, seeks the easy way out; it tends to make things easy for itself (*Erleichterung*, GA 61 108-10).[1] Thus, philosophy for the young thinker must become a "hermeneutics of facticity" (SZ 72, n.1/BT 490 n.i),[2] by which he meant a reading of life which catches life at its game of taking flight and thereby restores factical existence to its original difficulty. This hermeneutics of facticity then will follow the opposite course of "metaphysics" which, ever since its inception, and in accord with the inclination inscribed in factical life itself, has been making light of the difficulty in existence. Metaphysics, to use Derrida's felicitous phrase, has all along been a metaphysics of presence. From the start, it has been giving us eloquent assurances about Being and presence even as factical existence was being tossed about by *physis* and *kinesis*. Metaphysics has been trying to sell us the same bill of goods, the same *ousia*, ever since it opened for business. But a hermeneutics of facticity, convinced that life is toil and trouble *(Sorge)*, would keep a watchful eye for the ruptures and the breaks and the irregularities in existence. This new hermeneutics would try not to make things look easy, to put the best face on existence, but rather to recapture the hardness of life before metaphysics showed us a fast way out the back door of the flux.

That is the notion of hermeneutics with which I wish to begin: hermeneutics as an attempt to stick with the original difficulty of life, and not to betray it with metaphysics. It was just such a hermeneutic energy that irrupted with a fury in *Being and Time* and the radical questioning which that work initiated. Philosophy must begin by putting Being as presence in question—and by holding it there. For we have been through this before. Metaphysics always makes a show of beginning with questions, but no sooner do things begin to waver a bit and look uncertain than the question is foreclosed. The disruptive force of the question is contained; the opening it created is closed; the wavering is stilled. But Heidegger wanted to try something new, something revolutionary (even unacademic, for it undermined the magisterial mode of the professor): to raise

1

the question of Being as presence and let it hang there and to resist the temptation to cut it down when it starts to look a little blue. He unleashed a radical force in *Being and Time*, a deeply critical power which was intent on keeping the question of Being open, on letting Being as presence begin to tremble so that the whole would shake *(sollicitare)* and give way to movement *(kinesis)*. In *Being and Time*, the hermeneutics of facticity assumed the dimensions of a deconstruction of the metaphysics of presence and of a new raising of the question of Being; it had come to mean restoring the original difficulty in Being.

And that, it turns out, is what was going on in the young Heidegger's startling rereading of Aristotle: to read the *Nichomachean Ethics* as a story about factical life and its difficulties and the *Metaphysics* in such a way as to read the *kinesis* back into *ousia*, to read *ousia* back down into its kinetic components, to deconstruct *(ab-bauen)* it down to *(auf)*, the turbulence that meta-physics was trying to smooth over, still, arrest.[3] And he saw Aristotle as doing both these things at once, so that Aristotle is at odds with himself. All his life Heidegger would try to do just that one thing, to keep Being as presence in question. And that meant to resist the inclination to make things easy, to treat Being as the stable stuff and fullness of presence which the metaphysicians were trying to make it out to be.

But that project evokes another scene—of Johannes Climacus sitting in the Frederiksberg Garden of a Sunday afternoon, puffing on a cigar, and mulling over the fact that all over Europe thinkers were making things easier, writing compendia to explain the System, giving clear summaries of Hegel's metaphysics. So Johannes conceives the idea that his life's task must be to make things difficult. There is nothing else to do—the other thing, the *Erleichterung*, taking the easy way out, is already under way, is almost complete, will be finished in just a few weeks. And so Johannes Climacus and the other Kierkegaardian pseudonyms—Constantin Constantius is the most important for me—clearly belong to this hermeneutic undertaking, to the great project of hermeneutic trouble-making.

In *Repetition* (1843), Constantin begins by posing a Heraclitean problem of how the existing individual is to make his way in time and the flux. One solution, he says, is frankly to acknowledge that the individual has no business in the flux and, after making one's excuses, to make a quick exit. That is the Greek theory of recollection. Christianity, on the other hand, summons up the nerve metaphysics has lost. Taking time and the flux as its element, it puts its hand to the plow of existence and pushes ahead—for eternity lies ahead, not behind—to create for itself such identity as life allows. That is what Constantin calls "repetition." Recollection is a backwards movement (because the Greeks think we have lost eternity and have to regain it), while repetition moves forward (because Christianity thinks we have been put into this life to see if we have the mettle to earn eternity). The only exception to this, Constantin allows, is Aristotle, who had a theory of *kinesis*. Repetition thus is not the repetition of the same, Greek re-production, but a creative production which pushes ahead, which produces *as* it repeats, which produces *what* it repeats, which makes a life for itself in the midst of the difficulties of the flux.

Hermeneutics thus is for the hardy. It is a radical thinking which is suspicious of the easy way out, which is especially suspicious that philosophy, which is meta-physics, is always doing just that. For even when it makes a lot of noise about motion (Hegel), all that philosophy ever comes up with is a noiseless shuffle of concepts, like a mime moving in place and never taking a single step forward. Hermeneutics wants to describe the fix we are in, and it tries to be hard-hearted and to work "from below." It makes no claim to have won a transcendental high ground or to have a heavenly informer. It does not try to situate itself above the flux or to seek a way out of *physis*, which is what the fateful "meta-" in meta-physics always amounts to, but rather, like Constantin, to get up the nerve to stay with it.

Hermeneutics starts out in Heidegger as radical thinking, and it is the process of its radicalization that I want to pursue in the pages that follow. I do not approach hermeneutics in the usual way, by following its historical genesis from Schleiermacher and Dilthey; that has already been done well and elsewhere.[4] I am concerned here not with its historical genesis but with its radicalization, not with where it came from but with its innermost direction and momentum. That is why the protohistory of hermeneutics for me is to be found in radical thinkers like Kierkegaard and Husserl, Nietzsche and Meister Eckhart, and why its late history has to do with the late Heidegger—who drops the term from his vocabulary and criticizes hermeneutic phenomenology—and Derrida, who is an outspoken critic of hermeneutics. For hermeneutics always has to do with keeping the difficulty of life alive and with keeping its distance from the easy assurances of metaphysics and the consolations of philosophy. What I call here "radical hermeneutics" pushes itself to the brink and writes philosophy from the edge, which is why it sometimes speaks of the "end of philosophy." For it does not trust philosophy's native desire for the *Erleichterung*, its desire for presence, and it will not entrust movement and the flux to the care of philosophy, just as Constantin and Johannes Climacus did not.

But I also number Husserl among these radical thinkers and protoher-meneuts. I regard Husserl as an important philosopher of the flux, even though he is worlds removed from thinkers like Kierkegaard and Nietzsche. I read Husserl too with Constantin's question in mind, whether anything can survive the flux, i.e., whether and how it is possible to build up unities of meaning and stable objects in and through the flow of time. If Kierkegaard addressed the question of the constitution of the self in the flux, Husserl raised the question of the constitution of meaning and objectivity. Husserlian constitution is the epistemic parallel to existential repetition, a repetition which pushes forward and produces what it repeats. Husserl understood as well as anyone that we have to do with contingent unities of meaning, with constituted products, that nothing has dropped from the sky. For Husserl everything rises slowly from below, is formed and reformed, and remains subject always to discreditation, to what he called, in an uncanny experiment, the possibility of the destruction of the world. The one "thing" which alone resists this destruction is no thing at all but the pure flux of internal time.

Radical hermeneutics turns on that gesture, on some version or other of a hermeneutic epoché which questions the authority of whatever calls itself "present," which denies whatever is "given" metaphysical prestige, for presence is constituted. This is not to say that Husserl did not close off with one hand what he opened up with another, that he did not do his best to bury his revolutionary side under the most traditional metaphysics of subjectivity and transcendental reflection. But Derrida better than anyone has shown us the ambiguity of this text and unearthed the radical, more deconstructive side of Husserl which we enlist in our support in the project of a radical hermeneutics.

With the mention of Derrida we touch upon the turning point in this study. For Derrida—along with a few other Parisian philosophers—is exceedingly good at throwing difficulties in the path of metaphysics, at blocking off the superhighway that metaphysics seeks to build across the flux, at disturbing the consolations of philosophy. In the view which is defended in these pages, Derrida does not overthrow hermeneutics but drives it into its most extreme and radical formulation, pushes it to its limits. Heidegger was the first to put the question of Being as presence to the whole tradition, from Anaximander to Husserl. But Derrida, situating himself within the opening created by Heidegger's questioning of presence, pressed the issue even harder, making the difficulty of life even more difficult. Derrida shows that presence is the "effect" of a process of repetition, that re-presentation precedes and makes possible the very presence it is supposed to reproduce, that repetition is "older" than what it repeats, and that this is what Husserl himself says. Derrida makes it plain that Husserl belongs to this project of restoring the difficulty of things, even though he also tends systematically to repress what he has discovered.

But then things take a surprising and uncomfortable turn, for we were all comfortable criticizing Husserl's Cartesianism. Now the force of the Derridean critique is turned on the father himself, on Heidegger, on the analysis of "authenticity," on the "truth of Being," on "hermeneutics" itself. Derrida brings the whole weight of the critique of presence to bear on the fundamental words in Heidegger's vocabulary. He brings into question the very terms by which Heidegger himself tried to make metaphysics tremble, so that Heidegger too is made to waver. He shows that Heidegger's critique of the metaphysics of presence is itself filled with monuments to presence: *Eigentlichkeit* and

Ereignis turn on the metaphysics of the proper, *aletheia* on the metaphysics of truth, and the whole "onto-hermeneutic" project turns on a Platonic gesture of "retrieving" the "originary truth" of Being prior to its "fall" into metaphysics—more Greek recollection. Whence for Derrida the critique of presence pushes us beyond the Heideggerian hermeneutic of Being into the forbidding regions of *différance*, where things really get difficult.

Still, from the point of a radical hermeneutics, that is all part of the way, part of keeping the question of Being as presence under way, which, as the final page of *Being and Time* tells us, is the one thing essential in the book. The essential thing is the opening it creates, not the resolution. Derrida's critique of onto-hermeneutics belongs to the hermeneutic project more radically conceived. He does not undo Husserl; he unfetters him. He does not undo hermeneutics; he releases its more radical tendencies. Or rather, deconstruction is an "un-doing," a kind of *Ab-bauen*, which does not raze but releases and which is ready for what is difficult, indeed ready for the worst. Deconstruction trains its sights on the insinuations of presence wherever they appear, even in radical thinkers like Husserl and Heidegger, and it is able to show the *différance* by which things are inhabited. With deconstruction, hermeneutics loses its innocence and in so doing becomes even more faithful to the appointed way, which, as the young Heidegger said, means to remain faithful to the difficulty in life. *Différance* is very good at making things difficult. It puts in the place of the solemnities of Heideggerian hermeneutics a nontheological, nonrabbinic, more freewheeling, impious, poetic kind of reading; and in the place of Heidegger's Greco-Germanic poets it puts Artaud and Bataille, James Joyce and Mallarmé.

Derrida is the turning point for radical hermeneutics, the point where hermeneutics is pushed to the brink. Radical hermeneutics situates itself in the space which is opened up by the exchange between Heidegger and Derrida, an exchange which generates another and more radical reading of Heidegger and another, more hermeneutic reading of Derrida. It lets Derrida whisper in Heidegger's ear and then switches their roles and puts Derrida in the writer's chair, letting Heidegger whisper in Derrida's ear. "Radical hermeneutics" operates a shuttle between Paris and the Black Forest, a delivery service whose function is not to insure an accurate and faithful delivery of messages, like a good metaphysical postmaster (it has its doubts about masters of the post and masters of any other sort). Rather, it engages in a creative rereading of the postcards each sends the other, in a repetition that produces something new.

That also explains why Gadamer (and *a fortiori* Ricoeur) plays only a second-ary role and has but a minor voice in the following study. From the point of view of radical hermeneutics, Gadamer's "philosophical hermeneutics" is a reaction-ary gesture, an attempt to block off the radicalization of hermeneutics and to turn it back to the fold of metaphysics. Gadamer pursues a more comforting doctrine of the fusion of horizons, the wedding of the epochs, the perpetuation of the life of the tradition which sees in Heidegger only a philosophy of appropriation and which cuts off Heidegger's self-criticism in midstream. For Gadamer the matter to be thought is the fundamental content of the metaphysical tradition—the notions of dialogue in Plato, *phronesis* in Aristotle, dialectic in Hegel—all of which are put to work in a metaphysical effort to preserve and cultivate the truth of the tradition which is closer to Hegel than Heidegger. Even though it contains a useful critique of "method," the question of "truth" in *Truth and Method* remains within the metaphysics of truth. Constantin warned us about those friends of the flux who make a lot of noise about becoming, when what they have up their sleeve all along is the noiseless hush of *Aufhebung*.

The "hermeneutics" in *Radical Hermeneutics* is to be traced back to the project Heidegger announced in the twenties of a hermeneutics of facticity, which means the hermeneutics that writes from below, that renounces *Erleichterung*, and that wants to describe the irregularities and differences by which we are inhabited. In earlier drafts I thought of entitling this book "Hermeneutics as the Recovery of Man,"[5] but I soon abandoned that, for "recovery" suggests "recollection" and "man" suggests both sexism and humanism. But I never gave up on the word "hermeneutics," which ever since Heidegger has meant a critique of the hollow assurances and tranquilizing powers of the metaphysics of presence and which by that fact "restores" the difficulty of things. This hermeneutics exposes us to the ruptures and gaps, let us say, the textuality and difference, which inhabits everything we think, and do, and hope for. I want to show, however, that what I call here radical hermeneutics is not an exercise in nihilism, which wants to reduce human practices and institutions to rubble, but an attempt to face up to the bad news metaphysics has been keeping under cover, to the fact that Hermes is also a well-known trickster and liar. All of this is, I claim, hermeneutic work. For it describes the fix we are in, what in a more innocent day we might have called the "human condition." It provides an approach to the question of human existence that does not fall through the trap door of subjectivism and humanism. It opens us up to the question which we "are," as Augustine wrote some time ago ("quaestio mihi factus sum"). It gives us a chance to rewrite "*Eigentlichkeit*" as a work of "owning up" to the fix we are in, and if it is insisted that we can never do that, then owning up to that, too. It clears some of the smoke metaphysics has been sending up for over two millennia, ever since Plato took it upon himself to answer all of Socrates' questions, whereas the hermeneutic point was to keep them open, to let them waver and tremble a bit. Socrates was a master at making things difficult. He produced a wonderful hermeneutic disturbance—until Athens swatted him out, which is often the fate visited upon radical hermeneuts.

The book which follows has three parts. In part 1, I tell the story of the radical tendencies that feed into and culminate in *Being and Time*. As I said, this is not the usual story which begins with Schleiermacher but a story that grinds a philosophical axe about writing from below and making things difficult. That is why I start things off by turning to Kierkegaardian repetition and Husserlian constitution, which, I hope to show, are fused in a remarkable and original way in *Being and Time*. The latter has already become a "classical" text for contemporary philosophers and represents the central document in the development of hermeneutics in this century.

In Part 2, I take up the deconstructive critique of hermeneutics issuing from Derrida, which I treat as firing the steel of hermeneutics, "radicalizing" it, making it ready for the worst. I am interested first in how the Derridean critique releases the Husserlian text and then how it sets Heidegger's text into a motion of which it did not know itself to be capable, and thus allows the formulation of what I call here a "cold" or "radical" hermeneutic.

Finally, in Part 3, I am interested in showing that pursuing such radical intentions does not abandon us to the wolves of irrationality, moral license, and despair and does not succumb to nihilism and anarchism. The point is to make life difficult, not impossible—to face up to the difference and difficulty which enter into what we think and do and hope for, not to grind them to a halt. Indeed, it is the claim of radical hermeneutics that we get the best results by yielding to the difficulty in "reason," "ethics," and "faith,"[6] not by trying to cover it over. Once we stop trying to prop up our beliefs, practices, and institutions on the metaphysics of presence, once we give up the idea that they are endowed with some sort of facile transparency, we find that they are not washed away but liberated, albeit in a way which makes the guardians of Being and presence nervous. Far from abandoning us to the wolves, radical hermeneutics issues in far more reasonable and indeed less dangerous ideas of reason, ethics, and faith than those that metaphysics has been peddling for some time now. Curiously enough, the metaphysical desire to makes things safe and secure has become consummately dangerous.

But enough of these promissory notes; enough indulgence in the illusion induced by prefaces that one is the master of one's text. I must take Constantin's advice and have the courage to press ahead.

PART 1

Repetition and the Genesis of Hermeneutics

ONE

Repetition and *Kinesis:* Kierkegaard on the Foundering of Metaphysics

For Kierkegaard, the question is whether movement in the existential sense is possible, whether it is possible for the existing individual to make progress. Taking his point of departure from the Eleatic denial of motion, which is for him the paradigmatic gesture of philosophical speculation, Kierkegaard argues on behalf of existence and actuality. He takes his stand against philosophy and metaphysics, for which movement is always a scandal, and argues the case for existential movement. Thus, Constantin Constantius—the immobilized one, the one suspended in Eleatic constancy—raises this serious philosophical question in the most whimsical terms.

> When the Eleatics denied motion, Diogenes, as everyone knows, came forward as an opponent. He literally did come forward, because he did not say a word but merely paced back and forth a few times, thereby assuming that he had sufficiently refuted them. When I was occupied for some time, at least on occasion, with the question of repetition—whether or not it is possible, what importance it has, whether something gains or loses in being repeated—I suddenly had the thought: You can, after all, take a trip to Berlin; you have been there once before, and now you can prove to yourself whether a repetition is possible and what importance it has. (SV III 173/R 131)

This hoary philosophical issue is thus to be posed in a farcical form, by way of the "jest of an analogous conception" (SV IV 290/CA 18n), by deciding whether Constantin can repeat his trip to Berlin. This is to be a parody of the real question, which is whether it is possible for the individual to move forward, to get off dead center and make existential progress. Repetition is an existential version of *kinesis*, the Aristotelian counterpoint to Eleaticism, a movement which occurs in the existing individual.

Kierkegaard thinks that philosophy—metaphysics—inevitably undermines movement. Philosophy, as Nietzsche says, is Egyptianism: "All that philosophers have handled for millennia has been conceptual mummies; nothing actual has escaped from their hands alive. . . . What *is*, does not *become;* what becomes, *is* not."[1] Philosophy is scandalized by motion and thus tries either to exclude movement outright from real being (Platonism) or, more subversively, to portray itself as a friend of movement and thus to lure it into the philosophical house of logical categories (Hegelianism). Kierkegaard objects to the mummifying work of philosophy, not because he thinks that eternity—the sphere of that which lies outside of time and movement—is an illusion, that the real world is a myth *(Fabel)*, as does Nietzsche,[2] but because he thinks that philosophy makes things too easy for itself. It is ready to sneak out the back door of existence as soon as life begins. It does not have the courage for the flux, for the hard work of winning eternity in time, of pushing forward existentially for the prize which lies ahead. It is not eternity as such (Nietzsche's "real world") to which he objects but philosophy's effete manner of seeking it. He takes the side of becoming against Being, of existence against thought, of existential "interest" against metaphysics. For it is on the basis of interest that philosophy founders, that metaphysics comes to grief (SV III 189/R 149).[3]

Kierkegaardian repetition is the first "post-modern"[4] attempt to come to grips with the flux, the first try not at denying it or "reconciling" it, in the manner of metaphysics, but of staying with it, of having the "courage" for the flux. Kierkegaard wants resolutely to avoid turning the world into a frozen *eidos*, stilling its movement, arresting its play, and thereby allaying our fears. He wants to stay open to the *ébranler*, the wavering and fluctuating, and to keep ready for the fear and trembling, the anxiety by which the existing individual is shaken.

In the succeeding chapters of part 1, I will show how the Kierkegaardian project of "repetition" enters into the heart of what Heidegger means by hermeneutics in *Being and Time*. Despite Heidegger's own failure to acknowledge his debt to Kierkegaard, and the tendency among Heidegger commentators to ignore Kierkegaard, the Kierkegaardian origin of what Heidegger calls *"Wiederholung"* (retrieval, repetition) cannot be denied.[5] When *Repetition* *(Gjentagelse,* 1843) was translated into German in 1909 in the Diedrichs edition, it bore the title *Wiederholung*. And it was that early edition, which Heidegger certainly knew,[6] which fashions in an essential way what "hermeneutics" means in *Being and Time*, as we shall show in chapter 3 below. For hermeneutics in the early sense always involves inscribing the figure of the circle on the surface of the flux—like Zarathustra's eagle—and that circular movement is the circle of repetition. By virtue of repetition the individual is able to press forward, not toward a sheer novelty which is wholly discontinuous with the past, but into the being which he himself is. By repetition the individual becomes himself, circling back on the being which he has been all along. Repeating the Aristotelian *to ti en einai* (that which a thing was to be), repetition is that by which the existing individual becomes what he was to be, that by which he returns to himself *(Pap.* IV A 156/R 326).

I begin with the attempts of metaphysics to deny or subvert the flux, right at its inception in Plato (1) and in its consummation in Hegel (2). Then I turn to Constantin's psychological-phenomenological experiment (3). Finally, after surveying the three stages of repetition (4), I address the question of repetition and the "foundering" or overcoming of metaphysics (5).

REPETITION AND RECOLLECTION

For Constantin Constantius, to ask if repetition is possible amounts to asking whether movement is possible, whether there is such a thing as *kinesis*, after all, or whether it is just an illusion. What we get from the philosophers is either the outright denial of motion, as in the Eleatics, or some spurious theory which takes the teeth out of motion, even as it professes to be on its side. In philosophy, becoming is always getting subverted by being. That is why Constantin opens his "report" with a little philosophical prologue on the distinction between recollection and repetition (SV III 173–5/R 131–3). Among other things, this report gives the lie to Heidegger's complaint that Kierkegaard is a merely religious writer who does not appreciate the ontological dimension of the questions he asks.[7] For, by opposing the Greek denial of motion implicit in the doctrine of recollection to Christian becoming, to the movement *(kinesis)* of "existence," Kierkegaard takes his stand with Aristotle's defense of motion against all Eleatic tendencies.

For Kierkegaard, movement in any really serious sense ought to be movement *forward*. It ought to make some progress instead of simply retracing past steps. Moving backward, if it is movement at all, is a kind of antimovement which undoes the progress that has been made. There is a certain comic quality in one who boasts that he is "on the move" when what he means is that he is backing up. But that is what the theory of "recollection" is, and that is the sort of thing that philosophers, who distrust movement, are always giving us when they speak in the name of movement.

Philosophy—immanence, speculation—opened its doors with a theory of pseudomovement, meant to take the sting out of the flux. The Being of the soul, Plato maintained, is to return whence it came. Its coming into the world in the first place was a fall, and so the essential thing is to undo the fall as quickly as possible, to redress the wrong which has confined the soul to the realm of change. The essential destiny of the soul is to recover its origins in the sphere of primordial Being and pure presence. Knowledge, accordingly, is not a discovery which forges ahead—for that would be real movement—but a recovery, a recollection, which recoups a lost cognition. Learning means to reestablish contact with a cognition that we have always already possessed, which quells the seductive aporia about how we can acquire something new. The philosopher is no friend of movement, and the Platonic account of motion is in fact a theory of antimovement, of undoing what motion there has been. Movement is falling, and hence the only movement of which speculative thought approves is the unmovement which undoes the fall. In Plato therefore everything moves backward: from the fallen to the primordial, from the sensible to the supersensible, from the copy to the original, from loss to recovery, from forgetfulness to recollection. In short, movement is governed by a dynamics of nostalgia in which movement itself is something to be overcome.

In the place of this spurious movement Kierkegaard wants to put real movement, genuine *kinesis*. Thus he pits the Christian notion of "repetition," which forges ahead, covers new ground, against Greek recollection. To the paleness of Platonic retreat, Kierkegaard opposes the hardiness of Christian, existential advance:

> Say what you will, this question [whether repetition is possible] will play a very important role in modern philosophy, for *repetition* is a crucial expression for what "recollection" was to the Greeks. Just as they taught that all knowing is a recollecting, modern philosophy will teach that all life is a repetition. . . . Repetition and recollection are the same movement, except in opposite directions, for what is recollected has been, is repeated backward, whereas genuine repetition is recollected forward. Repetition, therefore, if it is possible, makes a person happy, whereas recollection makes him unhappy—assuming, of course, that he gives himself time to live and does not promptly at birth find an excuse to sneak back out of life again, for example, that he has forgotten something. (SV III 173–74/R 131)

Recollection and repetition alike undertake the transition from time to eternity. But the Greek wants to retreat back to an eternal preexistence. No sooner has life begun than speculative thought wants to sneak back out, like a philosophy professor claiming that he has forgotten his umbrella![8]

For the Greeks eternity always already has been; it is a presence which we always already possess but with which we have lost contact. Eternity is a lost actuality. Thus the point of philosophical speculation is to ease oneself out of time, as one would back out of a deadend, to steal back into eternity:

> When the Greeks said that all knowing is recollecting, they said that all existence, which is, has been; when one says that life is a repetition, one says: actuality, which has been, now comes into existence. (SV III 189/R 149)

Recollection begins at the end instead of at the beginning, with the "loss" instead of the task (SV III 178/R 136). In the *Postscript* Johannes Climacus calls Platonic recollection a "temptation" to recollect oneself out of existence, and he says that the greatness of Socrates was to have resisted this temptation (CUP 184–85).[9] As the movement opposite to recollection, repetition is movement indeed. It is the path from time to eternity which is cut by existence itself. It does not try to escape time but to immerse itself in it, to persevere in time. In repetition, eternity is not something lost but something to be attained, not a lost actuality but a possibility yet to be seized, not something passed (past) but something to come, not something to recover but something toward which we must press forward. For the Christian, eternity is the prize which awaits those who keep the faith.

In Christianity eternity has the essentially *futural* meaning of the *vita ventura,* the life which is to come (and in this "to come" we hear Heidegger's "*zu-kommen,*" *Zukunft*). It is the life which is promised to those who set their hands to the plow without looking back. It has to do with the possible, with effecting new life, not with reawakening one who slumbers. Repetition starts at the beginning, not at the end. It means to produce something, not to reproduce a prior presence. For the Christian, time (temporality) means an urgent task, a work to be done. Metaphysics wants to think its way out of time, while in Christianity every moment is literally momentous, an occasion for momentous choice. In the moments of time everything—all eternity—hangs in the balance. The Christian sees time in terms of futurity and decisiveness. But in metaphysics time and motion are an imperfection, an imitation. Nothing is decided in time; the point is to learn how to put time out of action. The love of repetition is happy, an exhilarating and earnest struggle, while the love of recollection is a nostalgic, melancholy longing for a lost paradise, a dreamy wistfulness.

For Kierkegaard the Greeks do not understand time, and they lack "the concept of temporality" (SV IV 358/CA 88). "Greek culture did not understand the moment" and "did not define it with a forward direction but with a backward direction" (SV IV 358/CA 88). The Greeks do not grasp the momentum—from *movere*—in the moment nor the Pauline "twinkling of the eye" in which the world may pass away (I Cor. 15:52; SW IV 358/88). For the Greeks, time signifies no more than a passing away which should be resisted in order to regain the permanence of the lost presence. They were innocent of the radical tension within man between spirit and flesh and of the fundamental tendency to evil, error, and sin. They thought that man belongs essentially to the truth (CUP 183–85) and that he presently suffers only a temporary fall. Time is the temporariness of the fall, a passing imperfection. They have no notion of the urgency and decisiveness of time. But for the Christian everything is different:

> The moment is that ambiguity in which time and eternity touch each other, and with this the concept of *temporality* is posited, whereby time constantly intersects eternity and eternity constantly pervades time. (SV IV 359/CA 89)

Every moment of the Christian conception of time is touched by the eternal, has the eternal at stake, is charged with the energy and momentousness of an eternal—and that means of a future—possibility (*vita futura, vita ventura.*) The future is the incognito of the eternal which is incommensurable with time (SV IV 359/CA 89). The Greeks see the moment not in terms of the primacy of the future but in terms of a past conceived merely as passing away. The authentic notion of time, of the temporality of time, is the contribution of Christianity (SV IV 359–60/CA 89–90).

A whole ontology underlies this opposition between recollection and repetition. One wonders how Heidegger can possibly have taken Kierkegaard to be only a "religious writer" with no ontological concerns. One wonders how he could have written the ontology of "temporality," which constitutes the meaning of the Being of Dasein in *Being and Time*, without so much as acknowledging Kierkegaard, when the whole analysis, in my view, derives in its main lines from Kierkegaard![10] Kierkegaard wants to undo the prestige of the metaphysics of presence embodied in Platonic recollection and to have us think instead in terms of temporality and movement *(kinesis)*. Repetition is *kinesis*, the way the existing individual makes his way through time, the constancy with which he confronts the withering effects of time upon character and faith.

The old dispute between Heraclitus and the Eleatics thus has for Kierkegaard an ethico-religious significance. If Constantin's return trip to Berlin is a "parody" of existential repetition *(Pap.* IV B 111 269/294), the real question is whether existential movement is possible. Is it possible for the existing spirit to live in time without, on the one hand, being dissipated by the flux and losing his identity or, on the other hand, without retreating from time and existence into timeless speculation? His response to this question repeats the Aristotelian gesture of feeling around for the elusive reality of *kinesis* which "exists" in the interplay of potentiality and actuality, which is neither the one nor the other, for it is that in-between land which alone describes the dynamics of freedom:

> In the sphere of freedom, however, [as opposed to that of logic] possibility remains and actuality emerges as a transcendence. Therefore, when Aristotle long ago said that the transition from possibility to actuality is a *kinesis* (motion, change), he was not speaking of logical possibility and actuality but of freedom's, and therefore he properly posits movement. *(Pap.* IV B117 290/R 309–310)

Like Heidegger, Kierkegaard regarded Aristotle as the supreme thinker of the ancient world. Both Kierkegaard and Heidegger were drawn to the Aristotelian critique of Platonic intellectualism, to Aristotle's taste for the dynamics of concrete existence. Contrary to Heidegger's view of matter, Kierkegaard pressed a strictly ontological issue or, better, he pressed against the limits of ontology, precisely in order to make room for existential movement which ontology tries systematically either to exclude or to make over in its own image.

REPETITION AND MEDIATION

The theory of recollection at least has the virtue of honesty. Recollection is an intelligible and frank attempt to undo the movement of time and becoming because it understands the sharp difference between eternity and time, logic and existence, Being and becoming. Kierkegaard thought there really were only two ways to address the question of movement: either to affirm it, with the category of repetition, or to negate it, with the category of recollection. Either way one makes sense of the flux.

> The dialectics of repetition is easy, for that which is repeated has been—otherwise it could not be repeated—but the very fact that it has been makes the repetition into something new. When the Greeks said that all knowing is recollecting, they said that all existence, which is, has been; when one says that life is a repetition, one says: actuality, which has been, now comes into existence. If one does not have the category of recollection nor of repetition, all life dissolves into an empty, meaningless noise. (SV III 189/R 149)

Without either recollection or repetition there is nothing but the flux, nothing but a meaningless turmoil. Recollection stills the turmoil; repetition finds a way to maintain one's head in the midst of it. Recollection says that everything important has already been. Repetition says that actuality must be continually produced, brought forth anew, again and again. Identity must be established, produced. Identity, as Derrida would say, is an effect of repetition.[11]

The worst muddle, however, would be to look for a way to reconcile movement, to try to mediate it, with Being and eternity. Mediation, which attempts to find a third thing between recollection and repetition, is foolish chatter and a confusion:

> It is incredible how much flurry has been made in Hegelian philosophy over mediation and how much foolish talk has enjoyed honor and glory under this rubric. One should rather seek to think through mediation and then give a little credit to the Greeks. The Greek explanation of the theory of being and nothing, the explanation of "the moment," "non-being", etc., trumps Hegel. "Mediation" is a foreign word; "repetition" is a good Danish word, and I congratulate the Danish language on a philosophical term. There is no explanation in our age as to how mediation takes place, whether it results from the motion of the two factors and in what sense it is already contained in them, or whether it is something new that is added, and, if so, how. In this connection, the Greek view of the concept of *kinesis* corresponds to the modern category "transition" and should be given close attention. (SV III 189/R 148–49)

The Greeks either frankly denied motion (the Eleatic view) or produced an honest Aristotelian account of it (*kinesis,* which is taken over by the category of repetition). But mediation is a misguided attempt to accommodate motion to Being, which equivocates about whether there really is motion, about whether anything really new emerges, or whether motion is not kept all along under the constraints of necessity and timelessness.

Kierkegaard distrusted speculation, and he thought that metaphysics always ended up in a denial or subversion of time and motion. The project of "overcoming metaphysics," of the critique of the "metaphysics of presence," was launched by Kierkegaard, although he had to wait for philosophy professors like

Heidegger and Derrida to give his project conceptual formulation and thematic development. (He did, however, as we have pointed out, speak of the "founding of metaphysics.") Metaphysics cannot digest movement, becoming, temporality, genuine novelty, and the attempt to do so results in ludicrous logicizations. Plato understood clearly the incompatibility of time and movement with philosophical speculation and hence defined philosophy in terms of its capacity to remove itself from them. Platonism was more candid; it simply confessed the incommensurability of time and movement with philosophical thought and urged philosophy to learn to die to such shadowy realities. Hence while Kierkegaard criticized *anamnesis* because it was a direct attack on motion, he criticized Hegelian *Aufhebung* as a more insidious, subversive attack on motion, one which put up the front of being a friend of motion, the final effect of which was in fact comic. [12] To a great extent, I think, Derrida's readings of Hegel are a counterpart to Kierkegaard's, for they keep Hegel honest and make him stick to his guns about movement and difference instead of slipping quietly through the back door of metaphysics.

Hegel made a show of embracing time and *kinesis* even while subverting them to his own purposes. Hegelian time is not authentic, radical, Christian temporality, in which everything hinges on the "instant," the decision. It is a time which is not exposed to flux and contingency but precisely insulated from their effects. It is a time made safe by eternity, underwritten by reason, regulated by necessity. In Derrida's terms, Hegelian mediation wants to arrest the play even as it appears to affirm it. Hegelian time lacks what is truly proper to time: contingency, freedom, exposure to the future. It pays public homage to history and temporality while in private it subverts them, subordinating them to a rational teleology which monitors and controls their movements. Hegelian time is time reworked by metaphysics, made over into its image and likeness, and in which the groundlessness of radical freedom, which belongs to the essence of time and *kinesis,* is revoked.

Kierkegaard has a profoundly Protestant and voluntaristic conception of things. [13] The very Being of the world is contingent inasmuch as it originates in a free act of divine creation, and everything that happens in the world happens contingently. Not even the laws of nature give evidence of pure necessity since the phenomena which these laws govern might never have existed and since the laws themselves could be altered by the divine freedom. The Christian world is free; the Greek world is necessitarian. [14] When Kierkegaard speaks of the "transcendence" of movement, he means the absolute unpredictability of the next moment from the present, an Ockhamistic contingency in the successive moments of change, a Cartesian "conservation of the universe" from moment to moment thanks to the divine freedom. Aristotle alone among the Greeks recognized the contingency in things, although even he did not distinguish sharply enough between the necessary and the possible (PF 93).

Now whatever occurs in time occurs contingently, since at first it was not, and then at a later time it came to be. Coming to be "is *ipso facto* historical" (PF 93). Hence it is a sophistry to confuse the immutability of the past with any alleged necessity of the past. The past is the historical and as such contingent, i.e., it is something which has come into existence. Its contingency is not removed by the passage of time. The merely external fact that it is now a past event does not annul the truth that when it happened this event could have been otherwise. Indeed, to say that the past is necessary is equivalent to predicting the future, for if the contingency of the one is annulled, the contingency of the other must likewise be annulled.

Hegelianism is therefore fraudulent, for it arises from an intellectual illusion which is akin to an optical illusion.

> Distance in time tends to promote an intellectual illusion, just as distance in space provokes a sensory illusion. A contemporary does not perceive the necessity of what comes into existence, but when centuries intervene between the event and the beholder he perceives the necessity, just as distance makes the square tower seem round. (PF 98)

Indeed Hegelianism is comic, for it attempts to wed logic and existence, necessity and freedom, thought and *kinesis*. Hegel wants to affirm the reality of time and becoming, but his affirmation is half-hearted, for he insists that there is a logical necessity inscribed in time, that time unfolds in accordance with the categories of reason, or contrariwise, that time is inscribed in logic, that the categories move, that they undergo becoming and *kinesis*. But time and contingency, the conditions of reality, forever resist the idealizing efforts of thought. Thought can flourish only in the element of necessity and essence, and it can appropriate becoming only at the expense of what is definitive for it, viz., its very contingency. Whence comes Climacus's account of "Lessing's Thesis" in the *Concluding Unscientific Postscript* (§4): it is possible for thought to construct a system, but the price it must pay is high, viz., such a system can lay no claim to reality. Conversely, any account which is faithful to existence must be prepared to face the worst, to founder on the paradox, for an existential account moves in an element which is hostile to thought, viz., time and *kinesis*.

We are now in a position to understand the claims of Constantin Constantius about the difference between Hegelian "mediation" and repetition. We are here indebted to a review of *Repetition* published by the Hegelian theologian J. L. Heiberg, the banality of which so outraged Kierkegaard that he was provoked to respond, again under the name of Constantin, with an illuminating commentary on *Repetition* which he did not, however, publish but which we are fortunate to have available in the new English edition of *Repetition*.

Heiberg accuses Constantin of naturalizing repetition by treating it in terms of movement. But Constantin's argument is that movement in its truest and most radical sense belongs above all to the individual spirit. For Heiberg movement in the realm of the spirit is at best the movement of world history, which is in fact governed by necessity and mediation, a movement whose dynamics are controlled by logic.

> In logic, transition is movement's silence, whereas in the sphere of freedom it becomes. Thus, in logic, when possibility, by means of the immanence of thought, has determined itself as actuality, one only disturbs the silent self-inclosure of the logical process by talking about movement and transition. (*Pap.* IV 117 290/R 309)

The movement of logic is an unreal, noiseless hush. It is nothing more than an unfolding of necessity, no more than a quiet rustle among concepts. There is talk about movement but no real movement. "In the sphere of freedom, however," Constantin continues, "possibility remains and actuality emerges as a transcendence" (*Pap.* IV 117 290/R 309–10). Here possibility is followed by an actuality genuinely transcendent to the possibility from which it emerges. Here—in freedom, which is movement in the preeminent sense—something new in fact appears. The actuality is transcendent to the possibility, not determined, enclosed, and precontained by it. The transition is alive with all of the noise and bustle of existence and genuine *kinesis*. Thus the whole question for Constantin is whether repetition is *possible*.

> But as soon as the individual is viewed in his freedom, the question becomes a different one: Can repetition be realized? It is repetition in this pregnant sense as a task for freedom and as freedom that gives the title to my little book and that in my little book has come into being depicted and made visible in the individuality and in the situation. . . . (*Pap.* IV B117 293/R 312–13)

Repetition means the task set for the individual to persevere in time, to stay with the flux, to produce his identity as an effect. And this ultimately is the religious task. The highest expression of repetition is the religious movement in which the individual passes from sin to atonement. Here is the most dramatic instance of a qualitative transition, of a transformation of the individual in which something new and transcendent is produced. Atonement, which is completely transcendent to the sin which it displaces, is repetition in the highest sense, *sensu eminentiore* (*Pap.* IV B117 302/R 320). Sin cannot be mediated but only forgiven. The transition is not lodged on the level of immanence but is a genuine passage, a genuine movement of transcendence, one indeed which is possible only in virtue of the absurd, that is, of faith in the power of God to intervene and to effect what logic and mediation can neither understand nor carry out (SV IV B117 293–94/R313). No such radical *kinesis* is possible in metaphysics, in Platonism or in Hegelianism. Such a repetition has nothing to do with world-historical progress or astronomy:

In the individual, then, repetition appears as a task for freedom, in which the question becomes that of saving one's personality from being volatilized and, so to speak, a pawn to events. The moment it is apparent the individual can lose himself in events, fate, lose himself in such a way that he therefore by no means stops contemplating but loses himself in such a way that freedom is taken completely in life's fractions without leaving a remainder behind, then the issue becomes manifest, not to contemplation's aristocratic indolence, but to freedom's concerned passion. *(Pap.* IV B117 296/R 315)

Repetition is the power of the individual to forge his personality out of the chaos of events, in the midst of the flux, the power to create an identity in the face of the incessant "dispersal" of the self *(Pap.* IV B117 303/R 320), of the dissipating effects of the flux. There is always a "remainder" no matter how much is subtracted from the individual by the taxing business of everyday existence. Repetition is the exacting task of constituting the self as a self.

In sum, recollection retreats and repetition presses forward, but mediation makes a great show of movement, a grand but silent display of movement, like a mime who appears to be racing along while all the time he remains in place on the stage.

LETTERS TO CONSTANTIN

It is in the context of this elaborate ontological preparation that Kierkegaard's *Repetition*—his "whimsical" treatise, his little joke—should be read. I have concentrated so far on the ontology which is written in the margins, in occasional excursions which interrupt the narrative, and in the unpublished papers. The text itself is meant to illustrate this abstract ontology with a concrete example, a psychological, phenomenological case study.[15] The first part, "Constantin's Report," is an account of a distraught young friend of Constantin's, caught in the throes of a difficult love affair. The second part, "Repetition," consists of a series of letters from the young man to Constantin. The second half of the text, which repeats the title, is the "serious" part (but are we to take that seriously?), where we really get to repetition, while the first half is a parody of genuine repetition.

This is not the place to undertake a detailed account of Kierkegaard's narrative but only to highlight certain features of the text. We are introduced to a young man who has fallen deeply but unhappily in love, for the girl he loves is no more than an occasion which has awakened the poetic nature in him. He is not so much in love with the girl, as in love with love itself and the occasion this affair provides him for poetizing. He is thus already in a stage of recollection which keeps leaping over life. He begins with the loss of the girl. He is not ready for the day-to-day work of making love last a lifetime. His love of this girl keeps getting transformed into "Eternal Love," the "Idea" of love, of which she is but the "visible form" (SV III 182/R 141). While her love for him is naturally directed toward the ethical relationship of marriage, his love for her keeps being diverted into the poetic. She moves in the sphere of ethical actuality, he in the sphere of poetic ideality. Constantin devises a scheme aimed at dissolving the relationship in which the young man would make himself out to be an unfaithful womanizer. This would provoke the girl to break off the relationship herself, leaving her with her honor intact and the feeling that she had saved herself from a bad marriage. She would be in the right, and the young man would look to be in the wrong (SV III 183/R 142). But the young man lacks the nerve for the plan and simply absconds from Copenhagen to Stockholm.

The problem with the young man, Constantin conjectures, is that he may really be in love with the girl and not have the courage to follow the way of repetition out of his predicament (SV III 186/R 145). The young man faces the critical juncture between recollection and repetition. On the one hand, he may transform his concrete relationship with this girl into ideality and thus enter the poetic. On the other hand, he may press bravely ahead in the sphere of reality, making the real relationship work out with the hard work of a day-to-day faithfulness which would break with his poetizing, idealizing tendency. He may either retreat backward into poetic eternity or press forward to produce eternity in time, that is, a good marriage. In fact he just retreats, turning on his heels and fleeing.

At this point Constantin is driven to wonder whether repetition is possible at all, and so he undertakes the satiric experiment in repetition, whose seriousness is to be compared to Diogenes' attempt to refute the Eleatics merely by walking back and forth. He will undertake a return trip to Berlin, to see if he can repeat the pleasures of a previous holiday. The whole trip is a series of disasters, like the farce which he sees at the Königsberg Theatre, and proof positive that repetition is not possible. Constantin is humiliated. He who counsels the young man to repetition no longer believes in it himself (SV III 210/R 172).

Life is a swindle, Constantin complains. Instead of giving a repetition (*Gjentagelse*, literally: again-taking, re-taking, repetition), life simply takes everything back again (*tage Alt igjen*) (R 368, n. 79). Instead of providing us with a continuity, a repetition which enables us to move ahead, life just exposes us to the flux. The more we try to put life in order, the bigger the mess we create. We would be better off if we simply lived without care, like a child who is constantly being rescued from disaster by his nursemaid, and let things take their course.

The failure to achieve repetition throws us back into the flux, the Heraclitean stream. There are only two ways to come to grips with the flux: recollection and repetition. And Constantin is capable of neither.

Do not all agree, both ecclesiastical and secular speakers, both poets and prose writers, both skippers and undertakers, both heroes and cowards—do they not all agree that life is a stream? How can one get such a foolish idea [repetition], and, still more foolishly, how can one want to make a principle of it? . . . Long live the stagecoach horn! It is the instrument for me for many reasons, and chiefly because one can never be certain of wheedling the same notes from this horn. A coach horn has infinite possibilities, and the person who puts it to his mouth and puts wisdom into it can never be guilty of a repetition. . . . Praised be the coach horn. It is my symbol. Just as the ancient ascetics placed a skull on the table, the contemplation of which constituted their view of life, so the coach horn on my table always reminds me of the meaning of life. But the journey is not worth the trouble, for one need not stir from the spot to be convinced that there is no repetition. No, one sits calmly in one's living room; when all is vanity and passes away, one nevertheless speeds faster than on a train, even though sitting still. . . . Travel on you fugitive river. (SV III 212–13/R 174–76)

Constantin alludes not only to Heraclitus but also to Job. Like the Lord, life gives and takes away, and we would do better to live like a child—or the birds of the air, who sow not nor reap—ready to bless the name of the Lord, who will find a way to give-again *(gjen-tagelse)* what life takes away. The taking away and giving again, which defines repetition, is modeled after Job's famous declaration.

The story of Constantin's trip is a parody, a satire, of true repetition, which must be of a more inward, more religious character than was Constantin's effort to reconstruct a holiday in Berlin. Constantin's vacation is comically juxtaposed to the allusion to Heraclitus, Job, and religious repetition. We are thus to conclude not that repetition generally is impossible but only that "aesthetic" repetition, which is at the mercy of circumstances and accidental factors, is impossible. Constantin's journey proves that aesthetics, which is devoted solely to the interesting, should fear repetition and cultivate instead the art of variation, which always knows how to produce something interesting and hence to stave off boredom.

The question of the possibility of repetition has not been decided in the negative but raised up a notch, forcing us to discuss it in terms of the religious category. Thus the second half of the book—"Repetition"—repeats the title and repeats the question—whether repetition is possible—now by way of a series of letters to Constantin from the absconded young man. The question of repetition is repeated, not as a farce, not as a whimsical trip to Berlin, but on a higher level, as the drama of the ethico-religious fate of the nameless young man. For the young man is in a crisis; he has reached a crucial turning point, a fork in the road of life.

Constantin seems to have misjudged the young man. He thought him to possess only a dreamy, imaginative love which belongs to the category of recollection, but he finds him caught up in a real love, snared by actuality. The young man is left with no choice but to press forward—into marriage, love's ethical consummation—but being a poet, too, he is incapable of marriage. He must press forward, but he cannot—a dilemma whose only solution is religious.

> He has now come to the borderline of the marvelous [faith]; consequently, if it [repetition] is to take place at all, it must take place by virtue of the absurd. (SV III 220/R 185)

But again Constantin cannot help suspecting that it is really not the girl herself who matters. Perhaps the girl is still an occasion, not now for the poetic but for the religious. In either case, then, the young man would make himself an exception and have no business with marriage, the ethical universal (SV III 220/ R 185). The young man is in a crisis of repetition:

> The issue that brings him to a halt is nothing more nor less than repetition. He is right not to seek clarification in philosophy, either Greek or modern, for the Greeks make the opposite movement, and here a Greek would choose to recollect without tormenting his conscience. Modern philosophy [Hegel] makes no movement; as a rule it makes only a commotion, and if it makes any movement at all, it is always within immanence, whereas repetition is and remains a transcendence. It is fortunate that he does not seek any explanation from me, for I have abandoned my theory. I am adrift. Then, too, repetition is too transcendent for me. Fortunately, my friend is not looking for clarification from any world-famous philosopher or any *professor publicus ordinarius;* he turns to an unprofessional thinker who once possessed the world's glories but later withdrew from life—in other words, he falls back on Job. (SV III 221/R 186)

Then follow the young man's letters. The young man explains that Constantin's fraudulent scheme to deceive the girl was repugnant to his ethical instincts. He has found better counsel in Job who, driven to life's extreme, keeps repeating "the Lord gives and the Lord takes away; blessed be the name of the Lord." Job repeats the prayer of repetition, that is, of resoluteness in adversity, of the self-possession which knows how to press forward no matter what. In particular, Job resists the explanation that his suffering is a just punishment for his sins and insists upon his innocence. It is merely human wisdom, ethical rationality, which explains his situation in terms of guilt. Ethically, he is innocent. That is just the situation of the young man. Like Job he finds himself thrust into a situation not of his own making and then declared guilty. In a passage clearly anticipating Heidegger's notion of "thrownness" (*Geworfenheit*), the young man laments:

> I am at the end of my rope. I am nauseated by life; it is insipid—without salt and meaning. . . . Where am I? What does it mean to say: the world? What is the meaning of that word? Who tricked me into this whole thing and leaves me standing here? Who am I? How did I get into the world? Why was I not asked

about it, why was I not informed of the rules and regulations but just thrust into the ranks as if I had been bought from a peddling shanghaier of human beings? How did I get involved in this big enterprise called actuality? And if I am compelled to be involved, where is the manager—I have something to say about this. Is there no manager? To whom shall I make my complaint? . . . How did it happen that I became guilty? Or am I not guilty? Why, then, am I called that in every language? . . .

Why should she be in the right and I in the wrong? If both of us are faithful, why then is this expressed in human language in such a way that she is faithful and I am a deceiver? (SV III 234–35/R 200–201)

If he marries her, that will destroy her—because of his poetic nature. If he does not marry her, he is guilty. If he marries her, he is indeed guilty; if he does not marry her, he is declared guilty by human language. Here is an either/or which no judge can resolve. And so he offers a reward to anyone who can invent a word for his state, who can find a category which names the condition of being innocent and seeming guilty. His condition is nameless, even as he himself is nameless. He is at a standstill, immobilized; he sees no way to press ahead.

Clearly all the possibilities of rational human discourse have been exhausted. The only way out is religious. And that is why he reads the book of Job with the eyes of his heart, which is the only way to deal with his "nameless anxiety about the world and life and men and everything" (SV III 239/R 205). The secret to repetition is in Job (SV III 241/R 207). Job was able to press forward, even though the whole world disagreed; he had the power to resist the ethical explanation. He knew the whole thing was not punishment for guilt but an "ordeal" in which God was putting his faith to the test. That is a category which does not exist in science; it is a strictly religious category which exists only for the individual. Because of faithfulness, Job's thunderstorm passes (SV III 247/R 214), and he is given back double everything that had been taken away from him. That is his repetition (SV III 245/R 212).

Job, however, is not a hero of faith, properly speaking, but of the region which lies just at the outskirts of faith. ". . . Job's significance is that the disputes at the boundaries of faith are fought out in him. . ." (SV III 243/R 210). An "ordeal" is a strictly religious category—it cannot be invoked on just any occasion, as when the oatmeal burns!—but it does not yet touch upon the extremities of Christian faith. The absurdity Job faces is not the absolute paradox of Christian belief. An ordeal is a temporary condition, which is rewarded at the end by a worldly repetition. Christian faith runs deeper than that.

But the application of Job's life to the young man is clear:

All I know is that I am standing and have been standing *suspenso gradu* [immobilized] for a whole month now, without moving a foot or making one single movement.

I am waiting for a thunderstorm—and for repetition.

> What will be the effect of this thunderstorm? It will make me fit to be a husband. It will shatter my whole personality—I am prepared. It will render me almost unrecognizable to myself—I am unwavering even though I am standing on one foot. . . .
>
> In other respects, I am doing my best to make myself into a husband. I sit and clip myself, take away everything that is incommensurable in order to become commensurable. (SV III 247–48/R 214)

Unable of his own strength to enter into marriage—everything rational in him tells him that marriage would destroy the girl and destroy himself—he awaits a transformation by God which will make him a fit husband and restore his honor, which will render his exceptional condition commensurable with the universal ethical measure. He cannot make progress, cannot take another step further, cannot make a movement—except in virtue of faith.[16]

Now Constantin inserts a word, in between the letters, like an aside from offstage: he distrusts the whole thing; he does not believe in thunderstorms. He is sure the whole thing will come to grief—as it does in the next letter:

> She is married—to whom I do not know, for when I read it in the newspaper I was so stunned that I dropped the paper and have not had the patience since then to check in detail. I am myself again. Here I have repetition; I understand everything, and life seems more beautiful to me than ever. It did indeed come like a thunderstorm, although I am indebted to her generosity for its coming. . . . Let existence reward her as it has, let it give her what she loved more; it also gave me what I loved more—myself, and gave it to me through generosity. (SV III 253/R 220)

The repetition is that he is given himself back. But this is not religious repetition. His freedom is to be employed not in the service of God but in the service of the poetic idea. Despite the flirtation with the religious, the deeply religious tone of the thunderstorm, despite the invocation of Job, the young man becomes a poetic, not a religious exception to marriage (SV III 254–55/R 221–22).

But it is to Constantin that Kierkegaard gives the last word, and with good reason, for now Constantin confesses that the nameless young man does not exist, that he is an experiment devised by Constantin himself (SV III 262/R 228). Both parts of *Repetition* thus are a kind of farce, an imaginative construct, the end result of which is to show that repetition is nowhere to be found—not in Constantin, not in the young man, not in philosophy, not even, properly, in Job. Genuine religious repetition keeps deferring itself. It is nowhere to be found in this book, or in any book. It cannot be circumscribed by the margins of a book.[17] The young man was an analogue, a parody, of religious repetition (SV III 262/R 228).

The critical point the young man reached was the point of readiness for divine action, where he had completely surrendered his own sense of self-sufficiency and put himself at the disposal of God's action on him. He was ready to have his whole nature as a poetic exception destroyed and to be remade in God's image, according to God's plan for him. That is the point of religious repetition, when we are ready to let God make something new in us, effect a transcendence in us of which we are incapable ourselves. But when the thunderstorm came, he managed to break through, not to the religious, but to a poetic existence in which he is loosened from the universality of marriage and free to exist as a poetic exception, thanks to the girl. That is his repetition, which consists in "the raising of his consciousness to the second power" (SV III 263/R 229). But *that* repetition is but an imperfect analogue and transition stage to a higher repetition which he at times skirted but never attained (SV III 263/R 229). When the thunderstorm broke, he took the poetic way out, instead of weathering it out religiously (SV III 263/R 229–30).

The forward momentum of existence can be sustained only by the energy of faith. The passion of existence which remains faithful to the chosen way must be the passion of faith, which operates "with religious fear and trembling, but also with faith and trust" (SV III 263/R 230). In the end, repetition is possible neither for Constantin nor for the young man. The experiment undertaken in *Repetition* ends in failure, but this is meant, not to fill us with despair about the possibility of repetition, but rather to sharpen our sense of its illusive and self-deferring quality, of the demands it makes. It is meant to persuade us that repetition is not to be found within the margins of a book. It is a way of writing a book about repetition which arises from an understanding that we have reached the end of the book (cf. CUP, "A First and Last Declaration").

REPETITION AND THE STAGES OF EXISTENCE

We can clarify what Kierkegaard means by repetition by differentiating the well-known "stages" or "spheres of existence"—the aesthetic, ethical, and religious. Clearly, aesthetic repetition has proven to be a disaster. Repetition spells the end of aesthetics and hence must be feared, for repetition "has a magic power to keep [aesthetic] freedom captive" (*Pap.* IV B 117 281/R 301). It is the death of unqualified pleasure seeking. With each repetition the edge of aesthetic pleasure is dulled until it becomes tedious and vanishes. The trip to Berlin is an exercise in naive aesthetic repetition, simple reduplication. Constantin is unwary, naive; he thinks a pleasure can just be reenacted, reproduced. Had he been a little more clever he would have had the sense to fear repetition, to see in it the enemy of freedom-as-pleasure seeking.

Hence the despair of straightforward pleasure seeking generates a higher form of aestheticism equipped with a "sagacity," a finite, worldly wisdom illustrated by the famous "Rotation Method" (in *Either/Or*, vol. 1) meant to fool repetition (SV IV B 117 281/R 301–302). If the repetition of a pleasure dulls it, then freedom must learn to be more cunning. On the aesthetic level, the question is not indeed whether repetition is possible—that was Constantin's mistake—but whether it is *avoidable*. The whole problem for the aesthete then is to acquire the art of variation and constant alteration. The rotation method is a shrewd and systematic attempt to offset the fatal effects of repetition upon aesthetic life, a way to keep it at bay and avoid it, always altering pleasure so as to keep pleasure alive. But this too breaks down in despair, to the extreme of the Seducer and his repugnant treatment of Cordelia. Aesthetically speaking, the Seducer is a higher type—more reflective, more careful, and premeditating—but ethically he is cruel and diabolical. Ethically repulsed, we are driven to seek higher ground.

Freedom becomes itself, becomes truly free, not when it seeks ways to evade repetition, but when it seeks repetition itself, when it asks the guiding question of *Repetition:*

> Now freedom's supreme interest is precisely to bring about repetition, and its only fear is that variation would have the power to disturb its eternal nature. Here emerges the issue: *Is repetition possible?* Freedom itself is now the repetition. . . . What freedom fears here is not repetition but variation; what it wants is not variation but repetition. (SV IV B 117 281–82/R 302)

Here repetition is looked upon not as a fatal affliction which kills off the life of freedom but as freedom itself. The rotation method has as little to do with real repetition as does an alehouse keeper who happens to look like the king. We ought to smile at Constantin's trip to Berlin as we would smile at such a man. True freedom and genuine repetition converge; repetition has become inward, a matter of freedom, of "the individuality's own repetition raised to a new power" *(Pap.* IV B 111 270/R 294).

With that, the question of repetition enters the sphere of the ethical and religious. But it is important to distinguish the two. The ethical significance of repetition is embodied in marriage, whose aesthetic validity and higher ethical worth are defended by the Judge in the second volume of *Either/Or.* All of the books written just after the breach with Regine are addressed to her; they are explanations to her, and to Kierkegaard himself, of what he had done, of why he made of himself an exception and departed from the ethical-universal, whose Archimedean point is married life. The Judge, who represents conjugal fidelity, the paradigm case of ethical repetition, attacks the aesthete on the grounds that for him genuine love is impossible (E/O II 144).

The aesthete lacks substance and actuality. His relationship with the girl ends like a novel, at the point where the lovers are to get married, which is precisely the point where the ethical begins (E/O II 144). Marriage is eternity, not the moment; actuality, not flirtation; possession, not conquest. The aesthete is intoxicated with first love, by the charm of the first kiss, the first embrace, but the Judge knows that first love is unhistorical—it has not proved itself in time—whereas marriage is tested by time and ripened by development.[18] What the aesthete fears most about time is monotony (E/O II 128ff.)—boredom, it was noted in the "Rotation Method," is the *radix malorum*—for he cannot imagine love when it is not young and new. He dreads the repetition of marriage because of a defective understanding of time. He prefers the time which leads up to something and then is over and done with (E/O II 138). He knows nothing of ethical time, the toilsome process in which something is slowly built up and grows into the fullness of its being. The ethical individual has learned to do battle, not with dragons and lions, but with the most difficult enemy of all, time. He has learned to hold fast in time, both by finding constancy in the midst of the flux, and by finding novelty in the midst of the customary and everyday. Marriage and the ethical have a different conception of time and repetition, says the Judge, for where the aesthete finds monotony the ethical man finds preservation and increase.

Repetition is thus the centerpiece in Kierkegaard's "existential theory of the self." For the self is defined by choice, as something to be "won" (E/O II 167). This is an ethical, not a metaphysical, account of the self (which clearly anticipates §64 of *Being and Time*), which treats the self not as a substance, a permanent presence which endures beneath the changing fortunes of age and bodily change, but as a task to be achieved—not as presence but as possibility. Without choice, the individual lapses into the diversions of "half hour works" (E/O II 202). The aesthete lacks memory, not in the usual sense but in the sense of "memory of your own life, of what you have experienced in it" (E/O II 202). For the aesthete the past is simply over; it has lost all interest for him. But the ethical individual has long memory, stretching himself out toward his past, for which he assumes responsibility, even as he stretches himself out anticipatorily toward what is expected of him in the future, holding his entire life together in the unity and continuity of a self, thereby constituting himself as a self:

> Only when in his choice a man has assumed himself . . . has so totally penetrated himself that every moment is attended by the consciousness of a responsibility for himself, only then has he chosen himself ethically, only then has he repeated himself. . . . (E/O II 207–208)

To speak of choosing oneself is of course paradoxical, for the self does not exist until it is brought forth by choice, and yet the self must exist if it is to choose:

> . . . that which is chosen does not exist and comes into existence with the choice; that which is chosen exists, otherwise there would not be a choice. For in case what I chose did not exist but absolutely came into existence with the choice, I would not be choosing, I would be creating; but I do not create myself, I choose myself. (E/O II 219–20)

Kierkegaardian repetition, like Derrida's, is productive. It does not limp along after, trying to reproduce what is already present, but is productive of what it is repeating. The repeating is the producing—of the self. But not absolutely: One does not create *ex nihilo* but always beginning from a situated standpoint one gradually carves out an identity for oneself. The paradox is resolved, therefore, in a way which anticipates the hermeneutical paradoxes in §32 and §33 in *Being and Time:* by introducing a kind of existential circle, according to which the self by choosing the self comes to be the being which it all along has been:

> He becomes himself, quite the same self he was before, down to the last significant peculiarity, and yet he becomes another, for the choice permeates everything and transforms it. (E/O II 227)

He does not create something altogether new, but actualizes what he has been all along *(to ti en einai)*.

Repetition thus is not an ethical gymnastics which thinks anything possible. It begins with the situatedness in which one finds oneself. It is not abstract freedom but the freedom to actualize possibilities. It does not depend upon the favor of world history to give it an opportunity, but it knows how to find the possible in any situation in which it is put. It knows how to transform necessity (facticity) into freedom. The individual knows himself:

> . . . as this definite individual, with these talents, these dispositions, these instincts, these passions, influenced by these definite surroundings, as this definite product of a definite environment. But being conscious of himself in this way, he assumes responsibility for all of this. (E/O II 255)

If necessity thrusts him into a certain place, freedom chooses this place. Freedom knows that it is not possible always to have good fortune but that the essential thing is "what one sees in every situation, with what energy he regards it" (E/O II 257). The ethical does not require one to be in the right place at the right time, for the essentials of ethical repetition are at hand in any time or place. The aesthete requires good fortune, but the ethical requires only one thing, "and that is . . . his self" (E/O II 257).

In sum, repetition on the ethical level is the constancy and continuity of choice by which the self constitutes itself as a self, by which it returns again and again to its own innermost resolution and establishes its moral identity. Ethical repetition means the steadiness of the unbroken vow, the enduring bond of the lasting marriage, the capacity to find ever new depths in the familiar and self-same. It means a recurrent cycle of growth and development by means of which the self becomes itself.

But eventually the bravado of ethical repetition must come to grief. In the ethical, one needs only oneself, and that is its illusion. The ethical sphere is predicated on the false assumption that everything in life is weighed on the scales of human justice, that it means everything to be innocent. But what if a man were entirely innocent and yet still suffered? Furthermore, what if a man attributes such innocence as he has to himself, as if there were something to him of himself, independently of his God-relationship? Ethical repetition maintains the illusion that a resolute will with good intention is enough to constitute the self, to keep a man whole, that a balance is possible between the ethical and the aesthetic factors in the personality. The Judge's argument against the aesthete is that the self cannot be dependent upon external factors, upon the vagaries of good fortune. But that argument finally skews because it leads in the end to the illusion of the self-sufficiency of the will. What if a man were ethically whole, a just man, and yet is struck down and deprived of all aesthetic immediacy, which, according to the Judge, is an integral complement to ethical righteousness, part of the balanced whole of the personality? Ethics suffers from the illusion that repetition lies within its power.

Relative to the idle caprice of the rotation method, ethical repetition presses forward resolutely, makes progress, effects transcendence. But inasmuch as it calls upon nothing more than human resources, upon resolve and firmness of will, ethical repetition pushes ahead within the sphere of immanence. Repetition in its deepest registers, therefore, has to do with the exception, with the breakdown of the human, the loss of human compensation, a transformation which shatters the categories of immanence. It concerns that most extreme inwardness which arises only from the shipwreck of ethical humanism.[19] Genuine repetition, which is absolutely transcendent and effected in virtue of the absurd, occurs only when the individual does not see how he can go on, when every rational human resource is exhausted. Then the individual gives up everything and awaits the thunderstorm. The young man reached that point, but he had recourse to the poetic, not the religious, when the thunderstorm broke. The young man was caught in an ethical paradox; he was guilty but he had done no wrong. Here indeed was a stumbling block to confound the Judge's cheery moralism and ethical balancing act. That is the importance of Job, who saw his suffering not as punishment for a wrongdoing but as purposely visited upon him by God so as to accentuate the purely personal God-relationship and to diminish the juridical one.

Job and the young man reach the point of the breakdown of the ethical wisdom and sanguine rationality of the Judge. They enter a sphere not governed by the rule of credit and debit, investment and return, an economy of expenditure without reserve.[20] In this mad religious economy, if one gives up everything, everything is repeated, returned, even a hundredfold, in virtue of the absurd. Here there is not sound reason but a "play" in which the world, that is, the hand of God, is playing with man in order to humble his finite understanding and lead him into another and transcendent sphere. Repetition is reached not by achieving ethical steadfastness but by realizing that, from a human standpoint, everything is lost, that there is nowhere to turn (SV III 245–46/R 212). At that point we learn what we have all along heard in the sermons:

that unless a man loses his soul he cannot have it back, that of himself a man can do nothing. These are the first laws of the dynamics of religious repetition, of the religious way through the flux.

Indeed, even Job and Abraham fall short of this demanding sense of repetition. The paradox they faced was not the absolute paradox, and the repetition they were granted retained an earthly sense: the restoration of Job's goods and honor and the restoration of Isaac. Thus, the repetition had not been sufficiently interiorized, had not yet been driven inward. Repetition cannot have to do with the restoration of outward goods. Repetition is a law of inwardness which moves ahead precisely in virtue of outward loss. The outer loss is an inner gain; the detachment from the finite is progress toward the infinite. The whole question of finitude becomes a matter of indifference (SV III 263/R 230). Repetition takes place only if the finite is crucified and the individual surrenders everything in order to enter the divine absence, the dark night, the fear and the trembling. The individual takes his stand in the abyss, endures the withdrawal of presence, lets himself be led by God, who is alone the true teacher of repetition. In the abyss of the God-relationship the individual is able to move ahead. True repetition is the radical transition from sin to atonement. Therefore, the only authentic *kinesis*, which is repetition, is set in motion by eternity.[21]

REPETITION AND THE END OF METAPHYSICS

Kierkegaard inaugurated the delimitation of the metaphysical tradition—which today is spoken of in terms of "the end of philosophy," "the end of metaphysics"—and it is a great mistake on the part of the Heideggerians to write him off as a merely religious or psychological thinker. Far from having only a passing significance for the more "existentialist" elements in the "existential analytic," Kierkegaard set in motion the "destruction of the history of ontology" and hence anticipated the central ontological argument of *Being and Time* and the whole gesture of "overcoming metaphysics" in the later Heidegger.

By opposing existential repetition to Platonic recollection and Hegelian mediation, the beginning and end of metaphysics, he mounted a sweeping attack upon the whole history of metaphysics. Platonism makes light of time while Hegelianism offers a fraudulent version of time. Hegelianism is but a variation of Platonism which undermines the contingency of temporal movement, even as Platonism undermines time itself. Together they completely subvert *kinesis* and becoming; they turn them over to the rule of essence and necessity, to pure thought and disengaged speculation. Metaphysics is an exercise in disinterested *nous* looking on at the spectacle of *eidos* or of a phenomenological "we" serenely observing the logical unfolding of the formations *(Gestaltungen)* of the spirit.

For Kierkegaard everything turns on our ability to take our stand in the flux, to press forward in the element of actuality and becoming rather than to seek some way around it. It is a matter of "interest" in the literal sense of *inter-esse*,[22] of being-between, of firmly placing oneself in and amidst the strife of temporal becoming:

> If one does not have the category of recollection or of repetition all life dissolves into an empty, meaningless noise. Recollection is the pagan *[ethniske]* view of life, repetition the modern; repetition is the *interest [Interesse]* of metaphysics, and also the interest upon which metaphysics comes to grief; repetition is the watchword *[Losnet]* in every ethical view; repetition is the *conditio sine qua non* [the indispensable condition] for every issue in dogmatics. (SV III 189/R 149)

Repetition displaces the disinterested posture of metaphysical thought and sets in motion the "foundering" of metaphysics, the way it "comes to grief." In this foundering the Heideggerian gestures of *Destruktion* and *Überwindung* are already anticipated. For Kierkegaard, metaphysics, ethics, and theology—in short, the length and breadth of "onto-theo-logic"—shatter against the rocks of "interest."

"As soon as interest steps forth, metaphysics steps aside," Kierkegaard explains. Repetition forces metaphysics to the side in order to make room for the existing spirit. The existing spirit belongs to the sphere of actuality, for which the categories of logic are a bad fit. Metaphysics wants either to negate movement and make its way out the back door of time or to replace them with seductive logical counterfeits. Repetition cuts off all subterfuge, forcing the spirit to proceed without recourse to the fantastic constructions of *eidos* and *Geist*. Metaphysics puts becoming under the protective rule of essence so that nothing genuinely new can emerge. But religious repetition, which is the subjective passion that presses forward in virtue of faith, says with St. Paul, "Behold all things have become new" (II Cor 5:17).

Even ethics, which takes its stand in actuality and real choice, remains bound to the sphere of immanence and a logic of moral development. Hence even in the ethical sphere, nothing really new happens. Ethics functions within the range of law-governed change. Religious repetition, on the other hand, means a more radical transition—from fall to grace, from sin to at-one-ment—shattering all ethical continuity.

> Either all of existence comes to an end in the demand of ethics, or the condition [faith] is provided and the whole of life and existence begins anew, not through an immanent continuity with the former existence, which is a contradiction, but through a transcendence. (SV IV 289/CA 17n)

Religious repetition, as a discontinuous wrenching free from sin, does not arise immanently, from laws internal to moral development, but transcendently, from the intervention of God's saving act. Ethics does not make a single step forward out of the sphere of immanence. Here then is the end—the delimitation—of metaphysics and ethics, of ethical and metaphysical humanism, of any future metaphysics of morals:

> If repetition is not posited, ethics becomes a binding power. No doubt it is for this reason that the author states that repetition is the watchword in every ethical view. (SV IV 290/CA 18n)

Despite his talk of "subjectivity," what Kierkegaard has in mind is the foundering of all human categories, the shattering of the subjective and the anthropocentric. In the face of the fury of the flux, only faith can move forward. Faith intervenes just where everything human and rational, everything ethical and metaphysical, every form of humanism, comes to grief. And not only ethics and metaphysics but also theology ("dogmatics") too. For inasmuch as theology takes itself to be capable of making progress in sorting out the flux by means of its onto-theo-logical categories, it too is a kind of paganism:[23]

> If repetition is not posited, dogmatics cannot exist at all, for repetition begins in faith, and faith is the organ for issues of dogma. (SV IV 290/CA 18n)

The full range of onto-theo-logic—of metaphysics, ethics, and theology—is thereby delimited. There can be no mistaking the character of Kierkegaard's project. If it is "religious," as it certainly is, it proceeds by way of a religious delimitation of onto-theo-logic, a religous way out of philosophy and metaphysics, and hence belongs essentially to the project of the deconstruction or overcoming of metaphysics.

Without having this vocabulary at his disposal, Kierkegaard saw quite clearly into the shortcomings of the metaphysics of presence—the essential tendency of metaphysics to arrest the flux. He saw in the beginnings of metaphysics, in the doctrine of recollection, a philosophy of timeless presence which tells the story of the loss of presence and how presence lost can be restored. And he saw in its Hegelian completion the subordination of time and becoming to the immobility of logical necessity: In the beginning, an archeology of lost presence; at the end, a teleology of history rushing headlong into a historical *pleroma*, a *parousia*, a consummation of presence. In the one case, a nostalgia for a presence lost; in the other, a dreamy hope and rational optimism about presence promised. Metaphysics is essentially an archeo-teleological project.

Within the history of metaphysics, Kierkegaard saw only one alternative to its inveterate idealism, and that lay in the Aristotelian doctrine of *kinesis*. Against Plato and the Eleatics, Aristotle set his sights on movement and actuality, the real transition from the possible to the actual. But in fact Kierkegaard was pressing Aristotelianism, and philosophy generally, beyond its limits, putting demands upon it which it could not meet. That is why Kierkegaard always had to look for heroes *outside* metaphysics: Socrates, the great existing individual just before metaphysics who regarded the doctrine of recollection as a temptation to be resisted; Abraham and Job, on the outskirts of faith in the Old Testament; and finally the knight of faith himself, the Christian believer, St. Paul's "just man." The real, the concrete, the existing, the temporal, the free and contingent—these were matters for which the categories of metaphysics were in principle unprepared. Metaphysics always wants to keep a safe distance from the flux and to maintain its balance by means of an objectifying thinking. It maintains itself at a distance from the flux and thereby induces the optical illusion of stillness, even as from a distance the square tower looks round. It is always on the lookout for the stable essence, the law that constrains movement, the *eidos* and the *Begriff* which keeps the flux in check.

But as soon as metaphysics becomes interested, as soon as it is drawn into the flux and loses its protective barrier, it is forced to acknowledge the groundless play, the abyss, the absence inhabiting every claim to presence. What concerned Kierkegaard above all was the mysterious movement of faith, the midnight hour of faith, the abyss in which the existing individual, outside the protective shelter of the universal, takes his stand before God. What concerned Kierkegaard was the darkness of faith, not the light of reason, the abyss of freedom, not the reliability of logic. His thought takes place in the twilight zone between presence and absence, the point of intersection, of the interweaving of eternity and time.

Thus the deeply deconstructive element in Kierkegaard, which begins the work of dismantling the apparatus of metaphysics, belongs to a hermeneutic[24] attempt to restore the sphere of "actuality." Kierkegaard displaces the philosophy of Being and presence with *inter-esse,* with being-in-the-midst-of, with existence always already exposed to the flux. This deconstructive work leads us back to the human condition, not in the sense of the humanism which he rejected, but in the sense of a decentering of human willfulness which reveals the poverty of our circumstances. It leads us back to the original difficulty of life which metaphysics always wants to erase. In repetition we press ahead into what Derrida calls the *ébranler,* where the whole trembles *(sollicitare),* a region which is marked for Kierkegaard by "fear and trembling," from which, like the companion piece published on the same day, repetition cannot be separated.

TWO

Repetition and Constitution: Husserl's Proto-Hermeneutics

FROM THE GENESIS OF SELF TO THE GENESIS OF SENSE

Kierkegaard's notion of existential repetition is but one element in the attempt of twentieth-century hermeneutics to come to grips with the flux. I want to show now that what can be called here the "first essence" of hermeneutics, the sense that was set for it by *Being and Time*, is inseparable from Husserl's phenomenology. If hermeneutics is inconceivable apart from Kierkegaard and the project of existential repetition, of founding the self in the midst of the flux, it is also unimaginable without phenomenology and its own sort of epistemic repetition. In its first essence, hermeneutics is both existential and phenomenological, and it is just this existential, phenomenological substructure of hermeneutics which comes under attack in Derrida and the late Heidegger himself. What I call here "radical hermeneutics" is fired by the deconstructive critique of "hermeneutic phenomenology" and thus in an important way is postphenomenological and post-existential.

Husserl no less than Kierkegaard had a keen appreciation of the dynamics of the flux. His phenomenological method turned on the assumption that unless a way can be found to order and stabilize the incessant flow of experience, to feel about for its regularities, we would be at the mercy of the chaos and the "world" could never be "constituted." Husserl thus set out on an inquiry that could not have differed more from Kierkegaard's but nonetheless traced out a parallel orbit. It is part of the genius of *Being and Time* to have seen this, even as part of the difficulty of that book lies in the still-unresolved tension in it between this oddest of couples.

Kierkegaard and Husserl: on the one hand, the intensity of religious passion, a conundrum of witty, farcical, satiric, imaginative experiments, a Chinese puzzle box of pseudonyms and indirect communication; on the other, the dispassionate serenity, the austere *(streng)* self-discipline of science, the search for univocal language and direct communication. If Kierkegaard sought an existential conquest of the flux, Husserl sought to do epistemological battle with it. While Kierkegaard was concerned with the existing subject, Husserl was taken up with the "noetic" subject. If Kierkegaard was interested in the constitution of the existing self in the midst of the world flux, Husserl was concerned with the constitution of the world in the flux of internal time-consciousness. Two philosophies of life and becoming: existential life and becoming on the one hand, intentional life and genesis on the other.

In both cases we find a philosophy of productivity, of inscribing a pattern in an otherwise uncontrollable drift, and a philosophy of repetition, of the creative production of unity by means of a constituting act which, by repeating again and again, brings forth an existential unity in one case, and in the other, an ideal unity, the unity of meaning—in the one, the engendering of existential unity; in the other, of noematic unity. Here, the genesis of the self, there, the genesis of sense; existential genesis and sense-genesis; the choice of self and the constitution of meaning. In both thinkers we have to do not with a movement in reverse to a preexistent world but with one which pushes forward to the product to be engendered, with repetition and constitution, not recollecting. Two philosophies of becoming, two accounts of the Heraclitean flow, of the existential stream on the one hand, of the stream of conscious experiences (*Erlebnisstrom*) on the other.

In this chapter I want to show that, understood as a philosopher of repetition and the flow, Husserl contributes in an essential way to the strategy of hermeneutics. For hermeneutics in the broadest sense means for me coping with the flux, tracing out a pattern in a world in slippage. Hermeneutics is the latest form of the philosophy of becoming, the latest response to the Heraclitean challenge. For Husserl, the flux is at once the raw material of phenomenology and its constant opposite. It is at once that which requires fixation, stabilization, regularization, and so gives phenomenology the work it has to do, and it is that which threatens the whole enterprise of phenomenology, that which, left unchecked, will break down its entire scientific edifice. I will argue that Husserl finds the means to fix the flux in a doctrine of constitution which has a particularly hermeneutic resonance. I mean by this that everything in Husserlian constitution turns on a certain *anticipatory* movement, a gesture of regularizing the flow by means of anticipating its regularities, of sketching out beforehand the patterns to which it conforms, of trying in effect to keep one step ahead of it. The flux is not raw and random but organizes itself into patterns which build up expectations in us about its next move, and this "building up" of expectations is the key to the "constitution" of the world. Experience is the momentum of such expectations, their progressive confirmation or disconfirmation, refinement or replacement. Experience moves ahead by the repetition of patterns, which builds up their credibility, or by modifying them so as to make them credible.

Husserl's "anticipatory" theory of constitution is an essential ingredient in the "hermeneutic" method Heidegger practices in *Being and Time*, a point which will be confirmed in the next chapter. And that, it turns out, throws into confusion the familiar way we have of distinguishing Husserl's "pure" or transcendental phenomenology from Heidegger's "hermeneutic" phenomenology. Husserl, we are told, insisted upon the primacy of "intuition," upon the privilege of the "given," and upon the ideal of presuppositionlessness in his characterization of phenomenology. But for hermeneutics objects are not given but interpreted, not intuited but construed, and the point is not to get free from presuppositions but to find the right ones. We are in the habit of opposing "phenomenology" to "hermeneutics," or pure transcendental phenomenology to hermeneutic phenomenology, and of pitting Husserl against *Being and Time*. I want to show that there is something importantly misleading about that standard dichotomy and that Husserlian phenomenology has an essentially hermeneutic component.

But that raises the question of how Heidegger and Husserl genuinely differ, a matter which is focused for me on that point in Husserlian phenomenology where it backs off from its own hermeneutic tendencies. In a sense one can say, to borrow Deleuze's phrase, that Husserl does not want to "pay the price" for a philosophy of the flux *(supra,* n. 25). I mark the true divide between Husserl and *Being and Time* just at that point where Husserl tries to insulate phenomenology from the flux.

At that point Husserl's project falls into complicity with Platonism and is subverted by a philosophy of recollection, of making-present-again, and hence by what we nowadays call the metaphysics of presence. For Husserl thinks it possible to surmount the hermeneutic conditions he himself has laid down and to lay hold of consciousness in a perfect return that violates everything he has to say about predelineation. In this regard, Kierkegaard will emerge as the more radical thinker who was all along concerned with delimiting metaphysics, while Husserl aspires to a phenomenology that is the secret dream of Western metaphysics, the fulfillment of the Western *telos* for science. Husserl and Kierkegaard thus both address the "end" of philosophy, but Husserl was interested in the end as *telos,* Kierkegaard in the end as foundering.

Husserl's phenomenology represents at best a kind of "proto-hermeneutics": a "hermeneutic" because it shows how we make our way through the flow of experience by means of certain anticipatory cuts which adumbrate its structure and predict its course, which give us a reading or interpretation of things; but a "proto-hermeneutics" because in the end it backs off from the full implications of its own discovery. At that point we will be in a position to examine the confluence of Kierkegaardian and Husserlian themes in *Being and Time*, to see how Heidegger was able to bring together two philosophies of repetition—the Kierkegaardian doctrine of the genesis of self and the Husserlian theory of the genesis of sense—in a uniquely powerful "hermeneutic phenomenology" and "historical repetition."

Then, in part 2, we will see how this synthesis is itself subjected to a new and surprising critique issuing in part from Heidegger himself and in part from Derrida, where for the first time we will hear the voice of Nietzsche who is the most outspoken advocate of the flux and of the innocence of becoming in our time. At that point we must ask whether the whole project of hermeneutics is dissipated or whether it can survive, albeit in a more radicalized form.

EXPLICATING INTENTIONAL LIFE

For Husserl, the work of phenomenology consists in unpacking the prereflective, prethematic, or, as he puts it, the "horizonal" structures which are at work in the "wakeful cogito." He takes consciousness to be a composite of focal and marginal components and the work of phenomenology to be an "un-folding" or "ex-plicating" of this marginal life, which is what he meant by *Auslegung*. This is the same word, of course, which is used by Heidegger in *Being and Time* and rendered in the English translation as "interpretation." *Aus-legen* means to lay out, or make explicit, the tacit structures of intentional life. The English "explicate"[1] means literally to unfold the plies or folds in the manifold constitution of intentional life. Intentionality is not a simple or blank looking-at, as the German *an-schauen* suggests, but a complex, highly structured interpretive act. To say that consciousness is always consciousness *of* is not to invoke some magic by which a simple and unfettered consciousness is borne into a pure given. On the contrary it is to point to a complex activity in virtue of which objects are enabled to appear at all. The "principle of all principles" (*Ideas I*, §24) is not a call to naked intuition, which is how it sounds, but a summons to understand givenness in all its complexity.

Experience of the thematic object is made possible by certain fore-structures which provide its antecedent conditions of possibility. These fore-structures correspond to what in hermeneutics is called the "pre-understanding," and it is the task of phenomenological explication to ferret them out. Phenomenological reflection uncovers the antecedent conditions already embedded in experience. As "analysis" (*Analyse*) of the complexity of intentional life, phenomenological explication does not reach atomic elements, bits and pieces of experience, which need only to be separated out and then shown to be combinable according to certain laws (Hua I 83/CM 46). Rather, intentional analysis has to do with a subtle blending of the potential and the actual, the implicit and the explicit. For every actual intentional experience is inhabited by a ring of potentialities which play a decisive role in structuring that experience. Intentional analysis sets forth the mute components of intentional life, for the intentional object is always *more* than it first presents itself to be. The principle of all principles thus is no endorsement of a shortsighted empiricism which constricts experience into isolable atoms of experience. Rather, it implies a wariness of the "pretentiousness" of experience, which "continually pretends in fact more than it can do in accordance with its own essence" (Hua XI 11). Experience always contains a *plus ultra;* it always means more than "what is meant at that moment explicitly" (Hua I 84/CM 46).

Properly understood, the principle of all principles is a principle of suspicion which suspects that there is more to what is given than it gives itself out to be. Thus the phenomenon is not taken by Husserl to be pure presence—and this bears on the Derridean critique of Husserl which we will discuss in chapter 5 below—but a complex of presence and absence or, better, the explicit and the implicit, the actual and the potential. The only way to stay with the given as given is to appreciate that it is always more than it gives itself out to be. "Consciousness of . . ." is always consciousness of something *more*, of hitherto unnoticed factors.

If intentional acts and their correlative objects are not isolable, atomic data, that is because they are always bound about by what Husserl calls a "horizon-structure." The perceptual object, indeed the intentional object generally, is bound about by a ring of horizons which provides it with an inherently contextual meaning.[2] The conscious act and the intended object belong to a concatenation of acts and objective aspects which it is precisely the work of intentional analysis to uncover (Hua I 86/CM 48). Everything focal implies a margin or horizon (Hua I 81–82/CM 44). At any given moment the side of the object "immediately given"—we require scare quotes, for that is something continuously vanishing as well—is gird about with a fringe of cogiven, mediately present sides which belong integrally to its structure, sides which, while not directly perceived, are nonetheless "ap-perceived," "perceived-with." The full perceptual object is thus a complex of perceived and apperceived, present and copresent, focal and horizonal. The object appears in the interplay "between" them. Were this not so the object would be a facade and we would be surprised to encounter its other sides. Contextuality, or horizonality, is constantly, marginally "retained." A writer sitting at a desk in a cabin in the woods would be astonished, say, to hear the roar of traffic outside the window, although that is not an astonishing noise "in itself."

Horizons are not vacuous and wholly indeterminate potentialities; they are not *absent* but "predelineated" (*vorgezeichnet*): "The horizons are predelineated potentialities" (Hua I 82/CM 45). This notion of predelineation, *Vorzeichnung*, is one to which I attach a great deal of importance. *Vor-zeichnen* means to trace or sketch beforehand, to trace something lightly in advance. One thinks of a light pencil sketch which a painter might then fill in with his oils. It is in fact a word with Derridean resonance (or, to keep the chronology straight, a Husserlian resonance in Derrida). The marginal trace is neither there nor not there, neither present nor absent, but an implicit, marginal factor which contributes in an essential way to the structure of the given, of what does appear and is there, so that what is present is an effect or product of the trace. (Husserl is groping for something like Aristotelian *kinesis*, a between-land which is neither presence nor absence.) Taken in conjunction with *Abschattung*, which means a certain shadowing or adumbration, the word *Vorzeichnung* betokens the central role of the fore-structure in Husserl's theory of intentionality. Intentionality is possible only to the extent that the object is adequately foreshadowed, traced in advance, prepared for by what we can only call here a certain hermeneutic fore-structuring which provides the preliminary or anticipatory preparation for the actual appearance of the object. In *Erste Philosophie*, the outer horizon which surrounds the perceptual object is called a *Vordeutung:* a preinterpretation, foremeaning (Hua VII 149).

Vorzeichnung is a suggestive hermeneutic theme in Husserl's phenomenology. The intentional object is possible only to the extent that it is prepared for in advance by an anticipatory fore-structure. The progress of experience is not a matter of continually being amazed by what is ever new, or of being confounded by the flux, but rather of filling in *(Erfüllung)* already predelineated horizons (or, alternately, of revising expectations when we are indeed surprised). The object then is never some raw given; rather, it is always an entity which can appear only under the condition that it can insert itself within a frame of expectations—that is to say, only if we know how to "take" it, to construe it.

The intentional object for Husserl is always something interpreted, even as intending has always meant interpreting. Despite his own rhetoric, Husserl clearly rejected the idea of a "pure given" and always understood intentionality as interpretation. The whole point of his many detailed investigations into intentional life was precisely to show that experience takes place only under a subtle structuring and rendering on the part of consciousness which weaves the world into a unity of meaning. To perceive for him is to know how to take a thing, to know how to render it.

Here, in this work of tracing and synthesis, of the building up of the preconditions under which it is possible to produce the object, Husserl is clearly elaborating a philosophy of a repetition which moves forward, which is able to weave out of the progress of experience the progressive result of the object, the noematic unity, the interwoven result. The object is the synthetic unity of its ingredient noemata, a "system" of noemata, which is something of a Husserlian equivalent to textuality in Derrida—the object as interwoven, from *texere*. Consciousness builds up and constitutes, makes up the object by making up for what is missing at any given moment—and this by a retention (repetition) which is compounded with protention in such a way as to bring the flow of *Erlebnisse* to a contingent rest.

This was already plain as early as the notion of *Auffassung* in the *Logical Investigations*. To intend is to "apprehend" or interpret *(auffassen)*, to seize or take *(prehendere, fassen)* something up *(auf)* in a determinate way, to take it as a particular such and such. He used the example of a word written in a script which is unknown to us. At first, we take it to be a kind of pleasing arabesque until we realize that it is writing, that is, until we come to take it *as* writing. The same kind of shift occurs when we hear a strange sound only to discover that it is a word. *Auffassung* is the "surplus" *(Überfluss)* between simply looking at something and taking it *as* the thing which it is, so that it is not a mere subjective sensation but the scent of flowers (LU II/1 385/LI 567). We perceive already-interpreted objects. The sensate raw material—of itself unin-terpreted—is not perceived at all, although it is a certain component of the psychical process *(Erlebnis)* in which an object is apprehended. This appercep-tive, interpretive act is identical with intentionality itself (LU II/1 385/LI 567–68). It is by means of *Auffassung* that a certain buzzing in the ear becomes the act of hearing the automobile motor idling outside the window.

This is by no means to say that Husserl has recourse to the empiricist schema of sensations-plus-interpretation.[3] For Husserl, the empiricist notion of a sensa-tion is displaced by the perceptual intention of an object whose work is to construe the perceptual object as the thing which it is. To lack this interpretive moment is to be left not with some uninterpreted given but with no "object" at all. And that occurs only on rare and aberrant occasions (when, e.g., we are thrown into confusion by a sip of "milk" which turns out to have been milk of magnesia). In that intervening moment—between the perception of two recog-nizably different and distinguishable objects—there is only subjective confusion and consternation, when the subject is robbed of his intentional thrust into the world and thrown back upon a purely private *Erlebnis*.

At this moment in Husserl's phenomenology, and speaking from our Heracli-tean perspective, we are exposed to the flux, which for Husserl is the *Erleb-nisstrom*, a pure flow of subjective acts, a river of sensate materials which have not been stabilized, organized, grasped about, and interpreted. Here experi-ence runs out of control, and for one disconcerting moment we lose our bearings, our momentum into the world. Then phenomenology finds itself exposed to its opposite—whence the absolute necessity for the interpretive act to intervene. Without the moment of interpretation we are given not a pure datum, an uninterpreted given, but a kind of Husserlian equivalent of the primeval chaos. Husserl thus rejects the theory of sensations (which are for him uninterpreted sense data) in favor of a theory of intentional perception.[4]

We ought therefore to be wary of Husserl's rhetoric about returning to pure givenness in the famous "principle of all principles" (Hua III.1 51/*Ideas I* 44). For even here, where Husserl's intuitionism reaches its most extreme formulation, there is still mention of taking the given "as what" (*als was*) it gives itself to be. The self-giving of the thing is never detachable from its as-structure. To be given is to be given *as*; to take up the given is to take it *as*.

We are not arguing that there is no given in Husserl or that he has no theory of intuition, but only that these notions are not naively formulated by him, that he has a critical sense of the limits of intuitionism. For him, to intuit the given means to know how to construe what presents itself, failing which there is only the flux. The injunction to remain with the given includes the reminder that the given is given only *as* something. This hermeneutico-interpretive moment in Husserl's theory of intentionality resolves the tension between Husserl's intuitionism and his theory of constitution by reading the former in terms of the latter. Properly understood, *reine Anschauung* means knowing how to interpret.

The role of hyletic data in Husserl's theory—which have a special significance in our Heraclitean problematic—is to explain what happens when the intentionality of perception breaks down. But the matter/form theory of interpretive act and hyletic matter is at best incomplete. As Sokolowski points out, it serves to *locate* meaning in intentional life, not to explain its *origin*.[5] If intentional life is a flowing stream, the matter/form theory isolates, synchronically, a cross-sectional slice whose structure it describes, while leaving out of consideration its temporal, progressive development.

As Husserl developed his account of intentionality, the interpretive element, far from disappearing, developed accordingly. The intentional object, Husserl argued, is not merely "apprehended" (*aufgefasst*) but, in order to be apprehended, must be construed or apprehended "in advance" (*aufgefasst im voraus*) (Hua I 83/CM 45). And that leads us directly to the notion of "horizon" and "predelineation" on which my account of Husserl's "proto-hermeneutics" is centered.

THE "PREDELINEATION" OF EXPERIENCE

In the famous discussion of the annihilation of the world (*Weltvernichtung: Ideas I*, §49), Husserl wants to demonstrate that every object is the correlate of the act in which it is apprehended or constituted. And he does this by means of an imaginative experiment which shows that even if the world were varied away, consciousness would remain. The whole discussion has a misleadingly metaphysical tone set by Husserl's highly Cartesian language.[6] Still, he is not arguing a metaphysical idealism (that an immaterial consciousness would survive the physical annihilation of the world) but an epistemic or phenomenological point: an object is an object for consciousness only inasmuch as consciousness has been motivated to constitute it as such. He is addressing the phenomenology of "motivation," not proving the metaphysical subsistence of consciousness.

Because of the regular concatenations of experience, consciousness is moved to pick out particular formations and endow them with "objectivity." Were the clouds in the sky suddenly to organize themselves into ferocious animals and then descend upon the landscape devouring everything in their path, were the surfaces of the streets suddenly to burst into flames, were everything in general capable of the wildest and most unforeseeable transformations, and were such things as this to happen incessantly and unpredictably, then the "world" would break down. For the "world" is a unity of meaning, a collection of more or less stable objects, in which indeed transformations follow the rule of law. Were that order disrupted, Husserl contends, consciousness would not vanish but survive, left to survey the disaster. It is this wild irregularity, not some metaphysical annihilation, that Husserl means to describe by *Vernichtung*. He has in mind not the real or metaphysical destruction of the world but the breakdown of the world-as-phenomenon, the world as a unity of meaning. The outcome of this thought-experiment is to show the extent to which "objects" are the product of the synthetic, concatenating life of consciousness which, moved by the regularity of their appearance, "constitutes" them in a synthetic unity.

This is a suggestive hypothesis from the point of the present study. Husserl has an acute appreciation of the "contingency" of the world and of mundane arrangements, of the alterability of constituted objects and of familiar configurations. Indeed, Husserl's sensitivity to contingency, extending as it does not merely to "cultural" objects but to physical objects themselves, is really quite radical. He takes not merely local cultural practices to be alterable but natural objects themselves. Only the regularized structures, the constituted patterns which the transcendental subject is motivated to form by reason of the regularity of their appearance, separate us from the abyss, from the flux into which things would otherwise be thrown. And indeed the flux is always there, on the horizon, as a constantly outstanding possibility into which the world is always able in principle to degenerate.

The real world is the world which, motivated by actual concatenations of experience, has actually taken shape in experience. And corresponding to this are the real and more or less likely "possibilities" opened up by the actual course which experience takes. Thus the possible in the primary sense means the experienceable (*erfahrbar*), not merely some abstract, logical possibility (Hua III.1 101/*Ideas I* 106–107). The "possible" in this sense is the realm of experiences whose possibility has been sketched out beforehand, to a more or less complete extent, by the course of actual experience—the possibility to walk on the surface of the moon, to explore the depths of the ocean, to assume a new role in life, etc. These are possibilities whose essential content has been more or less prefigured and predelineated—Husserl uses the important word *Vorzeichnung* here—by actual experience. We have already projected the horizon within which such an experience can take place. Were we unable to carry out this predelineation, it would be quite impossible even to conceive such possible experiences. They belong to "the undetermined but *determinable* horizon of my experiential actuality at the particular time" (Hua III.1 101/*Ideas I* 107). The object which is able to appear has been prepared for in advance *(im voraus)* by the horizons which have been projected beforehand. These objects represent not empty but motivated possibilities whose "essential type" *(Wesentypus)* has been predelineated beforehand.

Such predelineation makes all subsequent experience possible. It is a universal law of intentionality, therefore, that every object of possible experience depends upon a prior projection of its essential type or, to use Heidegger's language, a prior understanding of its Being. This prior projection is no Kantian a priori (GA 24, §22c), for it is drawn from and motivated by the actual course of experience, and it is furthermore subject to ongoing temporal revision, as former horizons are filled in and new ones are opened up. In other words, it is a gradually accumulated a priori, the product of repetition, of the repetition of the regularities of experience, and not some metaphysical prior presence, some a priori form or preexistent idea. It is a creative, not a recreative or representational, repetition.

Such motivated possibilities are significantly different from merely formal or logical possibilities, that is, possibilities for which we have not the slightest evidence other than the thought that they involve no formal contradiction. Consider, e.g., the possibility that there is a world entirely different from ours. It is a world for which we have no projective interpretation, no predelineated horizon, and hence it remains an entirely unmotivated possibility. Indeed I think that Husserl holds to a "fusion of horizons" theory on this point. Any possible being must, in principle, be locatable somewhere on the outer horizonal limits of actual experience. Even commerce with extraterrestrial beings must be prepared for on the basis of actual experience, which means a constant moving back and forth between our experience and theirs, assimilating their experience within our horizons, revising our horizons on the basis of their experience, even as they on their part do the same—until finally some point of convergence and fusion can be reached (Hua III.1 102–103/*Ideas I* 108). Gradually, by means of a back-and-forth movement between assimilation and revision, carried out on both sides of the dialogue, a chain of experiences can be constituted which would link one experience with the other within the unity of a single world.

That makes non-sense, or what Husserl calls, quite precisely, "material counter-sense" *(sachlicher Widersinn)*, out of the hypothesis of a world of experience which is absolutely heterogenous from ours. Such a world, while it is not formally incoherent, the way a square circle is, makes no material, real, substantive sense.[7] Our powers of projective thought, of horizonal predelineation, fail before it, and we find ourselves confronting a merely "transcendental object = X," as Kant puts it, an object to which we can give no possible shape, that we cannot prefigure or sketch out beforehand in even the remotest way, with even the slightest of tracings (Hua III.1 103/*Ideas I* 108–109).

Nonetheless, experience is always and necessarily inhabited by the transcendental possibility of the breakdown of the concatenations of experiences to which we have become accustomed. Any worldly object, as indeed the world as a whole, remains always a "presumptive" unity, a tentative organization of the flux upon which we cannot absolutely rely:

> It is instead quite conceivable that experience, because of conflict, might dissolve into illusion. . . . [I]t is conceivable that there might be a host of irreconcilable conflicts not just for us but in themselves, that experience might suddenly show itself to be refractory to the demand that it carry on its positings of physical things harmoniously, that its context might lose its fixed, regular organizations of adumbrations, apprehensions, and appearances—in short, that there might no longer be any world. (Hua III.1 91/*Ideas I* 109)

What then is absolute? Is there anything about which we can have absolute assurance that it is solid and unshakable? Husserl's surprising answer is that it is only the flux itself which remains constant. The only constancy is the flow; the only thing which will not change is change itself. Even the stability of the transcendental "ego" is not absolute, for it is constituted, he says, in "what is ultimately and truly absolute" (Hua III.1 182/*Ideas I* 193). For this truly absolute absolute Husserl refers us to the Göttingen lectures on internal time-consciousness where, in §§34–36, Husserl distinguishes three levels of constitution, which proceed, as it were, from the outside in (to internal time-consciousness) or from the surface down (to the profound and deep-lying [*tiefliegend*] subject.

First, he marks off objects in "objective" time, transcendent objects in the straightforward sense of objects which are outside, or transcendent to, the conscious stream. An object is defined by its persistence in time, its capacity to maintain its identity throughout a time-flow. The house, as a material object, is a unity of meaning built up in time-consciousness as something transcendent to time-consciousness. Second, the immanent unities, or "immanent transcendencies," which are built up within the conscious time-flow itself, are the structural configurations which are built up *in* the time-flow, the subjective acts—say, of perceiving, remembering, or desiring the house—which belong to the life of the ego as the overarching, highest immanent unity. But finally there is that in which even such immanent unities are themselves constituted, the time-flow itself, the absolute stream, the absolute streaming of the stream, the flux *(Fluss)* itself:

> We can only say that this flux is something which we name in conformity with what is constituted, but it is nothing temporally "Objective." It is absolute subjectivity and has the absolute properties of something to be denoted metaphorically *(im Bilde)* as "flux," as a point of actuality, primal source-point, that from which springs the "now," and so on. In the lived-experience of actuality, we have the primal source-point and a continuity of moments of reverberation. For all this, names are lacking. (Hua X 75/PIT 100)[8]

Indeed, were one able clearly to distinguish literal and metaphoric, something which has become problematic today, I would be more inclined to say that it is "absolute subject" which supplies the metaphor here for what is much more properly described as "flux." Husserl is right to say that this ultimate matrix in which all unities of meaning, including all word-unities, are constituted does not itself have a proper name. But if it did, I would rather call it the pure stream.

In Husserl's image, the flux "underlies" the unities of meaning which accumulate, including even the "internal" or immanent unities of the ego and its properties. Even these subjective acts are to be understood as contingent stabilizations of experience, ways of ordering the flux which are as vulnerable to annihilation *(Vernichtung)*, that is to say, to a disruption of their harmonies, as are their worldly counterparts. If the remembered house is dissipated, the correlative remembering is dissipated too. All that "endures," all that "remains" is the flux itself, the streaming and flowing of conscious experience. It alone survives the breakdown of hermeneutic order, the failure of the hermeneutic harmonies.

Here is the transcendental, epistemic equivalent, the Husserlian counterpart, to Constantin Constantius's lament in *Repetition* that life is a meaningless stream and that the stagecoach horn is his symbol. Here both Husserl and Kierkegaard face the possibility that there is no repetition, no movement forward in which a stable unity—of self or sense—is constituted. Both catch glimpses of a point where the harmonies of metaphysics founder. For Husserl there is nothing but this flux, nothing given, without the dynamics of predelineation which we have been describing here. The dynamics of intentional life turn on a *Vorstruktur,* a prestructuring, which clearly paves the way for the "hermeneutic fore-structures" which Heidegger takes up in *Being and Time* and which I will examine in detail in the next chapter. By reason of these fore-structures, we are able to "fix" (Hua III.1 103/*Ideas I* 108) the flux and stabilize it within predelineated constraints which make it possible for something to appear in the first place.[9]

THE HISTORICAL GENESIS OF SENSE

For whatever reasons—perhaps it was the impact of *Being and Time*[10]—in Husserl's last writings, the work of inscribing pattern in the flux takes on a historical dimension, and the object of phenomenological investigation switches from the internal history of the ego to the movement of Western history at large. In the *Logical Investigations*, constitution was static and atemporal; in *Ideas I* it achieved a temporal but still ahistorical sense. Finally, in the thirties, constitution becomes the work of an intersubjective, historical community. The genesis of sense becomes a sense-history, and constitution acquires a historical coefficient.

But the history which Husserl proceeds to write is of a most extraordinary sort, for it has nothing to do with history in the usual sense, with tracking down ancient documents or historical episodes (Hua VI 366/*Crisis* 354). It is answerable only to a higher phenomenological authority, to the demands of essence and *a priori* necessity. It is a history written to cure a cultural crisis with an epistemic antidote, to heal a morbidity which infects the very *eidos*—the founding intentions—and *telos*—the ultimate goal—of Western Europe, viz., the dream of universal science (Hua VI 319/*Crisis* 273). It is a history meant to right a tradition which has begun to drift from the infinite idea which gives it life.

This is accomplished by an extraordinary retelling of the story of Galileo, one which ignores completely the strife between science and the church and one which has nothing to do with any "scientific revolution" or paradigm switch. On the contrary, on Husserl's telling, what Galileo did arises precisely from the naïveté with which he simply takes over the inherited scientific—here geometric—tradition and proceeds to build upon it as if it dropped from the sky. Husserl's historical reduction consists in suspending the inherited self-evidence of geometry and, by way of a meditation which proceeds in reverse (*Rückbesinnung:* Hua VI 16/*Crisis* 17–18), to dig back into the founding acts (*Urstiftung*) which give geometric constructions their sense. And that produces the remarkable notion of an *a priori* history which proceeds by way of a reenactment (*Nachstiftung*) bent on recovering the forgotten beginning (*Crisis*, §15). The first geometers *must have* lived in a world of material and cultural objects and of fellow human beings. Such bodies *must have* been spatiotemporal and qualitatively determined. The early geometers *must have* had practical needs which could be met only by a *praxis* whose task was to make these bodies conform to human need. They needed to make surfaces smooth, edges square, lines straight—if they were efficiently to tend their fields and erect their buildings, to sew and cook and meet their other needs. But for this technical praxis an ideal praxis was first required, one which could carry out these operations without the resistance offered by empirical reality (Hua VI 383–84/*Crisis* 375–77; cf.

§9a). If a historical novelist can add an imaginative touch or two to enrich his factual store, the phenomenological historian injects lines of a priori necessity into his story with which the facts must accord.

Having shown (a priori) that these original geometric constructions did not spring full-grown from the breasts of the first geometers, Husserl points to the laborious and cumulative historical process by which ideality was layered upon ideality so that simpler idealities became elements in more complex ones and the work of one generation became the matter out of which new structures were devised by succeeding generations. It is only "natural"—there is a kind of historical natural attitude—that after a long process of development and repetition, the original moorings of these idealizations would drop out of sight. By the time of Galileo the beginnings had been forgotten, and the origin of these higher-order geometric structures in the life-world lay in oblivion. Thus arose the myth of objectivism, that this mathematical account of nature is independent of transcendental subjectivity. The life-world, which lies on the margin of the sciences, and with which the early geometers moved in easy and familiar commerce, became a horizon which receded more and more out of sight with the progress of idealization. And that is the basis of the current crisis which requires transcendental cure.

As Derrida points out, the story Husserl is telling catches him up in a new understanding of the role of language.[11] Husserl had always done his best to hold language at a distance from the inner reaches of phenomenology. In *Ideas I* language is described as a merely expressive stratum layered over the primal intentional relationship of meaning. He distinguished a founding level of pre-linguistic meaning *(Sinn)* from a superstratum of *"logos"* or signification *(Bedeutung)*, which simply gives expression to meaning (§§124–27). Still, one can find a soft spot even in the hard line Husserl adopts in *Ideas I*. For, while refusing to grant *logos* any productive role, he does concede that, as a mirroring *(Spiegeln)* or picturing *(Abbilden)* of primal intentionality, signification is not a perfect mirror or a simple reduplication. If the signification does not add to the founding intentionality, it can at least clarify it by simplifying it. The expression is always a partial reproduction of the original meaning, yet this incompleteness is not a failure of language but the key to its power and economy. For without general terms, which purposely leave out particulars, language would degenerate into an infinity of proper names. Language gives the founding intentionality a sharper, more focused, and more articulate sense.

Founding experiences therefore get "deposited" in linguistic expressions and hence can be "passed on," thus constituting the possibility of a "tradition." But in such a process the ties between the original experiences and their carriers weaken. Thus the task of the historical "reduction" is to keep these founding and animating bonds alive by retracing the track from the primal experiences to the expressions which bear them through the historical process. The economy of language—it is not efficient to have constant recourse to founding intuitions or to repeat original experiences every time a word is used—is its very danger (*Gefahr:* Hua VI 372/*Crisis* 362). For without this economy a scientific tradition, indeed a tradition of any sort, is impossible. But in such an economy expressions may become hollow shells, more and more detached from their original sense, thus generating a "crisis" in that tradition.

Clearly the work of historical constitution depends upon the power of language to package and deliver (to use Derrida's postal metaphor) these original idealizations. The original moment in which an ideal structure is brought forth will come to naught unless it can be brought forth at will, again and again, unless it is "repeatable" (*wiederholbar:* Hua VI 370/*Crisis* 360) by any geometer, anytime. Now it falls to language to bestow this objective, repeatable, communicable form upon the founding act, so that it can become part of the established human community, so that it can enter the company of public science. The great economy of language is to give us a means of repetition so that the self-same ideal structure, the Pythagorean theorem, let us say, may be indefinitely repeated, first within the confines of the same consciousness, then across the entire scientific community of the day, and then throughout all time. Thus, despite his own metaphysical prejudice against language, Husserl is acutely aware of its productive, creative, constitutive power. And it is in just this space between Husserl's critical and his metaphysical moments that Derridean "deconstruction" situates itself.[12]

Husserl goes still further in recognizing the "productive" role that language plays in historical constitution by pointing out that the summit of objectivity/ repeatability cannot be reached without writing. Without writing we cannot insure the persistent existence (*verharrendes Dasein:* Hua VI 371/*Crisis* 360) of these ideal structures, which means their capacity to survive when no one is thinking them or bringing them to self-evidence (Hua 371/*Crisis* 360–61). Writing is language in which neither the speaker nor the one spoken to need be present. The summit of repeatability is to so embed meaning in a sign that anyone, anywhere, may at some time reenact it, even though the original author and audience have long since vanished. Writing then—presumably the most removed and distant stratum in the meaning/expression (*Sinn/Bedeutung*) stratification—is here assigned a central role at the heart of transcendental constitution. The "dead letter," which the metaphysical Husserl would presumably want most to exclude—this is the point of the Derridean reading of Husserl—is here given a central and irreplaceable function in transcendental life.

But that daring act of making writing important is at the same time the source of the danger. For writing makes the living meaning virtual; it reduces it to a state of dormancy which is the very means of passing it on. The power of its extension is directly proportional to the power of the sign to reduce meaning to a merely dormant (signified) state. Hence writing requires a correlative awakening and actualization, which is the role of reading. But when, by reading, we experience the meaning of written signs, thus making the virtual actual, we undergo a passive experience, of receiving meaning by way of an associative process guided by the written text (Hua VI 371/*Crisis* 361). And that puts an important demand upon the reader to transcend his merely passive state, to convert passivity into activity, to *reactivate* the original founding act in which the written sign was constituted in the first place:

> . . . what is passively awakened can be transformed back, so to speak, into the corresponding activity: that is the capacity for reactivation that belongs originally to every human being. (Hua VI 371/*Crisis* 361)

The reader bears the responsibility to reactivate the sedimented, to bring the meaning back to life.

That is why the transcendental cure for the crisis is indeed a *pharmakon*, for language, and especially writing, is as dangerous as it is necessary. If the originary intuitive life which constitutes meaning is entrusted to language, it simultaneously can be victimized by it. Thus Husserl warns against falling "victim to the *seduction of language*" (Hua VI 372/*Crisis* 362). Intentional life falls more and more under the spell of empty forms which just get repeated and passed along. Genuine discourse becomes chatter *(Gerede)*, to borrow the term which Heidegger borrowed from Kierkegaard. And the only antidote to the narcotic seductiveness of language is reactivation which, in its totality and completion, remains an infinite idea, belonging integrally to the infinite idea of universal science (Hua VI 373n/*Crisis* 362–63n).

Hence, while historical-linguistic constitution is an originary repetition— repeating, consolidating, complexifying, and handing on built-up meanings—in a teleological drive to fulfillment and perfect scientific rationality, it also demands of us an archeological return to beginnings. The creative process of historical constitution is a self-endangering but also a self-accumulating progress. It can be kept alive and full of the sense it harbors and passes on only by the meditation that goes in reverse. If the constitutive work of repetition goes forward, phenomenological reflection goes in reverse, retracing its steps. In Husserl's later writings, there is both a theory of repetition—the creative advance of a historically accumulating tradition—and a theory of recollection— the phenomenological historian retracing the steps of the tradition back to the founding acts.

In its last form the Husserlian conquest of the flux is necessarily an intersubjective, historical, and linguistic work, too much to expect of the transcendental individual. It is the labor of the generations, a work of historical repetition. The work first entrusted to a simple act of *Auffassung*, and then to the time-consciousness internal to the individual ego, finally becomes the work of a transcendental community. But however constitution is formulated, phenomenological reflection is always a work of *Auslegung*, of intentional explication, unfolding the implicit and mute factors which enter into the constitution and preformation of the world, whether they are conceived ahistorically, in terms of predelineation and the internal time stream, or as historically buried sedimentations, as in the *Crisis* period. The fundamental work of phenomenology is to make explicit what is implicit in transcendental constitution, to ferret out these mute performances, bring them into the light, make them explicit, lay them out: *aus-legen, legein ta phainomena*.

That is why I speak of Husserl's "proto-hermeneutics," for it is a philosophy which says that consciousness reads off the world in terms of a built-up complex of intentional factors, a highly complicated network of presuppositional structures, and that the task of phenomenological reflection is to flush these out into the open. That goes to the heart of what Heidegger means by hermeneutics in *Being and Time:* that understanding proceeds from preunderstanding, from fore-structures which provide a projective clearing of the field of entities which are to be understood. Hermeneutics copes with the flux by anticipating its next move, adumbrating the objects with which we will be confronted, trying always to keep one step ahead of the stream. It deploys an anticipatory strategy to address an old Eleatic puzzle.

HUSSERL'S DEPARTURE FROM HERMENEUTICS

According to the received reading, Husserl undertakes a presuppositionless inquiry into the pure given, while Heidegger looks for the right presuppositions in an interpretive, hermeneutic phenomenology. Now if the preceding discussion has any merit at all, it is to show that that is too facile and simplistic a rendering. Husserl's theory of constitution turns on the notion of fore-structures—of anticipatory predelineation, of horizon, of historical-linguistic acquisitions. Far from differing on this point, Heideggerian and Husserlian phenomenology are in fact precisely in agreement.

Intentionality for Husserl, and understanding for Heidegger (GA 24/BP §11–12), must always be guided beforehand by a preparatory grasp of what is to be understood, failing which they are left disoriented and cut adrift in the flux, unable to seize the matter at hand. Were consciousness unable to sketch beforehand the main lines of what is to be perceived, perception would break down, abandoned to a chaos of uninterpretable, unintended hyletic data or of internal time-flow. Were Dasein not equipped with a projective understanding of the Being of the entity to be interpreted, Dasein would be at the mercy of the most commonplace, publicly available framework of understanding, lest Dasein understand nothing at all. That is why, if we read "presuppositions" in the sense of "anticipatory predelineations," Husserl too can say with Heidegger:

Philosophy will never seek to deny its presuppositions but neither may it simply admit them. It conceives them, and it unfolds with more and more penetration both the presuppositions themselves and that for which they are presuppositions. (SZ 310/BT 358)

For both Husserl and Heidegger the work of phenomenology is a work of unfolding *(Entfaltung)*, explicating, laying out the implicit fore-structures which make explicit experience possible. Phenomenology is for both the *subtilitas explicandi*, unfolding the horizons without which no entity or object can appear. Derrida was quite right to say that in Husserl and Heidegger everything turns on the logic of implicit and explicit, which is why there is nothing vicious in the circular logic of phenomenology (cf. W&M 173/T&M 163; *Marg.* 151/126).

This is not to say, however, that Husserl does not, in the end, resist the hermeneutics which he himself sets in motion, that his thought does not, finally, fall victim to certain quite traditional metaphysical and antihermeneutical impulses. After all is said and done, it is only a "proto-hermeneutics" which I attribute to Husserl, not hermeneutics in a fully developed sense. At a critical point, Husserl backs into a traditional, antihermeneutic position.

In Heidegger the projective character of the understanding is itself rooted in the more profound ontological make-up of Dasein. The structure of the understanding reflects the Being of Dasein as care, existence, and temporality (a point which we will examine in more detail in the next chapter). It is precisely at this point that the ontology of Kierkegaard intervenes in *Being and Time* and in a particularly decisive manner. The hermeneutic circle in Heidegger thus is rooted in the Being of Dasein as care (SZ 315/BT 363). The projective character of understanding for Heidegger is a function of the Being of Dasein as a project. Understanding proceeds by way of projective predelineation *because* Dasein's Being is always ahead-of-itself. Heidegger's conception of hermeneutics is founded on an ontology of Dasein as existence. Whence the very notion of presuppositionlessness is an ontological paradox for Heidegger. To acquire presuppositionlessness Dasein would, *per impossibile*, have to undergo a change of Being such that it would no longer be Dasein but something else which is neither futural nor projective. It furthermore follows, according to the basic meaning of care, that Dasein is thrust or thrown into its presuppositions, for care means that Dasein is thrown as well as projective, factical as well as existential. Hence Dasein always moves about within a certain historically situated, factical understanding, or rather preunderstanding, from which it neither can nor wants to extricate itself. That, as we will see below, is the point of departure for Gadamer's extension of *Being and Time* in the direction of a "philosophical hermeneutics."[13]

In the case of Husserl, however, this Kierkegaardian ontology of care is nowhere to be found. Husserl makes no effort to root the analysis of predelineation in an ontological subsoil. It is his intention that the theory of *Vorzeichnung*, indeed the entirety of his phenomenological view, be ontologically innocent, unencumbered by ontological presuppositions. Phenomenology ought to have a purely descriptive status; it ought to arise only from the independent work of phenomenological reflection, without drawing from the well of ontology. Husserl thinks that the reflective life of the phenomenological ego can make its way without ontological guidance, and hence that the discovery of intentional predelineation is not itself ontologically predelineated but ontologically *neutral*.[14]

But with that gesture toward *ontological neutralization* Husserl shows his hand, and the issue between Heidegger and Husserl comes out into the open. It has to do with the question of *ontological* presuppositions rather than with the concrete life of the worldly ego (= Being-in-the-world). For Heidegger, Husserl's commitment to ontological neutrality does not escape ontology but rather harbors within itself a concealed ontology of the Being of consciousness (the *Sein* of *Bewusstssein*). By seeking ontological "neutrality," Husserl takes the Being of consciousness to be such that it *can* neutralize itself or purify itself of worldly contamination. At this point Heidegger thinks that Husserl wants to walk on water. Heidegger thinks that every attempt to proceed without ontological bias ends up being subverted from behind, driven by ontological presuppositions at work on it behind its back. The very attempt to proceed without ontological guidance is itself an ontological project, inspired by a Cartesian ontology which supposes the separability of reflective consciousness from concrete first-order experience which is embedded in language, historical tradition, and culture. *The very project of neutralization proceeds from an ontology of consciousness as self-neutralizing*.[15]

Husserl does not deny—indeed I have argued that this is his express teaching—that first-order intentional acts are made possible by a ring of enabling presuppositions. He differs with Heidegger on the capacity of consciousness to effect a second order, reflective extrication from such conditioned, predelineated acts. Explication demands extrication. Husserl thus is put in the inconsistent position of holding that reflective consciousness is conducted under conditions which he precisely denies of first-order experience. Husserl clings to the ideal that the reflective ego enjoys a mode of intentional life—free from potential, implicit, horizonal, historical, and predelineatory factors—which he otherwise insists belongs to the make-up of intentional life at large. For Heidegger this inconsistency arises from Husserl's ontological presuppositions, from his acceptance of the self-neutralizing capacity of the Being of consciousness, of the possibility of pure reflection, that is to say, of transcendental consciousness. For Heidegger, on this point at least—which could not be more decisive—Husserl simply succumbs to the metaphysics of modernity. Husserl's view of the self-neutralizing power of consciousness, of the capacity of consciousness to effect a neutrality-modification which neutralizes the effect of the world, is laden with ontological deposits and belongs to the mainstream of Western metaphysics from Plato to German idealism.

Heidegger's critique of Husserl can also be put as follows. Whenever Husserl undertook to describe the concrete functioning of intentional life, he invariably resorted to a hermeneutic schema—that is, he sought out the fore-structures which made it possible. Whenever he actually practiced the phenomenological method, he ascribed to consciousness a hermeneutic, contextualized composition. The life of the living ego was always ringed about by a border of horizonal fore-structures, always temporally situated within a stream of protended and retained moments, laced with potential and implicit factors which make it impossible to "interpret" or "construe" (*auffassen*), that is, to intend the intentional object. The notion of a presuppositionless grasping of the intentional object, of grasping it without the support of these intentional fore-structures, is unheard of on this level and would turn intentionality into magic for Husserl.

The idea of presuppositionlessness arises only when Husserl wants to characterize the nature of phenomenology as a science. At this point he has recourse to the inherited idea of a Cartesian science, not in the sense of a deductive system, from which he expressly departs, but rather in the sense of achieving an absolutely indubitable and presupposition-free beginning. This ideal does not arise from concrete phenomenological inquiry. It has no correlate in the way intentional life is lived in ordinary, prescientific experience. Husserl asks us to believe that scientific consciousness is free from the very conditions which make consciousness in general possible in the first place. He asks us to believe, in effect, in two selves, one conditioned and finite, the other unconditioned and free from limitation. And while he means to say that there is but one self, he ends up unable to deliver on that claim.[16] He asks us to believe, thus, in one self caught up in the flux, like the rest of us, and one which has managed to escape it, to anchor itself in something stable, absolute, unchanging, present, and self-present. And that is where I locate Husserl's flight from the flux, from the difficulties of intentional life, and hence from his own hermeneutic discoveries.

I do not mean by all of this to oppose hermeneutics to science, but only to Husserl's misconception of science. As I hope to show below (chapter 8), recent philosophy of science confirms that hermeneutic conditionedness, the need to have a point of departure in guiding preconceptions, which Husserl readily concedes to the life of prescientific consciousness, is of the very essence of scientific life as well. The Cartesian conception of science seriously misrepresents the character of science itself, as the best work in recent years in the philosophy of science—natural, social, and human—has persuasively argued.

Husserl's Cartesianism does not issue from his concrete phenomenological inquiry; rather, it is invoked as a way of settling the ongoing debate about

psychologism, naturalism, and historicism. But this ideal has no phenomenological credentials. Consciousness is inherently hermeneutic, and the
goal of presuppositionlessness is a foreign import, a graft from the metaphysics
of modernity which, from Descartes on, has put its faith in the idea of transcendental consciousness.

But if Husserl's Cartesianism did not derive from his phenomenological work,
his concrete work was not untouched by his Cartesianism. His lack of an
adequate ontologically guiding idea of consciousness could not fail to influence
his concrete investigations. And that is only as it should be. If hermeneutics
claims that concrete experience must be directed beforehand by guiding presuppositions, then a fault at the level of ontological fore-structures would have to
show up on the level of concrete work. And that is just what happens. For it can
hardly be denied that on the level of his descriptive analyses Husserl failed to
give the hermeneutic element in his thought full play. Instead, diverted by this
Cartesian ideal, he allowed the interpretive element which he himself invoked
to be subdued by the favor he showed toward the theoretical attitude. And this
affected his account both of the intentional object and of consciousness itself.

For Husserl, the primary intentional object is the physical object given in
perception. Now it is true that the physical object can appear as a physical
object only if it is adequately prepared for in advance, only if it is adequately
predelineated in its essential type, delivered to us in its familiar external
horizon, situated within a protentional-retentional frame, etc. It must meet the
hermeneutic requirements which Husserl sets forth in order for it to be
properly interpreted as the thing which it is. Husserl, however, never gave this
"as-structure" its full play. He does not see that we rarely "perceive" physical
objects as "physical objects" but rather are constantly "dealing" with items of
use in one pragmatic setting or another. The sizes, shapes, colors, and other
properties of extended objects are abstractions from the items of use in concrete
life. Husserl criticized the antihermeneutic, empiricist theory of "sensations" as
an abstraction, a theoretical construction, vis-à-vis the concrete life of perception. But he failed to see that "perception," too, is an abstraction vis-à-vis the
hermeneutics of everydayness.

As Gadamer points out, this argument had been made clearly by Max
Scheler and the American pragmatists, and even more decisively by Heidegger,
but Husserl never owned up to it.[17] And that is why Gadamer, conceding with
Oskar Becker that there is "a hermeneutic element *in* Husserl's analyses of the
experience of consciousness," nonetheless complains, and rightly I think, that
the primacy of the perception of physical objects undermines Husserl's most
important descriptive accounts. On the most crucial occasions Husserl lapses
into the naive, prehermeneutic schema of givenness-plus-interpretation, of a
physical object which then gets overlaid by an interpretive frame, to account for

the experience of items of use, of other persons—first I perceive a material object which then is interpreted (ap-perceived) as another person—and even of my own body. Clearly a fully hermeneutic rendering of these experiences would rewrite them in terms of an interpretive experience of things just *as* the things which they are, something which is possible only in a hermeneutics of facticity.

But if this Cartesianism misled Husserl about the character of intentional objects, it misled him even more seriously in his account of consciousness. Husserl allows that physical objects are always construed, interpreted, under one set of adumbrations or another (and Gadamer's complaint is that this interpretive moment is not radical enough in Husserl.) But Husserl would never concede that these restrictions applied to consciousness itself. As the well-known argument of *Ideas I* (§§44–46, 54–55) maintained, the difference between the world and consciousness is precisely that worldly objects—be they physical objects or items of use—are always adumbrated, partial, presumptive unities of meaning, while consciousness is given to itself in an unadumbrated, absolute, uninterpreted fashion. Consciousness returns on itself in so perfect a manner that nothing requires interpretation. The need for interpretation arises in Husserl only from a failure of absolute givenness, a failure which does not beset the givenness of consciousness to itself. Hermeneutic interpretation arises from a defect in givenness; it is the recourse of a being which lacks identity with the world. Thus, Husserl's neat division of the intentional sphere into the transcendent and the immanent amounts to a division into the pre-sumptive and hence interpreted givenness of the world to consciousness and the absolute and hence uninterpreted givenness of consciousness to itself. [18]

Husserl in effect asks us to believe in two selves: one situated in the world and the other, its transcendental double, as Foucault calls it, [19] capable of reflecting on that situation, taking hold of it and laying it out. *Auslegung* is a power of perfect return which makes consciousness transparent, exposing all of the preconditons under which it labors. The repetition which repeats backward is unimpeded in its regress. It is able to seize consciousness in its beginnings and hold it fast. But that is just what not only Heidegger but nearly all of those who come after Husserl have denied. The point of undertaking this regressive movement, Merleau-Ponty said in his memorable preface to *The Phenomenology of Perception*, is just to find out that it cannot be done. [20] The origin always regresses, recedes, withdraws, defers itself, Derrida would say. [21] I cannot improve upon Foucault's formulation:

This is why modern thought is doomed, at every level, to its great preoccupation with recommencement, to that strange, stationary anxiety which forces upon it the duty of repeating repetition. . . . Modern thought makes it its task to return to man in his identity, in that plenitude or in that nothing which he is himself, to history and time in the repetition which they render impossible but which they force us to conceive, and to being in that it is.[22]

Repetition backward, Constantin learned, is a dream.

TWO PHILOSOPHIES OF REPETITION

We have thus, at this point in our story, encountered two works of repetition. The first, the Kierkegaardian, repeats forward, by a creative act of sustaining a commitment from day to day. The "re-" of Kierkegaardian repetition means to keep coming back in the future to the self which one sets out to be. It occurs in the arena of existence, not meaning, and indeed in its most inward and passionate moment goes ahead precisely without, even against, meaning. It is an ethicoreligious act of faithfulness, of constituting and creating a moral self. Kierkegaardian repetition is existential, futural resolve, turned toward the possible and contingent, exposed on all sides to the vertigo of freedom, to anxiety before the possible, anxious about the *vita ventura*. Its product is an ethical self, woven of the fabric of existential resolve.

In Husserl there is a comparable energy of repetition, deployed, however, not in the genesis of self but in the genesis of sense and meaning. Repetition has the epistemic sense of the constitution of meaning; it is a process in which the moments of experience are woven together into a fabric of expectations such that consciousness is able always to keep one step ahead of the flux, oriented and directed in the flow of experience and flexible enough to learn from its frustrated expectations. It is a theory of the creative constitution of history by an ascending series of intentional acquisitions.

But the energy of repetition is always subordinated by Husserl to the metaphysical gesture of recollection, to the return to origins, to the self's return to itself in reflection, to the repetition which wants to repeat backward. At this point Husserl retreats to a posture of disinterest—in conformity with Constantin's warning that it is always upon interest that metaphysics founders—of disengagement from the world in order to take reflective possession of it. He succumbs to the metaphysical dream of perfect return, of infinite goals. He resists the flux and looks for a standpoint outside it, where consciousness is insulated from its effects and keeps company with ideal unities of meaning and infinite projects. Even his account of history takes place in terms of meaning and of necessary structure, not existence and the possible. Kierkegaard would have seen in this side of Husserl another spurious friend of the flux, another fraudulent way to take the side of *kinesis* and becoming, another flight of metaphysics which wants to put the flux to sleep, to arrest its play. This Husserl—this metaphysical, antihermeneutic, Cartesian Husserl—does the work of "philosophy," of "speculation," in the Kierkegaardian sense, and represents another version of Platonic *anamnesis* and Hegelian *Erinnerung*.

Kierkegaard understood that metaphysics turns on the nostalgia for presence lost, that it defines itself as a work of recollective recovery, of the repetition which repeats backward, and on this point Kierkegaard is the more radical, deconstructive thinker. Genuine repetition repeats forward and bears the responsibility to produce what it would become. Genuine repetition always operates in the element of becoming and *kinesis* and learns to makes its way though the flux.

Now it is the claim of the present study that in *Being and Time*—which defines what we today understand by "hermeneutics"—these two quite different philosophies of repetition are brought together. Heidegger fused the Kierkegaardian project of the genesis of self with the Husserlian project of the genesis of sense. He deployed an existential ontology of the self as a being of becoming and temporality in concert with the Husserlian theory of a constitution which proceeds by way of forestructuring and predelineation. He thus laid the fore-structures of consciousness upon an ontological ground. He broke with the residual Cartesian ontology in Husserl, with the metaphysics of "consciousness" which, as the metaphysics of modernity, represented the latest form of Platonism. He thus recommitted phenomenology to the difficulty of life, rooted it in an ontology of care, and so fashioned what has come to be known as "hermeneutics" in the contemporary, post-Diltheyian sense. Our task now is to explore that Heideggerian undertaking in greater detail, and then to see what became of it when it itself was charged with being in complicity with Platonism, when it itself was taken to be still another form of the metaphysics of presence, and another faint-hearted friend of the flux.

THREE

Retrieval and the Circular Being of Dasein: Hermeneutics in *Being and Time*

THE CIRCULAR BEING OF DASEIN

In Heidegger, the Kierkegaardian project of "repetition" *(Gjentagelse)* becomes one of "retrieval" *(Wiederholung)*, and the structure of *kinesis*, of the movement in which Dasein's Being is caught up, is taken to be circular. As an "existing" being (in the Kierkegaardian sense), the meaning of Dasein is to move *forward*, to press ahead toward its authentic future. But this forward movement is taken by Heidegger to be at one and the same time a movement *back* to the being that Dasein all along has been. The movement forward is thus also a movement of recovery or retrieval. Kierkegaard had already recognized this problem when he discussed the paradox of the "self": repetition, which is productive of the self, is itself possible only in virtue of the self. Repetition both arises from, and is productive of, the self (E/O II 219–20). But Kierkegaard tended to portray repetition in progressive, linear terms.

Heidegger, on the other hand, gives a special play to the "circular" movement of Dasein's Being in *Being and Time*, linking in an ontological loop Dasein's forward and backward movement, its futural projection and its already having been. *Wiederholung* in *Being and Time* means a repetition/retrieval, a pressing forward which recovers something hitherto latent, *in potentia*, harbored in the possibility-to-be *(Seinskönnen)*, of Dasein. Dasein's own Being "circulates" between its "futurity" *(Zukünftigkeit)* and its "having been" *(Gewesenheit)*. The Being of Dasein is constantly projected ahead, never in a free-floating and absolute way, but always toward possibilities into which it has all along been inserted. Whence Heidegger speaks of "the circular Being of Dasein" (SZ 315/363) whose *kinesis* therefore takes the form of an existential circulation.

Thus, the felicitous English translation of *Wiederholung* as "retrieval"[1] adds the nuance of recovering something hidden, lost, or fallen, which we do not hear in "repetition." In its Kierkegaardian accents "repetition" stresses a linear future—repeating forward, resolving always to be faithful in the future, to do again and again what one does now. The Kierkegaardian notion was crafted in opposition to Platonic and Hegelian metaphysics and stressed the free emergence of something new. Heidegger's notion was fashioned in a struggle with the metaphysics of transcendental consciousness and stressed the sense of recovering factical possibilities.

But this existential circle, deriving from the ontology of repetition in Kierkegaard, is linked together in *Being and Time* with a phenomenological circle deriving from the Husserlian doctrines of explication *(Auslegung)* and anticipatory predelineation *(Vorzeichnung)*. Whence another level of circulation, another circulatory system, is set in motion in Dasein, not merely alongside but deriving from the first. To understand means to project a certain horizonal framework within which the being is to be understood. Entities can appear only insofar as a certain horizon of Being has already been laid out for them in advance. We can learn something new only on the condition that we have already been appropriately oriented to begin with. We can understand only if we already pre-understand. There are no pure, uninterpreted facts of the matter but only beings already set forth in a certain frame, projected in their proper Being.

In *Being and Time* the projective structure of the understanding (the Husserlian principle) derives from the Being of Dasein as repetition (the Kierkegaardian principle), from the forward momentum of "existing" Dasein, as we have seen in chapter 2. Understanding is projective because the Being of Dasein is projective, and its projects are contextual because its Being is characterized by thrownness and having-been. The hermeneutic circularity of the understanding is a subsystem of the ontological circulation in the Being of Dasein.

Heidegger thus gives the "hermeneutic circle"—which previously bore only an epistemological or methodological sense—an ontological weight. We understand as we do because we exist as we do. Understanding follows Being: *intelligere sequitur esse*. There is no field of "pure epistemology" for Heidegger but only an ontology of knowing or understanding.[2] Hermeneutics cannot be understood in ontologically neutral terms. The "hermeneutic circle" in its peculiarly contemporary and post-Diltheyan sense arises from a creative rereading of Kierkegaard and Husserl, from an extraordinary wedding of Constantin Constantius's farcical trip to Berlin and the sober work of phenomenological "explication."

Heidegger thus means to get a fix on the flux by inscribing a circular pattern on it which identifies the "logic" of movement, not in the fraudulent Hegelian sense which Kierkegaard criticized but in the sense of *logos* as letting be seen.

This logic traces the back and forth movement in the Being and understanding of Dasein. Issuing as it does from the *logos* of phenomen-ology, it wants not to undermine motion but to track its movements.

Now the movement which defines the Being of Dasein is the movement of "care." But the movement of care, he says (§63), involves a fundamental drift (*Zug*), a tendency to fall in among things and to fall outside the proper concerns of Dasein's own Being, to take the "easy way" out (*das Leichte*, GA 61 108–10). Dasein is always "falling" where "fall" has the strictly ontological sense of a degeneration in virtue of which Dasein becomes more and more removed from its own primordial Being.[3] We tend to drift farther and farther away from ourselves ontologically, even though ontically we *are* this very being (SZ 311/BT 359). Fallenness is a *Zug*, a pull away from the center of Dasein toward dispersal and dissipation.

If there is a fall in the Being of Dasein, there is a corresponding fall in Dasein's "understanding" by which Dasein falls into a commonplace and superficial understanding of itself and of things in general. Because existing Dasein is always being drawn off course in an "ex-orbitant" movement which pulls it out of orbit and disrupts its circulation, understanding too is constantly being waylaid.

Ontologically, falling means that Dasein is weighed down by the actual or present, which cuts short its futural projection, on the one hand, and cuts it off from its heritage, on the other, cutting off its existential circulation. By the same token, falling subverts the circulatory life of the understanding. Instead of the projective work of authentic understanding which recovers the primordial meaning, Dasein is lured into complacency with the prevailing public interpretation of things. Dasein and, ultimately, Being itself are understood in terms of what is immediately present (*vorhanden*). Even as inauthentic Dasein allows itself to be preoccupied with the concerns of the present moment (*Gegenwart*), to be tranquilized by what is actual and subverted from the possible, understanding is lured into a reading of the world in terms of actuality and presence, the always available stuff of things (*Vorhandensein*).

Now existing Dasein breaks the spell of the present by exposing itself to its most extreme possible absence (death) and thereby recovers its Being as *possibility*, as a potentiality for Being (Aristotelian potency and *kinesis*), as a potentiality to become itself. Correspondingly, for the understanding, the task is to break the spell of the metaphysics of presence, to make a deeper reading of the Being of Dasein, and of Being generally, in terms of temporality and time.

To be alert to what is happening in *Being and Time*, we must keep these two movements constantly in view. We must keep in mind that the much-discussed "hermeneutic circle" in *Being and Time*—the circle of understanding—proceeds from the ontological base of an existing-falling being-in-the-world. That alone explains one of the most important and easily misunderstood features of the hermeneutics we find in *Being and Time,* namely, that for Heidegger hermeneutics always requires "violence." Hermeneutics means interpretation *(Aus-legung),* but interpretation—because it is the work of falling Dasein— must always be a forceful setting free *(Frei-legung)* of the matter to be understood which counters Dasein's own tendency to fall and take the easy way out. "The laying free of Dasein's primordial Being must rather be *wrested* from Dasein by following the *counter-tendency (im Gegenzug)* from that taken by the falling ontico-ontological tendency of interpretation" (SZ 311/BT 359). Interpretation proceeds by reversing the drift, by swimming against the stream. It is always working against the dead weight of a fall.

The work of hermeneutics is to lay out the depth structures, first of Dasein and then of Being itself, which tend by their own ontological weight to sediment, to recede from view, in favor of the surface phenomena that are rooted in them. Hermeneutics is the countermovement to the pull of withdrawal, concealment, and fallenness. It sets about undoing the damage that fallenness does. Indeed, the words "phenomenology" and "ontology" bear the mark of this hermeneutic "logic" *(logos)* bent on reversing this drift. "Phenomenology" means the *logos* which lets that be seen which primarily tends to hide itself, to remain concealed behind what is overtly manifest. "Ontology" means the *logos* which lets Being itself be seen, that Being which is concealedly revealed in beings, which are what is primarily accessible (§7c). The matter *(Sache)* is inherently self-concealing, self-withdrawing. The falling of Dasein out of its primordiality is but a case of the more general falling of Being into beings and hence out of sight *as* Being. For Heidegger, the primordial is always concealed; Being is always subject to *lethe* and self-concealment. *Physis* loves to hide.

In the face of such a self-concealing matter we require a method which does not shrink from "violence":

> Dasein's *kind of Being* thus *demands* that any ontological interpretation which sets itself the goal of exhibiting the phenomena in their primordiality, *should capture the Being of this entity, in spite of this entity's own tendency to cover things up.* Existential analysis, therefore, constantly has the character of doing violence *(Gewaltsamkeit).* (SZ 311/BT 359)

The "violence" of hermeneutics is "natural," for it is dictated by the structure of self-withdrawing Being. Hermeneutics is able to "retrieve" the primordial only insofar as it dismantles the overlaid accretions and derivative understandings of the world, of Dasein—and of Being—that have accumulated in the history of metaphysics. This violence governs "the task of the destruction *(Destruktion)* of the history of ontology" (§6).[4] "Destruction" is hermeneutic violence. It not only resists the prevailing understanding but also runs counter to it. Destruction rejects the prevailing tendency to understand Dasein in terms of common and everyday conceptions and to understand Being itself in terms which have dominated metaphysics for centuries. Hermeneutics thus means both recovery and violence, both restoration and destruction. More precisely, it involves violence *because* it is bent on retrieval. For the work of recovery cannot proceed except by clearing away the superficial and commonplace understanding of things which systematically obscures our view and subverts the understanding.

The necessity of hermeneutic violence in *Being and Time* raises one of its most central problems. How are we to discriminate the violence which is genuinely hermeneutic—which means restorative—from merely arbitrary violence? How are we to tell the difference between the violence that, exerted on secondary and derivative interpretations, *recovers* the things themselves in their primordiality and the violence that *violates*, that does an injustice to the matter at hand? The viability of the way that *Being and Time* travels depends upon answering that question, as Heidegger is acutely aware.

Furthermore, this destruction cannot simply declare its independence of the traditional concepts and proceed in the naive belief that it has thereby won its freedom. Every radical attempt to begin again is subverted by an inherited framework of concepts—concepts that keep working their way back into the destruction:

> It is for this reason that there necessarily belongs to the conceptual interpretation of being and its structures, that is, to the reductive construction of being, a *destruction (Destruktion)*, that is, a critical deconstruction *(Abbau)* of the traditional concepts, which at first must necessarily be employed, down to the sources from which they were drawn. (GA 24 31/BP 22–23)[5]

The work of *Abbau*—we today cannot resist translating this as "deconstruction"—cannot expect to proceed apace. It must remain vigilant about its own need to use traditional conceptual instruments, that is, a philosophical conceptuality in which are embedded the very de-generated, derivative, and fallen interpretations which it hopes to uproot. Hermeneutic work must be an *Abbau*, a deconstructive violence that is alert to the subversiveness of the traditional conceptuality which it must "at first" provisionally (strategically) deploy. The notorious complexity of the language of *Being and Time* is a function of this deconstructive vigilance, which sets about loosening the sedimented sense of traditional philosophical vocabulary in order to wrest loose the primordial experiences it conceals. "*Ab-bau*" is a suggestive and less misleading word than *Destruktion*, which implies a sheer leveling or razing. *Abbau* means a dismantling or undoing of a surface apparatus which has been allowed to build up over an originary experience—a dismantling not in order to level but in order to retrieve. Its function then is positive, to break through the encrusted in order to recover the living experience, which has since grown old and stiff.

In *Being and Time* the work of destruction or deconstruction is deployed on two levels. In the first place, it must break through the accumulated, metaphysical commonplaces which envelop Dasein, whose Being is always interpreted in terms of the present, in order to exhibit the deeper Being of Dasein as a being of temporality. Dasein tends constantly to interpret itself in terms of the present and to turn away from its more radical being-toward-the-future. Hence, the first work of deconstruction is to disrupt the predominance of Dasein's self-interpretation as a being of the present *(Gegenwart)*. And that leads to its second work: to disrupt the concomitant interpretation of Being itself in terms of presence *(Vorhandensein, Anwesenheit, Praesenz;* the "metaphysics of presence"), where time is taken as a sequence of now's and true being as a stationary now. The deconstruction of the prevailing tradition will open the doors to a radical recovery of Being itself in terms of time, not the temporality *(Zeitlichkeit)* of Dasein but the temporality *(Temporalität)* of Being itself.

In *Being and Time* hermeneutic recovery and phenomenological destruction or deconstruction work hand in hand. They are collaborators in the work of hermeneutic phenomenology. The recovery of the meaning of Dasein, and ultimately of Being itself, cannot be effected without deconstructive violence, even as deconstructive violence is not to be undertaken except in the service of a positive program of retrieval. In *Being and Time* the recovery of Being or Dasein is necessarily a deconstruction of the traditional overlays, even as violence toward the tradition is not a violation of it but a natural violence which wrests free its primordial contents.

There is no hermeneutic recovery without deconstruction and no deconstruction not aimed at recovery. That is a principle which guides *Being and Time* and which we too take as a guide throughout this study, in the project of formulating a "radical hermeneutics." Its seeming evidence is not disturbed until the work of Derrida and his radicalization of Heideggerian deconstruction. For Derrida, deconstruction functions not hand in hand with hermeneutics but as a deconstruction *of* hermeneutics. The confrontation with Derrida's critique of Heidegger is complicated even further by the later Heidegger's own self-criticism and hence deconstructive radicalization of his own earlier hermeneutic standpoint. At that point we will be driven to ask whether the work of retrieval, and therefore hermeneutics itself, can survive in the midst of this deconstructive energy and whether the formula we here propose does not itself invite disruption.

THE CIRCULAR STRATEGY OF *BEING AND TIME*

There is one last twist, one more complication of the already complex circulatory system of *Being and Time*, beyond the ontological circle in the Being of Dasein and the hermeneutic circle in its understanding. And that is what I will call here the "strategic" circle of the text of *Being and Time* itself. Like Nietzsche's reader, the reader of *Being and Time* requires a certain light-

footedness—the ability to insert oneself into the work's back and forth movements without stumbling or declaring the whole operation "vicious." I mean by
this the textual strategy deployed in *Being and Time*, in which Heidegger puts
into practice, in his own treatise, the theory of the circular movement of
understanding. This last circle thus is strategic, tactical, and methodological.

Here we see a certain convergence of the matter *(Sache)* which *Being and
Time* addresses and the method which the treatise employs. In Kierkegaard,
the matter was existential repetition, but the method was oblique indirection in
a complex aesthetic thrusting and parrying. In Husserl, the matter was the
anticipatory constitution of the object, and the method was a reflective, scientific explication. In Heidegger, the matter is the circular Being of Dasein itself,
and the method follows the lead of the matter and puts the circle into practice.

Accordingly, the interpretive effort undertaken in the text of *Being and Time*
itself is launched by means of an anticipatory projection of the Being of Dasein,
that is, the treatise begins with its own outcome, the determination of Dasein
which it seeks. The text simply sets out by *defining* Dasein as "existence"—"the
'essence' of Dasein lies in its existence" (SZ 42/67; cf. SZ 12/32)—whereas that is
what is to be *shown*. But what appears to be a kind of dogmatic high-handed-
ness is in fact only the initial "projection" of the Being of Dasein, a gesture
made in accordance with the nature of the understanding itself. It is not
dogmatic but hermeneutic violence.

Everything in *Being and Time* turns on getting this initial projection right.
Dasein must be cast in the appropriate terms, projected upon the Being which
lets it be the being which it is, lest the whole subsequent discussion founder.
But how we are to find the appropriate projection? How are we to go about
making such a decisive determination?

> Where are ontological projects to get the evidence that their "findings" are phe-
> nomenally appropriate? Ontological interpretation projects the entity presented to
> it upon the Being which is that entity's own, so as to conceptualize it with regard to
> its structure. Where are the signposts to direct the projection, so that Being will be
> reached at all? (SZ 312/BT 359)

What leads us to project Dasein one way rather than another? And how can we
ascertain that a projection truly seizes a being in its primordiality and origins?
What warrant is there for such confidence in the fecundity of "existence"? How
can we be sure that "existence" touches bottom, that it taps into the primordial
sources of Dasein's Being? Does *Being and Time* simply begin with an intuition?
Is the hermeneutic circle only an elaborate device for justifying a private
preference?

Heidegger's answer to this constellation of difficulties is at once simple and
disconcerting: we are all along possessed of the appropriate understanding of
Dasein. It is something we already understand, even if we have not adequately

conceived it and put it into words. We raise the question of Dasein, to begin with, only because we all along possess an understanding of what is in question.[6] The question arises from and returns to this prior understanding. We do not "know" *(wissen)* what Dasein and *a fortiori* Being itself mean; we lack a conceptual fix *(begrifflich fixieren)* on them. But we always and already move about within an "understanding" of them (SZ 5/BT 25). And the task of hermeneutic phenomenology is to raise this concrete preunderstanding to the level of an ontological concept.

Being and Time articulates something which we already understand about ourselves. No matter how faultily we explicate our Being in terms of mere objective presence *(Vorhandensein)*, no matter how badly we misinterpret our self-understanding, even if we degenerate into purely magical accounts of the Being of Dasein, we nonetheless always and already understand ourselves. What has gone astray in a bad reading of the Being of Dasein is not self-understanding *(Verstehen)*—for that is constitutive of our existence—but self-interpretation *(Auslegung)*, which has failed adequately to tap into the prior understanding of Dasein (cf. SZ 15/BT 36, 58/85, 59-60/86, 289–90/336, 313/361).

Still, we want to know, does *this* beginning, *this* initial projection of the Being of Dasein as "existence," seize upon the Being of Dasein itself (and will it ultimately lead us to the concept of Being itself)? Only the subsequent course of *Being and Time* itself will reveal whether this beginning has disclosed the entity which it investigates, has wrested the Being of Dasein free from commonplace and superficial interpretations or has simply done it violence. Only by being worked out in detail can the projection of existence prove its worth.

There is no other way to proceed. It is the very nature of the understanding—as we have already learned from Husserl—to proceed projectively, to forge ahead and clear the ground within which entities to be investigated make their appearance. True to its own ontology of the understanding, *Being and Time* begins not by clearing away all presuppositions but by stating them explicitly and clearly in order to penetrate them all the more fully. Its aim is to insure not that the treatise is free of presuppositions but that its presuppositions are deep enough and ample enough to encompass the matter at hand. In short, the beginning of *Being and Time* must be rich enough to see to it that we do not assume too little.

One thing is clear, however, and that is that the strategy is free of any formal fallacy. Clearly a deductive system which tries to solve for p by presupposing p is trivial and logically vicious. But *Being and Time* is no such deductive system. Here there is no formal, deductive movement from premise to conclusion but a regressive, hermeneutic movement bent on explication, *aus-legen*, on unpacking the implicit components of an everyday functioning preunderstanding. The point is to raise a vague understanding to the level of an explicit concept, to move along a line from implicit to explicit. All the dilemmas surrounding the formal validity of the hermeneutic circle are solved as soon as this is recognized, as Derrida rightly points out.[7]

The entire strategy of *Being and Time* turns on its ability to "tap into" this operative, pretheoretical understanding of Dasein (and of Being in general). The initial positing, or projection, of existence is the form which this tap takes. The projection supplies not a metaphysical first principle, an axiom in a deductive system, but a first cut, an initial casting, an anticipatory sketching out or predelineation, of the Being of Dasein which is meant to let Dasein be the being which it is, to let it emerge gradually into appearance, as the sketch is filled in in the course of the treatise. Thus, the subsequent account of Dasein in *Being and Time* is governed by this initial projection of existence, even while, at the same time, this projection is put to the test. Existence is not the axiom in Heidegger's system but the horizon within which all subsequent phenomenological investigation is conducted. It is the way Dasein will be "cast" (a good English equivalent for Heidegger's use of *Entwurf,* projection). Existence stakes out in advance an initial predelineation of the Being of Dasein, of the region to which it belongs. We cannot have recourse to just any "dogmatic construction" but we must "choose" an "access" to Dasein which lets it "show itself in itself and from itself" (SZ 16/BT 37).

Having launched its movement by way of this anticipatory sketch of the Being of Dasein, *Being and Time* proceeds to trace out a back and forth motion of circling over, and then over again, the staked-out terrain (§66). In its first phase, *Being and Time* consists in an "existential analytic" which culminates in the determination of the "meaning" of the "Being" of Dasein in terms of temporality (§§9–65). But then the entire analytic needs to be "repeated" in a "temporal analysis" (§§65–83) in which the temporal sense of the elements disclosed in the existential analytic can be spelled out, item by item. Finally, the temporal analysis itself must in turn be "repeated" in another run through the Being of Dasein, one in which "the whole turns itself around" and we are led to a determination of the meaning of Being in terms of time (the famous, but missing, "Time and Being," Division III).

Thus the very method of the book, the progress of the treatise, follows the downward-spiraling path of repetition. With each new turn, with each new pass over the same terrain, the whole is deepened and radicalized, the hermeneutic sights and foresights are sharpened and refined, and the investigation makes its way further down, further back into the preunderstanding from which it proceeds. With each repetition we penetrate all the more radically the presuppositions from which we set out. It is not a question of escaping these presuppositions but of unfolding and penetrating them, of tapping into their latent wealth, a method importantly anticipated by Husserlian *Auslegung*.

Being and Time is thus a complex circulatory system in which these circles weave and interweave in an effort to inscribe pattern and sense in the move-ment of Dasein's Being. The circle is at one and the same time the model for the ontology of Dasein (and of Being itself), for the work of the understanding, and for the strategy of the text. Our task is to track down and retrace the course these circles follow. To do so, let us take up the circle of the understanding, the famous "hermeneutic circle" itself.

THE CIRCLE OF UNDERSTANDING

As an "existing" being, Dasein is always "more" than it factually is. It is never "present" or fully *"actual" (ousia, substantia)*. Rather, it continually stretches out toward the "possible." On the level of its "everydayness," Dasein is pro-jected into the world of day-to-day concerns, the complex of relationships among the tools or items of equipment with which it is involved and the ends which these tools serve. But over and beyond the world of everyday concerns, Dasein is stretched out to that for the sake of which there is a world, to Dasein itself. In this second, more radical projection, Dasein is projected upon— directed toward—its own deepest possibility to be the being which it alone is or can be. On either level, Dasein "understands" what it is about, that is, it predelineates for itself an anticipatory sketch of its world, casts itself forth into a sphere or horizon of existence within which it must make its way about (§31).

"Understanding" *(Verstehen)*—which is pragmatic and existential and never primarily a theoretical matter—is the projective sketch of the horizon within which things are set free to be the things which they are. "Interpretation" *(Auslegung)* is the working out *(Ausarbeitung)* of understanding (§32). Under-standing is related to interpretation in *Being and Time* as the less determinate to the more determinate, the preliminary to the more fully developed. Interpreta-tion is the way understanding gets developed, filled in, articulated. Under-standing and interpretation differ, not in kind but in degree of completeness. Interpretation makes the possibilities projected by understanding determinate and specific. When an interpretation is made of a hammer, say, the hammer is taken up explicitly in its "in order to" *(um zu)* and hence "laid out" as the tool which it is. In being understood as the thing which it is, which can only be done in an adequate way by actually hammering, the tool is interpreted. Those coming from a non-Western culture, e.g., may "understand" the world as a system of involvements, for that is an ontological structure of Dasein in general. They may lack a developed, articulate interpretation of this world and hence of this hammer. They may fail to grasp the particular "as-structure," the her-meneutic peculiarities, of our cultural objects, even though they know what cultural objects in general are.

The fact that interpretation is more determinate than understanding does not mean, however, that it is explicit, thematic, conceptual knowledge. One who has an articulated grasp of his cultural world need hardly be supposed to have given this interpretation conceptual form. Interpretation, like understanding, is something we "always already" possess. The distinction between preconceptual and conceptual cuts across the distinction between understanding and interpretation.

The working out of understanding into a fully developed interpretation consists in accumulating the hermeneutic "fore-structures" which together make up what Heidegger calls the "hermeneutic situation" (SZ 232/BT 275). In §32 Heidegger illustrates these fore-structures in terms of our prethematic interpretation of the world of everydayness; in §45 and §63, he treats the fore-structures which constitute Dasein in its authentic Being, thereby radicalizing and deepening the interpretation of Dasein. There are three such fore-structures.

(1) Fore-having *(Vorhabe)*. In order adequately to project a being we must have the being in our possession, have a hold on it. Fore-having refers in particular to having a hold on the *whole* object, getting it into our possession as a whole. We do not have it if we do not have it all. In §45 (SZ 232/BT 275), Heidegger adds that fore-having is concerned with the *constitution* of the Being to be projected *(Seinsverfassung)* and thus with having its whole constitution or makeup in hand. In order to have an interpreted grasp of the system which makes up our world, therefore, we need to have the whole scope of that system in view. We cannot interpret a hammer unless we have a grasp of the scope of the system to which it belongs. In order to grasp the Being of Dasein, we need to have the whole of Dasein in view. Understanding thus is essentially holistic.

(2) Fore-sight *(Vor-sicht)*. In order to project a being appropriately, it is necessary to have an initial grasp of the kind of Being *(Seinsart, SZ 150/BT 191; 232/275)* which belongs to it, so that we understand the sort of thing with which we have to do. We need to know that the hammer is ready-to-hand, not merely present, and specifically that it is something used for hammering. If, on the other hand, we are to interpret Dasein adequately, then we must understand Dasein neither as ready-to-hand nor as present-at-hand but precisely in terms of existence itself.

(3) Fore-grasping *(Vor-griff)*. The "-*griff*" in "*Vor-griff*" is derived from "*Begriff,*" that is, concept. Hence, to have a fore-grasp is to have a fore-conception of the projected being, which Heidegger describes as having at one's disposal an articulated system of concepts with which to grasp the being. Fore-grasping is to fore-sight what the articulated is to the general schema. Fore-grasping spells out and articulates the kind of Being which is caught sight of in fore-sight. Fore-grasping supplies the appropriate conceptual system or table of categories into which the being is entered. It has to do with articulated structures *(Seinstrukturen, SZ 232/BT 275)*. Fore-sight supplies an overview of that for which fore-grasping supplies a categorial table.

It is in virtue of this theory of fore-structures that Heidegger can offer a theory of meaning *(Sinn)* (SZ 151–2/BT 192–93). To know the "meaning" of something is to know that in terms of which it is to be projected, the horizon in terms of which it should be cast, the sphere to which it belongs. This horizon is set by the fore-structures. Meaning is not, as in the Husserl of the *Logical Investigations,* an eternal objective structure but an existential of Dasein. Meaning is supplied by Dasein when Dasein projects a horizon which gets filled in by entities. Meaning is found only so long as there is Dasein. Outside of Dasein there is not absurdity but non-meaning. Only Dasein can experience meaningfulness or meaninglessness. *Being and Time* itself is concerned with the meaning of Being, first of all, and to that end, the meaning of the Being of Dasein. That, Heidegger says, does not mean anything "deep," but simply that we are looking for the right horizon within which to project Being itself—which will turn out to be time—and Dasein—which will turn out to be temporality.

The warranty or basis of the anticipatory projection depends upon whether the fore-structures are "drawn from the entity itself" or just forced upon it (SZ 150/BT 191). They must seize the entity in its proper Being and not simply be imposed upon it from without. They are also revisable *(vorbehaltlich),* which is why Gadamer speaks of a back-and-forth movement between understanding and interpretation until the right "fit" is found between the fore-structures and the entity (W&M 251–52/T&M 236–37).

Far from wanting to approach things without presuppositions, understanding is precisely a question of finding the right presuppositions, i.e., the right fore-structural complex. When a textual exegete appeals to what is "there" in the text, the one thing we can be sure to find is the presupposition under which the exegete is laboring (SZ 150/BT 192). And we are not to think that this is something to be deplored. Rather, it belongs to the very nature of interpretation. We must, however, be on the alert for presuppositions which force the issue, which compel the being into a mode of Being which violates it. Heidegger is not endorsing the thoughtlessness, e.g., which fails to realize that other ages and cultures differ from ours and hence that our own presuppositions cannot be imposed upon them. He is making the ontological point that whatever access we gain to other cultures or ages will be gained by the presuppositions we deploy.

In a clear reference to Dilthey, Heidegger adds that we must not think that the task is to find an objectivity for the human sciences which rivals that of the natural sciences (SZ 153/BT 194). For both the natural and the human sciences proceed by way of understanding and interpretation. The issue is not to secure presuppositionlessness but to see how fore-structures belong to the very possibility of knowing: "What is decisive is not to get out of the circle but to come to it in the right way." We do not have to do with a "vicious" circle which must merely be tolerated; rather, "in the circle is hidden a positive possibility of the most primordial kind of knowing." And so everything comes down to securing the presuppositions themselves, not to securing an interpretation which is free of presuppositions.

> . . . our first, last and constant task is never to allow our fore-having, fore-sight and fore-conception to be presented to us by fancies and popular conceptions, but rather to make the scientific theme secure by working out these fore-structures in terms of the things themselves. (SZ 153/BT 195)

Understanding requires presuppositions in order to get underway. It requires fore-structures, a presuppositional matrix, within which it functions—or else it will not function.

Everything comes down to finding the appropriate fore-structures, projections which are not "free-floating constructions" (SZ 28/BT 50) arbitrarily imposed from without. When Descartes posed the problem of the worldless ego, when he projected a "consciousness" denuded of a relationship with the world and with its own body, Heidegger says, he presupposed not too much but too little (SZ 316/BT 363). The Cartesian *cogito* is a contrivance, a free-floating construction which is drawn not from the things themselves but from the artificialities of "epistemological consciousness."

The fore-structures which are drawn from the things themselves elucidate these things, illuminate and disclose them, set them free. This hermeneutic is phenomenological because it has to do with disclosure, with opening things up, with freeing them from distorting misconceptions. That indeed is what the existential analytic itself comes down to and what is invested in the idea of "existence." Heidegger's hermeneutic wager in *Being and Time* is all along that the projection of Dasein in terms of "existence" represents the most fruitful hermeneutic presupposition, that it has the widest range and makes the deepest penetration, in short, that it has the *greatest elucidatory power*. The wager is that the momentum of this project will catapult us into the meaning of the Being of Dasein and ultimately into the meaning of Being itself. And if this bet pays off, Heidegger owes a massive debt to Kierkegaard, where he first found this suggestive hermeneutic principle.

Therefore, we must be able to recognize ourselves in the account which *Being and Time* gives. Everything turns on the fact that we already "understand" who we are, even when we interpret ourselves as a thinking thing, a bundle of perceptions, absolute spirit, or in the terms of any other metaphysical construction. Everything turns on our ability to say that *this*—the existential analytic—is the account which brings to words what we have all along understood but have been unable to say because of traditional metaphysical prejudices. The existential analytic articulates, lays out and sets free, who we are and what our mode of Being is. And that is because "any interpretation which is to contribute something must already have understood what is to be interpreted" (SZ 152/BT 194).

THE DANGER OF THE ASSERTION

No interpretation is safe. Even after an authentic projection has been drawn from primordial sources, we cannot assume it will be preserved. On the contrary, we must assume that the incessant pull of fallenness will set to work on it, threatening to turn it into something second-hand, derivative, used up. Interpretation is always threatened by the pull *(Zug)* of fallenness, the withdrawal *(Entzug)* of authentic self-understanding. The opposite pull *(Gegenzug)* of projection, which makes authentic interpretation possible, is always liable to degenerate. It is just this threat that is posed when interpretation passes over into the "assertion" (§33 and §44b). Once again—we have already seen this in Husserl—phenomenology's concern with the primordial leads to the notion of the danger of language. Both Heideggerian and Husserlian phenomenology move within the same orbit of the originary experience and the derivativeness of the language which, in passing the originary experience along, at the same time imperils it.

For Heidegger, the assertion, which traditionally has enjoyed a primacy as the privileged locus of truth, is subordinated to a more primordial kind of truth. Understanding and interpretation are not thematic acts. They belong not to the level of explicit conceptualization and judgment but to the prethematic, pre-predicative, operative, or functioning level of Being-in-the-world. They can however be seized upon thematically and articulated propositionally. But that very seizing of the interpretation in the assertion poses the threat. For predication is a derivative occurrence which runs the risk of allowing the more primordial experience to deteriorate or degenerate, even if, in the first assertion, it was seized upon authentically. By the pre-predicative, we hasten to add, Heidegger does not mean the prelinguistic. On the contrary, discourse *(Rede)* belongs to the essential constitution of the disclosedness of the "there" (§34). He is distinguishing pre-predicative from predicative *discourse*.

The assertion has a threefold structure (§33). (1) It is an *apophansis*, a showing forth, in which something (the "subject") is pointed to or pointed out. (2) It is predicative, so that what is pointed out (the subject) is given a definite character (a predicate) in the assertion. Something pre-predicatively manifest is given explicit predicative form. This occurs by way of a certain stepping back from the matter at hand, a "dimming it down" *(abblendend, entblendend,* SZ 155/BT 197), by means of which we focus precisely on the predicate. (3) Finally, what is thus constituted in the judgment may be passed along to others so that it may be shared with them *(mit-teilen,* that is, communication). But this is the chink in the wall of discourse. The constitution of communicable assertions creates the possibility of *extending* understanding by allowing us to share it with the other who is not in a position to experience it himself. But it also creates the possibility of the *degeneration* of understanding by allowing "mere hearsay" to take root. For the assertion allows for telling and retelling, widening the scope of the sharing to the point that the original assertion is diluted of its originary sense. The assertion thus takes on a "pharmacological" quality, in the Derridean sense: it is both necessary and dangerous.

Insofar as it exhibits the threefold hermeneutic fore-structure of fore-having (of the subject which it points out), fore-sight (of the predicate, which determines the subject), and fore-grasping (it articulates an understanding in a certain way), the assertion enters into the very act of interpretation. And so long as it retains the sense of the primordial experience from which it is drawn and to which it gives articulation, it performs a worthy hermeneutical function.

Heidegger illustrates this in terms of a hammer. In our functioning, pre-predicative Being-in-the-world, we can articulate the heaviness of a hammer "without wasting words" (SZ 158/BT 200), perhaps merely by a facial gesture. But in the assertion there is a certain standing back from the world of circumspective concern in which Dasein speaks *about* the hammer and determines it predicatively. Now, instead of being an inconspicuously reliable item of use, the hammer becomes a thematic object with properties. The "as-structure" of the interpretation has been modified from the prethematic "hermeneutic as" of circumspective concern to the thematic "apophantic as" of the assertion. We have toned down our Being-in-the-world in order to take up the disengaged posture of the predicative assertion. We no longer seize the tool as a tool but look at something present-at-hand as having the property of being usable. The thing is uprooted from its involvement in the totality of tools, isolated, objectified as the object of a pointing out which just looks ("puren hinsehenden Aufweisens," SZ 158/BT 201). There are, Heidegger points out, numerous intermediate cases between the pure cases of hermeneutic and apophantic discourse, between the physicist, who is interested in the hammer purely in terms of its mass, and the working carpenter. (One can imagine, e.g., the discourse of two carpenters engaged in an after-hours conversation about the best kinds of hammers or of hardware store salespeople comparing the features of various hammers.)

Understood properly, assertion plays a derivative, but legitimate, role in understanding and the bringing about of truth. Although Heidegger does not think that the assertion is, as the tradition holds, the locus of truth, he does think that truth is the locus of the assertion, inasmuch as the assertion secures a derivative mode of truth. Truth means disclosedness, uncovering, and the assertion is a mode of uncovering. A statement discloses a state of affairs, even as a defective statement covers things over. The difficulty with the assertion, however, arises from its derivative character. For if disclosure has the mode of

Being of Dasein, which is existence, the assertion is something ready-to-hand (SZ 161/BT 204). It is an entity within-the-world, whereas uncovering and discourse have the mode of Being-in-the-world itself. That means that the assertion can be passed along, by word of mouth or in written texts, like something ready-to-hand (SZ 224/BT 266). And though the possibility of being repeated is an advantage which the assertion offers, it is also its undoing:

> Even when Dasein speaks over again what someone else has said, it comes into a Being-towards the very entities which have been discussed. But it has been exempted from having to uncover them again, primordially, and it holds that it has been thus exempted. (SZ 224/BT 266)

This is the logic of Husserl's "Origin of Geometry."[8] Dasein which repeats, which gets the word that is passed along, need not reenact the original experience which funds the assertion. This "repetition" is not the authentic circular Being of Dasein but precisely its falling, its degeneration. The process of uncovering becomes a process of hearsay. We become lost in words and fail to enter into relationship with the things themselves. And, once the assertion is sufficiently emptied of its disclosive power, once it fails to uncover, then and only then can the question arise as to how and whether the "assertion-thing," on this side, is related to the "object-thing," on that side. The "epistemological" problem arises only on the basis of the deteriorated Being of the assertion. Truth then is misunderstood in its Being and is taken to be a relationship of objective presence *(Vorhandensein)*, like correspondence or likeness, between assertion-things and object-things.

The object of Heidegger's critique, then, is not the assertion as such but the fact that assertions can be passed along—that they can be repeated—and divested of their original life. Heidegger moves within the framework of a Husserlian theory of sedimentation: the originary experience drops out, leaving us with the empty shell of an assertion. Everyday communication then becomes a shell game in which we match shells with things or pick out the shells which stand for things. The "correspondence" theory then arises from privileging assertions, which are derivative, over originary experiences.

There is a logic of the primordial and the derivative at work in *Being and Time* and hence a notion of phenomeno-logic as the recovery of the primordial. Primordial hermeneutical understanding takes place on the level of our concrete, prethematic engagement with the world. From that primal level arise authentic assertions, which, fresh from their contact with concrete existence, still retain their quality of uncovering. Finally, at the uttermost remove from the primordial understanding, is the assertion which just gets passed along, which is bandied about, to the point where it no longer discloses anything but has become a commonplace, part of the common stock of everyday discourse.

And that tells us something about *Being and Time* itself, as a treatise. Because

Being and Time is itself made up of assertions which are meant to have disclosive power and to be drawn from primordial sources, it is also exposed to the danger that its own assertions may simply get passed along and emptied of their originary force. The task of the reader, accordingly, is not to hold himself exempt from uncovering for himself what these assertions disclose. On the contrary, the reader must ascertain for himself what *Being and Time* has accomplished by drawing upon his own primordial self-understanding, by consulting his own preunderstanding in a Heideggerian analogue to Husserlian "reactivation." Do we understand ourselves in terms of "existence"? Is this indeed the articulation for which we have all along been searching?

RESETTING THE "HERMENEUTIC SITUATION"

Heidegger's hermeneutic strategy in *Being and Time* comes to a head in Division II. Although the entire investigation was launched by the projection of Dasein in terms of "existence," Division I is given over to a hermeneutic of everyday existence. Hence the fore-structures in Division I are always those in virtue of which we "have sight" and articulate Dasein's everyday world. But that is all along only a preliminary to gaining access to Dasein's primordial Being. Hence our hermeneutical sights need to be reset; the hermeneutical situation needs to be both widened and deepened (§45). The presuppositions by which we have been guided thus far do not have within them either the range or the depth to seize upon Dasein in its originary Being (*Ursprünglichkeit*, SZ 231/BT 275). We have thus far *assumed too little*.

(1) The hermeneutic situation developed so far has failed to take into account the *totality* of Dasein's Being. By restricting itself to Dasein's everydayness Being, the analytic omits what Jaspers calls extreme or limit situations, those situations of profound crisis in which Dasein runs up against the finitude of its Being. In hermeneutic terms, we have not yet brought the whole of Dasein into our fore-having. We have concerned ourselves with how Dasein is from day to day, "between" birth and death, but we have not yet taken into account Dasein's end.

This hermeneutic failure is remedied in the analysis of Being-toward-death in which Heidegger exhibits the structure of "anticipation" (*Vorlaufen*), by means of which Dasein runs forth, or is projected toward, its own end or death (§53). The structure of Dasein as projective understanding is seized as a totality only when Dasein is understood to be projected upon its own uttermost, final possibility, which is the possibility to be no more ("nicht mehr Dasein"). Dasein is made a whole, not by being rounded off in the manner of something merely present but only projectively, as a being of care. Dasein is a whole by keeping itself open to its possible end precisely as something possible, by cultivating and sustaining it, as a possibility (SZ 261/BT 306). In this way we get beyond the preliminary analysis of Dasein's everydayness, in which Dasein is at best distracted from, and at worst evasive of, its own final possibility. In anticipatory projection Dasein is brought back to itself from its dispersal in the world and from its evasiveness of death, brought home to its own proper potentiality for Being, recalled from inauthenticity to authenticity. Authentically projected upon death, the Being of Dasein is properly set in motion, properly recovered in its Being as motion, and dislodged from the false security engendered by the comforting and "easy" presence of what is all around it from day to day.

(2) The hermeneutic presuppositions which guided the analysis of everyday Dasein also lack *radicality*. For although Dasein was held in view (fore-sight) in terms of existence and not in terms of objective presence, still it was everyday existence which was kept in view, not radical, originary, authentic existence. Now one might think that this failure too has also been remedied by the introduction of Being-toward-death, and in fact I think it has. But Heidegger here adduces, largely to my mind for architectonic reasons, an "attestation" or phenomenological confirmation that Dasein is indeed capable of the authentic potentiality for Being called for by the phenomenon of anticipation. This attestation is found in the call of conscience which, Heidegger shows, is the call of care (§ 57). The middle term between the "call" and "care" is the phenomenon of "uncanniness," an uneasiness which tears us away from the tranquilizing comfort of everydayness and puts us face to face with the nothingness of Being-in-the-world. The call issues from thrown, anxious Dasein, in the mode of a discourse which summons Dasein back to itself, out of the fallenness of the "they." Dasein thus experiences a call in which it is ready for anxiety and called back to itself. Hearing this call is termed "wanting to have a conscience," and its existential structure is "resoluteness" (§60). In resoluteness Dasein reticently projects itself upon its own potentiality for Being—that is, it seizes itself, and discloses its Being, in its authenticity.

It is then a short step to show that the structure of anticipation and the structure of resoluteness are the same, for Heidegger never really succeeded in showing that they are different. Hence the analysis of "anticipatory resoluteness" (§62) comes as no surprise and indeed verges on redundancy.

Now the hermeneutic stage is set. All the hermeneutic preparations have been made, our hermeneutic sights have been reset, and the shortcomings of the hermeneutic situation remedied. Now we have the Being of Dasein as a totality within fore-having and the radicality of Dasein's mode of Being, which is existence, in fore-sight, which in turn puts a table of existentialia at the disposal of fore-conception (SZ 311/BT 358-59). Now, in §63 (an extremely important discussion of the hermeneutic strategy of *Being and Time*), Heidegger pauses to reflect upon the hermeneutic course which he has followed as the existential analytic nears its climax in the demonstration of the temporality of care (§65).

The path of this hermeneutic inquiry has all along been violent. It has been forced to move against the tendency of this being to cover itself up. As the counterthrust to the pull of fallenness, the hermeneutic inquiry has projected that which tends to withdraw, cast forth a sketch of that which tends to sediment, and violently drawn out that which tends to be withdrawn, all in order to wrest this being free in its very Being, which the being tends to conceal.

But before passing on to the analysis of temporality, Heidegger wants to know if every precaution has been taken to see to it that this hermeneutic violence has not been wanton and arbitrary. That is the central strategic difficulty which haunts the investigation throughout and which threatens to undermine the whole operation of a projective hermeneutic. "What are the signposts to direct the projection, so that Being will be reached at all?" (SZ 312/BT 359). What is to protect this projection from being arbitrary (*Belieben*, SZ 313/BT 360)?

> Where does this Interpretation get its clue, if not from an idea of existence which has been "presupposed"? How have the steps in the analysis of inauthentic Dasein's everydayness been regulated, if not by the concept of existence which we have posited? And if we say that Dasein "falls," and that therefore the authenticity of its potentiality for Being must be wrested from Dasein in spite of this tendency of its Being, from what point of view is this spoken? Is not everything already illumined by the light of the "presupposed" idea of existence, even if rather dimly? Where does this idea get its justification? (SZ 313/BT 361)

Once again Heidegger responds: we *are* the beings to be investigated. As such we stand in a certain self-understanding without which the present investigation would have neither beginning nor end. There is nowhere else to turn but to our self-understanding. No matter how badly it may have done so, Dasein "has already *understood itself*" (SZ 313/BT 360).

To understand ourselves is to set forth fore-structures which are drawn from our own prior self-understanding. And we have chosen to go the way which is guided by the fore-structure of existence; whether this has been the right choice "can be decided only *after one has gone along it*" (SZ 437/BT 487). We have chosen to "presuppose" the idea of existence:

> But what does "presupposition" signify? In positing the idea of existence do we also posit some proposition from which we deduce further propositions about the Being of Dasein, in accordance with formal rules of consistency? Or does this presupposing have the character of an understanding projection, in such a manner indeed that the Interpretation by which such an understanding gets developed, will let that which is to be interpreted *put itself into words for the first time, so that it may decide of its own accord whether, as the entity which it is, it has that state of Being for which it has been disclosed in the projection with regard to its formal aspects?* (SZ 314–15/BT 362–63)

And to this Heidegger responds:

We cannot ever "avoid" a "circular" proof in the existential analytic, because such an analytic does not do *any* proving *at all* by the rules of the "logic of consistency." What common sense wishes to eliminate in avoiding the "circle," on the supposition that it is measuring up to the loftiest rigour of scientific investigation, is nothing less than the basic structure of care. (SZ 315/BT 363)

The network of hermeneutic fore-structures is the very condition under which objective understanding is possible; it is not an obstacle to objectivity. To "avoid" this circle would be to short-circuit the very dynamism of understanding, to resist its ontological makeup, and render it mute, wordless, without a trace of an idea, "without a hint," as we say in English, as to the makeup of the being to be understood. Avoiding the circle would be to deprive understanding of a "way to go" and so leave it stalled. Hence both the prethematic, operative understanding, as existing Being-in-the-world, and the thematic work of *Being and Time* itself must go the way of the circle—or not move at all:

> When one talks of the "circle" in understanding, one expresses a failure to recognize two things: (1) that understanding as such makes up a basic kind of Dasein's Being, and (2) that this Being is constituted as care. To deny the circle, to make a secret of it, or even to want to overcome it, means finally to reinforce this failure. We must endeavor to leap into the "circle," primordially and wholly, so that even at the start of the analysis of Dasein we make sure that we have a full view of Dasein's circular Being. (SZ 315/BT 363)

In this passage is encapsulated the whole of the present analysis of *Being and Time*. Here Heidegger addresses at once the circular motion of Dasein's Being, which guides the circular motion of the understanding, which provides the rule for the circular motion of the textual strategy of *Being and Time*, for the way *Being and Time* moves. Thus the point is not to escape the circle but to acquire a certain light-footedness which knows how to join the ring-dance, to enter it "primordially and wholly" ("ursprünglich und ganz," SZ 315/BT 363) and to project the things themselves in terms which befit it.

Might we not concede to Heidegger everything that he has said thus far and still insist that he has not yet given us the means to know whether we have projected Dasein in the Being which is appropriate to it? Let us concede everything: that to understand is to project, that to project is to set forth the fore-structures under which understanding occurs, and hence that there is no question of denying the circle but only of entering it primordially. Can we not still deny the appropriateness of any *particular* projective understanding? Can we not, e.g., deny the suitability of projecting man in terms of anticipatory resoluteness, as it is done in *Being and Time*? What is to fix the suitability of *this projection*, this particular articulation or interpretation of Dasein?

For Heidegger himself, to accept the methodology of the hermeneutic circle is already to commit oneself to the ontology of "the circular Being of Dasein"

("das zirkelhafte Sein des Daseins," SZ 315/BT 363) upon which it is based. The
hermeneutic circle is simultaneously the method of the investigation and the
Being of Dasein. One cannot, as far as Heidegger himself is concerned, separate the two. *Being and Time* proceeds by way of hermeneutic projection
because the Being of Dasein is projection, care, existence, temporality.

But that argument can be pushed only so far. It is true that if the Being of
Dasein is projection, understanding must proceed projectively. And it would
certainly be a misunderstanding of Dasein's Being, in that case, to want to deny
the circle. But the reverse is not true. It does not follow that if one has adopted a
hermeneutic and projective method, one would be committed to the ontology
of *Being and Time*. One can perfectly well conceive the use of this *method* as a
purely heuristic device, which could be deployed, e.g., in conjunction with an
idealist ontology. One would then not want to deny the circle but simply the
existential ontology with which it is linked by Heidegger.

What response can be made to one who does not want to deny the circle but
who denies that it has been entered primordially and wholly in *Being and Time*
itself? To answer this question we must return to the text cited above, in which
Heidegger tells us that hermeneutic presuppositions ". . . will let that which is
to be interpreted *(das Auszulegende)* put itself into words for the very first
time, so that it may decide of its own accord ["es von sich aus entscheide"]
whether, as the entity which it is, it has that state of Being [which has been
projected]" (SZ 314–15/BT 362). The expression "to decide for itself" means to
let the thing itself speak for itself. The matter to be "decided" is whether the
projection "fits." As we saw above, projections are revisable, or "provisional."
Hence a decision has to be made about the appropriateness of the projection. In
the case of inner-worldly entities, letting them decide for themselves means
determining whether they are disclosed or distorted by the projection. And in
the case of Dasein itself, where we are ourselves the being to be interpreted, we
must decide *for ourselves* whether the projective account is elucidatory or
obfuscatory. And the only possible means we have at our disposal to do so is to
consult the preunderstanding of our Being in which we always and already
move about.

Has Heidegger entered the circle "primordially and wholly"? Has he disclosed Dasein in its authenticity and totality? (SZ 313/BT 361). There is no other
answer than to let *Being and Time* play itself out, let it go the way which it has
chosen to go. Whether this is indeed the way to go can be determined "only
after one has gone along it" (SZ 437/BT 487). Thus the harder we press this issue
the more we are led to see that in *Being and Time* everything comes down to our
capacity to recognize ourselves in the finished account, in the "story" of human
existence which is recounted there. Everything depends upon the preunderstanding which we possess. The legitimacy of the projection is secured only if,
when the account is given, the projection reaches back and links up with the

preunderstanding. This linking up is the only possible control in hermeneutic phenomenology. We can insure that the projection is not wanton violence, but a violence which wrests loose and sets free, only by insisting that the projection, the casting forth, is at one and the same time a movement back to the preunderstanding. In short, the projection must be a retrieval. The projection of the Being of Dasein must be a retrieval of the preunderstanding which we already have of that Being.[9]

As a hermeneutic analysis, the existential analytic succeeds only if it brings to words what we have all along understood about ourselves but have thus far been more or less unable to say. No one else can make that decision for us. Nor can the formal laws of consistency do any more for us than rule out obviously inconsistent accounts. Everything in *Being and Time*, or any exercise in hermeneutic interpretation, comes down to its ability to provoke in us the ultimate hermeneutic response: "*That* is what we are looking for. That puts into words what we have all along understood about ourselves." The *hermeneuein* is either a *legein*, which lets something be seen, or it is not.

Hermeneutics in *Being and Time* invokes a strategy of recovery, of *re-cognitio, Wieder-erkennung*, of knowing again, bringing back on a cognitive level something which is already obscurely understood. Interpretation (*Aus-legung*) is the working out, the unfolding of a preunderstanding. Hermeneutics is the recovery of a prior understanding for which we have hitherto lacked the words. Hermeneutics uncovers because it recovers, brings us to stand in the place where we already are, a place of mysterious proximity. There is no proving and disproving in hermeneutics but only a certain letting-be-seen in which we find (or fail to find) ourselves in the account.

Hermeneutics does not throw everything back into an ineffable, nondebatable intuitionism. On the contrary, it opens up a "conflict as to the Interpretation of Being" (SZ 437/BT 487), one which, far from being resolved, has hardly even been enkindled. The point of *Being and Time* is not to still this conflict but to set it in motion, to let the *question* of Being as presence tremble (first as regards Dasein, then in general), to upset the complacency of metaphysics which prefers the easy way out. The point of *Being and Time* is to put us "on the way" (*unterwegs*) to an adequate hermeneutic, to stir up a hermeneutic conflict (*Streit*), not to put it to sleep. Hermeneutics cannot be reduced to the veridical intuitions of a Cartesian ego, on the one hand, or to sheer irreconcilable conflict, on the other. At this point, one might invoke Gadamer's notion of an ongoing work of correction and refinement by means of hermeneutic dialogue. Heidegger does not himself make such a move because he would take it to be premature. He has much less interest at this point in resolving the conflict than in engendering it. There is already too much peace and rest in metaphysics, an excess of the fusion of horizons to the neglect of a genuine questioning and radical thinking out of the question of the horizon. Heidegger has a radical, deconstructive streak which Gadamerian hermeneutics does not pick up on. Gadamer started out looking for ways to reconcile the *Streit*, which Heidegger spent his life trying to enkindle.[10]

We might also wonder whether all this talk of recognition and recovery constitutes a new philosophy of recollection. If so, it is of a strange sort indeed, for it brings us *back* from the comforts of everyday presence to the fear and trembling of a being which is essentially being-possible. And this is to suggest the possibility of a more "radical" hermeneutic, which I hope to defend in the second part of this study.

TEMPORALITY AND THE AUTHENTIC BEING OF DASEIN

Having widened and deepened its presuppositional framework (the "hermeneutic situation"), Heidegger is prepared to characterize the authentic Being of Dasein in terms of temporality (§65) and hence to bring the "existential analytic" to a head. That analytic must, in turn, be subjected to a "repetition" in which the full temporal and historical Being of Dasein is made plain. The repetition of the existential analytic will issue in the ontology of repetition itself. The repetition of the provisional analysis of the Being of Dasein discloses the Being of Dasein as repetition—which expresses in a formula the convergence of matter and method in *Being and Time*. The ontology of repetition is defined and defended in §74, which is the heart of the chapter on the historicity of Dasein in which, it is not often pointed out, the published text of *Being and Time* culminates. That discussion depends directly upon the elaboration of the "temporality" of Dasein, which is itself prefaced by an important discussion of the "constancy" of the self (§64).

Heidegger's dependence on Kierkegaard, which I have insisted upon in this study, is more decisive at this point, in my view, than in any other place in *Being and Time*, including the better-known use of Kierkegaard's analysis of "anxiety." For repetition goes to the heart of Heidegger's ontology of the circular Being of Dasein. It confirms the hollowness of his criticism of the merely "ontic" and religious nature of Kierkegaard's writings, as I argued in chapter 1.[11] Heidegger not only understates his dependence on Kierkegaard, he misstates it. In borrowing upon Kierkegaard's theory of repetition—without acknowledgment—he invokes Kierkegaard at the most crucial ontological juncture in the published text of *Being and Time*. And when he does mention Kierkegaard, it is always to dress him down as an ontico-existentiell author. Yet the three central sections we have singled out—§64 (the constancy of the self), §65 (temporality), and §74 (repetition)—are directly drawn from Kierkegaard's writings. The treatment of the constancy of the self comes from the discussion of the "continuance of sin" in *The Sickness unto Death*.[12] The analysis of temporality is dependent upon the analysis of existential temporality in the second volume of *Either/Or*. And the all-important discussion of repetition is based quite directly upon Kierkegaard, as I have been arguing throughout.

It is clear that Kierkegaard's contribution to *Being and Time* goes right to the heart of the ontology which is defended there. Heidegger differs from Kierkegaard, not as an ontological thinker from an ontic, as he likes to make out, but principally in terms of the degree to which Heidegger has formalized and articulated Kierkegaard's ontology in a more systematic, professorial manner. Kierkegaard remains the academic renegade, the tormented "exception," the anti-establishment figure who lives on the margins. Heidegger, on the other hand, is very much the German professor, a type about which Kierkegaard had not a few things to say. Stylistically, as a piece of writing, the complexity of *Being and Time* is more like that of Hegel's *Phenomenology of Spirit* than that of the *Concluding Unscientific Postscript*. *Being and Time* is written in a difficult, unconventional but, from Kierkegaard's point of view, "direct" manner. The complexities of its hermeneutic circulation are still dimensions of what Kierkegaard would call direct communication. It shares none of the paradoxicality of Kierkegaard's pseudonymous, indirect communication. The "Kierkegaardian" ontology which Heidegger defends is borrowed from the pseudonyms, and hence we cannot be sure where Kierkegaard himself actually stood in regard to this ontology. If Heidegger's prose is complicated, so that we are not sure if we understand him, Kierkegaard's is ironic, so that we never know whether to believe him. Kierkegaard might well have declared *Being and Time* a dupe of the pseudonyms for having taken Johannes Climacus at his word.[13]

And this is not merely a historical or exegetical issue. For Kierkegaard's philosophy of repetition represents an important and decisive break with metaphysics: repetition is the interest upon which metaphysics founders. On the other hand, Husserlian phenomenology, in its original setting and sense, is very much a part, indeed it is even a certain culmination, of the deepest tendencies of metaphysics (*Cartesian Meditations*, §63). Now some of the difficulty with the Heidegger of the Marburg years is that he remained partly under the spell of Husserl's dream of a universal phenomenological science (BP, §1–3) and did not yet fully appreciate the demands of a thoroughgoing destruction of the history of ontology. When he did, he would only be catching up to Kierkegaard who distrusted ontology from the start. When Derrida later criticizes Heidegger, he criticizes his phenomenological side, which forces Heidegger to be faithful to his Kierkegaardian, not his Husserlian, inspiration.

Heidegger initiates the analysis of temporality by first asking about Dasein's "constancy" (*Ständigkeit*). Heidegger wants to know in what sense Dasein is a unity, i.e., how Dasein is able to gather itself together in the midst of the flux, to maintain its identity in the rush of everydayness. For Heidegger has argued that to a great extent Dasein is *not* a unity, that it is not itself, but rather is scattered about in the inconstancy of the "they," dissipated by the pull of fallenness. And he rejects the traditional metaphysical conceptions of substance and of a pure transcendental subject, because both treat Dasein as something present-at-hand. The unified self for him is neither substance nor subject, but neither is it the inauthentic self of average everydayness.

The only constancy which can be attributed to existing Dasein is the "anticipatory resoluteness" which stands against the wavering of inauthenticity (the Kierkegaardian determination of the "self" as an ethicoreligious unity, a product of the freedom of repetition). Dasein is neither subject *(Subjekt)* nor object *(Vorhandensein, substantia)*; it is a resoluteness which commits itself to a course of action and abides by it. Dasein unifies itself in the unity of a projection in which it binds itself to what it has been all along. And in order to explain how Dasein can thus "bind itself," Heidegger requires, in turn, the theory of temporality presented in §65, in which it is shown that temporality is the "meaning of the Being of Dasein."

On the basis of the provisional analysis of Dasein (Division I), we have determined the Being of Dasein as care. In §65, we determine that the meaning of care is temporality. This points out an important distinction in Heideggerian hermeneutics between the *Being* of a being and the *meaning* of that Being, a distinction which turns, it seems to me, upon an implicit distinction between primary and secondary phases of the work of projection. The being is projected first in a preliminary way upon its "Being" and then in a second and determinative way upon the "meaning" of that Being. Heidegger writes:

> What does *"meaning"* signify? In our investigation, we have encountered this phenomenon in connection with the analysis of understanding and interpretation. According to that analysis, meaning is that wherein the understandability *[Verstehbarkeit]* of something maintains itself—even that of something which does not come into view explicitly and thematically. (SZ 323–4/BT 370–71)

Meaning is not the object of understanding, *what* is understood by the understanding, but, more exactly, the organizing component *in* what is understood, that upon which the understandability depends, around which it is organized and "maintained" *(sich halten)*. Thus we see a distinction between understandability and the organizing center of the understandability. " 'Meaning' signifies the 'upon-which' *[das Woraufhin]* of a primary projection in terms of which something can be conceived in its possibility as that which it is" (SZ 324/BT 371). The organizing principle or center of reference in the understandability is called the "upon-which" of the "primary"—or first phase of—projection. We are thus to distinguish in the projective understanding of any being the initial projection—of the being in its Being—from that upon which the projection was carried out (that upon which it maintains itself, that which organizes and structures the projection). When we have determined the meaning (the "upon-which," the second, determining element) of the Being (the primary projection, the initial or provisional determination) of a being, we will understand that which makes that being possible as a being. "To lay bare the 'upon-which' of a projection amounts to disclosing that which makes possible what has been projected" (SZ 324/BT 371).

We can thus distinguish among (1) the being which is to be understood or projected, which is, however, never a bare fact and which never makes an appearance apart from a determinate projection; (2) the projection of that being in virtue of a certain initial determination of its Being; and (3) that upon which the projection was carried out, that which guided and organized it, albeit in an implicit and prethematic manner. We are thus distinguishing the *being*, its *Being*, and the *meaning* of its Being or, again, the *being*, the *projection* of that being upon its Being, and that *upon which* the projection was carried out. We have to do here not with two different projections but with two different phases of one and the same projection: an initial or provisional phase and a final or radical phase.

Thus the thrust of this hermeneutic undertaking, this penetration to the meaning of Being, is already beyond Being, as Heidegger himself points out in *Basic Problems* (GA 24 399–400/BP 282). Hermeneutics is on the way beyond Being, is already engaged in a destruction of ontology, an overcoming of the metaphysics of Being as presence. It seeks to determine and to delimit Being as presence, to think that which, itself beyond Being, lets Being come to pass, "produces" Being as its "effect," to speak like Derrida, and hence is not itself a captive of the metaphysical project, which is always defined by Being. To think Being is to remain within the first projective cut, but to think the meaning of Being is to make a hermeneutic determination of so radical a sort that it leaves metaphysics and its "Being" behind. When the hermeneutic situation is fully radicalized, we are carried beyond Being to that in which it "maintains itself," to that which produces Being as an effect. As the medieval author of the *Liber de causis* wrote, "Being is the first of all creatures" ("esse primum creaturum").

It is significant that the later Heidegger crossed out the word "Being" in favor of various alternatives like the "open," *Unter-Schied*, and above all *Ereignis*. Heidegger was never concerned with a simple Being/beings distinction, despite such misleading expressions as "the question of Being," the "oblivion of Being," the "ontological difference" between Being and beings. The genuine *Sache* for thought was never *Being* but always the meaning, or truth, of Being or the "It" which gives Being. There was always a third thing, beyond Being, which ultimately held his interest. In *Being and Time*, it was the beings/Being/meaning structure, and in the later works it was, variously, beings/Being/truth of Being; beings/Beingness/Being; and ultimately beings/Being/*Ereignis* or, even more radically, what is present/presence/that which gives presence. Hence there is already here, in *Being and Time*, the makings of what we call "radical hermeneutics." I will return to this important point in chapter 6 in my discussion of Derrida's relation to Heidegger.

Now the initial determination of the Being of Dasein, the first projective look, the first cut into its Being, issued in the definition of care (§41). The task which Heidegger undertakes here is to determine the "meaning" of care (existence). That amounts to seeking the "upon-which," the nourishing principle, which lets care be care. And that of course turns out to be "temporality," which has all along been implicitly guiding the provisional projection of Dasein's Being but only now gets laid out (*ausgelegt*).

Now the temporal "meaning" of the threefold structure of care (SZ 192/BT 237) is written all over it. (1) As projected, Dasein "comes toward" (*zu-kommt*) itself, toward its own deepest possibilities, and hence is futural (*zukunftig*). (2) As a factical being, thrown into the world, Dasein carries its past with it, not in the sense of that which is over but in the sense of what Dasein has been (*gewesen*) all along. Futurity and having-been are conceived not as opposites but as a reciprocal reaching-over into each other. So when Dasein comes *toward* itself in its authentic potentiality for Being, it comes *back* to itself and *retrieves* that which it has been all along (SZ 325–26/BT 373). In stretching *forth*, it comes *back*. That is the heart of "the circular Being of Dasein" and the cornerstone of Heidegger's theory of repetition. (3) Finally, as being-alongside-other-entities, Dasein either comes back to itself authentically or fails to do so. That is to say, the "present moment" is either a moment of vision—a situation in which Dasein acts decisively, in which, as Heidegger says, Dasein "makes-present" (*gegen-wartigen*)—or a moment of fallenness in which Dasein is immersed in the present and allows itself to be dictated to by the circumstances in which it finds itself. In the first case, the "there" (*da*) of Dasein is open and free, and in the second, it is closed off and hemmed in by what is "present" all around it. Dasein fails to be loyal to itself—that is, to its Being as "existence" or "anticipatory resoluteness"—and falls victim to what is "objectively present" (*vorhanden*) around it. Dasein either comes back to itself futurally (projectively retrieves its possibilities) or idles away its time. Thus the structure of existential temporality proves to be the "upon-which" of the projection of the Being of Dasein as care—that which, at work all along in care, makes its possible for care, and hence for Dasein, to be what it is.

With that, the "existential analytic" (§§9–65) concludes, but the work of *Being and Time* is far from over. For a twofold task of "repetition" still remains (§66). In the first place, the existential analytic itself requires a repetition in a "temporal analysis" (SZ 331/BT 380). Having determined that the meaning of care, and of anticipatory resoluteness itself, is temporality, Heidegger must now confirm this analysis by showing how it is so. He must exhibit, item by item, the temporal sense of every structure uncovered in the existential analytic. That leads him, in chapter 5 of Division II, to a determination of the "historicity" of

Dasein, in which the full temporal meaning of Dasein is laid out. At that point the determination of the meaning of the Being of Dasein is complete.

But a second and still more decisive task remains, and that is the repetition of the temporal analysis in terms of the meaning of Being in general. "The existential-temporal analysis of Dasein demands, for its part, that it be repeated anew within a framework in which the concept of Being is discussed in principle" (SZ 333/BT 382). And that—the most famous unredeemed promissory note in contemporary philosophy—was, of course, to be the work of the unpublished Division III. The work of repetition was not finished; the analysis of Dasein was left un-repeated.

REPETITION/RETRIEVAL

Although it is central to the argument of *Being and Time*, the analysis of "historicity," inserted as it is in the middle of the last three chapters (devoted to the temporal analysis), appears architectonically as something of an appendix to the work. Yet without it we would sorely misunderstand the Being of Dasein. For if the existential-temporal analysis has tended to favor a somewhat individualistic interpretation of Dasein (in terms of existential temporality), this emphasis is balanced out in chapter 5 by a stress on the historicity of resoluteness. That in turn will reveal one important difference between the Kierkegaardian and the Heideggerian conceptions of repetition. Although Kierkegaard did see the historical situatedness of existential resolve, his battles with the Hegelians of his day prevented him from formulating a conception of historicity and tradition. Heidegger on the other hand has all along been building up to the historicity of Dasein and a theory of historical repetition.

Resolute Dasein projects upon possibilities that are uniquely its own. Still, Heidegger thinks, that remains too formal a determination of resoluteness. True, ontology has no business trying to decide "what Dasein *factically* resolves in any particular case," but that does not exempt it from asking "whence, *in general*, Dasein can draw those possibilities upon which it factically projects itself" (SZ 382–83/BT 434). Up to this point, *Being and Time* has had nothing to say about the actual content of Dasein's resolve, about what Dasein in fact resolves upon. The projection upon death assures that Dasein's resolve will be its own and will be made in the light of the totality of its Being, but this projection waves its hand at the question of how Dasein resolves upon one course of action rather than another.

To meet that demand, Heidegger turns to his notion of facticity (thrownness, having-been). For, as we have seen, in projecting forth toward the possible, Dasein is brought back to its factical self, to the situation in which it is always and already thrown. But thrownness more deeply considered, which means *repeated in terms of temporality*, turns out to be Dasein's "heritage" *(Erbe)*, so that Heidegger now speaks of what has been "handed down" to resolute Dasein (SZ 383/BT 435). Dasein's factical situation is no brutal factuality but a constellation of possibilities which have been "delivered over" or handed down (*überliefern*) to Dasein. There is some sense now of the "gift" which is implied by the "*dare*" in *trans-dare, traditio*. But it is hardly a gift which just drops from the sky; on the contrary, it depends upon the resoluteness of Dasein.

> The more authentically Dasein resolves . . . the more unequivocally does it choose and find the possibility of its existence, and the less does it do so by accident. Only by the anticipation of death is every accidental and "provisional" possibility driven out (SZ 384/BT 435).

The possibilities harbored within one's heritage must be *disclosed* or opened up by resolute Dasein lest Dasein simply be tossed about by circumstances which will seem to it entirely fortuitous. The possibility of death, which means the confrontation with one's finitude, is the condition under which facticity is transformed from a random chance into a hertiage ripe with possibility. Thus one's possibility is both inherited and chosen, which explains why Heidegger uses the active expression "handing down to oneself" (*ein Sichüberliefern*). To a limited degree, then, good or bad fortune is made by the resoluteness with which one comes to grips with the circumstances in which one finds oneself.[14]

Dasein's heritage may be either individual or collective. The possibilities which are sent to Dasein may be sent either to individual Dasein or to the larger historical group of which it is a part. The heritage of the individual is what Heidegger calls "fate" (*Schicksal*). We must not be misled by the translation of this term; instead we must hear the "sending" (*schicken*) in *Schicksal*. Heidegger does not mean that the individual with a "fate" is the victim of circumstances beyond his control, for only the resolute, authentic individual has fate, that is, can seize upon the possibilities that have been *sent* his way. But Dasein is never merely an individual, for Being-in-the-world is always Being-with, and historicizing is always cohistoricizing. And this collective heritage Heidegger calls "destiny" (*Geschick*, another derivative of *schicken*), a word which will itself play a central role in the later Heidegger's reflections of the destining of Being (*Seinsgeschick*). In *Being and Time* "destiny" means the heritage which is sent to collective Dasein, to a community or people, which it is up to the resoluteness of the community to seize upon (SZ 384/BT 436).

Together, fate and destiny, the heritage of the individual (the narrative of one's own life) and the heritage of the community (the history of the time) make up "the full authentic historicizing (*Geschehen*) of Dasein" (SZ 385/BT 436). And with that remark Heidegger is prepared to formalize the notion of Dasein's authentic historicity (*eigentliche Geschichtlichkeit*) in which, in my view, the entire argument of the published text of *Being and Time* culminates.

Only an entity which, in its Being, is essentially futural so that it is free for its death and can let itself be thrown back upon its factical "there" by shattering itself against death—that is to say, only an entity which, as futural, is equiprimordially in the process of having-been—can, by handing down to itself the possibility it has inherited, take over its own thrownness and be in the moment of vision for "its time." Only authentic temporality, which is at the same time finite, makes possible something like fate—that is to say, authentic historicality. (SZ 385/BT 437)

In this formula Heidegger fills in the historical dimension of the tripartite structure of temporality (which is itself the matrix of the tripartite structure of care), giving it historical flesh and concretion, so that there can be no question of an isolated "existential individual." Authentic Dasein must be authentic historicizing, which means that the moment of choice, of truth, of vision is above all a historical moment in which Dasein seizes upon the historical possibilities which it has inherited and which it alone, as resolute, has the eyes to see. Dasein's temporalizing *(Zeitigung)* is historicizing, and its historicizing is cohistoricizing in and with its "generation." It is just this historical dimension of authentic Dasein, the historicity which is essential to authenticity, that is often overlooked in the usual renderings of *Being and Time*, which have a tendency to treat everything which follows §65 as an appendix.

The *content* of Dasein's resolve is governed by its historicity, by the context or situatedness of Dasein in a particular complex of historical circumstances. And that is as close an approach to the existentiell situation as an ontological-existential analysis can make. From here on in, it is a matter of something like *phronesis*, which is the power, described by Aristotle, to find the universal in concrete circumstances, to know what is demanded by the particular situation. And, in *Being and Time*, "*phronesis*" is translated as "*Verstehen*," that is, understanding.[15] *What* is to be done is a matter of (1) authentic Dasein's insight into what is demanded *of* a being who has looked death in the eye and (2) what is demanded *by* the constellation of circumstances which make up the historical moment in which authentic Dasein finds itself.

In chapter 9 I will argue that there is here the makings of a Heideggerian ethics. Heidegger's antagonism to ethics is largely a hostility to modern value-theory, to its preoccupation with determinate rules of conduct for an ahistorical subject to the neglect of the considerations of historicity and *phronesis* which I have underlined in the present discussion. I will argue that Heidegger is hostile to modern ethics but not to a more profoundly historical ethics.

Having reached a formulation of authentic historicizing, Heidegger proceeds to show that authentic historicity is "repetition" (in the Macquarrie-Robinson translation):

The resoluteness which comes back to itself and hands itself down, then becomes the *repetition* of a possibility of existence that has come down to us. *Repeating is handing down explicitly*—that is to say, going back into the possibilities of the Dasein that has-been-there. (SZ 385/BT 437)

The circular movement of Dasein's Being is the movement between Dasein's futurity and its having-been: in projecting *forth* upon the possible, Dasein comes *back* to the possibilities which have been handed down to it and which can now be characterized as Dasein's heritage. What Dasein can be is a function of what it has been; what Dasein has been opens up a spectrum of possibilities for Dasein, so long as Dasein is resolute. That circular movement Heidegger calls *Wieder-holung*, which, as we have argued, has the sense of "retrieval" or "recovery," of retrieving a possibility which has been handed down to Dasein, of making actual a possibility which has all along been lingering in what Dasein has been. *Wiederholung* combines in one expression both the Kierkegaardian sense of pressing forward again and again (which has primarily a futural sense) and, a more historical sense of simultaneously returning to the factical, historical situation.

Repetition, accordingly, is not a matter of making actual again what has been previously actualized. It is not, then, what one ordinarily means, in English, by repetition—the simple reduplication of a previous act, as when one "learns by repetition." In Heidegger's terminology, repetition *(Wiederholung)* is not "bringing back again" *(Wiederbringen)*.

> But when one has, by repetition, handed down to oneself a possibility that has been, the Dasein that has-been-there is not disclosed in order to be actualized over again. The repeating of that which is possible does not bring again *(Wiederbringen)* something that is "past," nor does it bind the "present" back to that which has already been "outstripped." Arising, as it does, from a resolute projection of oneself, repetition does not let itself be persuaded of something by what is "past," just in order that it, as something which was formerly actual, may recur. (SZ 385–86/BT 437–38)

Inasmuch as Dasein itself is a being of possibility *(Seinskönnen)*, repetition is always focused on the possible. Dasein is Dasein, is authentically itself, inasmuch as it projectively anticipates or runs forth into the possible. The simple reduplication which reproduces something already actualized is precisely a movement away from the origin, precisely the *de-generation* which is the source of the inauthentic, the second-hand, the fallen. Repetition is always an originary operation by means of which Dasein opens up possibilities latent in the tradition, bringing forth something new. Repetition/retrieval thus has the productive sense which Derrida wants to emphasize. In repetition/retrieval Dasein is productive of what is repeats; it does not simply go over old ground. The self produces itself by repetition. In repetition Dasein discloses its own Being and that of the historical situation in which it belongs, that of its generation, *for the first time*. Repetition is a first, a breakthrough, a retrieval which pushes forward, which opens what was previously closed, liberates what was formerly held in check. Repetition is a new beginning which aims at the possible.

Far from being a fading echo of the past, repetition is for Heidegger an "*Erwiderung*," a reply, a retort, a rejoinder to what has up to now laid in wait, merely potentially.

> Rather, the repetition makes a *reciprocative rejoinder [Erwiderung]* to the possibility of that existence which has been there. But when such a rejoinder is made to this possibility in a resolution, it is made *in a moment of vision; and as such* it is at the same time a *disavowal [Widerruf]* of that which in the "today" is working itself out as the "past." (SZ 386/BT 438)

Repetition "answers" what is calling to it in what has been, "responds" to what is possible, makes a "rejoinder" which consists in bringing forth something for which Dasein has up to now only obscurely groped. The rejoinder (*Erwiderung*) is a rebuff (*Widerruf*) of the inertial weight of the past. It is a living response which speaks against, protests, disavows the weight of a tradition which has become leaden and lifeless; effecting the possible is "revolutionary," while clinging to the past is "conservative" (GA 45 37). There is thus a deconstructive moment in repetition, a moment of countermovement (*Gegenzug*), of rebuttal (*Widerruf*), which rejects that whose only authority is its prior actuality. Repetition aims at not the *actual* but the *possible*. Possibility is higher than actuality.

The directedness of Dasein's Being to the future accounts for its interest in what has been. The future is not an empty, purely logical possibility but the determinate possibility to retrieve what is handed down to us by what has been. And that holds too for the practicing historian whose work is otherwise an idle and uprooted objectivism (§76). If Foucault wants to write the history of the present, Heidegger thinks the historian's proper task is to write the history of the future.

It is thus possible to distinguish between Kierkegaardian repetition and Heideggerian retrieval in terms of the character of *kinesis* they describe and in a way which has nothing to do with dressing Kierkegaard down. For Kierkegaard repetition is repeating *forward*. It starts out from the point of decision and moves forward in a futural direction of resoluteness, vowing to remain faithful to the chosen path so as to acquire or constitute a self. But in Heidegger the movement is more properly *circular*, inasmuch as the movement forward is at the same time a movement back to one's inherited possibilities. Kierkegaard remains within the *linear* model but reverses its direction. For the prevailing metaphysical conception takes repetition to move backward because it puts eternity behind as the object of recollection, whereas Christian existence moves forward, putting eternity ahead, as the reward for keeping one's hand to the plow. Heidegger rejects the linear model because his interests in a radically temporal interpretation of existence lead him to a notion of the tradition. Heidegger's interest in Dilthey and Yorck drew him closer to a more fully historical conception of temporality. Kierkegaard certainly thought that by resolute choice and repetition the individual constituted himself as a self and actualized his possibility to be. But he conceived this primarily in terms of individual temporality and resisted the notion of historicity as an offspring of Hegelianism.

We have thus met up with three philosophies of repetition and *kinesis*, three ways to come to grips with the Eleatic condemnation of the flux, three ways to restore the original difficulty of life. In each case repetition functions as a way of establishing identity and of coping with the flux, not as a way of denying it. These efforts culminate in *Being and Time* and its account of the circular being of Dasein and the hermeneutic circle of understanding. The question to which we must now turn is whether this hermeneutics of the circle does not in the end fall into complicity with the Eleatics, with the well-rounded circle of Parmenidean *aletheia* in which Being clings to Being in a final gesture of self-presence.

PART 2

Deconstruction and the Radicalization of Hermeneutics

FOUR

Hermeneutics after *Being and Time*

THREE INTERPRETATIONS OF INTERPRETATION

After the publication of *Being and Time,* the idea of hermeneutics underwent three significant developments: in the work of the later Heidegger himself; in Gadamer's "philosophical hermeneutics"; and in the French structuralist, and then poststructuralist, critique of hermeneutics, of which Derrida's deconstruction is the form most pertinent to this study. After *Being and Time* there are, to modify a phrase of Derrida's, three interpretations of interpretation. [1]

The later Heidegger became his own most important critic. He submitted the notions of "horizon" and "fore-structure" to a searching critique with the result that he no longer described his work as hermeneutic at all. In the meanwhile, Gadamer (with whom we today most readily associate the word "hermeneutics"), almost without regard to this development in Heidegger himself, adopted the fundamental standpoint of *Being and Time.* He took over notions which had been brought under fire by the late Heidegger—preunderstanding, the hermeneutic circle, the phenomenological theory of horizons—and made them the basis of a "philosophical hermeneutics" which emphasized the restorative side of Heidegger, the philosophy of retrieval. Derrida, on the other hand, exploited the radically deconstructive side of Heidegger, the moment of critique and *Abbau,* and directed it against what he called the "metaphysics of presence," within which he included hermeneutics itself as a metaphysics of meaning and truth.

The hermeneutic project launched in *Being and Time* thus moved in three directions: to the right, in Gadamer's more conservative "philosophical hermeneutics"; to the left, in a Derridean "deconstruction" of hermeneutics; and finally, let us say, straight ahead, in the direction of the late Heidegger's startling repetition of his own project in *Being and Time.*

Heidegger came to see that "transcendental-horizonal thinking" belongs to the metaphysics of subjectivity and hence that "hermeneutic phenomenology" has its coat caught in the door of Cartesianism. He delimited the notion of horizonality in favor of what he called the open, and he said that the metaphorics of the circle were subjectivistic. But he meant by all of this not to abandon the fundamental project of hermeneutics altogether but to repeat it and transform it in a nontranscendental form and in a way which accorded with the dynamics of the "transformation of thinking." In the later Heidegger the hermeneutic project "turns itself around" in favor of a hermeneutics more deeply construed. The "circle"—which implies the notion of the projective preunderstanding—gives way to what Heidegger calls the hermeneutic "relation" which consists in the "belonging together" of Being and man. Being and man are related to each other in a primordiality which is endangered by metaphysics and which it is the task of "thinking" to recover. Thinking means to restore a unity which precedes objectification. We stand always and already in Being, in belongingness to Being. And it is just this nearness of the world, this closeness of things—from which modern *Technik* has alienated us—that must be restored, de-distanced. We are always and already in the world, in constant touch with the simplest things, and the task of thought is to re-cover that belonging in which we already stand.

The relationship between Being and Dasein is retained, but rather than linking them by means of hermeneutic fore-structures, according to which Being is a prepossession of Dasein's understanding, Heidegger speaks of the way in which Dasein is prepossessed by Being. Preunderstanding, as the fore-having of Being by Dasein, is replaced by the prepossession of Dasein by Being, a kind of prior invasion by, or prebelonging of Dasein to, the world. And the work of hermeneutics is to recover that sense of the world before it was disrupted by objectifying thinking, to restore the sense of what is close before it was made distant by objectification.

Gadamer understood everything that was healing and restorative about Heidegger's notion of retrieval but, as I hope to show, he lacked the heart for Heidegger's more radical side. He produced an impressive philosophy of the "tradition" and of the dynamics of its transmission. His concern was always with the horizons, with their mutual nourishment and interaction, with a certain wedding or joining of the horizons such that each draws strength from the other and all in the service of the present.[2] He understood what Heidegger had to say about the truth of Being and the experience of the work of art, but he had no interest in the more deeply critical side of Heidegger which had inspired Heidegger's talk of destruction and overcoming.

That produced the odd result that as Heidegger's own thought moved forward a kind of conservative Heideggerianism began to take shape on his right flank, a Heideggerian hermeneutics which remained under the spell of Plato and Hegel, the old nemeses of repetition, according to Constantin Constantius. Gadamer has a deeply Hegelian streak which leads him to search for some hermeneutic version of the *Aufhebung*—some way to fuse the horizons so as to bear fruit in the present—rather than to undertake the radical Heideggerian step-back *(Schritt-züruck)* from all horizonality. He is too much interested in garnering the accumulated goods of the tradition, the "truth" *(verum, alethea)* which it has stored up, to ask the question of the *a-letheia* process itself, which Heidegger never ceased to pose and pose again, which never gave the "path of thought" any rest.

But even the step back to *aletheia* itself is only so much metaphysics for Derrida—a metaphysics of nearness and proximity, of truth and shining presence—around whom a left-wing (a left-bank!) Heideggerianism began to form. For Derrida, the later Heidegger has succeeded, not in launching a deconstructive critique of hermeneutic phenomenology but only in raising it up another notch into an onto-hermeneutics of the truth of Being. Derrida has no taste for the circle or the "belonging together" of "Being" and "man" and no interest in the metaphorics of closeness, simplicity, unity, homecoming, and mystery which punctuates the later Heidegger. If Gadamer's work is a conservative hermeneutic, and the later Heidegger's a deeper repetition of hermeneutics, Derrida's means to be no hermeneutics at all but a delimitation, a deconstruction of hermeneutics as a nostalgia for meaning and unity. Of these three thinkers, Derrida is unquestionably the philosopher most faithful to the flux, most suspicious of every attempt to still its movements or, to use his own striking expression, to "arrest the play." There is a more Nietzschean side to Derrida than to Heidegger or Gadamer, a more deeply suspicious eye, a greater sense of the fragility of our thought constructions and the contingency of our institutions.

I want now to explore these three interpretations of interpretation in order to pose the question of a "radical hermeneutics." I will insist upon the necessity of the searching criticisms of hermeneutic phenomenology undertaken by the later Heidegger and Derrida. Deconstructive criticism is for me the gateway through which radical hermeneutics must pass. I am interested in breaking the spell of metaphysics where metaphysics means the attempt to arrest the play and to flood us with its reassurances. I am interested in letting the play play itself out. But I contend—and this goes to the heart of what I mean by radical hermeneutics—that after tracing out this deconstructive course, after allowing the disseminating drift its full play, we are in an odd way led *back* to ourselves, not in a moment of recovery and self-presence but in a deeper, less innocent way. Radical hermeneutics makes a pass at formulating what the French call *la condition humaine*, the human situation. I do not mean by this to incite another wave of the "humanism" which deconstruction has tried to put down but to evoke the notion of "facing up" to the limits of our situation, to the illusions of which we are capable, to the original difficulty of our lives. And I call this "hermeneutics" just because I think there is something liberating about all this, not dehumanizing (in the spirit of the hermeneutics of facticity launched by the young Heidegger). That at least is what I shall try to show.

In the present chapter I want to stake out the three paths that hermeneutics took after *Being and Time*. Then, in the rest of Part II, I will look more closely at the Derridean, deconstructive critique of hermeneutics and phenomenology. For what I call radical hermeneutics is not to be identified with the later Heidegger himself, because it arises from a certain interplay between Heidegger and Derrida, from letting each loose on the other, which produces an odd but emancipatory effect.

HEIDEGGER'S REPETITION OF HERMENEUTICS

There are two sides to what the later Heidegger has to say about hermeneutics: the delimitation of "transcendental horizonal representing" in the *Discourse on Thinking (Gelassenheit)* and the retrieval of "hermeneutics" in *On the Way to Language*. I will take up each in turn.

(1) The structure of "projection" so central to *Being and Time* would inevitably become suspect to Heidegger in virtue of the very momentum of *Being and Time* itself. Heidegger was engaged in dismantling the Cartesian subject. As his thought evolved, it became clear that a projective understanding, issuing from Dasein, rendering beings manifest in their Being, was a suspiciously transcendental notion. Heidegger had come to believe that Nietzsche's metaphysics of willing was the most extreme outcome of Cartesianism. Hence, what he called "thinking" defined itself in opposition to willing, as a suspension of willing. Willing thus has the wide sense, not merely of the exercise of human choice but of any imposition of human subjectivity upon things—whether by means of the will in the narrow sense or of the structures of the thinking subjectivity. Willing means the metaphysical structure of subjectivity itself, whether that subject be conceived in voluntaristic terms (existentialism, Sartre) or in epistemological terms (transcendental philosophy from Descartes through Kant to Husserl). So the *Discourse on Thinking*, which targets the transcendental subject, can be read as a companion piece to *A Letter on Humanism*, which targets the existential subject. In both treatises the remedy for subjectivism is to be found in locating the essence of man in something "beyond" man (or subjectivity).

Thinking is "willing" in the transcendental tradition because thinking is conceived in terms of "spontaneity" (G 31–32/DT 58–59), the active rendering manifest of things by means of the resources of the transcendental subject. If Descartes initiated this project and Kant was its high point, Husserl's "horizonal phenomenology" remains under its spell (although something else was at work in his phenomenological method, something which Heidegger wanted to radicalize.)[3]

Heidegger needed a determination of thinking that lay outside willing. And even if such a thinking must *begin* as a willing not to will, it means ultimately to terminate in a thinking which gets free of willing altogether (G 51–52/DT 73–74). Such freedom clearly is not anything which we effect by the force of our will, but it is something into which we are admitted *(zugelassen)* by means of our openness toward it. We are admitted into freedom, letting-be, releasement *(Gelassenheit)*, a word borrowed from Meister Eckhart, whom Heidegger regards as a master of thought, not of mystical obfuscation (G 36/DT 61; SG 71).[4] In Heidegger's sense, releasement means a thinking which proceeds in freedom from the constructs of the thinking subject, unobstructed by subjective constructions, a thinking which has deconstructed the works of subjectivity— precisely in order to gain access to the sphere which they obstruct.

Heidegger calls the thinking which is willing *Vor-stellen,* which means the way the subject "sets" *(stellt)* things forth *(vor)* for itself and which the English translators call "representational" thinking. Heidegger criticizes not only the *stellen,* the willfulness of setting things out in a way that suits us, but also the *vor,* the setting *forth,* putting things forward in an order of our own devising, a construction of our own making, made in our own image, made to suit us. There is no distinguishing here, as there is in *Being and Time,* between free-floating constructions and the constructions which release the things themselves into their own Being. Now releasing means releasement from willing and constructions of any sort.

The standpoint of "transcendental-horizonal representing" in the *Discourse* is presented by the "scholar" *(Gelehrter)*—is it Husserl?—for whom the appearance of a tree depends upon passing beyond the tree to the field or horizon which places the tree before us as a tree (and in that sense "lets the object be"). Now if it is true that this is the phenomenology of Husserl, it is also true that this is the very phenomenology, deriving from Husserl, which Heidegger himself defended during the Marburg period. But the teacher—is it Heidegger, the later Heidegger?—wants to go after, to delimit, the idea of horizon, because something in turn lets the horizon be.

> *Teacher:* What is evident of the horizon, then, is but the side facing us of an openness which surrounds; an openness which is filled with views of the appearances of what to our re-presenting are objects. (G 39/DT 64)

The horizon then is something derivative, secondary. For a horizon is the "look" or the "sight" *(Aussehen)* in terms of which we line up or sight objects, thereby making the objectivity of objects possible. And the teacher claims that this enabling condition is itself conditioned, because the look of things which supplies the horizon or field of vision does not originate with us, is not generated by a subjective source. Beyond the object-with-horizon, there is the open itself of which the horizonal view or circle of vision is but a perspectival or partial view. If the horizon lets the object be—as it does, that is what horizonal hermeneutics, horizonal phenomenology, shows—it remains true that something *lets the horizon be,* and that is the "open." When we look on something, and set it forth in a certain horizonal frame, we are simply carving out a space within the open, a space which we did not ourselves open up in the first place. Horizonal projection presupposes the open, which makes it possible for the horizon to be an open space. By projecting a horizon we shrink the open down to our size, so that it contains objects made to fit our subjective-human limitations.

Now Heidegger tries to push further into a more radically nonsubjective determination of the open by distinguishing two different aspects of the open (G 40/DT 64). The horizon supplies the condition (the look, *Aussehen*) under which the "object" (*Gegenstand*) appears. But if the horizon is itself made possible only by the open, then the open is a kind of meta-objective sphere, a sphere not of objectivity (*Gegenständlichkeit*) but of that realm in which it is possible for things to come over toward us (*das Ent-gegen-kommende*), that which makes possible the objectivity of objects, objects under their horizonal conditionality. This Heidegger calls the "region" (*Gegend*), not any particular region to be sure, but the region of openness, the region of all regions (G 39–41/DT 64–66). But the region, as the side of the open which is open to us, turned toward us, as the horizon's other side, remains defined relative to us (*quoad nos*). But for a radical delimitation of subjectivity, it would be necessary to think the open *in itself*, as it is for itself, not relative to us (*quoad se*). For this Heidegger adopts an old word, *gegnet*, that has a verbal sense derived by taking *gegen* as a verb—*gegnen* (as in *begegnen*)—and that is translated as "that-which-regions" (G 41–42/DT 65–67), which has the sense of the regioning of the region, the coming-to-presence of the region.

Thus the regressive, reductive movement, the movement back beyond transcendental horizonal thinking, may be portrayed as a double movement, or twofold step. First, there is the movement from objects (*Gegegenstände*, beings, the ontical), to their objectivity (*Gegenständlichkeit*, *Aussehen*, horizon, Being, the ontological); this is the movement of transcendence, which defines the sciences and horizonal thinking. Second, there is the more radical movement from the transcendental horizon to the open—first as *Gegend*, then as *Gegnet*—as that open expanse in which the objectivity of objects, that is, the Being of beings, comes to pass. This effects the delimitation of transcendental horizonal thinking, of metaphysics in general, and corresponds to the quest for the "meaning" of Being in *Being and Time*.

Once again we are driven to a tripartite scheme in order to get Heidegger's questioning right. That tripartite scheme, I keep insisting, is already to be found in *Being and Time:* from beings to their Being, from Being to its meaning (*woraufhin*). The step back is always the *second* step. The first step is always the step of metaphysical transcendence.

The *Gegnet*, the teacher says, is to be understood in the sense of the free, open expanse ("die frei Weite") which is also a space of time, of the lingering for a while in the open (*Weile*). The *Gegnet* thus is both *Weite* and *Weile*, open expanse and whiling (lingering, abiding). It is the realm, therefore, in which "things" *(Dinge)* can rest for a while, in which they find a space and a time to emerge, linger, and then drop back out of sight. Here things are things, not objects. They linger, abide, rest—rather than being stood up like objects against a horizonal screen or backdrop so that they can stand before us *(gegenstehen)*. Here things rest "in themselves," in the free and open expanse, not in a projective framework of our own devising. They linger in an opening which has not yet been domesticated by our human, conceptual (or perceptual) frames, framings, or frameworks. Although Heidegger does not make the connection here, we can see a link between *vor-stellen*, setting things up within a framework of our own devising, and *Ge-stell*, as the encompassing frame of modern technology.

"*Gelassenheit*" thus has a twofold force. On the one hand, it refers to a kind of thinking, to the way man must be in the face of that-which-regions. But on the other hand, it refers to the *Gegnet* itself, which lets be not only the horizonal look of objects but also "things" in the special sense that Heidegger reserves for that word. *Gelassenheit* refers not only to thinking but also to that which grants thinking, which admits thinking into its sphere, which lets things *(Dinge)* be, and, finally, as the other side of the horizon, which lets the horizon of objects be (cf. SD 40–41/TB 36–37).

There is a sense in which it would be misleading to say that this movement is a movement from transcendental-horizonal thinking to the open expanse, for that makes it sound like we have moved from one place to another, while in fact we are always and already in that expanse (G 50/DT 72). Indeed, we are both in the open expanse and outside it: outside it insofar as we are explicitly taken up and preoccupied with the business of transcendental-horizonal projection, and yet inside it, insofar as we have not yet realized that the horizon is but the horizonal constriction or contraction of the open. We fail to open ourselves to that in which we already are. These are the familiar dynamics of the hermeneutic circle: we stand already (implicitly) in a sphere of which we are not (explicitly) cognizant. And it is the task of "thinking" to take stock of that implicit sphere, which is to be understood no longer as an implicit horizon but as that of which the horizon is itself a certain constriction or closing off.

Man "belongs originally" (G 51–52/DT 73) to the open. The thinking which is admitted *into* the open is itself brought about *by* the open which, as it were, draws thinking back to itself, gathers thinking to itself. We belong to the open region from the start, prior to everything *(im vorhinein)* (G 63/DT 83). And the open itself, the *Gegnet*, is something which thought cannot get beyond. Heidegger calls this the *Un-vor-denk-liche* (G 63/DT 83), that is, that prior realm to which we always already belong but which thinking cannot get beyond or behind, which thinking cannot somehow or another get ahead of and bring within the grips of its fore-structures.

But that spells the end of the version of hermeneutics defended in *Being and Time*, which I have called here the "first essence" of hermeneutics. In this unfore-think-able the hermeneutic fore-structures of *Being and Time* collapse, giving way to a certain acknowledgment that we are always and already held in advance in the hold of Being or, better, the *Gegnet* (or *Ereignis*, the clearing, language, etc.). Transcendental preunderstanding has been transformed into (deconstructively retrieved as) a post-transcendental prepossession of thought by Being, a prebelonging of thought to Being. The transcendental "pre-," the hermeneutical fore-structure, is transformed into an aletheological belonging of man to Being.

Heidegger calls this original belonging of man to the *Gegnet* the process of *Vergegnis*, that is, of the appropriating, taking possession, of thought by the *Gegnet* (G 54/DT 75). The *Gegnet* thus takes possession of thought and releases it from transcendental horizonal thinking, letting thinking be what it is. *Vergegnis*, which retains a phonic proximity to *Ereignis*, means our original being-owned *(ge-eignet)* by the open. But *Gegnet* also takes possession of things, letting things be things, not objects; this Heidegger calls *Be-dingnis*, literally be-thinging or conditioning (G 56/DT 77). The *Gegnet* lets thinking *(Vergegnis)* and things *(Bedingnis)* be. It admits *(einlassen)* thinking and things into their own. Thinking not only must be free of willing and become letting-be, but that also must be preeminently true of the *Gegnet* itself.

We do not end up in some new place, but we recover the place, or region, in which we have been all along. We must, however, guard against the illusion that this recovery is something brought about by human effort. It is "acquired," Heidegger says, by "waiting" upon the *Gegnet*, not by rushing it, by trying to take it by storm, by launching an assault, but by a surrender of the projective attempts we make to surround and encompass the open. We are admitted into the open only in the experience of the breakdown of such attempts. Now here is a point where Heidegger is beginning to catch up to Kierkegaard who said that repetition is possible only with the experience of the thunderstorm, or the breakdown of human efforts at repetition. We experience the "unencompassable" character of that which horizonal thinking wants to surround, encircle, and encompass by its horizonality. We are ourselves encircled and encompassed by the open; we cannot horizonally encircle and encompass it (G 52/DT 74).

And that is the central point for me: genuine thinking, according to Heidegger after *Being and Time*, is effected only by relinquishing horizonal projectiveness, which means willing, constructing, projecting horizonal schemes. Although such horizonal schemes are the stuff of which scientific thought is made, they must be superseded in the more radical notion of "thinking" which the later Heidegger cultivates. In chapter 8 I will return to the question of the sciences and ask how, having been thus delimited and displaced, we are now to conceive them.

(2) All of this explains why the later Heidegger lets the word "hermeneutics" drop after *Being and Time* (US 98–99)/OWL 12), but Heidegger always puts us on notice that he never really drops anything but reworks or repeats it in accord with the dynamics of the "way" which is mentioned on the last page of *Being and Time* (SZ 437/SZ 488). The term was dropped to keep thinking under way (US 121/OWL 29). "Hermeneutic phenomenology" retains a residue of transcendental ontology and so must, in the interests of thought itself, be surrendered in order to approach that for which metaphysics has no name. The notion threatened to block the way to the more primordial experience which Heidegger seeks.

Then what remains of "hermeneutics" after it has been exposed to the relentless self-criticism of the "way"?

Inq. The expression "hermeneutic" derives from the Greek verb *hermeneuein.* That verb is related to the noun *hermeneus,* which is referable to the name of the god Hermes by a playful thinking that is more compelling than the rigor of science. Hermes is the divine messenger. He brings the message of destiny *(Geschick);* *hermeneuein* is that exposition which brings tidings because it can listen to a message. Such exposition *(Darlegen)* becomes the interpretation *(Auslegen)* of what has been said earlier by the poets who, according to Socrates in Plato's *Ion* (534c), *hermes eisin ton theon*—"are messengers of the gods." (US 121–22/OWL 29)

Heidegger does not entirely jettison the word "hermeneutics" but suggests a deconstructive retrieval of it which, he admits, has a playful sense. No longer to be conceived in terms of interpretive fore-structures which render the being manifest, hermeneutics now is thought of in terms of the destining of Being *(Seinsgeschick),* so that the hermeneut is to be compared to the messenger-god Hermes, bearing the tidings of the gods to men. By the tidings of the gods Heidegger means the various epochal destinies, the configurations which are given to Being, in the diverse epochs of Being. The hermeneut is one who can read and interpret *(auslegen)* and then present *(darlegen)* those destinies, understanding them as destinies. He reads in Hegel's words not only Hegel's philosophy but a certain epochal configuration, a certain shape which Being takes in Hegel. The hermeneut is awakened to the history of metaphysics as a history of *Being,* as an unfolding movement of the *aletheia* process, so that the essential thing is to attend not merely to Hegel's words but to the epochal coming to pass *(Ereignis)* which takes place in them. Hermeneutics then is not a question of supplying an anticipatory projection of the Being of beings but of hearing a message ("eine Botschaft zu hören") that is not about supplying anticipatory horizons but about listening to what is sent our way in the words of the great metaphysicians.

This later "postal" conception of the hermeneutics, however, will not be good enough for Derrida, who is a critic not only of the hermeneutics of *Being and Time* but also of this later notion of receiving the message of Being. If Heidegger criticizes transcendental hermeneutics—the attempt to project the appropriate projective fore-structures—as subjectivistic, Derrida also criticizes the hermeneutics modeled after Hermes, which waits for the mail to be delivered, for the meaning of Being to be sent one's way as a message from the *Seinsgeschick*, the sender of onto-hermeneutical messages. Thus from Derrida's point of view, the later conception of hermeneutics is no less metaphysical than the earlier.

There is, nonetheless, another side to the later Heidegger's retrieval of hermeneutics that will prove quite important when I undertake below to set in motion the interplay between Heidegger and Derrida. For this late Heideggerian hermeneut reads off not precisely the messages of Being but rather of the "two-fold" or the difference between Being and beings:

> *J:* Man then realizes his nature as man by corresponding to the call of the two-fold, and bears witness to it in its message.
> *I:* Accordingly, what prevails in and bears up the relation of human nature to the two-fold is language. Language defines the hermeneutic relation. (US 122/OWL 30)

The hermeneut heeds the call of the two-fold *(die Zwiefalt)*. Man exists as a certain hermeneutic relation to the two-fold. The hermeneut hears in the language of the metaphysicians not merely their determination of the Being of beings (= the first step back) but an unfolding of the two-fold, a particular way in which the Being/beings distinction is elaborated (= the second step back). The essential thing for hermeneutics is to think not the metaphysical conception of the Being of beings but the very coming to pass of the differences *(Unter-Schied)* in the diverse metaphysical systems.[5] The hermeneut thinks the two-fold *as* a two-fold. He hears in the words of the great metaphysicians the movement of the history of Being, of the *Ereignis*, of the two-fold which unfolds in them. And this constitutes a more thought-ful relation with past thinkers, a more radical hermeneutical "dialogue" with them. This is one of those points in Heidegger, incidentally, which is altogether missing from Gadamerian "dialogue."

Man is to be understood as a hermeneutic relationship to the message which is sent his way. And that means that man is needed and required to preserve the two-fold as a two-fold (US 125–26/OWL 32). The two-fold unfolds the distinction between presence and what is present in any given age, and man is the being who responds to and hears the unfolding of that message.

> *J:* . . . [the two-fold] cannot be explained in terms of presence, nor in terms of present beings, nor in terms of the relation of the two.
> *I:* Because it is only the two-fold itself which unfolds the clarity, that is the clearing *[Lichtung]* in which present beings as such and presence can be discerned by man.
> . . .

J: . . . by man who by nature stands in relation to, that is, is being used by, the two-fold. (US 126/OWL 33)

The two-fold is a *differentia differens* (the dif-fering which opens up the difference), not a *differentia differentiata* (the difference which is opened up), and man is the being who hears and preserves this *differens* (US 136/OWL 40).

In this dialogue with the Japanese, Heidegger wants to know how the Japanese give words to what Europeans experience as "language." After a hesitation which lasts almost the whole length of the dialogue, the Japanese finally volunteers the expression *Koto ba. Ba* means petals, like the petals of peach or cherry blossoms. *Koto* means a source of delight, a moment of grace. Hence, if we can think what is contained in these Japanese words, we will experience what Heidegger himself calls, in his own language, the gentle or still realm of the open, the realm of graciousness *(Anmut)* in the sense of the gracious bestowing upon us of what comes-to-presence (US 140/OWL 43). In a particularly suggestive phrase, Heidegger writes,"*Koto*, the event *[Ereignis]* of the lightening message *[lichtenden Botschaft]* of the graciousness *[Huld]* which brings forth" (US 144/OWL 47). So the realm of *Koto* in "The Dialogue on Language" is very much the same as the sphere of the "open" (or the "region") in *Gelassenheit.* And it is in order to gain entrance to that realm, to be admitted to it, that the project of a deeper hermeneutics, as message bearing from the gods, is undertaken. Hermeneutics is admission to the sphere of the two-fold, the opening up of the clearing in which things come to presence.

The Japanese was always reluctant to give this word for language, and now that he has brought it forth, he wants to guard against the illusion that everything has thereby been made clear, when the whole idea is to experience the sway, the power, of the mystery. Heidegger feels the same reluctance about his own word "saying" (*Sagen*, US 148/OWL 50). The essential thing is to awaken to the mystery and to shelter *(hüten, bergen)* it in its mystery. In the "Dialogue on Language," the mystery is the mystery of language itself, and what threatens it is discourse *about* language, which threatens to turn language into an object. We speak about language instead of speaking *from* it, from out of its own essential nature.[6]

Japanese: It seems to me that now we are moving in a circle. A dialogue issuing from language must be called for from out of language's reality. How can it do so, without first entering into a hearing that at once reaches that reality?
Inquirer: I once called this strange relation the hermeneutic circle. (US 51/OWL 150)

However much we have removed ourselves from a horizonal conception of hermeneutics, it appears that we cannot escape the dynamics of the circle. But the circle does not move between our preunderstanding and what is understood, as in *Being and Time*. Rather, the whole turns itself around and now moves between the *Sache selbst* (in this essay, language) and man, who belongs to the *Sache* (here, to language):

> *J:* The circle exists everywhere in hermeneutics, that is to say, according to our explanation of today, it exists where the relation of message and message-bearer prevails.
> *I:* The message-bearer must come from the message. But he must also have gone toward it.
> *J:* Did you not say earlier that this circle is inevitable, and that, instead of trying to avoid it as an alleged logical contradiction, we must follow it?
> *I:* Yes. But this necessary acceptance of the hermeneutic circle does not mean that the notion of the accepted circle gives us an originary experience of the hermeneutic relation. (US 150/OWL 51)

It is at this point that Heidegger feels compelled to distinguish between the hermeneutic *circle* and a more originary hermeneutic *relation*. The ready acknowledgment made in *Being and Time* that there is no escaping the preunderstanding in which we always and already stand—which is the hermeneutic circle—does not go far enough toward understanding this more radical hermeneutic relation. The circle of preunderstanding and what is understood is not radical enough.

> *Japanese:* In short, you would abandon your earlier view.
> *Inquirer:* Quite—and in this respect, that talk of a circle always remains superficial.
> *Japanese:* How would you present the hermeneutic circle today?
> *Inquirer:* I would avoid a presentation *[Darstellung]* as resolutely as I would avoid speaking *about* language. (US 150–51/OWL 51)

The image of the circle, as it is offered in *Being and Time*, still suggests a transcendental and methodological gesture, some kind of prior, subjective determination. We must be prepared to give up talk about a circle—which is now taken by Heidegger to be an image of transcendental-horizonal thinking—in order to recover the more primordial belonging together (*Identität, Zusammen-gehören*): of Being and thought; of the *Ereignis* and the thinking which is appropriated by it; and—in the case of this essay—of originary language itself and the human speaking which strives to speak from out of an experience of it. The more originary hermeneutic relation is the intertwining of originary saying—or the essential nature of language—and human speaking. Only when this is understood will human speaking cease to set itself up at a distance, holding court over language; only then will it give itself up to originary saying and let "language" itself come to words in it.

The circularity of the circle to which Heidegger objects is not the belonging-together of Being and Dasein but the suggestion of a transcendental a priori, a prior holding of Being by Dasein within a pre-established framework or horizonal fore-structure. Accordingly, the circle is subjected to a deconstructive retrieval which radicalizes its intent and divests it of its transcendental remnants. Now instead of a circle, Heidegger speaks of a more originary hermeneutic relation, which is conceived in a nontranscendental form, in keeping with the dynamics of the reversal.

It is this intertwining of originary language and human speaking, and not the relationship between two human speakers, that Heidegger calls a "dialogue" (US 152/OWL 52). And as if to anticipate the later charge of logocentrism, Heidegger adds that the structure of what he is calling "dialogue" is not affected by whether it is written or spoken. The one thing necessary is that this dialogue issue from originary saying itself and that it remain suitably reticent, free of chatter, silent even about silence.

The hermeneutic circle thus is transformed into a more radical circulation between Being and Dasein, an intertwining of message and messenger, of the call issuing from the god (the destiny of Being, the call of the two-fold, of originary language itself, for these are all, in the end, the same *Sache*) and the being who, like Hermes, is used to bear that message to men. This circulatory system is the Heideggerian postal system criticized by Derrida, a sending of missives between the originary sending itself *(Seinsgeschick, Schickung)* and men, by means of the hermeneutic message bearers. But does Heidegger, in thinking the hermeneutic relation a relation to the two-fold, entertain the dream of finding the secret code, the final message, the master name of Being? Or would it be enough, in a more radical hermeneutic, simply to stand in this relation and let the names of Being fly up in disarray without thinking that there is a single, decisive meaning to be heard? Is that what he means by *Ereignis* and *Seinsgeschick?* Or is *Ereignis* meant to be a master name? The whole confrontation with Derrida turns on the answer to this.

Thus both "hermeneutic" and "hermeneutic circle" disappear as terms from Heidegger's lexicon. All that remains is a more primordial relation between the speech of mortals and the originary address to which it should respond— between messenger and message. This is the same relation, discussed in *Gelassenheit*, between the open and man and the relation that Heidegger made his first attempt to think under the title being-in-the-world. It is the first, last, and constant concern—the *Sache*—of Heidegger's thought. It is the primordial bond of Being and man, which every effort by objectifying thought tends to distort or disfigure (*Verunstaltung*, US 147/OWL 49). Heidegger seeks to make his way back into the deep structure of that bond and to bring it to words—not words *about* it but words spoken *from* it, words whose adequacy is not to be measured by their success but by their vigilance about their own inadequacy.

All of the strangeness of the later Heidegger—the exotic constructions, the poetic, even mythological, formulations—consists of so many efforts to bring this deep bond to words. One cannot get free from this primordial linking and bring it under an objectifying scrutiny. Thus the only appropriate "method"—and this is the strictness of thought which consists in being faithful to the "way" (*meta-odos*)—is to surrender that pursuit, to abandon all efforts at objectification, in order to reestablish contact with this originary circulation between Being and man so that one's words issue from out of an experience of it and are spoken at its bidding. It is not a question of establishing a technical vocabulary—quite the contrary—or of finding a final formulation of this relationship. It is a question rather of plasticity, of incessant reformulation, of a virtuosity which seeks innumerable ways to evoke the simplicity of the simple. It is a question always of staying under way (*unterwegs*), where the essential thing is the way and where the illusion of a final formulation and resting point is dispelled as so much metaphysics. It is a question of awakening to the mystery of this primordial relationship which defines and sustains us, not in order to remove the mystery but to preserve it as a mystery, to shelter it from the withering glare of metaphysical conceptuality. The difficulty of life has become more a matter of the mystery of the simple. The task of this more exotic hermeneutics that we find in the later Heidegger is to keep open to the mystery as a mystery, a mystery which sustains us and is the unencompassable source of scientific and prescientific life.

The later Heidegger's repetition of the hermeneutic project of *Being and Time* is but one of a number of ways of continuing what was set in motion by that book. And even though it is Heidegger's own way, we have nowadays learned the lesson that an author has no special privileges. Thus I want now to mark off two other paths down which *Being and Time* has been taken, one swinging off to the right, the other to the left.

GADAMER'S PHILOSOPHICAL HERMENEUTICS

Gadamer's philosophical hermeneutics occupies an important spot on the path I am tracking from the first essence of hermeneutics—let us say, a horizonal hermeneutics—toward a hermeneutics more radically conceived. And my interest is to determine the way in which Gadamer takes up, transforms, and in the end, as I will argue, constrains and domesticates the hermeneutic project "under way" in *Being and Time*.

Truth and Method is concerned with the movement of the tradition, the *kinesis* at work in it, the "dynamics" of its *trans-dare*. Gadamer wants to show how the tradition communicates its goods, passes on its wealth. He describes a process in which horizons are formed and reformed, in which they mutually enrich and expand one another. He is emphatic about the continuity of the tradition process and the way in which it is extended, renewed, and perpetuated in an ongoing and incessant process of retrieving and repeating its age-old contents.

Gadamer draws out the implications of *Being and Time* for a contemporary theory of the humanities (and, by extension, of the social and natural sciences). He convincingly attacks the dogma of the disinterested investigator capable of ahistorical and unprejudiced objectification. He goes a long way toward breaking the spell of the Enlightenment illusion of unprejudiced knowing by means of an insightful account of *Vorurteil* which is drawn both from a close historical study of the humanist tradition and from a creative use of Heidegger's notion of the hermeneutic fore-structures (although it was Bultmann who first staked out that terrain). He provides an illuminating elaboration of Heidegger's claim, in "The Origin of the Work of Art," that the work of art is not an aesthetic object but a transforming experience in which we come to a richer understanding of ourselves and of our world. In a provocative and controversial account of historical understanding, he takes up Heidegger's notion that we are capable of historical study only insofar as we are historical and belong to the very history we seek to understand. He demonstrates that the distance which separates us from the past is productive, not destructive, allowing us to filter out what is classical and enduring from what is merely idiosyncratic and time-bound. He offers an impressive defense of the authority of the text over and against that of the author or of the first audience. He offers an illuminating account of the dynamics of dialogue, of the expanding and essentially revisable nature of knowledge which grows only by exposure to the other.

But perhaps the most important contribution which Gadamer makes is his treatment of the Aristotelian notion of *phronesis*, which he first learned in a seminar with Heideggger in 1923, in those creative years when Heidegger was rereading Aristotle in terms of a hermeneutics of facticity:

> We studied the analysis of *phronesis*. . . . Today it is clear what Heidegger found in it, and what so fascinated him in Aristotle's critique of Plato's idea of the Good and the Aristotelian concept of practical knowledge. They described a mode of knowledge [an *eidos gnoseos*] that could no longer be based in any way on a final objectifiability in the sense of science. They described, in other words, a knowledge within the concrete situation of existence.[7]

In *Being and Time*, *Verstehen* is precisely that know-how which informs Dasein's most concrete involvement with the world. Dasein knows what it is about without having explicit conceptual knowledge to fall back upon. *Verstehen* is the capacity to understand what is demanded by the situation in which Dasein finds itself, a concrete knowledge which gets worked out in the process of existence itself. It is the grasp which Dasein has of its own affairs but which cannot be reduced to formalized knowledge and rendered explicit in terms of rules. Aristotle's objection to the Platonic idea of the Good was that it lacked the one thing which rendered such knowledge effective, namely, a grasp of the accidental and fortuitous circumstances which shape the situation in which it must be put to work. What is required in the concrete situation is a kind of practical insight and knowledge whose special merit is its ability to grasp what is demanded by the circumstances at hand. *Verstehen* is the hermeneutic act par excellence—in the sense that it provides the primordial interpretive insight into the demands of existence.

Heidegger's interpretation of Aristotle thus goes to the heart of Gadamerian hermeneutics, providing it with its pivotal conception of "application." *Phronesis* is the paradigm after which the hermeneutic act is patterned (W&M 295–307/T&M 278–93). For the hermeneutic act involves an act of application analogous to the moral agent's application of a general schema to a particular situation. The "timeless" value of the classical text, its value for all times, requires of the humanist a corresponding capacity to understand what the text says here and now, in this historical situation. This is not to say that application is a kind of routinizable or formalizable method of instantiation of a universal in the particular. We might do better to use "creative appropriation," not the English "application," to get at Gadamer's view. Like moral knowledge, hermeneutic judgment takes on meaning only in the concrete situation, outside of which it is just a more or less empty schema.[8] Unlike the architect who produces a fully formed idea of the thing to be made for the construction engineer before work begins, the moral agent only knows "in general" what bravery is outside the concrete circumstances in which he is called upon to be brave. Bravery is not a detailed blueprint but a general schema requiring skillful application—*phronesis*—in a particular situation. The "truth" of moral and hermeneutic knowledge eludes "method" (whence the title of his book). Hermeneutic knowledge, like moral knowledge, becomes more perfect in the application, whereas the real building is always an imperfect compromise with the blueprints. Indeed, in application, understanding becomes what it is, just as, in *Being and Time*, understanding *(Verstehen)* becomes more perfect in interpretation *(Auslegung)*.

Gadamer's hermeneutics is an insightful repetition of the standpoint of *Being and Time*, that is to say, of a hermeneutic centered on horizon-intentionality and *Verstehen/phronesis*. Gadamer is extremely good at defending the idea of a mobile, flexible tradition which never congeals into timeless, canonical formulations. "Philosophical hermeneutics" turns on a principle of creative repetition, of the endless reenactment of the tradition which, by repeating its age-old contents, is perpetuated, renewed, and thereby kept "on the move." It is both a philosophy *of Wiederholung*, as Kisiel argues, and a good example of applying not only Heidegger but also Plato and Hegel.

In the years since *Truth and Method* first appeared (1960), it has become clear that his insights about the humanities are shared by those who, like Polanyi, Kuhn, Feyerabend, Hanson, Winch, Geertz, and others, see a fundamentally "hermeneutic" moment also in the natural and social sciences.[9]

Gadamer's has become an important voice in the attempt to formulate a more reasonable, post-Enlightenment idea of reason. Indeed I think it is a weakness in the later Heidegger that his penetrating critique of the *Gestell* is not accompanied by an alternative—nonmetaphysical—account of "rationality." That can only weaken his important delimitation of the irrationality of the *Gestell* because it leaves him with little to say about how we are properly to conceive the rationality of the sciences.

But there are strings attached to Gadamer's project. At a crucial point, he backs off from the deeper and more radical side of Heidegger's thought. In the end, I think, Gadamer remains attached to the tradition as the bearer of eternal truths, which in a way does nothing more than modify Plato and Hegel from a Heideggerian standpoint. Gadamer's hermeneutics is traditionalism and the philosophy of eternal truth pushed to its historical limits. He offers us the most liberal form of traditionalism possible. He introduces as much change as possible into the philosophy of unchanging truth, as much movement as possible into immobile verity.

Plato said that truth is eternal and that we require a dialogue among ourselves in order to make the ascent to the forms. Hegel put the forms into time and required that they pass through dialectical development, that they prove their eternal worth in time, in the hard work and negativity of historical becoming. Gadamer delimits the Hegelian project of setting the truth into time, not by denying eternal truth but by protesting that there is no one final formulation of it. He insists that there is always a plurality of articulations of the same truth, that the selfsame is capable of an indefinite number of historical expressions. But that is another way of reassuring us that no matter how great the transformations of the tradition may be, its deep unity is always safe. Gadamer's whole argument turns on an implicit acceptance of the metaphysical distinction between a more or less stable and objective *meaning* and its ceaselessly changing *expression*.[10]

For Gadamer, the only real question is how meaning and truth get passed along and handed down *(trans-dare)*. That is why the Platonic conception of dialogue and the Hegelian doctrine of dialectical mediation are so important to him. These are the principal means of the transmission of meaning and truth. The one difference he has with Hegel is his contention that this selfsame and unchanging truth can always be understood *differently* and that there are no grounds for saying it is understood *better* by one of its finite bearers than it is by another. Gadamer is a more egalitarian Hegelian, a Hegelian with the good sense to know that the absolute never assumes absolute and canonical form, that the very structure of historicity prevents the absolute instantiation of the absolute. His is not a Hegelianism without the absolute but a Hegelianism where the absolute lacks absolute expression.

Gadamer wants to hold the flux in check, to ease the difficulty in history, to keep the tradition under the rule of an unchanging base content *(Gehalt)* which is constantly being transmitted, to see to it that the transformations of the tradition are contained by its essential content. The truth of the tradition is never put in question, only the dynamics of its communication, extension, renewal, and constant revivification. Gadamer puts the *logos* into time, the forms into historical matter, but he qualifies this with a Heideggerian factor of historical finitude. If, as he says, this is very much a philosophy of finitude, his conception of the "finite" remains within a binary metaphysical opposition to the infinite, upon which his conception of finitude in fact depends. Gadamer provides us with the best possible explanation of how the "infinite resources" of the tradition get passed along and renewed in finite but indefinitely new forms. For it is good strategy for a metaphysics of infinity—which is what I think Gadamer's project amounts to—to insist on the finitude of any finite expression. The best way to protect and preserve the infinite resources of the tradition is to insist upon the finitude of any historical understanding of it.

He describes the continuity of the tradition, but he leaves unasked the question of whether the tradition is all that unified to begin with. He never asks to what extent the play of the tradition is a power play and its unity something that has been enforced by the powers that be. His "tradition" is innocent of Nietzsche's suspicious eye, of Foucaultian genealogy. He does not face the question of the ruptures within tradition, its vulnerability to difference, its capacity to oppress.

In the manner of all metaphysicians, Gadamer wants to give us comfort in the face of the flux, to reassure us that all is well, that beneath the surface of historical transition an unchanging, infinite spirit labors. He wants to allay our fears and to say that the selfsame eternal truth is capable of assuming many forms, of speaking in many tongues, of producing an indefinite variety of finite expressions of its infinite content. The same word keeps getting spoken across the ages, and the only question is to know how to hear and "apply" it.

So Gadamer turns out to be another questionable friend of *kinesis,* perhaps an even wilier one than Hegel. Plato defined the truth in frank opposition to movement. Hegel, posing as the friend of the flux, tried to introduce movement into truth and to reconcile the two. Gadamer refines the Hegelian thesis by insisting on the indefinite plurality of moves which the unchanging truth can make. For a while we take him to be on the side of movement, as indeed he is, up to a point. But at that critical point he bails out on us, invoking the doctrines of recollection and mediation, the age-old narcotics of metaphysics designed to let us sleep through the thunderstorm, to curb our restlessness, and assures us that it is always the same eternal truth which is on the move. Plato and Hegel: the very metaphysics which Heidegger set out to deconstruct and which Kierkegaard hoped to bring to grief.

Gadamer speaks of the "play" in which things are caught up—and it is the play of the flux that hermeneutics must face up to—but it is always a play made safe by the constraints of unchanging truth. In the analysis of the work of art, for example, Gadamer speaks of play between the observer and the work by means of which we enter the world-horizon which the work opens up, not in such a way as to leave our own world behind but in order to expose our world to it and come away transformed and enriched, that is to say, to effect the fusion of horizons. We neither can nor want to reconstruct the world to which the work of art originally belonged, as Schleiernmacher hoped to do; rather, with Hegel, we want to integrate it with our own (W&M 159–61/148–50). But this *play* carries out the *work* of *Er-innerung*, of making the art-work our own inner possession, of a mediation *(Vermittlung)* which mediates its genuine content *(Sache)* to the present, which is in fact what the "fusion of horizons" amounts to (although it is not mentioned until somewhat later in *Truth and Method.)* Here is a "play" made safe by recollection. It is not the ominous world-play of Heidegger (SG 186–88) or the uncontrollable play of dissemination in Derrida. It is a play governed by the dynamics of truth and communication, as is the playful movement of the word in a genuine dialogue. In this play the ball always remains in bounds.

Although Gadamer rejects the ahistoricality of the Hegelian project, insisting that understanding is always historical and finite, he proposes in its place a kind of finitized project of *Aufhebung*. He seeks not an *Aufhebung* which reaches or even aims at a final canonical state but an ongoing and continual *Aufhebung*, a more humble and authentically historical one, which consists in the continual appropriation and reappropriation of the ageless contents (the *Sache)* of the tradition. Gadamer's work represents a kind of modified Hegelianism, a meta-physics of infinity constantly monitored by Heidegger's analysis of the finitude of the understanding. It is a Hegelianism for the hermeneutic phe-nomenologist. *Verschmelzung* (fusion) is the Gadamerian version of *Vermittlung* (mediation) and assumes its rightful place alongside *Aufhebung, anamnesis,* and *Erinnerung*—in a last-ditch effort to hold off the foundering of metaphysics.

Gadamer is extremely good at hearing what Heidegger says about the truth of Being, but there is another, more radical side to Heidegger which gets no hearing at all. [11] He makes no effort to come to grips with the later Heidegger's delimitation of, and movement *beyond,* "horizon" in favor of the open of which it is the circumscription. He does not see the radical hermeneutic gesture in *Being and Time* itself which consists in going *beyond* Being to its "meaning," where meaning means not the one true sense which Being has but that in reference to which *(das Woraufhin)* the diverse meanings of Being arise, the hermeneutical key to their constitution. On that reading of *Being and Time,* Heidegger is not interested in Being at all, much less in "fusing" the diverse sorts of things that metaphysics has been saying about Being in an ongoing renewal of ontology. Rather *Being and Time* is "on the way" to a delimitation of metaphysics which steps outside, and tells the story of, what metaphysics is doing all the time with its Being/beings schemata.

In the later Heidegger this finally issues in the thought of *"Es gibt,"* of the It which gives the metaphysical epochs, so that *what* is given in the diverse metaphysical constellations never interests him. What does interest him is the *giving* itself, the rising up and flowing off of the epochs. This is the thought of the *Ereignis*, the happening which sends Being into the epochs and lets them unfold there. "Thinking" is never "taken in" by any one of the epochs or by any fusing or combination of them. It does not allow itself to think that there is any master name, or fusion of master names, or ongoing renaming with a series of "finite" names for the "infinity" of Being itself.

As we have just seen, Heidegger described the hermeneut as one who hears the message of the two-fold, of the difference, that is, of the way in which an ontological spread is opened up in any epoch. In the succeeding chapters I hope to show that, more radically conceived, Heidegger is concerned not with the actual metaphysical grid which is spread out in any particular sending of Being but with reading that metaphysics *as* such a spread, with seeing in it a way that Being is sent and articulated within a certain epochal constellation. Heidegger wants to effect the step back, not from beings to Being, which is what metaphysics does, but from Being to the *Aus-trag*, that which "carries out" the distinction between Being and beings in any given epoch. Accordingly, Heidegger's critique of Hegel in "The Onto-theo-logical Nature of Metaphysics" applies to Gadamer's modified Hegelianism as well. Gadamer, like Hegel, is interested in the *Auf-hebung*, the step up—let us say here the step-forward, the progress of the tradition in the sense of its progressive, albeit finite, elaboration and unfolding—and not the step back, the regressive return to that which gives the tradition, which both reveals and conceals itself in the various epochal sendings. Gadamer's thought is historical, but it is not Being-historical, not thought in terms of the *Geschick*, of Being's sending-withdrawal.[12] It is historical but not epochal, for it does not see the *epoché* of the *Seinsgeschick* in any given epoch. Gadamer remains within the tradition, which he regards as an inescapable facticity, but he sees no need to think *through* the tradition to that which is at work, or at play, in the tradition.[13] He is concerned with *what* is given in the tradition—with keeping it alive, with passing on the word and teaching us to listen—but not with the giving process itself, the event of unconcealment itself which comes to pass in and as the tradition. He does not seek that thought which effects a certain *closure* or delimitation of the tradition as a whole, a gesture which, he complains, Heidegger picked up from Nietzsche. Indeed he even wonders whether Heidegger's attempt to think the tradition as a whole differs, on this point at least, from Hegel's attempt at totalization.[14]

For Gadamer the *Sache* is the expressed content of the tradition, the metaphysical content *(Gehalt)* of Platonic, Aristotelian, and Hegelian thought which he wants to bring to a synthesizing fusion. The matter is what these philosophers have to say and how we are to hear it. But for Heidegger the *Sache* is not any particular metaphysics or fusion of metaphysical standpoints but the very happening of metaphysics as such, of the epochs, the *Aus-trag* or *Zwie-falt* which opens up the epochs and gives them their epochal spread. Heidegger is not interested in the "truth" *(Wahrheit)* of Plato or Aristotle or in how, by the exposure of our epoch to theirs and theirs to ours, we can enrich our truth. He wants to think the truth-event itself, the happening of truth and untruth, which is what *a-letheia* means. Gadamer is interested in the *verum, alethea,* what is true here and now and ready for our consumption (application), not *a-letheia,* the event of concealment and unconcealment.

For Heidegger, in the end—I will have to show this—there is only the springing up and passing away of the metaphysical epochs, the happening of the truth-event, the coming to pass of the epochs, the event of opening or clearing—not the content which fills up any epoch or horizon circumscribed within the open. Heidegger thus exposes us to the abyss, to the play of the epochs, to their movement and flux, in a much more radical way than Gadamer allows. Heidegger offers us no comfort that the great "classical" systems of metaphysics possess an ageless truth which will keep on addressing us, consoling us, providing us direction and guidance. He thinks all the trouble started with Plato, culminated in Hegel, and is about to explode in our faces in the *Gestell*. He does not believe in ageless truths but in the historicity of the truth-event, of *a-letheia,* of its endless flux and transiency. There can be—in a fully radicalized Heidegger, one who has become suspicious of his talk of the truth of Being—no golden ages which shine like beacons in our dark times. There is only the dark play of the epochs. It is always and everywhere the *Abend-land*. We are always and everywhere exposed to the play. That at least is a neglected side of Heidegger which I want to demonstrate.[15]

But Gadamer has no taste for this deconstruction of metaphysics. His thought operates within fundamentally traditional constraints, although he has had the good sense to loosen their death grip and give them historical, contextual flexibility. He offers us the most liberal possible version of a fundamentally conservative idea. He allows as much movement and play as will not disrupt the ageless truths of the tradition or cause it too much difficulty. His is a kind of Heideggerianism without the scandal of the *Ereignis* and the play of the epochs. Gadamer proposes a more conservative hermeneutic, a gentler repetition, a continuation of the hermeneutic project of *Being and Time* which remains fundamentally attached to the metaphysics of recollection and mediation and which dulls the edge of destruction and deconstruction. It is separated by a chasm from the philosophy of *différance*, which is, in a sense, another but much wilder post-Heideggerian sibling to which we turn now.

DERRIDA'S "DECONSTRUCTION" OF HERMENEUTICS

Derrida is the philosopher of the flux par excellence, the one thinker who, to use Deleuze's expression, is ready to pay the price exacted by a philosophy of movement and becoming. Everything in Derrida turns on a Nietzschean affirmation of becoming and its innocence, on an irrepressible play which Derrida wants above all to preserve. The "metaphysics of presence" (for him a redundancy) is defined by its opposition to movement and becoming, by its constant effort to "arrest the play." Derrida accordingly wants to follow to the end the project launched in *Being and Time* (which is, according to its last page, only getting "under way"), to put Being as presence into question, to uproot the desire of metaphysics to stabilize, ground, and center beings in an onto-theological ordering, in a system of permanent presence *(stetige Anwesenheit)* which takes its clue from the temporality of the "present" *(Gegenwart)*. To that end Derrida enlists the deconstructive energy of Nietzsche, the pitiless Nietzschean critique of metaphysics as Egyptianism and a mummification of life which declares becoming guilty. Indeed, so pitiless is the Nietzschean/Derridean critique that it is in the end brought to bear against Heidegger himself.

In a piece published in 1964 on Edmond Jabes, the Jewish author of *The Book of Questions*, Derrida distinguishes the "rabbi" and the "poet." The Jews are the people of the Book which was handed down by God, of Laws engraved on stone tablets, and of the tradition of commentaries whose sole function is to elucidate the Book, to help pass it on, and in so doing to remain as faithful to the original Book as possible. In a nation and culture organized around a sacred writing, the writing of the poet is secular, a weed which grows up between the crevices of the broken tablets. Like the Jew himself, the poet is suspect, an outlaw, in constant exile.

> In the beginning is hermeneutics. But the *shared* necessity of exegesis, the interpretive imperative, is interpreted differently by the rabbi and the poet. The difference between the horizon of the original text and exegetic writing makes the difference between the rabbi and the poet irreducible. . . . The original opening of interpretation essentially signifies that there will always be rabbis and poets. And two interpretations of interpretation. (ED 102/WD 67)[16]

Just as Heidegger points out the originally theological aim of hermeneutics (US 96–97/OWL 9–10), so Derrida takes the hermeneutic impulse to be "rabbinical." Hermeneutics stems from a religious subordination to an original text and conceives itself as humble commentary, explication. Like any good and faithful servant, like everything heteronomous, receiving its direction from without, from the original, it wants to be transparent and ultimately dispensable, superfluous. The poet on the other hand is impudent and autonomous, an outlaw. He does not bow his head to the sacred original. If he is involved in interpretation at all, it is in a wilder, freer, antihermeneutic way which lacks the

piety of rabbinical hermeneutics. There will always be rabbis and poets, interpretation which is bound to hermeneutics and interpretation which wrests free
of it, that is to say, two interpretations of interpretation.[17]

Two years later, in a well-known essay on Lévi-Strauss, Derrida says that
Lévi-Strauss shares the rabbinical instinct, despite his decentering of Western
ethnocentrism. He seeks the primitive, the native, the "natural"; he still
believes in primeval innocence, the pristine, untouched originary. Lévi-Strauss
dislodges European ethnocentrism only to recenter it on another original text,
an unspoiled land which is being spoiled by the anthropologist.

> Turned towards the lost or impossible presence of the absent origin, this struc-
> turalist thematic of broken immediacy is therefore the saddened, *negative*,
> nostalgic, guilty, Rousseauistic side of the thinking of play whose other side would
> be the Nietzschean *affirmation*, that is, the joyous affirmation of the play of the
> world and of the innocence of becoming, the affirmation of a world of signs without
> fault, without truth, and without origin which is offered to an active interpretation.
> (ED 427/WD 292)

Derrida flaunts this humble respect for the origin—the original and uncor-
rupt—with a Nietzschean affirmation of the innocence of everything derivative,
plural, multiple, acculturated, an affirmation which culminates in undoing the
very distinction between original and derivative, so that the "true world," the
originary, can at last become a fable. And that brings us back to rabbis and
poets.

> There are thus two interpretations of interpretation, of structure, of sign, of play.
> The one seeks to decipher, dreams of deciphering a truth or an origin which
> escapes play and the order of the sign, and which lives the necessity of interpreta-
> tion as an exile. (ED 427/WD 292)

The hermeneut is an exile longing for the native land. Like Constantin, who
complains of the melancholy of recollection, the exiled exegete dreams wistfully
of an unencumbered truth where interpretation gives way to perfect and
unmediated contact. The purpose of hermeneutics is to return to the original
and convey it whole and undistorted back to the present. Its task is to crack a
code, decipher a hidden truth.

> The other [interpretation], which is no longer turned towards the origin, affirms
> play and tries to pass beyond man and humanism, the name of man being the name
> of that being who, throughout the history of metaphysics or of ontotheology—in
> other words, through his entire history—has dreamed of full presence, the reassur-
> ing foundation, the origin and the end of play. (ED 427/WD 292)

The other interpretation is a Nietzschean affirmation of the free play of signs, an
impious, poetic, antitheological,[18] antihermeneutic interpretation of interpretation. It denies all deep meanings, all hidden truth, indeed truth itself. It

denies that there is anything originary, that the originary is anything more than a linguistic illusion induced by grammar. In the absence of something originary, interpretation ceases to be derivative, heteronomous, in exile, because the very distinction between the original and the derivative, between nature and culture, autonomy and heteronomy, native land and exile, comes undone. This other interpretation of interpretation knows that truth is a woman, a Dionysiac who does not even believe in truth, who thus does not even believe in herself.[19]

On this interpretation of interpretation there is nothing original to interpret, and hence the very distinction between the message of the original text and the message bearing of hermeneutics breaks down. Writing and reading are ensnared in each other. Every text resonates with other texts, "originals" no less than "commentaries." And the task of interpretation is to keep the trembling and endless mirror-play of signs and texts in play, to see to it that metaphysics does not have its way with texts—by arresting the play, recentering the system, stabilizing the flux, breaking the code, reintroducing the nostalgic longing for the origin. This is not a purely negative act—of remaining alert *against* the metaphysics of presence. Above all, it is an affirmation of the innocence of becoming—that there never was anything originary, primeval, undistorted, that nothing was ever guilty. This other kind of interpretation abandons the distinction between home and exile and affirms the innocence of the whole earth, affirms the play and the ring-dance—"for all joy wants eternity."[20]

Thus, if there is in Gadamer a certain conservative extension of the philosophy of retrieval first announced in *Being and Time*, there is in Derrida a wholly different voice, a wilder and more Nietzschean tone, a philosophy not of retrieval but of a more impious and free-wheeling repetition, a repetition whose antics might leave Constantin himself staring wide-eyed. If Gadamer pursues everything healing and restorative about Heideggerian *Wiederholung*, Derrida unleashes the Heideggerian motifs of *Destruktion* and *Abbau*, pushing the delimitation of metaphysics to its limit.

For Derrida, even Heidegger himself—to the extent that he is still involved in a hermeneutic project, piously bent over the sacred (*Seinsgeschichtlich*) texts—is implicated in metaphysics and its dream of the master name. Heidegger is caught within the hermeneutic frame, still a victim of the nostalgia for a truth—if not truth as *adequatio*, still truth as *aletheia*. Heidegger is after an originary experience, a deeper truth. He does not quite see that Nietzsche's truth is a *woman*, that Nietzsche does not *believe* in the will to power, much less that it is the Being of beings and eternal recurrence is its essence. That is to be deceived by a wench. "Almost."[21] For Derrida always hesitates to enclose Heidegger within an enclosure that Heidegger better than anyone else has marked off. Derrida is the first to say that deconstruction can begin only by first situating itself within the space opened up by the Heideggerian questioning.

Derrida and Heidegger: it is in the space which opens up between them, in their interplay, that "radical hermeneutics" springs up.

How does it stand with hermeneutics after *Being and Time?* On the "left" is the impious, poetic transgression of metaphysics and the hermeneutic dream, happy to pay the price of becoming in order to keep the flux in play. On the "right" is the theological reverence of philosophical hermeneutics. In the "center" is the father, the repetition of *Being and Time* carried out by Heidegger himself, whose authority we are not sure we should concede. Like Nietzsche/Derrida, Heidegger has undertaken the closure *(Ende)* of the tradition, but he joins to this moment of active forgetting a work of return, retrieval *(Wiederholung)*, and memorialization *(Andenken)*.

As for us, we are swarmed with questions. What is the Derridean gesture? What is its aim and end(s)? Can it be carried out? Is it any more possible to face the flux than it is to see the face of God? Is facing the flux itself another dream? Does this Derridean project pronounce the final word on hermeneutics? Will the project of "radical" hermeneutics, which we are patiently staking out, turn out to be just another compromise, another insidious *"Aufhebung"?* Is "radical hermeneutics" one more wily friend of the flux, more cleverly disguised than ever but ready, at the opportune moment, to arrest the play? Can there be a hermeneutics beyond "hermeneutics," beyond the "first essence" of hermeneutics, beyond the hermeneutics which looks for meaning and stability, a hermeneutics which takes the measure of deconstructive critique? Can there be a hermeneutics which, contrary to Derrida, is not metaphysics, indeed which is born of the "foundering of metaphysics," a hermeneutics which wants to remain true to *kinesis*, which does not repress the fear and trembling? Is Derrida right about Heidegger, that not even Heidegger lives up to his own demands about overcoming metaphysics, that the Heideggerian project requires deconstruction in order to overcome its own residual metaphysical desire for rest and comfort and for making things easy?

These questions go to the heart of the present study. And they require a closer investigation of the great transgression of the hermeneutic project effected by Derrida. The question of radical hermeneutics must pass through the fire of the "deconstruction" of hermeneutics.

FIVE

Repetition and the Emancipation of Signs: Derrida on Husserl

I begin with the surprising rereading of Husserl by Derrida, which succeeds in showing us another face of Husserl, a more radical side, and enlists him in the service of a more critical enterprise. I take Derrida's work to be not an attack upon Husserl but a liberation of Husserl's deepest tendencies. I see Derrida trying not to raze or level Husserlian phenomenology but to free it from itself. In general, I take Derrida not as an antagonist in the project of a radical hermeneutic but as effecting a breakthrough essential to its emergence, providing it with its thunderstorm.

Under Derrida's hand the Husserlian *Vor-zeichnung*, the systematic pretracing of the intentional object which we discussed in chapter 2, becomes a more radical arché-tracing which traces out and thereby produces its effects. This rereading of Husserl is made possible not by rejecting the notion of constitution but by shifting its focus from consciousness to semiotics, from the subject to signs. And with this shift we meet up with another operation of repetition, another and Derridean way of addressing the question of whether and how repetition is possible. We never get far from Constantin's question.

THE GRAMMATOLOGICAL REDUCTION OF PRESENCE

There are two sides to Husserl, and it is in the gap between them that Derrida carries out his rereading of phenomenology. The first is a philosophy of "constitution," of the *production* of meaning and the constituted object. For this Husserl, nothing is given apart from the labor of the transcendental life. The work of phenomenology is carried out by means of the *epoché* as the suspension of natural belief and the subsequent reduction of the object to transcendental subjectivity. The other side of Husserl is the philosophy of givenness, of intuitive contact, of the in-person presence of the things themselves. Here phenomenological work is conducted under the principle of all principles as the demand for what is self-presenting (a principle which, as we saw, it is dangerous to take at face value). The first side proceeds from a critical imperative which admonishes us to take nothing for granted; the second has recourse to the rhetoric of the granted, given, self-presenting.

Derrida works within the distance that opens up between this critical imperative and what he regards as a metaphysical laxity. His "deconstruction" of Husserl—like all deconstruction—does not result in utter destruction but in a critical rereading, a reading differently. By playing one side of Husserl against the other, setting the critical philosophy loose on the metaphysics of givenness, deconstruction produces a creative repetition of Husserlian phenomenology.

For Derrida, Husserl's discovery of the reduction is at once the isolation of the fundamental operation of philosophy and the undoing of its claim to provide foundations and assured presence. The reduction is the name of philosophy's critical power, the imperative to get beyond naiveté and already constituted products. Deconstruction cannot take a single step forward without its help. Indeed deconstruction is itself a certain rewriting of the reduction. Derrida is not out to get the reduction but only to get it right, to see that it is carried out far enough, that its work of critique is not subverted in advance by a teleology of presence and fulfillment. He wants thus to carry on what Husserl set in motion, to work with and not just against Husserl, to extend the work of reduction—that is, to be even more ruthless about the reduction. For in Husserl himself phenomenological vigilance is satisfied with presence, intuition, self-showing—when these are precisely what need to be questioned. The teleology of fulfillment curtails Husserl's achievement and causes him to lose sight of a more radical reduction, let us say a semiological or grammatological reduction.

Husserl is acutely sensitive to the contingency and alterability of the constituted world, and he understands perfectly the need for a work of constitution/repetition to bring stability to the flux. But he lets this critical instinct get waylaid by a desire for presence which reduces repetition to the metaphysics of re-presentation. In Kierkegaard authentic repetition always moves forward, producing what it repeats, while recollection is a kind of bad repetition which repeats backward, which begins with the loss, looking back wistfully at the time when presence was perfect. Now Derrida's rereading of Husserl turns on a comparable distinction between two kinds of repetition (OrG 104–105/102–103), which correspond closely to the two kinds of interpretation, the poetic and the rabbinical. There is a repetition which comes later, which is *reproductive* of a *prior presence*—let us say a metaphysical idea of repetition, which moves backward. This is opposed to the repetition which moves forward, which is *prior to presence* and *productive* of it, and which, as a kind of reading, is therefore free to produce as it reads—let us say a critical idea of repetition. According to Derrida, Husserl discovered this more radical repetition but always kept it under the close guard of a metaphysics of presence. The aim of deconstruction, then, is to liberate Husserl's own most radical discoveries from the house arrest under which Husserl kept them. As the liberation of phenomenology, deconstruction is a rereading which reads both with and against Husserl.

Derrida's earliest work, it seems to me, is best construed as a kind of left-wing

Husserlianism (as well as a left-wing Heideggerianism) which defends Husserl's critical views against his metaphysical ones, advocating precisely what Husserl discovered but also repressed. Husserl always refused to take meaning and objectivity "as manna fallen from a heavenly place *[topos ouranios]*" (ED 233/ WD 157). Meaning is never "fallen from the sky" *(tombées du ciel)* but "constituted" (cf. *Pos.* 18/9; 39/27; ED 233/157). It would be a naiveté to think that objects somehow drop into our lap, ready made. Nonetheless, Derrida thinks, Husserl stops short in locating the constitutive activity productive of these structures. He rests content with laying a foundation for them in a self-present subjectivity. Derrida urges phenomenology further, toward a grammatological reduction which sees even the self-presence of "consciousness" *(con-scire)* as a constituted effect.

Even as he discovered the principle of productive repetition, Husserl wanted phenomenology to come to rest in presence and exclude repetition as a secondary re-presentation. In violation of its own critical imperative, phenomenology persists in trying "to save presence and reduce the sign, and with it all the powers of repetition . . . "which comes to living *in* the effect—the assured, consolidated, constituted effect of repetition and representation, of the difference which removes presence" (VPh 56–57/SP 51).

In what I am calling Derrida's grammatological reduction, both the object and the subject are constituted products, the effect of synthesis and repetition, of a systematic iterability which is what Derrida means by "sign" or "trace." And he argues this not only against Husserl but also with Husserl, on the basis of Husserl's own most searching and critical analyses, analyses which reach an "incomparable depth" (VPh 94n/SP 84n). Transcendental subjectivity, no less than transcendent objectivity, is a stable unity of meaning, a synthetic amalgamation forged from the flow itself and as such traceable to a more radical repetition, retraceable to a system of tracing. Indeed all the most honored words of metaphysics—not only object and subject, but also Being, truth, and history—are similarly constituted effects.

But that is just where phenomenology chooses to come to rest and to let down its critical guard. Phenomenology is content to live in the safe, assured, reassured, constituted effects—"vivre dans l'effet—assuré, rassuré, constitué"—of repetition, oblivious of the constituting, repetitive system which generates or produces those effects. Phenomenology nourishes a natural attitude of its own. Its very vigilance is conducted on the terms which metaphysics sets: presence, evidence, perception, intuition, subjectivity (VPh 3–4/ SP 4–5). It contents itself with evidence and the self-presenting instead of bringing "evidence" and "presence" before the bar of transcendental *différance*.

Thus, the Derridean rereading of Husserl is conducted under the rule of a principle of repetition which reverses the roles of presence and re-presentation:

"The presence of the present is derived from repetition and not the reverse" (VPH 58/SP 52). Something "is," i.e., takes on the unity of an object or a subject, to the extent that it is brought forth by repetition; being is proportionate to repetition. In metaphysics, on the other hand, the reverse, mirror image has always prevailed; something is "repeatable" to the extent that it "is." The meta-physical principle which has dominated our understanding of repetition from Plato to Husserl—and against which, up to now, only the voice of Kierkegaard has been raised in protest—the principle which has determined being as presence and repetition as a representation of presence, is subverted by a more radically Husserlian/Derridean principle of the "constituting value" of nonpresence (VPh 5/SP 6–7) in virtue of which presence is a function of repetition. To be sure, reversal is to be followed by displacement (*Marg.* 392–93/329), so that in the end the whole binary opposition between presence and representation will be displaced and Derrida will seek other ways to write and to name that which is not a name or a concept but is always already productive of both.

Thus, at least as a start, it is helpful to see Derrida's celebrated notion of "*différance*" as a rewritten and more radically critical version of Husserlian constitution, the result of a more radical reduction, which—also just as a start— we are calling here a "grammatological reduction." As Derrida says, he wants "to interrogate that which precedes the transcendental reduction," to question "the possibility of the transcendental reduction" (ED 251/WD 167), and hence to enter a sphere which, being prior to transcendental life, represents a kind of death.

Derrida's struggles with Husserl always have to do with the role of signs, which always do the work of repetition. In his first sweep of Husserl's terrain (OrG) he argues that Husserl cannot have a notion of transcendental history without signs. Then (in SP) he gets bolder and says Husserl cannot even have an idea of transcendental, monological interiority without signs. But in the end, I will argue, it is not the *work* of repetition that signs do that interests him, but their *free play*. Hence I will conclude these remarks with a discussion of Derrida's emancipation or "liberation" of signs, which sets them loose in a kind of celebrative repetition. And it is here that I locate the pointed tip of Derrida's pen.[1]

THE WORK OF REPETITION IN TRANSCENDENTAL HISTORY

By choosing the "The Origin of Geometry" Derrida has, to a certain extent, made things easy for himself. For he has chosen to show that the whole project of a transcendental, a priori history is inherently dependent upon language and signs, a point which Husserl himself actually makes quite explicitly. But that of course is all the better, for nothing pleases Derrida more than to show just how baldly metaphysics has recourse to what it excludes. Thus empirical, natural languages, which are excluded by Husserl from the transcendental sphere, are also called upon by him to do transcendental work and hence must be granted at least temporary visas into the transcendental domain. It is by pressing this shifting between what is internal to (included in) and what is external to (excluded from) the transcendental sphere that Derrida effects his first and, to my mind, his clearest, most exemplary piece of deconstruction. This also leads to a second central deconstructive claim in this essay, about the inevitable postponing, or deferral, of the results of transcendental work to which Husserl must confess. We are reminded of Climacus's satirical predictions in the *Postscript* that the system is just about to be finished, that we can expect delivery of the last, missing pieces in just a few weeks!

There are two senses of repetition in "The Origin of Geometry." The first refers to the productive process of the historical sense-genesis by which geometric ideality is constituted—and against that Derrida argues that it cannot proceed a single step forward without the help of signs. The second refers to the reproductive process of reactivating the founding acts of the first geometers—and against that Derrida shows that every step-in-reverse it takes is caught up in deferral. Let us consider each point in turn.

(1) A transcendental, a priori history (a sense-history, we recall from chapter 2) pursues the historical genesis of ideal formations—in this case of geometry—the rules in conformity with which the ideal structures of geometry "must have arisen." The method is historical inasmuch as it is structured in a narrative form and a priori inasmuch as it has to do with eidetic laws rather than empirico-historical information about how the first geometers actually went about their work. Derrida, as I have already indicated, is interested in Husserl's explanation of idealization in terms of "repeatability" (*Wiederholbarkeit*, Hua VI 370/*Crisis* 360), and of repeatability in terms of language and, ultimately, of writing. On the metaphysical reading of Husserl, repeatability is directly proportionate to ideal objectivity. The higher the level of ideality enjoyed by the object, the wider the extent of its empirical repeatability. The more perfect the ideal unity of the object, the more diverse its empirical repetitions. But in the Derridean rewriting—which is also, we may not forget, another motif *in* the Husserlian text—this metaphysical formula is written backward as a critical one: the greater the power of repetition, the higher the level of ideality which is achieved. On the critical reading, repeatability is displaced by repetition, and ideality is made a function—a genetic function—of repetition.

A particular expression (*Ausdruck*)—say, the English word "lion" or the German word "*Löwe*"—possesses a certain ideality. No matter whether it is spoken or written, whether it is spoken with an accent or in the queen's English, whether it is written sloppily or elegantly, typewritten or displayed on a green phosphorous screen—no matter how many times it is reproduced, it is always the *same* word. In the critical version, it is precisely the repetition or iteration that produces the unity of the expression and makes it the word that it is. Now what holds for expressions, which are embedded in natural languages, holds also for meaning or signification *(Bedeutung)*, for lion itself, that which is commonly meant by the expressions "lion," "*Löwe*," "*leo*," etc.

The highest level of ideality is absolute ideality—the ideality of a geometrical object, say, which is absolutely free from empirical constraints (the meaning "lion" derives from empirical experience). The Pythagorean theorem exists but once, no matter how often and variously it is repeated, whether by Euclid or by all the commentaries on Euclid over the centuries. Such an ideality is not relative to a particular natural language or to language in general. It is absolutely free. Thus we move from the ideality of an expression *(Ausdruck)* to that of a meaning *(Bedeutung)*, to that of an ideal state of affairs *(idealer Sachverhalt)*. And it is this final, highest stratum of ideality which supplies the condition of possibility of history, the basis of a transcendental historicity, and the foundation for a scientific tradition (OrG 56–69/66–76). If Gadamer locates the condition of the tradition in a more or less unified meaning which keeps getting heard anew and reformulated, Husserl, who thinks that the "West" is fundamentally a scientific unity, not merely a cultural one, wants to locate it in a univocal ideal unity.

Now Husserl claims that such ideality is achieved by means of language even though, in itself, it is independent of language. And it is into this crack that Derrida slips in order to effect his rewriting. The ideal geometric principle (the pure presence) is in itself, as a matter of principle, *de jure*, independent of language. But as a matter of pragmatic fact, *de facto*, there is no way the principle could actually be passed on, delivered, and re-presented from one member of the community to another without language. Does the presence precede the re-presentation, or does the representation produce the presence? For Husserl, it is not the ideality but the communication of the ideality that requires language.

Now the particular advantage which Derrida has here is that Husserl has chosen to discuss a transcendental *history* in which, of course, communication and tradition are essentially ingredient. If there is to be any "science" of geometry at all, the originally founding act in the mind of the first geometer must be made to reach beyond his empirical limits in order to establish a community of geometers, stretching over space and time. For geometric truth makes an unrestricted claim to truth, transcending the limitations of space and time, of culture and age. In the language of the *Cartesian Meditations*, whatever has been egologically constituted achieves full objectivity only by means of intersubjective constitution, that is, by becoming a communal object. But that requires that the primordially founding act *(Urstiftung)* of the first geometer be lifted up beyond the particularity of his own ego-life and given universal validity in the intersubjective community, an operation which cannot be performed without language. For the prelinguistic ego is solitary.

> Without this pure and essential possibility, the geometrical formation would remain ineffable and solitary. Then it would be *absolutely bound to the psychological life of a factual individual,* to that of a factual community, indeed to a particular moment of that life. (OrG 70/77)

Now there is an important point to be made here in Husserl's defense. Derrida is not entirely right to say that without language meaning would be confined to the psychological life of the individual, for Husserl does allow for an *individual* but still transcendental ego, so that prelinguistic constitution would indeed be a bound ideality, but it would be bound not to the empirical (or psychological) individual but to the transcendental *solus ipse,* to monological interiority. On this hypothesis, truth would remain solitary, but it would not be psychologized. Husserl could still maintain the ideal status of the geometric truth but concede that, without language, it is deprived of its means of transportation. It has lost only its delivery service, not its ideal status.[2]

But Derrida is right enough, for all he needs to show here is the impossibility of transcendental *history* without language and signs. For if truth is confined to a transcendental but still solitary ego, then the full, absolute ideality which Husserl requires cannot be achieved and transcendental history is rendered impossible. And that is also why *Speech and Phenomena* is ultimately the more interesting book. For it seeks to show the necessity of signs at the heart of transcendental life, within the monological sphere itself, and thereby to cut off the only retreat which transcendental phenomenology has left.

Husserl thus cannot exclude language as something exterior to transcendental history. It is not merely an outer expression *(Ausdruck)* or exteriorization *(Äusserung)* of an already constituted meaning. On the contrary, it is now enlisted in the service of constitution itself, "supplying"—making up (constituting), making up for (supplementing)—a necessary condition of possibility of *intersubjective* constitution, which is what gives rise to a scientific tradition for Husserl. Signs are not useless in transcendental history; on the contrary, they have essential work to do. What the metaphysical Husserl wants to exclude as exterior and contingent, the critical Husserl regards as intrinsic and necessary. Husserl calls upon what he excludes; he requires help from what he declares superfluous. Language is the "supplement" of presence: it starts out looking like an extra and ends up with a central role in the production (and is not a mere second, a stand-in, a reproduction). Language does transcendental work and is assigned—contrary to Husserl's remark in *Ideas I,* §124—a productive job.

Furthermore, such a transcendentally productive work is not only granted to speech—to the apostolic community of the first geometer and his immediate followers—but also *a fortiori* found even more rigorously in writing, in geometry's scriptural tradition. For it is in writing that the power of language to transcend the limits of the original audience is raised to its highest level. By means of writing, the ideality of the object is so well established that it can survive the death of its first author and of the original community that he addressed. Here ideality and repetition reach their maximal proportionate perfection.

And that of course sets into motion the logic of danger and crisis which we discussed above. For in writing truth is transmitted in a "virtual" state, awaiting the life-giving act of a reader, the "reactualization" it will receive at the hands of subsequent generations. Such depositing of truth in the letter exposes the truth to danger, opens up the possibility that it will be lost, forgotten, buried over, that the mail will go astray. Truth then becomes subject to the risk of a "graphic catastrophe": documents can be lost, stolen, burnt, or (nowadays) destroyed by a sudden surge of electricity. More subtly, the significance of the founding acts themselves can be lost, so that signs are passed on lifelessly, like dead and sedimented structures which we no longer understand. And that of course is precisely the "crisis" of foundations which affects modernity.

And that leads Husserl to introduce a metaphysical repetition which "reactivates" and reanimates the originally founding acts that gave birth to these ideal formations in the first place. Thus two operations of repetition appear on the scene of geometry. First, creative, productive repetition—the forward progress which science makes by building up layer by layer—involves the corresponding risk of accepting what has been handed down as if it fell from the sky. Second, reproductive repetition, the re-activation of these originally founding acts, is introduced precisely to counter the threat which the first involves. The two kinds of repetition belong in coordination. The first is productive but endangering; the second is re-productive and saving. In the danger grows the saving. Reproductive repetition must save us from the danger which has been precipitated by the very success of productive repetition. The danger is active, the saving re-activating. The first presses forward and makes progress possible; the second reaches back, is memorial, recollective, salvific.

(2) With the introduction of a second kind of repetition, an openly recollective one, Derrida's argument shifts. Against the first, productive repetition he argues only that it is not possible without signs. Against the second, reproductive kind, he argues that is not possible at all.

Husserl's neat opposition between the original founding act and its reactivation leads him into a dilemma about just how a tradition is supposed to move, how meaning is to get communicated, how anything can be under way. For there are, Derrida says, two ways for repetition to follow, two ways to repeat a tradition and "recollect" (in the Hegelian sense of *Erinnerung)* its resources, that is, to collect the mail. Here we meet up with the poet and the rabbi again, this time disguised as James Joyce and Husserl. The one follows a kind of generalized equivocity, exploiting all the buried potential in every word and proposition—actualizing links that even cross over natural languages—all the consonances and associations, "settling into," rather than "reducing," this "labyrinthine" field.

> The other endeavor is Husserl's: to reduce or impoverish empirical language methodically to the point where its univocal and translatable elements are actually transparent, in order to reach back and grasp again at its pure source a historicity or traditionality that no de facto historical totality will yield of itself. (OrG 104–105/102–103)

Actually, both positions involve a dilemma. Were one to pursue the path of perfect univocity, as Husserl wants, were the protogeometers, indeed were scientists of every kind and age, able to encode their creations in a rigorously univocal manner, and were later workers simply to reenact and repeat their productions with perfect fidelity, there would be no "tra-dition" because nothing would ever *move*. Were a statement to succeed in being absolutely univocal, it would be so flattened out, so deprived of depth and nuance that, while it would be able to be passed on, it would lack suggestiveness and fertility enough to encourage historical *progress*. (As Kierkegaard complained, in meta-physics, nothing new or novel can emerge.) On the other hand, unbounded Joycean equivocity would render the tradition impossible in the opposite way, by so scattering it to the four winds that nothing would be passed on and "the very text of its repetition" would be "unintelligible" (OrG 105/103). Joyce requires a concession to univocity, or he risks unintelligibility, even as Husserl requires fluidity and vague suggestiveness, or he risks total sterility. (Given some of the things that are said about Derrida nowadays, it is worth remember-ing that he wants to put the brakes on Joycean repetition, and he does not think that it can get a tradition going.)

We can wring from Husserl only a concession of a certain de facto inev-itability of equivocity. But univocity remains the ideal, the infinite idea, to be pursued in principle, even though it is not achieved in fact. Univocity is the goal and the horizon of historical equivocity, the task it pursues, the end it aims at, and hence it is always in place, keeping these associative drifts—what Derrida will later call the disseminative drift—in check.

But Derrida thinks that this metaphysical gesture of waving one's hand in passing recognition that, after all, one cannot do what one says one is doing, is at best a dream, at worst a kind of bad faith.[3] Reproductive (metaphysical) repeti-tion (reactivation) pursues an ideal which cannot be achieved but which it refuses to renounce, even while it denounces the alteration of meaning upon which it depends for the production of meaning. It practices the repetition which it denies even while it concedes the impossibility of the repetition which it pursues. The Husserlian project is thus inhabited by an economy of "deferral"—one of the two important senses of the word *différance* for Derrida[4]—that is, an irreducible delay, a confessed failure to achieve what it sets out to do, a failure which it tries to hold off by distinguishing de facto and de jure.

The Husserlian researcher thus is caught up in the endless to and fro of an archeological-teleological circle, constantly drawn back to ever-receding beginnings, constantly lured forward to an endlessly withdrawing telos, caught between a lost beginning and an infinitely distant ideal (OrG 141/131). Metaphysics never takes history seriously (OrG 123/116); it always turns it into an image of itself, putting it under the custody of the Idea. That is why phenomenology is so much taken with the idea of "horizon": horizons contain the future within the reach of the past, prevent anything truly novel from happening, return the future to what was there all along. The horizon is the "always-already-there" of a future which insures that beginning and end, archeology and teleology, *Urstiftung* and *Endstiftung* coincide (OrG 1123/117)—if only as infinite, unrealizable tasks.

Thus even as language and writing belong to the first sense of repetition, a radically nonintuitive principle belongs to the second. There can be no phenomenology of this Idea. It never makes an appearance, is never the object of a possible intuition. Phenomenological presence is never delivered but only promised, dangling as it does between the lost origins and the impossible hope of fulfillment, all the while making use of the very instrument which it wants to expel. We are too late for the protogeometers, too early for realized science. We are unable to constitute ideality alone and unable to constitute it together without passing through the danger of writing. Presence is unable to present itself without the danger of delay and detour. The now—*maintenant*—cannot maintain itself but constantly gives way to delay and *différance*.

The absolute has lost its innocence in Derrida, and if we are to speak of a transcendental—which Derrida, in keeping with what he would later call his "paleonymy," is willing to do—then the transcendental must be that very difference, or division, of consciousness against itself in virtue of which nothing is ever firmly, fully present, that division of consciousness from its own *arché* and *telos*, which is dependent at every step upon signs. Things make their appearance only in such a divided, *différant* consciousness and "that," says Derrida, "is perhaps what has always been said under the concept 'transcendental'" (OrG 171/153).

Husserl wants to rescue the *arché* and the *telos* by reinstating them as ideas in the Kantian sense, looming goals from which we are divided only by a kind of fall. Derrida on the other hand builds these limitations into the very structure of consciousness, treating them as structurally necessary, not as factual accidents which have somehow or another befallen the essence of pure consciousness.

Indeed for Derrida they become principles of creativity. Geometry, art, philosophy, any historical formation, makes its way by a creative repetition, by a series of creative misunderstandings, by repetitions which alter. That is the only way to get any motion into the tradition. Were Husserlian reactivation even possible, it would not be desirable. For it would bring the tradition to a halt. The more perfect the reactivation, the more sterile the product.

Consciousness is "always already" differentiated, and that is why Derrida says that this is perhaps what the transcendental has meant all along. Difference is not the external, the accidental, but a kind of a priori which inhabits things from the start. Nothing is or ever was innocent, integral, undivided. The repetition which repeats forward does not make promises it cannot keep. It does not build *excuses* into the transcendental structure of consciousness in a kind of transcendental apology for not being yet, or for not being any longer, what we say we are "in truth." It recognizes that this "not" is built right in, that it is no merely temporary inconvenience which we hope to remove by the first of the month. It recognizes that we are caught up in the flux, breached by the "not," that the only honest thing to do, indeed the only thing to do at all, honest or not, is press forward. Indeed it does not even feel bad about all this. It understands full well that it is by means of this repetition-which-alters that we make any progress at all, that *différance* is not a humbling reminder of the finitude of one who has infinite tasks, not a mark of transcendental melancholy, but the only way anything ever gets done.

THE USELESSNESS OF SIGNS AND THE
USES OF REPETITION

As I have pointed out, Derrida's argument has not cut off every escape route for phenomenology. It could still be maintained that ideality is constituted in its purity and without recourse to language at least within the limits of solitary, monological consciousness and that transcendental consciousness has recourse to language only as an expediency in order to communicate ideality over space and time. In "The Origin of Geometry," Derrida was able to demonstrate the dependence of transcendental *history* upon language and writing. But he has a taller order in *Speech and Phenomena*, which is to show the way that language is required by transcendental *consciousness* itself, even in its monological interiority.

He has shown that ideality cannot be communicated without language; now he must show that ideality cannot be constituted at all without language or, as he now says, without "signs." He has demonstrated the dependence of intersubjective constitution upon signs; now he must show the dependence of constitution in general upon signs. Thus Derrida's argument takes its most radical form here, and deconstruction sets its sights on the very essence of transcendental life. Perhaps that is why he later described *Speech and Phenomena* as the work he valued most *(Positions* 13/4).

So this time he will take aim at internal time consciousness and the kind of commerce it has with its neighbors and show that both invoke—against phenomenology's own desire, its *vouloir-dire*[5]—the constitutive value of the differential, which in this perversely Derridean phenomenology is what the transcendental means:

> [P]henomenology seems to us tormented, if not contested from within, by its own descriptions of the movement of temporalization and of the constitution of intersubjectivity. At the heart of what ties together these two decisive moments of description we recognize an irreducible nonpresence as having a constituting value, and with it a nonlife, a nonpresence or nonself-belonging of the living present, an irreducible non-primordiality. (VPh 5/SP 6–7)

Despite the rhetoric (and the metaphysics) of in-person presence, Husserl in fact accounts for the temporality of internal consciousness and for consciousness of others in terms of distance, division, and nonpresence, which then are assigned a decisive and indeed constitutive role in the production of what we take to be present. Thus *différance*, the differential, is given in this reading "a constituting value" *(une valeur constituante)*: that, it seems to me, is the focal point of the Derridean, deconstructed Husserl, the Husserl against himself, the Husserl liberated from himself.

The effect of this is further to confound Husserl's argument in "The Origin of Geometry," namely, by subverting the very idea of "origin." In treating "The Origin of Geometry," Derrida insisted that the principle of deferral, disguised metaphysically by Husserl as the "Idea in the Kantian sense," ought to be confessed outright and built into the very structure of consciousness as a principle of *différance*. Now this argument too is given a still more radical twist, and he argues not only that the origin is infinitely removed but also that there never really was anything originary, that repetition is *always already* at work. It was, in effect, at work on the first geometers, and whatever it was they did, it was not an *Urstiftung* but a *Wiederholung*, a creative repetition or reorganization of an already established system of signs into which they inserted themselves. He argues for the nonoriginary character of the origin and for the priority of repetition over what it purportedly follows or repeats.

Derrida's investigation focuses on Husserl's claim in the *First Investigation* that, within solitary life, "indicative signs" are "quite useless" ("ganz zwecklos," §8).[6] This claim turns on the central distinction between two kinds of signs, expressions *(Ausdruck)* and indications *(Anzeigen)*. A sign is anything that stands for something else *(für etwas)*. An expression is a sign that bears a meaning, of which there is only one example, which is human language itself. Expressions are inherently meaningful signs. Indications, on the other hand, are empirical pointers that refer from the sign to the signified without bearing an intrinsic meaning in themselves. There is a purely empirical connection between them such that, upon the experience of the indicator, we are motivated to pass to the indicated. Indications do indeed have meaning *for* a consciousness which apprehends them, but they are not inherently meaningful. Smoke "indicates" fire, but it does not "mean" fire.

This is not to say that an expression cannot acquire an indicative function. That indeed is just what communication is: an expression that by its own essence simply gives expression to a meaning within the limits of solitary life and is passed on or shared with another by means of the indicative signs employed in the various natural languages. Now the solitary ego enters upon intersubjective life. "Meaning" occurs essentially in transcendental solitude, in the soliloquy which one holds with oneself when one "thinks to oneself." But when one communicates, something other than meaning and its expression is brought into play, and that is what Saussure would call a certain graphic or phonic substance. Then a piece of the empirical world is joined to meaning in the service of indicating, not merely of expressing, meaning. In communication, the ego shares its mental life with another by means of mundane signs, worldly instruments—sound and writing, marks in the air or on paper, traces in time and traces in space—which do not belong to the reduced essence of linguistic expression. In communication, meaning is not merely expressed (given linguistic shape) but also borne into the world, given a material body (graphic or phonic).

Derrida astutely points out that this distinction clearly prefigures the distinction which Husserl made over a quarter of a century later, in *Cartesian Meditations,* Part V, between the sphere of ownness *(Eigenheit)* and the sphere of the other who is grasped only appresentatively (VPh 42/SP 39). The purity of expression occurs in the sphere of ownness, whereas in communication expression ventures out into the world where it is threatened with the loss of meaning, with forgetfulness, with death.

But do not indicative signs make their way into the solitary sphere when we engage in "interior monologue"? Husserl resolutely denies this. He insists that the purity of monological life excludes contamination by indicative signs. And in this exclusion Derrida sees the anxiety of metaphysics, the anxious gesture of expelling its other and opposite, of casting its other and opposite into exile. Husserl thinks that any such dialogue of the soul with itself is strictly imaginary, of a purely "pretended" sort. One does not "really" communicate anything to oneself. And that is because indicative signs in the inner sphere would be entirely useless *(zwecklos)*, without purpose. We do not use them because we do not need to use them.

Derrida argues that the distinction between "real" communication, in the intersubjective sphere, and "imaginary" communication, in the monological sphere, is just one more metaphysical apparatus which comes undone. Real communication is not really real, effective communication. It is an illusion to think that in communication one makes naked contact, that mind is joined to mind in perfect immediacy. On the contrary, "real" communication is a work of signs and mediation and hence beset with confusion and exposed to misunderstanding and failure to communicate. It is caught up as much in the medium of "representations" (and hence likeness, image, the imaginary) as is the so-called imaginary dialogue within inner life. "Real" communication can be every bit as fictitious as "inner soliloquy" can be a work of productive clarification.

Repetition and representation cut into the very essence of signs, and it is never possible to separate out an original and a representative element within them (VPh 56–57/SP 51). One cannot take communication with others to be real and effective while making an interior monologue a mere image of a real dialogue. An inner soliloquy is not an image of a real dialogue because nothing can guarantee that a dialogue will be real and effective in the first place, for it too is a tissue of signifiers, any one of which can go wrong (in Austin's term, "misfire," that is, be misunderstood). Signifiers never deliver the things themselves. They are always placeholders in a differential system, a system of repetitions. In short, outer communication is beset with fiction and confusion—every bit as much as inner communication is likely to come up with something new, which leads to the next point.

Husserl thinks that there is no need to indicate one's own mental life to oneself because "the acts in question are themselves experienced by us at that very moment" (LU, §8). Consciousness, which is defined by immanence, by its own self-presence to itself, is always already there, on the spot, at the moment that a mental act takes place. There is no need for the act to be represented to itself by means of a sign, no need for transcendence in the sphere of immanence, no need to communicate one's own mental experience (*Erlebnis*) to oneself, since consciousness already is that very stream of experiences (*Erlebnisstrom*). Consciousness is already there at that very moment ("im selben Augenblick"). Not the blink of an eye (*Augen-blick*) intervenes between the act and our consciousness of it. Nothing divides the pure medium of consciousness from itself.

But that is a view of consciousness which has been refuted out of Husserl's own mouth, by his own theory of internal time consciousness. For there Husserl shows that the now is not altogether now, is not a simple unity or pure self-identity. The whole argument about the uselessness of signs stands or falls on the undividedness of the now. "Self-presence must be produced in the undivided unity of a temporal present so as to have nothing to reveal to itself by the agency of signs" (VPh 67/SP 60). But Husserl has himself shown that such absolute instantaneity is impossible for a consciousness embedded in the temporal "flux." On Husserl's own terms, the instantaneous "now" is merely part of a larger weave. In his view "now" must be continuously compounded with "now" (VPh 72/SP 64) in order to make up (constitute), in order to make for (supplement), the "present" in a wider and richer sense. The instantaneous now is to be distinguished from the wider, more pregnant "present," which is a product of a protentional-retentional synthesis of now's. The present in the pregnant sense, therefore, is not originary but produced by a more radical operation (synthesis, *différance*). Hence, even if retention is a modification of the "now" in the narrow sense, still the "living present," the present in which we "live" and which is accordingly privileged by phenomenology, is an effect, a product, a woven text, a work of synthesis and *texere*, transfixed with the structure of textuality. Presence in the pregnant sense is the effect of re-tention, re-presentation, repetition. Repetition does not repeat presence, by making it present again, but produces it in the first place. Repetition does not come afterward, does not repeat backward. On the contrary, it is always already in place, producing what metaphysics, which dwells naively in the products of repetition, calls being, presence, what-is.

But such a theory undoes the self-identity of consciousness which Husserl requires in order for consciousness to be present to itself "in the same moment" that a mental act elapses:

> If the punctuality of the instant is a myth, . . . and if the present of self-presence is not *simple*, if it is constituted in a primordial and irreducible synthesis, then the whole of Husserl's argumentation is threatened in its very principle. (VPh 68/SP 61)

If Husserl concedes the distinction between the moment in which one reflects and the moment upon which one reflects, the moment which has "just lapsed," he also understands how much damage this concession can do, and he takes measures to contain its effects. He insists that there is, in principle (de jure), a distinction between "retention" and "reproduction." When we hear a melody, or listen to a string of words, or watch a moving object, what is "given," what we experience or "live in," is a synthetic unity composed of a core source-point or now united with the immediately lapsed and the immediately pending moments. Otherwise one would not hear a melody but simply a series of discrete sounds. Now retaining the immediately lapsed moments in the melody which is presently being played is different in kind from remembering the piece which was played before the intermission. Retention (or "primary" memory) maintains itself in the element of presence, does not leave it for a moment, holds its place in the present in the "pregnant" sense—the present which is compounded, enriched, and fortified by retention and protention. Reproduction (or memory in the ordinary sense), however, has to do with the past, with a discrete noematic sequence, which has a unity of its own and which is now "over" (*vorbei*).

Thus the "moment" in which consciousness is present to itself is the moment which includes retention within itself and is not a subsequent moment farther on down the temporal stream. What is immediately retained thus participates in the surety and apodicticity of the immediately present, as opposed to the merely relative trustworthiness of secondary memory. Hence the return of the subject to itself in self-reflection is not threatened by the gap, ever so small, between the reflecting moment and the moment reflected upon. For the reflecting ego grasps itself in the immediately retained now, that is, within the safety net of the present in the broader or enriched sense.

But for Derrida the present in the pregnant sense is a little bit like the old saw about being a little bit pregnant. What is the difference *in principle* between what has just lapsed and what has been lapsed for some time? What is the difference, if the standard by which we are to judge such matters, the standard laid down by Husserl himself, is presence, immediacy, intuitiveness, apodicticity? A moment is not essentially or generically qualified as just "slightly" lapsed. That is not an essential, categorial, qualitative difference—a difference in kind or in principle—but a quantitative, practical difference, defined by the relative place of the now which is sinking away in the stream of retentions. Retention and reproduction then are but differing cases of re-presentation in general, differing only in terms of their relative distance from the now-point, and the case which Husserl makes for their difference in essence fails.

But if the so-called living present is the effect of retention/repetition, if it is invaded in its very core by nonpresence, then there is work for signs to do, and this is the heart of Derrida's demonstration. "The fact that nonpresence and otherness are internal to presence strikes at the very root of the argument for the uselessness of signs in the self-relation" (VPh 74/SP 66). For the work of signs is to stand for another *(für etwas)*, to take the place of the other, for what is not present now. The work of signs is the work of place taking, *tenere*, tenancy, the work of pro-tention and re-tention. Signs are the *pharmakon* which provides the remedy for memory. They make consciousness stronger, more tenacious. They help hold *(tenere)* it together *(con-)*; they are the bond of the synthetic unity of consciousness *(con-scire)*. Contrary to Husserl's claim that signs are useless, Derrida finds employment for them in the very heart of internal time consciousness. They are at work at the most primordial levels of transcendental consciousness where consciousness gives birth to objectivity, both the immanent objects within the stream and the transcendent objects without. There is no prelinguistic stratum, no private sphere of self-consciousness in which the self is in naked contact with itself. There is no private realm of ownness in which consciousness constitutes pure *Sinn* without the cooperation of signs. There is no unmediated self-identity which precludes the need to inform itself of its own doings. On the contrary, the inner life of consciousness is a flux, constituted by the gaps and interstices of flowing time which needs constantly to be repaired by the work of synthesis, which for Derrida is the work of signs. Derrida does not mean to deny that self-consciousness or self-reflection occurs, but only that it ever occurs in an unmediated way, without recourse to signs. Reflection for him is a mediated and limited process, at once made possible by, yet constrained within the limits of, the system of signifiers within which it occurs.[7]

After showing the dependence of self-consciousness and self-presence upon the movement of repetition, Husserl insists on reappropriating the element of otherness into a presence more largely, more amply understood. After masterfully exposing the otherness which inhabits the present, Husserl tries to cover it over. What unites retention and reproduction—which Husserl wants so much to distinguish—is repetition, which is, Derrida says, their "common root" and a more original constitution:

> . . . the possibility of re-petition in its most general form, that is, the constitution of a trace in the most universal sense—is a possibility which not only must inhabit the pure actuality of the now but must constitute it through the very movement of difference it introduces. Such a trace is—if we can employ this language without immediately contradicting it or crossing it out as we proceed—more "primordial" than what is phenomenologically primordial. (VPh 75/SP 67)

This more primordial movement of repetition is the movement of reiteration which is illustrated by Husserl in his diagram of the form of inner time consciousness, that sliding graph or flow chart which Husserl draws to track the movement of protention through the now into retention (PIT, §10, §43). That is the form of indefinite repeatability which shows the way in which repetition makes a noematic unity possible. The flow of internal time consciousness is a system of repetition which constitutes the presence of what is present. That is why Derrida says that repetition is "older than presence" (VPh 76/SP 68).

Monological life, the life of consciousness within itself, in the sphere of immanence, when one merely "thinks to oneself," is, for Husserl, a realm of *pure linguistic expression*, free from mundane interference and opacity. An "expression" for him is not a matter of expressing oneself *to* another, but the way in which consciousness expresses something to itself *about* an object. Its "expressive" power then consists simply in giving a linguistic shape or categorization to a prelinguistic meaning *(Sinn)*. That is why Husserl thinks that the work of expression is entirely unproductive *(Ideas I*, §124), simply stamping an already constituted meaning *(Sinn)* with linguistic signification *(Bedeutung)*, but not adding anything to it.[8] Expression is unproductive repetition. Hence the categories of signification agree perfectly with the categories of meaning. But Derrida denies that there is any such sphere, prior to the play of the impure, empirical, indicative linguistic signifiers, and free of their influence. On the contrary it can be shown that the categories of meaning *(Sinn)* are, contrary to Husserl's argument, in fact functions of the categories of linguistic signification.

Husserl entertains such an illusion, Derrida thinks, because he has taken over uncritically an old metaphysical conception of the "pure voice" as a kind of pure and diaphanous medium. We think things over within ourselves in a voice which is not spatial, mundane, contaminated by the world. Pure expressions are constituted in this inner voice which keeps silent, which goes about the work of repetition noiselessly, in silent acts of repetition exercised in inner soliloquy. There, in these hushed chambers, meanings are forged in the midst of inner time-flow and then shaped into ideal unities (with an ideality relative to the monological sphere). The special quality of this voice is its capacity to disappear, to give way instantly to its intentional objects, as if there were no voice at all. The voice is heard as soon as it speaks, in "absolute proximity" to itself, in perfect self-affection: "My words are 'alive' because they seem not to leave me: not to fall outside me, outside my breath, at a visible distance" (VPh 85/SP 76). This voice gives way instantly ("im selben Augenblick") to the things themselves, as if there were no voice at all. Speech remains in proximity to the speaker. My words seem not to leave me, to fall outside into the world. The inner voice effaces its own presence and induces the illusion of a thought operating in a pure medium. In inner soliloquy I speak to myself, but I do not write to myself. Writing is an irreducibly worldly operation. Speech is more pure, more ideal, than writing. This seeming self-presence of speech, its instantaneous reception as soon as it is spoken, is carried nicely by the French expression "je m'entende," "I understand/hear myself." Hearing oneself speak appears to effect the reduction of everything worldly, the removal of every worldly danger, in a medium of absolute self-proximity.

Such privileging of speech over writing, such "phono-centrism," is a transcendental-phenomenological illusion for Derrida, a metaphysical credulity which believes that speech is somehow free of the element of "writing," which dwells within speech and the inwardness of thought (VPh 92/SP 81–82). Husserl's phenomenology remained fundamentally naive about the invisibility of the voice, and as with all naiveté, it is the task of the reduction—here a grammatological, or semiotic, reduction—to root naiveté out by making the work of signs conspicuous, for signs are not useless. It is this naiveté which allows Husserl to think that the expression is not productive, that language is transparent. Still, because of the tension within the Husserlian text between its critical and its metaphysical motifs, this reduction of language never quite succeeds; it remains uneasy "because an underlying motif was disturbing and contesting the security of these traditional distinctions from within and because the possibility of writing dwelt within speech, which was itself at work in the inwardness of thought" (VPh 92/SP 82).

The more naive Husserl is already subverted by the more radical, critical

Husserl who makes it plain that presence is a constituted product and hence that the primordial comes to be under the hand of the trace. For the production of presence requires the work of retention which in turn requires the work of signs, although, Derrida adds realistically, "doubtless Husserl would refuse to assimilate the necessity of retention and the necessity of signs" (VPh 74/SP 66).

The possibility of writing which dwells within speech and which dislodges this phonocentrism is the systematic deployment of signs upon which all consciousness depends, including internal time consciousness itself. The *Bedeutung* is not the unproductive mirror-image of a pure prelinguistic *Sinn*, for there is no *Sinn* which is not already constituted as a unity by the semiotic system which produces it.[9] Even the most interior monologue is already infiltrated by the historico-cultural categories of language, which exert their invisible influence everywhere, "tracing" out the unities of meaning within which we think. Speech deploys a particular chain of signifiers, structuring and articulating the world by its means. Speech is already structured as an articulation, already invaded and differentiated by a system of categorization and syncategorization. It would not be enough to say that thought "cannot escape" from the chain of signifiers, that it must learn to tolerate the interference of signs, as if language were a prison and not a "house," as if différance were only a limiting condition and not an enabling one. The chain of signifiers makes thought possible in the first place and hence "liberates" thought.

It is this tracing and pretracing out of the world according to a differential system of signifiers that Derrida calls "writing," in the sense of "arché-writing," or, as one would say in left-wing Husserlianism, transcendental writing. Archéwriting is just as much at work in speech as in writing in the narrow sense; indeed at this point the difference between these two ceases to be of any importance, ceases to be anything more than an empirical difference in the "substance" of the signifiers. Whence the Husserlian "pre-delineation" (*Vorzeichnung*), a kind of fore-sketching, which we discussed in chapter 2, is rewritten by Derrida as a transcendental arché-writing. Speech is already inhabited by writing, not because people learn to write before they speak, but because both speech and writing, in their ordinary senses, are made possible in the first place by arché-writing, by a differential system of signifiers, which is essentially a system of iterability and repetition. In arché-writing, abstraction is made from the phonic or graphic substance of the signifier in order to attend to the deeper formality of a system of tracing, of making marks of whatever sort, in space or in time. Derrida wants to isolate that form and, having isolated it, to set it free. And it is to the character of this liberation that we now turn.

REPETITION AND THE EMANCIPATION OF SIGNS

It is not when signs have been put to work that their usefulness is established for Derrida but when they have been put into play. It is not the work they do but their free play that is most important to him. Thus after he has shown the uses of signs, both with and against Husserl, Derrida sets about their emancipation and liberation, freeing them from the restraints of the "*a priori* grammar" (itself already a "bold" liberation) which Husserl imposes upon them. In keeping with the logic of deconstruction, this emancipation of signs is to show how signs have been liberated by motifs already set in motion by Husserl himself. Thus the argument of *Speech and Phenomena* culminates in an emancipatory gesture which marks the whole of Derrida's work and not simply his interpretation of Husserl.

As we have seen, the "re-" in repetition, representation, reproduction does not come second, as a re-presenting of a prior presence, but first, as an enabling condition of possibility, as a code of iterable, repeatable signs, which generates presence (perceptual objects, ideal objects, and indeed every possible unity of meaning). We might call this an "originary" repetition, inasmuch as repetition functions like a transcendental condition of possibility, except that the point of this analysis has been to undo the notion of something originary, if that means something purely present which then gets copied by more or less inadequate reproductions. Repetition as a nonoriginary origin is the repetition which moves forward, as Constantin would put it.

Derrida deals with this somewhat elusive state of affairs by speaking of the "supplement of the origin." This means that the origin, the realm of alleged phenomenological givenness and first-hand experience, is in fact deficient and in need of help. Ideal objects, perceptual objects, other persons, are not fully given; they do not fall whole from the sky. Rather, they stand in need of the generative, productive work which is supplied *(supplié)* by *différance*. "The supplementary difference vicariously stands in for presence due to its primordial self-deficiency" (VPh 98/SP 88). The supplement, instead of being added on as a secondary accretion, appendage, or extra, is in fact productive of presence in the first place, originative of that to which it is said to be added on, supplying what is missing in the origin. Derrida thus exploits the ambiguity of the word "supplement," according to which it means both (1) something added on or extra, merely appended to what is already full, which is its usual sense in metaphysics, and (2) that which supplies what is missing, contributes a needed supplement without which what is in itself deficient would not survive or function (as do artificial organs, limbs, life-support systems). There is a fluctuation in the word "supplement" between these two senses that Derrida is exploiting here or, rather, that he thinks has played tricks with metaphysics, which imagines that it has reduced and excluded the supplement (in the first sense) just when it surreptitiously invokes it (in the second sense). This is the first of the "undecidables" *(pharmakon,* hymen, etc.) which Derrida will discuss more fully in *Dissemination.* The much-vaunted sphere of "originary presence" to which phenomenology lays claim is in need of help, stands in need of supplementation, not of a little extra addition at the end but of an essential

supplying and rendering possible which makes the presence which phenomenology desires possible. Phenomenology thinks that it has reduced and
excluded "re-presentation" just when it calls upon its help.

That is why the Husserlian discovery which Derrida most cherishes—and
this must seem a sheer perversity to Husserlian orthodoxy—is the possibility of
intention *without* intuition, that is, of unfulfilled intention. Husserl saw not
only that expressive intentions *can* function in the absence of their objects, but
also that this is their essential function. He saw that one can speak without
seeing, that one can speak without having the truth, and indeed that one can
speak without avoiding contradiction. Speech, in order to be speech, in order to
be "well-formed," is bound only by purely formal laws of linguistic configuration, organized by a theory of linguistic signification *(Bedeutungslehre)*. Even if
speech is deprived of an object, of truth, or of consistency, it can remain good
speech. [10]

Fulfillment *(Erfüllung)* is contingent; it does not belong to what Derrida calls
the "structural necessity" of signs. In Husserl's terms, such fulfillment is a
variant which can be varied away in order to isolate the invariant structure.
What is structurally necessary to the sign is the capacity to take the place of
another, to stand for something else *(für etwas)*, to hold the place for what is
absent. The whole merit, the great power and productivity of signs, is precisely
their ability to function in the absence of their object. Were we always saturated
by presence, signs would indeed be useless. Conversely, were signs bound to
fulfillment, we could not communicate unless we stood in the presence of the
object under discussion, and that would immeasurably impoverish the capacity
of language to constitute objectivity, making the constitution of ideal objec-
tivities and the scientific tradition itself impossible.

The motifs of presence, intuition, and fulfillment which so dominate Husserl's texts then arise from a metaphysical teleology which is imposed by
Husserl from without. They represent an external *telos* to which he subjugates
the *eidos* of language. They bury the eidetic structure of signs, which is laid
bare by his reduction, under an ideology of presence and thereby efface what is
truly unique to language and signs.

> [T]he language that speaks in the presence of its object effaces its own originality or
> lets it melt away; the structure peculiar to language alone, which allows it to
> function entirely *by itself* when its intention is cut off from intuition, here dissolves.
> (VPh 103/SP 93)

Thus, after unlocking the unique structure of language, Husserl proceeds to
bind it up again under metaphysical constraints: "Husserl describes, and in one
and the same movement, effaces the emancipation of speech as non-knowing"
(VPh 109/SP 97).

It is this liberation or emancipation of signs from intuitive fulfillment and even from truth and objectivity, according to Derrida, which liberates them from metaphysical constraints and releases the play of *différance*. Signs and traces are what they are when they are liberated from intuition and allowed to produce their own effects, *sui generis*, in a free play of their own. Husserl saw this, and one of his most impressive achievements from Derrida's point of view was to have inaugurated a progressive reduction to this radical freedom of the intention from fulfillment, of the form of signification from truth-content.

> The whole originality of this conception lies in the fact that its ultimate subjection to intuitionism does not oppress what might be called the freedom of language, the candor of speech, even if it is false and contradictory. One can speak without knowing. And against the whole philosophical tradition Husserl shows that in that case speech is still genuinely speech, provided it obeys certain rules which do not immediately figure as rules for knowledge. (VPh 100/SP 89–90)

Speech is still good speech (well formed) even if it has no present object, as when I speak truly of a distant time or place. It remains good speech even if I speak of a place I have only visited in my imagination, like the land of Oz. It persists in being good speech even if it is false and even if it is flatly contradictory, a *Widersinn*, like "the circle is square." Good speech requires neither fulfillment nor truth nor even consistency.

But then Husserl loses his nerve. Despite the "boldness" of the project of a pure logical grammar, Husserl calls off his reduction and puts a halt to the isolation and liberation of the pure form of signs. Now he invokes the rule of law, rules of a priori grammar, which draw a line with the *Widersinn* and mark it off from absolute non-sense, the pure *Unsinn*, "excluding" expressions like "green is or" and "abracadabra." The wild agrammaticality of these expressions marks an ultimate breakdown in speech. On what grounds? They are not of a *form* such that, were we to replace them with other expressions of the same form, intuition could result. The expression "the circle is square" is well formed because, given the proper substitution instances, it could be rendered true and intuitive. But for Derrida this is to import a foreign demand into signifiers, to subject them to the rules of another sphere, to subjugate to the rule of intuitiveness that whose peculiar structure is its ability to function without intuition. Husserl's critical, reductive impulse is brought to a halt by a metaphysical desire for presence, a will to let the rule of presence hold sway (VPh 110–11/SP 98–99).[11]

But Derrida wants to continue where Husserl broke off, to extend the liberation, to insist upon the essential freedom of signifiers from metaphysical demands. He wants to free up the play of signifiers in order to let "green is or" loose in all of its associative play, to let it produce its effects, leave its comet tail of sign making behind it, let it effect modes of sense which are not confined to knowledge, let loose a *logos* not held captive by intuition and objectivity. For "green is or" produces indefinitely new effects and this precisely in virtue of its *repeatability*. It can be repeated and thereby altered in another language, say in French ("verre est où/ou") in which it is caught up in a new concatenation. And it can be repeated and thereby altered in a new context (in a logic game, say, where disjunctives are color-coded), where the possibilities of recontextualization are indefinite. Indeed, contrary to Husserl's aim, Derrida defies us to find a semiotic string which cannot in principle produce an effect.

The "formality" (Derrida uses the scare quotes: VPh 110/SP 98) is not laid bare by the laws of a priori grammar but by the pure form of repeatability, iterability, *différance*, which lies deeper than this rational grammar and indeed conditions its possibility. To repeat is to produce and to alter, to make and to make anew. Repetition is a principle of irrepressible creativity and novelty; it would be impossible to repeat without making and without altering what is already made. Even to repeat "exactly the same thing" is to repeat it in a new context which gives it a new sense. But Derrida, unlike Husserl, does not think that everything comes to grief because of that. On the contrary, it is liberative— that is how "science progresses," is it not?—and hence nothing to repress. Signs are a "system" (we still require scare quotes) of repeatable traces whose very repeatability makes it possible to generate sense in the first place and impossible to stop altering whatever is produced. This repetition is to be systematically free, a repetition which is Joycean not Husserlian, poetic not rabbinical. And this is the only sense of "interpretation" he embraces: to interpret is to repeat, and to repeat is to make and remake. And if interpretation always involves a hermeneutic, this is a hermeneutic of productivity, alteration, and re-reading.

It is Derrida's point—the pointed tip of his stylus—to set this liberation in motion. He liberates signifiers from being, truth, and presence, not only by showing that they are constituted effects but by affirming the power of signifiers to create beyond them, to produce in a way which is not bound by being and presence. To be sure, this is no absolute act of creation which shatters its bonds with what precedes it. On the contrary, as a repetition which alters, it is always "bound" to its *repetendum*, both in the general sense of requiring a *repetendum* to begin with and in the particular sense of the particular constraints imposed by the *repetendum*. Its freedom is to exploit every latent connection, every associative bond, every phonic, graphic, semiotic, and semantic link, every relation of whatever sort which exists among signifiers, in order to set forth the power of repetition in all its productivity, inventiveness, and freedom. (Joyce is always the best example of this in English.) Derrida wants to show that what is traced out in signs is not set in stone but has entered into a concatenation of signifiers with connecting lines reaching out in every direction and that these links cannot be cut off or excluded—not by authorial intention, rules of a priori grammar, or any other instrument which metaphysics devises to still the flux.

Husserl himself had a glimpse into this abyss of productivity and irrepressible repetition, as I pointed out in chapter 2, in the famous discussion of the destructibility of the world. Here Husserl seems to acknowledge this deep play, this uncontrollable flux which, if it is ultimately put in metaphysical harness by Husserl himself, is boldly exploited and cultivated by Derrida. He is discussing the very contingency of a system constrained by the demands of "fulfillment," the radical alterability which is built into any intention which is put in a position of dependence upon presential completion. The discussion of the annihilation of the world leads in turn to the irreducibility of transcendental subjectivity which—in a discussion of "incomparable depth"—is then itself reduced to the truly irreducible flow of internal time. Derrida singles out the discussion of internal time in a long note, but he does not advert to the destructibility of the world, though it seems to me that both texts belong to his rereading of Husserl.

The destructibility of the world is not merely a surface disruption, which would only clear the way to a deeper reorganization of experience, but also a radical one in which there just would not be a world any longer (Hua III.1 91/*Ideas I* 109). The orderliness of the world is a contingent matter, not anchored in anything deeper than past experience, not secured absolutely against disruption. This is Husserl's most Kafkaesque moment, his wildest imaginative variation, meant to show the possibility of uncontrollable metamorphosis. It is little wonder that Derrida has recently turned his attention to Kafka. There is a road which leads from Husserl to Kafka.

But if the world is not secured against indefinite slippage, what then? Is anything "absolute," that is, insulated against alteration? If nothing mundane is absolute, there is nowhere to turn but consciousness. But even consciousness itself reduces to a flow, for the transcendental absolute effected by the reduction, the ego, is not truly absolute but is itself constituted on a deeper level by what is "ultimately and truly absolute" (Hua III.1 182/*Ideas I* 193). The unity of the ego is constituted, produced in the time-flow as a certain congealing and temporary thickening of internal time. Not only transcendent objects but also the objects immanent in the time-flow itself are produced, and alterable effects are generated in and by internal time and hence by a certain radical process of repetition/alteration.

Derrida points out this most radical of all the Husserlian conceptions in an important footnote at the end of *Speech and Phenomena* in which he emphasizes both the radicality of Husserl's intention and Husserl's attempt to contain "the incomparable depth of this analysis within the closure of the metaphysics of presence." What is released by this deep analysis is immediately contained and encased within the categorial stability of the metaphysics of substance and subject: it is absolute, not relative; subject, not object.

[I]t is not by chance that he still designates this unnameable as an "absolute subjectivity," that is, as a being conceived on the basis of presence as substance, *ousia hypokeimoneon:* a self-identical being in self-presence which forms the substance of a subject.

This most fluid of processes is stabilized, reified. Thus, what Husserl discovered needs to be set free.

> This determination of "absolute subjectivity" would also have to be crossed out as soon as we conceive the present on the basis of difference, and not the reverse. The concept of *subjectivity* belongs *a priori and in general* to the order of the *constituted.* (VPh 94 n1/SP 84 n9)

What is "ultimate" and "originary"—language which immediately encloses the analysis within metaphysical parentheses—is a certain nonderived re-petition, the spacing out process of internal time itself, which bears within itself the structure of signs, that is, of standing in for and taking the place of what is continually flowing off. In that space arises both subjectivity and intersubjectivity as well as all ideality and objectivity. That spacing, which is just as much a timing, that is, a nonderived repetition process, is what is ultimately productive.

> This being outside itself proper to time is its *spacing:* it is a *proto-stage (archiscène).* This stage, as the relation of one present to another *as such,* that is, as a nonderived re-presentation *(Vergegenwärtigung* or *Repräsentation),* produces the structure of signs in general as "reference," as being-for-something *(für etwas sein),* and radically precludes their reduction. There is no constituting subjectivity. The very concept of constitution itself must be deconstructed. (VPh 94 n1/SP 84–85 n9)

Accordingly, this "ultimate" cannot be reduced to the dimensions of one of its products—like "absolute" or "subject" or "Being" or "presence." As that which produces everything which gains name and stablity within the flow, it does not itself bear a name. It is the very power of producing names; hence, if it is to be named at all, it is with paleo-nymns like "writing" and "supplement" or neologisms like *différance,* all of which are ways of holding up one's hands and saying that it cannot itself have either name or concept.

Under Derrida's pen, the thesis of the de(con)structibility of the world means that whatever unities of meaning are constituted in natural languages, whatever normalized form experience assumes, whatever institutionalization our practices receive, all are alike vulnerable, alterable, contingent. They have not fallen from the sky; they are structurally, eidetically vulnerable, however much they have tended to gain acceptance. And the striking thing is that the wildness of Derrida's disseminations is not without an echo in Husserl's sober discourse on the contingency of noematic sequences.

The one thing that "remains" in the midst of this disseminative drift, the Derridean analogue to the irreducible phenomenological "residuum" and so to the internal time-flow, is the differential chain itself. It is *différance* which makes possible the endless linkages of signifiers in an irreducible diversity of combinatorial and associative chains and interweavings. What is irreducible for Husserl is the flow of internal time. That is rewritten by Derrida as the irreducible spacing out of nonderived re-presentation, that is, the sheer open-ended power of repetition, the plurivocity of combinatorial possibilities, the impossibility of containing and dominating this drift, the inescapability of indefinite alteration.

Now, on one level, Derrida thinks that it is a matter of living with this drift, coping with it, so that what Heidegger would call our "average everydayness" may continue its undisturbed routine. Truth, after all, is necessary—that is to say, we need our fictions.[12] We cannot function without taming the wildness of the play, without *imposing* normality, without a certain measure of stilling the flux. Derrida does not object to such recourse to pragmatic fiction. His point is only to remind us of this coefficient of uncertainty attached to all such fiction/truths, to raise our level of vigilance about their constituted, contingent nature, lest we become so habituated to them as to forget that they are fictions—Nietzsche's definition of truth—and begin treating as "self-evident" what are no more than contingent effects of repetition, temporary stabilizations of the flow. We must not mistake our need for these "truths" as something which justifies or grounds normality in principle.[13]

Derrida thus keeps us ready for a kind of "grammatological anxiety" of his own, which breaks through the undisturbed surface of normality and routinized everydayness, in order to uncover the subterranean operation of transcendental *différance*. Derrida is good at exposing the unsettling contingency, the inextinguishable flux, which lies close to the surface of these creatures of signs. He issues a warning about falling into a natural attitude of a new sort, one which is semiotically naive, naive about signs, about the useful work they do, and about their play. He keeps a kind of grammatological reduction in place which shows the rewritability of whatever has achieved hoary prestige and the look of irreformability. He interrogates entrenched authority, the established powers that be, that pretend to be, that pretend to be present. He solicits the people of substance (of *ousia*). Such authorities, as he likes to say, have not dropped from the sky; they are contingent formations, constituted products. He is interested in producing a Socratic effect.

But Derrida goes further than merely coping with the flux and with acknowledging the need for pragmatic fictions to make our way around the world. He goes as far as one dares with the flux. He does not want, ultimately, to tame it or merely to tolerate it but positively to celebrate and cultivate it. Husserl discovers the flux and then represses it; Derrida wants to set it free and allow it the full scope of its freedom. If Diogenes wanted to refute the Eleatics by walking to and fro and Constantin by a resolute pressing forward, Derrida wants to refute them with a kind of Dionysian dance, with the rhythm of dithyrambic song. The

distinctively Derridean gesture, which exceeds all pragmatism, is always emancipatory, liberative, celebrative. The voice that does not keep silent in Derrida
is not Husserl's or Heidegger's but Nietzsche's. It is the song of Zarathustra, the
booming laughter of Zarathustra's shepherd for which Zarathustra himself
longs.

Derrida's stunning rereading of Husserl raises the question of a radical
hermeneutic. It deploys the resources of a new, more grammatological anxiety
which follows the structural laws of the old one, that is, which moves through
the sedimented and normalized structures of everydayness, the structures
which give us comfort, toward the abyss beneath. That indeed is the import of
what Derrida calls "solicitation," the *sollicitare* which shakes and disrupts our
tranquilized comfort. It is in this strategy of solicitation that I see a new form of
the hermeneutics of facticity, of a certain vigilance about the difficulty of life—
the life of signs and communication. And there is, in my view, a certain
communication between "trembling" and "repetition" in Derrida even as there
is in Kierkegaard, for whom the work of repetition is always conducted at the
borderlines of fear and trembling. In repetition, we are stripped of the illusions
of permanent presence, divested of its comforts, exposed to the *ébranler.*

Now it is in this work of dis-illusionment, this emancipation from the metaphysics of comfort, that I locate an element of a deep hermeneutic, that is to say,
a hermeneutic which breaks the spell of illusion and awakens us to the abyss, to
the flux in which we are caught up. We would say that such vigilance has the
effect of bringing about a deeper self-confrontation and self-knowledge—except
that we have been deprived of such discourse. For we have understood the
"self" to be itself a temporary inscription on the flux, and we have learned that
confrontation is never frontal, never naked and face to face, but always mediated
by signs and that such self-knowledge does not bring things to a rest but puts
them all the more radically into play. But what I call "radical" hermeneutics is
precisely readiness for that, to make that confession, to let go even of that
comfort, to live without illusion, without appeal—knowing that even life without illusion is not a pure state, not a region into which we can slip without
catching our coattails in the door behind us. What I call radical hermeneutics
involves just this *readiness* for this anxiety and solicitation, the readiness to be
shaken, the openness for *différance.*

Derrida himself remains—rightly—suspicious of any such formulation, even
if it calls itself radical hermeneutics, for formulations bring things to rest and
stabilize them. His willingness to use old names has never included "hermeneutics." And that is as it should be. For Derrida's work is one of vigilance
against the metaphysical desire for meaning and stability, the desire of metaphysics to get beyond the *physis,* the play and the flux. Speaking of hermeneutics, he says: "This style of reading which makes explicit, practices a

continual bringing to light, something which resembles, at least, a coming into consciousness, without break, displacement or change of terrain" (*Marg.* 151/126). Hermeneutics is the business of the rabbi, not the poet, of a Husserlian explication of horizons, not of Joyce. It always remains on the same ground as the *interpretandum*. It is not prepared for rupture, discontinuity, disruption. Its commerce with movement is always limited to assured movements which do not change terrain, whose results are more or less guaranteed from the start, in a coincidence of archeology and teleology. Hermeneutics for Derrida is another of those dissemblers who lead us on with all their talk about change and becoming and *kinesis* but who, in the end, sell it down the (Heraclitean) river.

And that is as it should be. For if there can be a hermeneutic more deeply construed, a more radical hermeneutic, then that can never be turned into the latest philosophical standpoint, the newest position in the history of metaphysics. For it has no standing and no position, and it makes no attempt to get beyond *physis*, beyond the flow. Such a hermeneutic comes to pass only in the element of movement and *kinesis,* and it requires ceaseless deconstructive vigilance to "maintain" itself there, so that it will not get off at the first stop, not slip out the back door of existence, as Kierkegaard said. For there is nothing to protect it against itself, nothing to stop it from asserting its own authority, from setting itself up in a position of power, from taking itself seriously. If there "is" such a hermeneutic it does not come after, or alongside, but only in and through ceaseless deconstructive analysis. Radical hermeneutics does not pass through a moment of deconstruction in order to get to the other side of the flow. Rather, deconstructive criticism belongs to its very makeup.

But the work of deconstruction is not work but play. That is the point of the Derridean stylus, and that is the "contribution" he makes to radical hermeneutics. We must understand that any talk of solicitation and anxiety in Derrida is subordinated to a Dionysian laughter and exuberance. He is no captive of the spirit of seriousness. He makes the austere pages of transcendental phenomenology rumble with deconstructive energy. He spirits the signifier across the borders of a priori grammar and sets it free to produce effects in its own region, without regard to intuition and objectification. Whatever solicitation and trembling is here is made to dance. Whatever anxiety is here has learned how to laugh. But when he turns his attention to Heidegger, he will find a text which is at once deconstructive and memorializing, disruptive and tranquilizing, and that will prove the more decisive confrontation.

DISSEMINATION: BEYOND THE EIDETIC REDUCTION

The liberation which the reading of Husserl calls for is put into practice in *Dissemination* (1972), a work which begins the transition to what Gregory

Ulmer calls Derrida's period of "applied grammatology."[14] *Dissemination* shows *in concreto* the drift, the slippage, the instability in the chain of signifiers. It moves beyond the eidetic reduction, which is a reduction *to* meaning, toward a more radical reduction *of* meaning, a grammatological liberation of the signifier, releasing it into its free play. Thus if hermeneutics in the Gadamerian sense turns on the communication of meaning, the way meaning gets handed on and reappropriated across the ages, dissemination is an undoing of hermeneutics, a disruption of its "postal" service and harmonious deliveries. By its reduction of the privilege of meaning, dissemination means to release all the hitherto suppressed powers of the signifier. Indeed, were Husserl's a priori grammar allowed to have its way we would

> . . . have to relegate to absolute nonsense all poetic language that transgresses the laws of this grammar of cognition and is irreducible to it. In the forms of nondiscursive signification (music, non-literary arts generally), as well as in utterances such as "Abracadabra" or "Green is or," there are modes of sense which do not point to any possible objects. (VPh 111/SP 99)

For metaphysics, with its built-in commitment to semantic privilege, "green is or" is an *Un-sinn*, just a sheer failure to mean, a semantic misfire, and hence of no further interest. But, for Derrida, that failure to conform to semantic or grammatical rule represents an important "reduction" which breaks the spell of a logico-natural attitude, of the naive belief in *logos* as reason, of logo-centrism. There are all sorts of phonic and graphic relationships at play in such chains of signifiers which authors like Lewis Carroll, James Joyce, and e. e. cummings would find of considerable interest. Husserl's examples actually serve to effect the reduction to grammatological form, "releasing" the hitherto repressed potencies of signifiers. "Dissemination" thus proceeds by way of the reduction of semanticism, a reduction opened up but not followed up by Husserl. Dissemination is opposed to semantics as grammatology is opposed to hermeneutics. (Because it exploits the *semen/semantike* connection, a relationship which is itself a purely phonic and not a semantic or etymological link, the very word "dissemination" illustrates the disseminative drift.)

From the point of view of meta-physics (which wants to move "beyond" the substance of the signifier to the signified meaning), Derrida systematically explores all the "surfaces" of language, all the possible graphic, phonic, rhythmic, and psychoanalytic linkages between words. He wants to exploit every connection, follow up every possible link that connects one word to another without regard to, in a defiant reduction of, meaning. From that point of view, then, dissemination is a kind of "phonetic phenomenology" (*Diss.* 287/255) of the surface of words made possible by the reduction of meaning, which is a reduction to the form of words, to grammatological form. And semanticism would not deny the virtuosity, the dazzling grammatological agility, of Derrida, that he is indeed a master of the game he chooses to play.

But Derrida wants to undermine the smug assurances of semanticism, to put into question the assumed priority of meaning—which then thinks it can contain the effects Derrida produces by situating them within a phenomenology of surfaces. Dissemination cannot be patronized by semanticism because the grammatological reduction shows that meaning is but one among many effects of *différance,* one indeed which has been unduly privileged by our metaphysical preoccupations. It is the privilege of meaning, and hence the very authority of semanticism, to judge dissemination that dissemination puts into question.

Derrida critiques the semanticist reading of Mallarmé by J. P. Richard (*L'univers imaginaire de Mallarmé*) as symbolistic (cast in terms of Ricoeur's theory of metaphor and symbolism), as an attempt to gain control over Mallarmé's polysemy. For Richard, Mallarmé is a genius of "association," whose "rule" the critic must discern. But Derrida wants to liberate Mallarmé from hermeneutic deciphering and to set his texts free in all their disseminative energy. We cannot contain what Mallarmé does by reducing it to certain uses of rhyme and verse. On the contrary, Mallarmé shows us the generalized sense of rhyme and verse as the possibility of literature itself, that is, of producing textual effects at large (*Diss* 309/277). (And this leaves no room for "philosophy" as a sphere of pure meaning, exempt from textuality, for philosophy too is a form of writing.)[15]

Dissemination effects a disruption of semantics, even when semantics tries to protect itself, when it tries to make concessions, with a theory of polysemy, such as those of Ricoeur and contemporary hermeneutical theorists. The reading of literature has been dominated by the rule of the semantic. It has assumed, for fundamentally metaphysical reasons, that there is a ruling "thematic" unity to a text, a single, unifying meaning by which the entire chain of signifiers is organized and to which it is subordinated. In the older version, this semantic unity was attributed to the unifying intention of the author. In its more modern form, in the "new criticism" and in the hermeneutics of Gadamer and Ricoeur, it is attributed to a system of meaning which operates in the text itself, which therefore exceeds and outlasts the original author and his original audience. For Derrida, this amounts to a retrenchment of semanticism which has the effect of allowing it to dig in even deeper. In either version, the task of thematic criticism is to finger this golden thread, to find the animating, unifying center.

Oppositions, rising crescendoes, climax and denouement, rhyme, imagery, tropes are, according to thematic criticism, but the various instrumentalities deployed in the service of meaning. Everything is governed by a wise architecture, a law of dialectics which resolves all the oppositions and restores equilibrium to the whole, which is "the phenomenological, hermeneutic, dialectical project of thematicism" *(Diss.* 281/249). And if it is conceded that one cannot succeed in this infinite task, that the text ultimately eludes the totalizing project, this is attributed by thematicism to its infinite depth, its richness, what Ricoeur calls the "surplus of meaning," not to the disseminative drift. As we pointed out in chapter 4, the hermeneutical concept of finitude is always located on the other end of a finite/infinite polarity, so that it becomes, in fact, not a confession of limits, that things are getting out of control, but a transcendental argument for an infinite which steers all things with a mysterious order. And it is this hermeneutic concept of finitude which Derrida wants to rewrite in a "textual" sense—that we are caught in a bind, in the weave of a knotted text with threads going everywhere. The disseminative denial of finitude—it rejects this metaphysical finitude—is the affirmation of a disseminative in-finity in the sense of an uncontrollable plurality of textual effects which can be inscribed in what Derrida calls the "transcendental space of inscription itself," of the blank, white *(blanc)* paper, which is *arché*-writing, the "differential-supplementary structure" *(Diss.* 285/253).

Hermeneutics (semanticism) assumes that an analogical unity rules over the polysemy, that difference is ultimately made safe by identity, that harmony rules over the strife. Thematicism is a violence exerted by philosophical criticism which, for metaphysical reasons, subordinates the structure of writing and textuality to the rule of meaning.

> It is certain that Mallarmé was fascinated by the possibilities inherent in the *word*, and Richard is right in emphasizing this, but these possibilities are not primarily nor exclusively those of a body proper, a carnal unit, "the living creature" that miraculously unites sense and the senses into one *vox*; it is a play of articulations splitting up that body or reinscribing it within sequences it can no longer control. *(Diss.* 286–87/255)

The signifier is not the embodiment of meaning, its outer surface and container, but the power which produces meaning as just one of its effects. Moreover, it is not one power but a complex interwoven matrix which runs off in a textual (not a deep metaphysical) in-finity.

Such an infinity means that the play of differences in a text runs out of control, into a maze of connections which cannot be disentangled except by a metaphysical violence which simply cuts off or excludes certain connections as irrelevant, exterior, in-significant, not contributing to the ruling meaning. Semanticism trims the edges of a text, giving it neat and clear borders, framing and enframing it, so that nothing is written in its margins. Such violence consists in making meaning privileged over every other effect of the differential system, by excluding phonic and graphic links as accidental. Once the privilege of meaning is put into question, the text is liberated, literature is freed from metaphysics, and we are able to enjoy the free play of endless textual effects made possible by *différance*, by the code of differential, repeatable signs. We have set repetition free. Then we are free to enjoy the endless generation of new words, the excitation of new linkages, the innovations which are possible if one situates oneself in the interstices, the fold, the hymen, *between* signifiers. As Derrida says in a recent interview, "I like repetition."[16]

The end run which hermeneutics attempts with its notion of "polysemy" must be checked by "dissemination" (*Diss.* 294/262). To the analogical unity of hermeneutics, Derrida opposes the disseminative abyss, writing *"en abyme"* (*Diss.* 297/265), which is the endless drift, the uncontrollable slippage, the labyrinthine connectedness and interwovenness of signifier with signifier. To the serene unity of the *semantike*, Derrida opposes the uncontrollable overflow of *semen*, sperm, lava, milk, spume, froth, seminal liquor (*Diss.* 298/266). To hermeneutic appropriation of the unity of meaning in the midst of polysemy, he opposes the dissemination of the seed, the loss of sperm, scattered emissions, onanism; to the hermeneutic deciphering of meaning, disseminative pleasure in the free play.

Dissemination is precisely productive repetition, a repetition which takes-again (*gjen-tagelse*) by taking differently, as opposed to re-productive, hermeneutic repetition which wants to escape the play by finding the high ground of the meaning which rules over any chain and keeps it in bounds.[17] Unlike the repetition which repeats backward, dissemination alters, modifies, transforms, links, transgresses, shifts—even as it understands that it is an operation which is always carried out on what is pre-given, a *repetendum*.

Deconstruction is something like Augustinian time: even if we know what it is, we cannot formulate it. For in our formulation—which thus must pose as siphoning out the thematic unity of Derrida—hermeneutics has been disjunctively opposed to dissemination, and hermeneutics has been shown to be an insupportable violence. But that makes dissemination the real truth and meaning of literature and the text (by a flawless disjunctive syllogism, the essence of decidability!). Dissemination is a field mined by the paradoxes of self-reference (it is either true or false, but, if it is true, it refutes itself). But I think that Derrida knows his way through the field, knows the pattern according to which the explosives are laid out, and knows how to step between them. He makes use of Nietzsche's woman-truth, the woman who is not fooled by herself, whose own truth is to know that there is no truth, not even the truth of the woman. Dissemination is not ultimate truth or meaning; on the contrary, "the quasi-'meaning' of dissemination is the impossible return to the rejoined, readjusted unity of meaning, the impeded march of any *reflection*" (*Diss.* 299/268). But it is no melancholy complaint about the *loss* of truth, about a *fall* from the higher world, but rather it *begins* by *affirming* "the always already divided generation of meaning. Dissemination—spills it in advance" (*Diss.* 299–

300/268). It claims to be neither the truth nor the loss of the truth, neither dogmatism nor scepticism. It claims that truth is a textual effect. As for itself, it remains but a textual practice which never sets itself up as true. Instead, it is expert in unseating those who lay claim to truth and the unity of meaning. It is a writing, a stylus, a stiletto, used to unseat metaphysical and apocalyptic horsemen. It does not claim to be true but is on the look-out for those who do.

But if dissemination has a quasi-meaning, does it then imply a quasi-hermeneutics, a postmetaphysical hermeneutics, a hermeneutics which has lost its innocence and no longer believes in the unity of meaning? That is the question of a radical hermeneutics. And it is obviously a question whose answer, and indeed whose proper posing, depends upon a careful investigation of Derrida's rereading of Heidegger. For the enormity of the Derridean disruption is visited upon us only when we realize that it not only pushes Husserl over the edge and disrupts his a priori grammar—we were ready for that; *Being and Time* had already instructed us about the liberation of language from logic and grammar—but also appears to sweep over Heidegger himself. For what is left of the Heideggerian project if "meaning" and "truth" are put into disseminative drift, if "Being" is an effect? After we are visited by the Derridean thunderstorm, what is left of the question of the "meaning" of "Being," of its "truth," of "*aletheia,*" or the "belonging together" of Being and man or of "man" or of all this talk about the primordial and originary? Do we find ourselves in the position of Constantin Constantius, who declared that repetition was too much for him and that he was not capable of it? Perhaps all this talk about liberating language from logic and grammar was just a lot of brave words, but when the shooting starts, we are nowhere to be found.

SIX

Hermes and the Dispatches from Being: Derrida on Heidegger

The challenge which Derrida issues to Heidegger could not be more fundamental. He puts into question the very terms in which Heidegger seeks to "overcome metaphysics." Heidegger challenges metaphysics about its failure to think the Being of beings, for stopping short with beings and not moving on to "Being" or to the "meaning" of Being or, later on, to the "truth" of Being, to *aletheia,* or later still to the *Ereignis* (the "event of appropriation") which sends both Being and beings into their own.[1] But Being, meaning, truth, and the proper are, for Derrida, so many produced, constituted effects, which it is a naiveté not to reduce. For Derrida, Heidegger has simply shifted the scene of hermeneutics from "meaning," in some sort of Husserlian or transcendental idealist sense, to "Being," resulting in what Derrida calls in *Spurs* "onto-hermeneutics," a hermeneutics of the meaning of Being rather than of meaning in the Husserlian sense. But this is still to remain on the level of effects of *différance* and to fail to make the grammatological reduction. If Heidegger criticized the idea of a transcendental-horizonal hermeneutics in *Being and Time,* this was only by way of a retrenchment which allowed hermeneutics to dig in all the more deeply and so survive the critique of subjectivity. The hermeneutics which tries to determine the "meaning of Being" by way of a projection of it in terms of its "upon which" is displaced by a less subjective but, on that account, more entrenched hermeneutics which receives messages sent by the gods, dispatches and letters *(envois, Schickungen)* addressed to mortals, disclosing the meaning of Being and delivered courtesy of Hermes in an onto-hermeneutical postal service.

Derrida's critique thus is aimed not only at putting a halt to the operations of a transcendental-horizonal hermeneutics but also at putting Hermes out of a job. Derrida undoes the notion of the "meaning" or "truth" of Being, of a primordial epoch which was granted a privileged experience of Being, of a postal service sending "dispatches" (communications) across the epochs, of a primordial sender *(Ereignis)* and a privileged recipient (man), of a special message which, after a period of oblivion, comes safely home again. Derrida's critique cuts right to the core: of Husserl and Heidegger, of early Heidegger and late, of horizonal hermeneutics and receipt of messages from Hermes, of truth as correspondence and truth as *aletheia,* of the transcendental subject and the privileges of man as the place needed by Being (the privileged recipient of Being's mail). In the thunderstorm of dissemination, the dispatches of Being are scattered to the four winds. Dissemination extends all the way to "Being," "meaning," "man," and "truth" and the concomitant privileging of nearness, unity, ownness, rootedness, origin, and primordiality which so punctuates Heidegger's text. For Derrida, Heidegger remains in complicity with the metaphysics of presence.

"Almost."[2] "We are not going to imprison all of Heidegger's texts in a closure that this text has delimited better than any other" *(Marg.* 147/123). Heidegger's text is not unambiguous; we do not have it under hermeneutic control. It is disrupted by another, profoundly provocative, profoundly deconstructive streak, a "great breakthrough" *(Marg.* 72/62) which works in constant tension with onto-hermeneutics, a radical questioning which has taken as its charge the delimitation of metaphysics as a whole, which is vigilant about the wiles of metaphysics, which exposes us to the abyss, the play, the flux. Again, Derrida is not out to lay low the work of Heidegger as the last metaphysician but to release its critical energies, to liberate it from itself, to set it free by writing with Heidegger against Heidegger.

Derrida owes his very project, the deconstruction of the metaphysics of presence, to Heidegger. The very idea of the delimitation of metaphysics, of a deconstruction of a logic and grammar which dominates everything, is not only Nietzschean but also Heideggerian. He does not write against Heidegger but in continuation and extension of Heidegger's work, radicalizing the critique of presence as it makes its way even into Heidegger himself, thereby keeping Heidegger *unterwegs,* en route, on the way beyond the metaphysical desire for presence, even if that means giving up nearness and *aletheia* as part of the trappings of the metaphysics of presence.

The truth of Being, the destiny of Being, the primordial beginning and the new beginning, *Gestell* and *Geviert,* are new and more subtly disguised ways, beyond an a priori grammar, to hold the play of signifiers in check. The Heideggerian project is one more profoundly subtle insinuation of metaphysics into the deconstructive project, one likely to deceive even the elect. And Derrida's plan is to liberate it from itself in order to set the deconstructive project free in all its disseminative, Dionysian energy.

I want now, in this chapter and the next, to set the text of Derrida over the text of Heidegger, letting each get entangled in the other—Heidegger in Derrida and Derrida in Heidegger—so that their texts interweave, each inter-twined with the other, each showing signs of the other's intervention. In this way I propose a rewriting of Heidegger from Derrida's standpoint, which results in a rewriting of Derrida from Heidegger's standpoint, a kind of double repetition, a productive double cross, a palimp-sestuous cross-semination which goes to the heart of what I mean by radical hermeneutics.

I will carry out this interweaving in a process which covers four points: (1) Derrida's critique of onto-hermeneutics; (2) Heidegger's eschatological hermeneutics; (3) Derrida's critique of eschatology as postal metaphysics; (4) a concluding "demythologizing" of Heidegger's eschatology. In the next chapter, I will continue this discussion with a presentation of the interwoven effect of Heidegger/Derrida, which I call "cold hermeneutics."

HEIDEGGER'S ONTO-HERMENEUTICS

Derrida's notion of *différance* has a profoundly Nietzschean sting to it. A good deal of the trouble Derrida makes for Heidegger comes from Nietzsche's critique of truth—as a set of fictions which life has devised for its own needs and self-enhancement. Thus, the notion of a semiotic effect, in the Saussurean sense, is fused by Derrida with Nietzsche's theory of fictions, so that whatever is privileged as "true" can be nothing more than a fiction produced by *différance*. And it is this semiotic Nietzsche which is visited upon Heidegger, whose critique of the metaphysical conception of truth as *adequatio* is carried out in the name of a deeper truth as *aletheia*. But clearly, on the Derridean-Nietzschean scheme, *adequatio* and *aletheia* share the same fate as constituted effects. And that spells sweet revenge (how unbecoming!) on Heidegger for his critique of Nietzsche as the last metaphysician, the one who announces that the proper name of Being is will-to-power. The laugh is on Heidegger who missed Zarathustra's joke. Nietzsche does not believe in anything, including the will to power. The will, too, is a fiction. Heidegger missed the point—or rather he got stung by it, nipped in an embarrassing place by Nietzsche's stylus.

The problem with Heidegger is that he does not pay enough attention to sex, and he keeps missing the sexual tunings of Nietzsche's truth (*Spurs* 109). That, of course, could never be said about Freud—but then Freud ends up in hermeneutics, too, not an onto-centric one, to be sure, but a phallo-centric hermeneutic. "Supposing truth to be a woman—what then?"[3] Well, so much the worse for the philosophers who, believing straightforwardly in truth, end up looking like maladroit courtesans (*Spurs* 55, 59), ineptly courting a woman with a laugh up her sleeve, breathing heavily with earnest hermeneutic aspirations for the deep truth.

Metaphysicians and hermeneuts lack style. They mount aggressive, virile assaults on the truth which succeed only in charging directly into an ambush. They never catch on to truth's playful, beguiling ways, to her alluring shadows and action at a distance. She leads them on by dangling before them truth itself—when it is all she can do to contain her laughter when the philosopher-knight charges. She has a secret, but it is not a hermeneutic secret.

> Because, indeed, if woman *is* truth, *she* at least knows that there is no truth, that truth has no place here and that no one has a place for truth. And she is woman precisely because she herself does not believe in truth itself, because she does not believe in what she is, in what she is believed to be, in what she thus is not. (*Spurs* 53)

The truth is that there is no truth, and she, being herself a creature of fiction, device, art, artifice, illusion, and ornamentation, cannot be fooled at her own game, fooled into believing that she herself has an essence and truth (*Spurs* 67). Thus, Derrida spins Nietzsche's patently sexist images around and draws from them a conclusion which would have astounded Nietzsche: the sexual difference is a fiction, an enforced, social violence, signifying nothing in the nature of things. This Dionysian woman is not even a feminist, for a feminist also wants to enforce the sexual difference, but in its inverted mode. Feminists, too, believe in truth—the truth of woman which they want to oppose to the truth of man. They, too, lack style (*Spurs* 65).

True style means to believe nothing, to be a sceptic (*Spurs* 57), to accustom oneself not to too few truths but to too many. Indeed, there is not even "style" but only many styles, each suited to the cause it must serve. We create as many truths as we require. Having style means to change with the changed, to invent what is required, to make nothing irreformable. It is to be liberated from the illusion of a single truth, a single meaning. It is to be liberated from both dogmatism and hermeneutics and to adopt a strategy of writing (*Spurs* 95), which means to write with the stylus, the stiletto which punctures the sails of metaphysics as it tries to keep a steady course over stormy seas.

But, just when we think this Derridean Nietzsche is going to win the day over Heidegger's last metaphysician, Derrida turns the tables. Neither text—Heidegger's or Nietzsche's—is unambiguous. We cannot get hermeneutic control over either. For Nietzsche suffers a relapse into metaphysics—just as we are given pause over a certain radical moment in Heidegger as well in which Heidegger, too, seems ready to make the move beyond truth.

There are at least three conceptions of women in Nietzsche's text (and he loves them all): (1) woman as falsehood and error, the opposite of masculine truth; (2) woman as Christian, as siren, luring man on from a distance with false hopes and cruel illusions of after-worldly truth.[4] Both of these conceptions are sexist, phallo-logo-centric, debased portraits of woman which enclose her within the economy of the man of truth, once as castrated, once as castrating. (3) Finally, there is the Dionysiac, the woman-truth who believes in nothing, who is the untamed power to produce whatever fiction-truths we need. It is only in this third conception that "woman is recognized and affirmed as an affirmative power, a dissimulatress, artist, a dionysiac" *(Spurs* 97; cf. 87–91). Here alone there is neither feminism nor antifeminism, neither woman castrating nor woman castrated, neither good nor evil, truth nor error, but only the endless free play of the teasing, dancing, artful weaver of fictions for every occasion—a figure like the signifier in the Husserl-readings which escapes across the borders of pure a priori grammar and which practices a productive repetition.

There is no hermeneutic resolution of this ambiguity, no way to dominate this text and get it under control. Even Nietzsche himself got a little lost *(Spurs* 101). Woman is an undecidable, a *pharmakon*, a remedy/poison, a supplement/ substitute, hymen, subject to "an undecidable oscillation" *(Spurs* 121) which we cannot arrest. But then that very plurality of styles is the point, the tip, the stylus tip, the Dionysian thrust of Derrida's and Nietzsche's text.

There is no truth of Nietzsche's text, no truth of man and woman, and hence no hermeneutics which plumbs the depths of truth. There are as many truths as one needs, too many truths, a surfeit *(Spurs* 103). There is no sexual difference, no psychoanalytic hermeneutic, no Being-historical hermeneutic, no hard and fast identities of any sort, no strictly differentiated and decidable essences, each keeping to their own proper boundaries. This woman spells the end of her-meneutics.

> The question of the woman suspends the decidable opposition of true and non-true and inaugurates the epochal regime of quotation marks which is to be enforced for every concept belonging to the system of philosophical decidability. The her-meneutic project which postulates a true sense of the text is disqualified under this regime. Reading is freedom from the horizon of the meaning or truth of being. . . . *(Spurs* 107)

But it is in virtue of this same law of oscillating undecidability that we cannot consider the books closed on Heidegger's text. Heidegger is indeed a deep hermeneut, not of a Freudian (or Gadamerian[5]) sort but of a Being-historical type. He is a reader of what is coming to pass *(west)* in the great metaphysical systems; he can hear the Word which is being uttered across the epochs. Heidegger is a hermeneut raised to the second power, the power of Being's own truth. *Almost:* "Heidegger's reading subsists, throughout the near totality of its trajectory, in the hermeneutic space of the question of the truth (of being)" *(Spurs* 115). In the near totality, almost entirely *(presque totalité),* but not quite. Heidegger's text, no less than Nietzsche's, does not slip quietly into place. The question is not settled just because he does not explicitly touch upon the sexual question. Heidegger may be making his way by other means. For there is something in Heidegger's text to give us pause, a bursting open which displaces Being and truth.

> Each time that Heidegger refers the question of being to the question of the
> property *(propre)*, of propriate, of propriation *(eigen, eignen, ereignen, Ereignis*
> especially) this dehiscence bursts forth anew. . . . The order of Heidegger's thought
> is, however, regularly disoriented by an oblique movement which inscribes truth in
> the process of propriation. *(Spurs* 117)

There is thus a certain movement *beyond* Being and truth—a displacing of onto-
centric, aletheological questioning—a movement beyond truth, beyond Being's
truth and truth's Being. Toward *Ereignis*. Still, Derrida says, that is nothing
new; it is already in *Being and Time*.

We are edging close to the point of contact of Derrida and Heidegger, that
point—already in *Being and Time*—where even Being and truth are put into
question in such a way as to set off in their limits over and against something
else, something "beyond" Being or the truth of Being. But then Derrida skews
his progress. Misled by his preoccupation with delimiting the proper, Derrida
points to the analysis of *Eigentlichkeit* in *Being and Time* as the antecedent to
this discussion—and not, as I pointed out in chapter 3, to the question of
"meaning" of Being and of the two-fold projection: of the being in its Being and
of Being in terms of its meaning. For, as we have seen, "meaning" in *Being and
Time* is to be understood not in a traditional sense, as either *Sinn* or *Bedeutung*,
but uniquely as *woraufhin*, as some sort of organizing point of reference *of* what
metaphysics calls meaning, so that the "hermeneutics" of *Being and Time* is
already on the way beyond what metaphysics calls Being, meaning, and truth.
On that reading, even the notion of the "proper" is delimited by Heidegger.
Still, Derrida is getting warm: "Although this process is as if magnetized by a
valuation or an ineradicable preference for the proper-ty *(propre)*, it all the
more surely leads to this proper-ty's abyssal structure" *(Spurs* 117). Although
Heidegger is always talking about Being and *Ereignis*, he invariably ends up in
a movement beyond Being, ground, presence, and truth, landing in an abyss
(Ab-grund) of dis-propriation *(Ent-eignis)*.

> Truth, unveiling, illumination are no longer decided in the appropriation of the
> truth of Being, but are cast into its bottomless abyss as non-truth, veiling, dis-
> simulation. The history of Being becomes a history in which no being, nothing,
> happens except *Ereignis'* unfathomable process. The property of the abyss *[das
> Eigentum des Ab-grundes]* is necessarily the abyss of proper-ty, the violence of an
> event which befalls without Being. *(Spurs* 119)

By making the move beyond Being, and hence beyond the whole hermeneutic
project of determining the *meaning* of Being or, later on, of its *truth*, Heidegger
appears to awaken to the Dionysian dissimulatress, to the play of truth and
untruth, to fiction making, to the Dionysiac truth. Well then perhaps Heidegger understands women after all. He sees the *Ent-eignis* in *Ereignis*, the
dissimulation in all unveiling, what Derrida calls "le coup de don," striking by

means of the gift, taking away by means of giving—which is, Derrida says, "the essential predicate of the woman" (*Spurs* 121).

> We are led to ask *if* truth's abyss as non-truth, propriation as appropriation/a-propriation, the declaration become parodying dissimulation, *if* this is what Nietzsche is calling the style's form and the nowhere of woman [my emphasis]. (*Spurs* 121)

We are then quite rightly referred by Derrida to "Time and Being," in which Heidegger develops the gift (*Gabe*) and the giving of the "it gives" (*es gibt*) which, because it gives time and Being, eludes the horizon of each and so of any possible onto-hermeneutics or onto-phenomenology.

And *if* that is true, then Heidegger's critique of Nietzsche is put in question, not by Derrida but by Heidegger himself. If Heidegger also knows that every truth is always already undone by untruth, as he seems to, then he knows, although perhaps without realizing it, that willing for Nietzsche is a fiction, that Nietzsche both believes it—uses this metaphysical fiction—and does not believe it—regards it as nothing more than fiction.

Heidegger, who appeared at first to be one more case of an unseated philosopher/hermeneut, now appears upon closer examination to know about the infiltration of the proper by the improper, of truth by the untruth. He knows the abyss in the essence of truth. He knows that the proper-ty of the abyss passes over into the abyss of proper-ty. So then Heidegger is not unseated after all, not *if* Heidegger's abyss of truth is what Derrida calls the "styles of Nietzsche."

Now that is a big "if," and I shall try to determine its cash value below. What is the relationship between Heidegger's *Abgrund* and Derrida's *abime*? Between Heidegger's *Un-Wesen der Wahrheit* (the un-essence of truth), *Ent-eignis*, and this Derridean-Dionysian dissimulatress? Is the *lethe* in *a-letheia* the "same" as the play of signifiers in Derrida/Nietzsche? Is the movement beyond Being to *Ereignis* the "same" as the grammatological reduction which makes Being an effect of *différance*? Are the "withdrawal" of Being and the slipping away of the thing itself (VPh 117/SP 104) the "same" (but not "identical")?

To answer these questions we must further pursue the issue which Derrida raises here: Is there a break with onto-hermeneutics in Heidegger which displaces the meaning and truth of Being and puts onto-hermeneutics into question? Does Heidegger do business with Hermes (another wiley sort)? Does he get messages from the gods, from the destiny of Being?

The best way to get at that in my view is to turn to the Anaximander fragment—about which Derrida has a few things to say (*Marg.* 24–29/23–27)—where this deep hermeneutics seems to be in full swing. If Nietzsche is the last figure in the history of Being, an *eschaton* in which the very essence of technology itself is revealed, Anaximander is on the other end of the line, as the *terminus a quo*, the beginning of this series of dispatches first issued from Miletus and whose signals we are still picking up. It is time to take a close look at Heidegger's postal, epistolary, eschatological hermeneutics.

THE ESCHATOLOGICAL CIRCLE

The postal principle is the principle of message bearing and hence the principle of all hermeneutics. Hermes, as the message bearer from the gods, is the first of all postmen, and it is to Hermes that the later Heidegger attaches the only possible sense that hermeneutics can have. "Only a god can save us now," he said, that is, only a dispatch carried by Hermes. Now it is just such an epistolary service that Derrida wants to show is always already confounded and thrown into disarray: letters are lost, messages garbled, and neither the proper senders nor the proper addressee can be identified. If the history of the West is the collected and collective (*Ge-*) history of Being's sendings (*Schickungen, Geschicke,* from the verb *schicken,* to send or mail), the confounding of the postal principle is likewise a confounding of Being's own delivery service.

According to Heidegger's epistolary principle, Being sent itself in a primordial way at the beginning, in a sudden flash which lit up the Greek countryside and just as quickly passed away, leaving behind only traces of itself in a series of later dispatches. These traces have grown so faint that we are now at the end, at the *eschaton,* in the most extreme oblivion of the original event, awaiting a new sending, which repeats the first and inaugurates a new and revitalized postal system. Heidegger's postal principle is eschatological: an original message is driven into the extremities of oblivion through a series of gradual erasures and ever fainter appearances,[6] which, by a logic of reversal, occasion a new dispatch. Such an eschatology—the way the beginning overtakes and outstrips the end—is essentially hermeneutical, for it demands endowments to decipher the saving message in the later dispatches. It demands the ability to read traces and retrace the long forgotten origin (*Marg.* 25-27/24–25), to understand how the oldest of the old communicates what is coming so that we can see the end as the transition to a new beginning.

That is just what Heidegger is up to in his interpretation of Anaximander. Getting in touch with Anaximander is *the* long-distance philosophical call par excellence, for what Anaximander says is the very earliest recorded message we have from the Greek thinkers, and we are the very last to hear it. But why bother about such an *old* message? Is it just a hermeneutic challenge to see if we can actually decipher a message that old? That would reduce the call to a kind of technological-hermeneutical feat, without substance or weight (GA 5 325/EGT 6), without a bearing on the *Sache.* It would reduce it to an exercise in philological-psychological technique, to see if we could get inside the head of a man named Anaximander who lived long ago at this address in Miletus (GA 5 328/EGT 18).

The authority (GA 5 325/EGT 16) of this message, in Heidegger's view, has nothing to do with its age or the idiosyncrasies of its author. The interest we have in stringing a line of communication between Anaximander and us should not center on its length, on mere chronological-historical distance. Rather, it arises because the early *(die Frühe)* has a claim on the later, especially the last, so that it is not merely a saying *(Spruch)* but a claim *(Anspruch)*. This is not just any call; it is a priority call with the right to interrupt the work-a-day conversations we are accustomed to have. And so it is not that the call is long-distance that matters but that there is a voice of authority on the other end. In fact, for one so far away, the voice is surprisingly near *(Nähe)*, speaking to us now, about something which is coming ("in das Kommende hinausspricht"), perhaps any day now. (We know neither the day nor the hour.)

Which means it may not come at all. And *that* is why Anaximander is calling: to serve up a warning/reminder, to put us on watch for something which needs hearing and heeding. He wants to set us to thinking, to recall to mind *(an-denken)* something which we tend to forget. We have preserved but one saying of Anaximander, but it contains a double message. For it tells us not only how it was in the beginning—it is a long-distance call—but also what is coming, maybe any day. And the power of this saying, the authority of this voice, lies in the fact that these are the same thing. The same *(dasselbe)* but not identical. Anaximander's call stretches from one end to the other, so that it looks like a standard tele-communication. But the end in question is not a *telos* but an *eschaton*. Not a linear *telos* but a more ambiguous, playful, circular *eschaton*.

The end in question is not a tele-linear goal and consummation in which the accumulated potencies of the Western tradition reach their fulfillment—quite the opposite. It is the emptying (not the filling), the spending and exhausting of a great beginning. The *eschaton* means we have reached the point where potency of the tradition has been spent, and the question is whether we will persist indefinitely in this dead end or whether the *eschaton* will turn itself inside out and become the point of departure for a new beginning, an opening on to what-is-coming. And that is the point of Anaximander's call, the force of his claim *(An-spruch)* on us: to remind *(an-denken)* us of this decision, to mark the decisiveness of the point we have reached.

Eschato-logy is not teleo-logy. Teleology is metaphysics, a rule-governed process in which the seeds of success are sown from the very beginning, in which the *rationes seminales* are planted at the start. Teleology insulates us from the contingencies of history, the dead ends and detours, just as in Constantin's complaint that Hegel's treatment of time was a fraud, that Hegel was a dealer in counterfeit temporal coin. In teleology the beginning is small, progress is steady, and the end is a great fulfillment and parousia, an *Aufhebung*.

But eschatology is a play. In eschatology, the beginning is great, a tremendous burst of lightning, a flash illuminating the whole countryside. But it vanishes as quickly as lightning, and then its memory is dimmed and erased, until finally, through a series of transformations which no one could have predicted, there is only night, only *Abend-land*. Then, in that dark night, there lies the possibility of another beginning, another sudden turn in which the lightning flashes again.

> Do we stand in the eve *[Vorabend]* of the most monstrous transformation of the whole earth and that era in which it is suspended? Do we stand on the eve of a night which heralds another dawn *[Frühe]*? . . . Is the land of the evening *[Abend-Land]* only now emerging? Will this land of evening overwhelm Occident and Orient alike, transcending whatever is merely European to become the location of a new but primordially fated history? . . . *Are* we the latecomers *[Spätlingers]* we are? But are we also at the same time precursors of the dawn of an altogether different age, which has already left our historiological representation of history behind? (GA 5 325–6/EGT 17)

It is not a question of reckoning what is coming ("rechnen das Kommende") through scientific historical research, through a calculus of possibilities carefully drawn from the past. That historical calculus systematically destroys our true relation to the future *(Zukunft)*, to what is arriving *(An-kunft)*, maybe any day. It is systematically blind to the coming dispatch, to the genuine message which is being sent across the epochs, systematically destructive of what is arriving in the mail ("die Ankunft des Geschickes," GA 5 326/EGT 17).

There is thus an essential difference between the tele-communications of teleology and hearing the call of the beginning in eschatology. The present epoch is an age of sophisticated historical research, of the most advanced historical consciousness, which is likewise the age of the most advanced and sophisticated system of nationwide and international communications. We have at our disposal the most advanced techniques for getting in touch with every-thing past and present. But it is in just such an age—which Heidegger calls an epoch of "historicism," for we are the most sophisticated historical researchers yet, the best able to reconstruct the past—that we have become deaf and blind to the *message* which is sent across the epochs, to the genuine dispatch of Being: "The technical organization of communications throughout the world by radio and by a press already limping after it is the genuine form of historicism's dominion" (GA 5 326/EGT 17).

The press is slower to pass the word along than the radio. The radio limps after the television that via satellite puts us on the spot, makes us eyewitnesses of events transpiring on the other side of the globe. The eye of the video is slowly becoming all-seeing in fulfillment of the synopticonism described by Foucault. It is a question of how quickly and how efficiently end can be joined to end, *telos* to *telos*, and that is what has doomed the newspaper and appears now to doom the book. Teleo-logy is the science of getting from end to end with maximal efficiency. In tele-communications, teleology reaches its peak but the lines of eschatology go dead. The more advanced the technology of tele-communications grows, the more deaf we become to the dispatch of Being. The clarity of the message that is sent in eschatology is in inverse proportion to the technical organization of tele-communications. The noise of technological communication systems drowns out the word which Being sends.

In eschatology the earliest is not a seed which slowly ripens into the last but a flash which, having been all but extinguished by the last, is capable of flashing again and turning darkness into light, the evening into a new dawn. In teleology the last always comes after the first, after a long period of maturation; but in eschatology the first can overtake *(überholen)* the last, and with a suddenness that could not be anticipated. But what if that which is early overtakes everything late; if the very earliest thoroughly overtakes and outstrips the very latest (GA 5 327/EGT 18)? Then we would be in an eschatological mode, able to hear something new, the stirrings of a new beginning. And that is the most decisive difference of all between eschatology and teleology. Teleology reaches fulfillment, satisfaction, peace, rest, when it reaches the *telos*. But, in eschatology, the *eschaton* is the transition to a new beginning, a new flash of lightning and the commencement of a new postal service. Whence Heidegger answers his own question: "What once occurred in the dawn of our destiny would then come, as what once occurred, at the last *(eschaton)*, that is, at the departure of the long-hidden destiny of Being" (GA 5 327/EGT 18).

The beginning would come again at the end, would overtake the end. And that is what we mean by eschatology: when we are driven into the end in such a way that the beginning can overtake it, so that the end turns itself around, reverses itself, and becomes a commencement. Valedictory and commencement, taking leave and beginning anew, all in one. Then the whole accumulated wealth of the history of Being is collected together in one glimmering moment of reversal. The *eschaton* of itself is but an end, a spinning out of possibilities, the danger of a dead end. But an eschato-*logy* means that the beginning overtakes the end, that everything harbored and hidden in the interval between the beginning and the end is gathered together and pushes the end beyond itself, outdistances and outstrips it *(überholt)* and precipitates a new beginning. This gathering-together *(logos, legein)* of the whole history of Being in the end *(eschaton)* is the eschatology of Being.

> The Being of beings is gathered together *[legesthai, logos]* in the ultimacy of its destiny. The essence of Being hitherto disappears, its truth still veiled. The history of Being is gathered in this departure. The gathering in this departure, as the gathering *[logos]* at the outermost point *[eschaton]* of its essence hitherto, is the eschatology of Being. As something fateful *[geschickliches]* Being is inherently eschatological. (GA 5 327/EGT 18)

In teleology there is a linear development from the seed to the mature form. In eschatology there is a circular reversal in which the beginning overtakes the end and precipitates a reversal. Eschatological thinking, then, is precisely the capacity to see in what is coming the coming again of the early. When the early overtakes *(über-holen)* the late, the late repeats and retrieves *(wieder-holen)* the early. "If we think in terms of the eschatology of Being, then we must someday await what once belonged to the early in what is one day coming. Today we must learn to ponder the former dawn on its own terms" (GA 5 327/EGT 18).

The overtaking *(über-holen)* is retaking, taking-again *(wieder-holen, gjen-tagelse)*. The circularity of Heideggerian repetition reappears, transferred now from the circular Being of care and temporality (and the hermeneutic circle which that implies) to the circular Being of the history of the West, of the *Seinsgeschick*, to the circular sending of Being, the circulation of the dispatches of Being in an eschatological circle. Heidegger does not abandon the circle; he reinscribes it in the history of Being. The circle is the code of repetition, the code in which the messages of Being are sent. It is by learning that Being writes in a circle that we can decipher its messages. For then we will see that what comes last, the very last, the most extreme last, is on the verge of coming back to the first, not in a literal reenactment—that would be foolish—but in some form of replay whose form we cannot foresee.

In eschatology the beginning overtakes the end and puts an end to the end; in teleology, the end fulfills the beginning and puts an end to the beginning. In eschatology the beginning outstrips the end so that the end is driven beyond itself. The most extreme end is consequently the point of transition to a beginning. And it is in virtue of this eschatological circularity that the most extreme end, as the greatest danger, is likewise the place of salvation. The very circularity of eschatology explains Heidegger's claim that the saving and the danger converge. We are saved by the circle. And that indeed is the note on which the essay on Anaximander conclude
comes when and only when danger *is*. Dang‹
its farthest extreme *[Letzte]*, and when th‹
itself reverses itself" (GA 5 373/EGT 58).

The *legein* in eschato-logy, the gathering
reversal, a movement in which the beginnin‹
then turns itself around into a new beginni‹
which is a primordial *logos* and not a met‹
onto-logic—is simultaneously a salvation hi‹
and night is turned into day, a way we can b‹
which reverses itself, by the grace of esch‹
repetition, which is to be distinguished fron

And *that* explains the claim that Anaximar
call meant to save us from the *eschaton*, to a‹

terminal illness. Anaximander has an urgent message to deliver, and he has placed an emergency call to us, though it comes in the form of a one-line telegram, an *envoi* in which the rest of the page has been ripped away, perhaps lost in a fire. We have not the whole message but a fragment. But we can tell from what we do have, if we decipher those words carefully with a care for Being's sending, that the message is important, that there is an alternative to the current impasse, a "rescue" from the "danger." And those are Heidegger's words. One needs the hermeneutic code, the code of the circle—which teaches us to decipher by reading backward *(andenken)*, by reading in the light of the rule of repetition, according to which all forward movement is likewise a movement in reverse—in order to decipher this message of salvation.[7]

BEYOND THE POSTAL PRINCIPLE

Constantin's brow would wrinkle in suspicion at this eschatology. He would suspect the recollective, backward movement in all this talk about what is coming, the nostalgia for the old days in the talk of the new dawn. He would suspect that it all begins with the loss, that repetition is being done in by one who speaks in its defense. It is as if Abraham knew that there was some law in virtue of which the Lord was not going to make him go through with it, or Job knew that he would be restored and that the Lord was not going to make him last this thing out. That would make it all too easy instead of restoring the difficulty. And that would destroy the repetition, the trembling, the *ébranler.*

For Derrida, too, all this eschatology is a still more subtle variation on teleology, a meta-teleo-logical meta-physics, an extraordinarily alluring way around *physis* and the flux. The whole thing has designs on bringing the flux under the rule of law, not a hard teleo-logical law but the more gentle and elusive law of the circle, which is, after all, the most reassuring image which metaphysics has yet devised, the most Platonic of all images, which throws all forward motion into reverse. It is a devious gesture by which we allow things to rush forward as furiously as possible while all the time we are reeling them back. There is no better way to arrest the play, no better way to reassure ourselves in the face of the flux, than to say that the ever-deepening darkness is the preparation for a coming dawn. The *eschaton* repeats the *arche*, retrieves the possible, saves us all just at that moment when all is dark, indeed darkest. Just when the sun has sunk the deepest we turn around to see the traces of the new dawn. There is a thought to still one's midnight fears. For all its overcoming of subjectivism, onto-centrism is no less a form of centrism, no less reassuring. The sun also rises in helio-centrism. Platonism has always been helio-tropic.

Eschatology means one has one's ear to the *logos* which holds sway over the *eschaton.* But the *logos* which gathers together is not as far removed from the metaphysics of unity and totalization, from the *logos* of onto-logic and theo-logic, as Heidegger likes to think. Everything turns on what Derrida calls "the unity of a destination, or rather of a 'destinality,' of being,"[8] an eschatological unity in which the selfsame sends itself out in a pristine form and then keeps sending itself in more or less erased forms, leaving behind only traces of itself. Eschatology is a heightened, sublated form of metaphysics, metaphysics put in higher relief (relève, aufgehoben); it is not an overcoming of metaphysics but a higher metaphysics, not a delimitation of humanism but a higher humanism (Marg. 148/124). For after all, where is one standing oneself when one talks about the end of metaphysics, of onto-theo-logic, of philosophy? Where does one get off talking like that? Literally, where did one get off, get out of the flux, in order to survey it in one totalizing sweep? How does one get outside metaphysics in order to enclose it, draw a circle around it, effect its closure?

Where does this eschatological, apocalyptic tone which thought has recently adopted get its rights—all this talk about the end of this and the end of that? There is just too much "apocalyptic eloquence" these days, too many hermeneuts who think they see the end of the world at hand.

> I tell you this in truth; this is not only the end of this here but also and first of that there, the end of history, the end of the class struggle, the end of philosophy, the death of God, the end of religions, the end of Christianity and morals (that was the most serious naiveté), the end of the subject, the end of man, the end of the West, the end of Oedipus, the end of the earth, Apocalypse Now, . . . and also the end of literature, the end of painting, art as a thing of the past, the end of psychoanalysis, the end of the university, the end of phallocentrism and phallogocentrism, and I don't know what else. (Fins 464/Apoc 80)

Now apart from the interesting self-criticism here (Derrida himself had his apocalyptic moments; he tried to outdo Heidegger with his talk of the end of man and logo-centrism), Heidegger is very clearly to be numbered among these apocalyptic hermeneuts.

> And if Heidegger thinks the Überwindung of metaphysics or of ontotheology, like that of eschatology which is inseparable from it, he does so in the name of another eschatology. Several times he says of thought, here distinct from philosophy, that it is essentially eschatological. That is his word. (Fins 465/Apoc 81)

Apocalyptic utterances demand insight into the deep essence of what is going on, a power of deciphering which sweeps from end to end (where is it standing when it makes this sweep?), which has a hold on the Wesen in the verbal sense, of what has all along been coming to presence and now is coming to an end. It has the wherewithal to see that a primordial first possibility is spent, has exhausted itself, has made all of its moves and now has nowhere to go, which is not to say that it will not persist indefinitely. Apocalyptics presupposes hermeneutics, deep hermeneutics, with a hot line to the gods.

There is no telling, however, where apocalypticism begins and ends itself. Sometimes apocalyptics are seers and *Schwärmerei* who have seen the light; sometimes they are rationalists, *Aufklärers*, when the light they have seen is the light of reason. And sometimes, as with Heidegger, they are thinkers who think the dispatches sent by Being in the letters of the great metaphysicians. Indeed, even telling the truth on apocalypticism, proclaiming the end of apocalypticism, is apocalyptic, declamatory. And, to complicate it even further, apocalypticism does not have a neat and decidable essence. For sometimes apocalypticism does some good, when it defies the ruling postmaster who prescribes just what messages can and cannot be sent. Then we are glad to have the mad voice of disruption of the apocalyptic, sending out over public lines what the postmaster wants to censor.

Apocalyptics think they have a message to get across which will save us, a message with a determinate sender and destination. And Derrida wants to get beyond the postal principle, not by a leap on his part *over* it but by pointing out how it itself keeps coming undone. (He does not de-construct anything. The postal principle deconstructs itself, and his job is to keep pointing this out— rather the way Hegel took "speculative" movement to be a movement in the things themselves, which the phenomenologist simply witnesses.) The postal principle uses a teleo-logical system: *logoi* (messages) are sent from *telos* to *telos*, from sender *(destinateur)* to addressee *(destinaire)*, in a system of sending and destination *(Geschick)*. But, given the arguments which Derrida has made against "effective communication" in the Husserl and Austin readings, given what he has to say about *différance* and the intervention of the chain of repeatable and alterable signifiers, given what he has to say about dissemination, the postal principle is a dream.

Even the *Apocalypse* itself, the one by John, shows that. Elohim gives a message to Jesus, which Jesus is to pass on to John. But Jesus uses an angel— *angelus*, messenger—to carry his message, the result of which is a confusion of speakers and messages in a very complicated dispatch. As on the cover of *La Carte postale*, somebody is always whispering in the ear of someone else who is doing the speaking, so that we do not know whose message we are hearing. The really apocalyptic thing about the *Apocalypse* is the way it shows the confusion of tongues and garbling of messages in any communication *(Fins 470–71/87)*. The principle of destination is confounded by errancy, and the postal principle becomes one of *destinerrance*, messages running wild *(Fins 474/Apoc. 91)*.

Apocalyptics practice a "conductive violence," which always wants to save us, to lead us somewhere—out of the dark into the light, out of oblivion into memorialization, out of the *Gestell* into the *Geviert*. Come, lord Jesus. Come, beyond Being, into *Ereignis*. But, if this "conductive violence" can be undone, then the "come" is released, transformed into a free play of letters, a drift without determinable destination or fixed source, a repetition which always already repeats, without being stretched out between the *teloi* of a first time and last time.

> Perhaps you will be tempted to call this the disaster, the catastrophe, the apocalypse. Now here, precisely, is announced—as promise or threat—an apocalypse without apocalypse, an apocalypse without vision, without truth, without revelation, of dispatches [*envois*] (for the "come" is plural in itself, in oneself), of addresses without message and without destination, without sender or decidable addressee, without last judgment, without any other eschatology than the tone of the "Come" itself, its very difference, an apocalypse beyond good and evil. "Come" does not announce this or that apocalypse: already it resounds with a certain tone; it is in itself the apocalypse of the apocalypse. "Come" is apocalyptic. *(Fins* 477/Apoc 94)

But, if we put this to Heidegger, if we release the *Ereignis* from the work it does of delivering the one selfsame message, the result is a free flying up of the *Geschicke*, a pure playing of the *Ereignis* for which Heidegger was not prepared. Then the *legein* does not have to labor to gather up the message across the ages and then to deliver it in an *Austrag* (ID 132-33/65), a bringing to birth, to term, to final issue, a final deliverance in which the message reaches the *eschaton* and turns itself inside out, in a momentous reversal and parturition which starts a new postal service going.

> Our apocalypse now: that there is no longer any place for the apocalypse as the collection of evil and good in a *legein* of *aletheia*, nor in a *Geschick* of the dispatch [*envoi*] of the *Schicken* in a co-destination that would assure the "come" of the power to give rise to an event in the certainty of a determination. *(Fins* 477–78/Apoc. 94–95)

Instead of just putting up with the difference, Heidegger wants his dif-ference to give birth, to be an *Aus-trag*, a delivery service in which a new life is born. For Derrida, the only apocalypse is an "apocalypse without apocalypse."

Postal systems come in different forms. In Husserl, an ideal and repeatable message, fully constituted in its ideality, is sent out across the epochs, borne by different translations, copied by different copyists, xeroxed, collated, and distributed and then entrusted to professionally trained couriers. The letter inscribed in the founding act is passed on and perfected as it is transmitted in carefully, univocally packaged form. But receiving this letter demands a response, the responsibility of sending a letter-in-return *(renvois)*, a return mail, by means of which we keep in touch with the protoauthor of the letter. In Gadamer, the concern is with the dynamics of transmission and communication: it is always the same letter, the selfsame *Sache* or contents of the mail, which keeps getting translated anew and cast in new language so that we know how the letter applies to us. Thus, if Husserl runs an archeo-teleological post office,

Gadamer deploys a practico-teleological postal system: we are awaiting instructions in the mail, guidance from the voice on the other end of the line about what to do.

But, in Heidegger, an eschato-logical postal principle is at work: an original letter is sent out, filled with words of primordial power, but it is immediately lost. Only traces of it remain, torn-up fragments, until finally, just when we think it has fallen altogether into oblivion, we awaken *to* the postal principle, to the eschatological code which tells us about the way that metaphysics writes in reverse, circling back upon itself. Then the original dispatch is recovered, retrieved, repeated. We are ready for the new dawn, the second coming, the new beginning, the saving power. Our return mail has reached its destination even as the original message has reached us.

For Heidegger, we stand at the end of a series of distorted and dangerous messages of presence—from *ousia* to *Gestell*—which in turn poses the task of "thinking," of thinking-back *(An-denken)*. This requires a deep hermeneutics which knows how to read backward, in reverse, and hence to read the saving message in the words and works of technology, thereby turning it into a saving message. Thinking knows how to decipher; it knows that the saving is the danger spelled backward. For Derrida, that knowledge does not make thinking any less metaphysical, not for all its apocalyptic, eschato-logical form.

Derrida poses the objection to himself that this reading of Heidegger has already been displaced by Heidegger. Does not the postal principle invoke the role of a form of technology, a communications technology, which Heidegger has delimited in advance? Do we not try to think the *Seinsgeschick* in terms of *Technik*, one of the forms it takes? Yet it is not Derrida but Heidegger who deploys the postal discourse, who speaks in terms of *schicken*, *Schickung*, and *Prägung*. And this is not to be understood as a "metaphor," except in the "catastrophic" sense of metaphor which Derrida sees in Heidegger, that is, in which the role of tenor and vehicle are reversed. (If Heidegger says that language is the house of being, that means that house is to be thought in terms of Being, not Being in terms of dwelling in a house.[9]) Thus, if *Ereignis* is a postal system, that does not mean that we are to think the *Seinsgeschick* in terms of letter sending but letter sending in terms of the *Geschick*. This means that, for Derrida, *Ereignis* occupies a place in Heidegger which is occupied in Derrida's own work by writing in the sense of arché-writing, which is the matrix within which all transfers, metaphors, correspondences, and communications take place. And his point is that this central processing unit has been jammed, scrambled, decentered, thrown into confusion, in a maze of crossed wires.

> If the postal (technology, position, "metaphysics") is announced in the "first" dispatch, then there is no longer "metaphysics", etc. (this I will attempt to say one more time and differently), nor even the "dispatch," but only *dispatches* without destination. For to order the different epochs, stations, determinations, in

brief, the whole history of Being, to a destination of Being, this is perhaps the most unheard of postal snares. There is not even post or dispatch, there are only posts and dispatches. (CP 73–74)

Even to think the "history of metaphysics" as a "destiny of Being" (*Seinsgeschick*), to enclose it thus within the unified and undivided essence of "metaphysics," is to remain within the project of metaphysics and to arrest the play, to tame the flux. It is to organize it into a history and to center that history on a destiny—when all there is (*il y a*) is the plurality and plurivocity of dispatches flying in every different direction. [10]

In such a history, it is the dispatch of the *Gestell* which is written all over everything. The postcard of the day has a picture of a loathsome smokestack belching into the sky. But we hermeneuts who know the code, who know how to read backward, are able to find in it another possiblity—like those trick cards which display different scenes when held at different angles. The *Gestell* would be transformed into *Geviert*, "the most beautiful postcard which Martin has sent us from Freiburg" (CP 74). That would bring the epoch of postal technology to an end. That would represent the end of the post, the end of the course, the end of all couriers (CP 37). Everything would flip into a new beginning. But, for Derrida, that is the dream of presence: eschatology now.

For Derrida, there is no history of Being, no "metaphysics" (as a unified essence), no guiding logic of reversal—only the free play of differences. "There is" only différance, postal agency, relays, delays, lost letters. There are only letters going back by return mail to letters that have themselves gone back by return mail in an endless, hopelessly entangled maze: no letter reaches its destination. One cannot even write the history of these dispatches because history, tradition, and transmission are all constituted effects of the postal play. The desire for a history is eschatological, metaphysical, apocalyptic.

And so we come back to the question of the emancipation of the signifier, the reduction of the rule of *logos* over the play of signs, whether this be the *logos* of a priori grammar or the *logos* of eschato-logy which gathers up the play in a "history" or "destiny" of Being, fencing it in, in a great eschatological roundup. Derrida's grammatological reduction is in place wherever the attempt is made to establish rule over the drift, to bring the drift under the control of a ruling paradigm, even in the name of "saving" us.

Then what is left? Are we simply cut loose into chaos and confusion? On the contrary, in keeping with this work of emancipation in which Derrida is involved, this postal reduction releases the *free* circulation of letters, the public reading of messages on postcards instead of messages secreted away in envelopes and sealed in wax. Getting over the postal principle means that we stop waiting for the mail as if it contained a private message coming special delivery. The postal reduction releases the free circulation of signs, the free repetition, which does not have to answer to some metaphysical, or meta-metaphysical principle and arché. And that will make for free literature, free writing, free thought, free science, freedom for whatever you need.

Just after the text cited above, Derrida adds a parenthetical remark: "And this movement (which seems to me at once very far and very close to Heidegger)" (CP 74). Here is the ever-recurrent "almost" which Derrida never fails to insert into his texts on Heidegger. Heidegger subjugates the play of signifiers to the rule of the *Seinsgeschick* and remains in complicity with metaphysics: almost. Heidegger misses the Dionysiac woman: almost. Heidegger's thought moves in the near totality of its trajectory within hermeneutics. Almost.

Is there a Heidegger beyond eschatology, a post-eschatological Heidegger? A post-postal Heidegger? A Heidegger who does not make eschatological deliverances, who does not expect an eschatological delivery, who does not run a Being-historical delivery service? "Deconstruction" does not mean destructive criticism but the releasing of another reading.

> In recalling the difference between Being and beings (the ontological difference) as the difference between presence and the present, Heidegger advances a proposition, a body of propositions, that we are not going to use as a subject for criticism. This would be foolishly precipitate; rather, what we shall try to do is to return to this proposition its power to provoke. (*Marg.* 24/23)

For does not Heidegger write:

> Das Ereignis ereignet (SD 24/TB 24). Es spielet, weil es spielet (SG 188).

And here we catch sight of another Heidegger, a more austere, more radical Heidegger beyond eschatology and beyond the postal principle. Is this Heidegger beyond hermeneutics? Or is this indeed the long-promised "radical hermeneutics"?

HEIDEGGER DEMYTHOLOGIZED

I have been insisting that the matter of concern in Heidegger, the *Sache*, is not Being but *beyond* Being. There is a moment of surpassing, transgressing, or delimiting Being which has been there from the start in the discussion of the "meaning" of Being in *Being and Time* and which emerges clearly in the later works in such expressions as the "truth" of Being (although that is ambiguous), the "open," the "Clearing," and, best of all, *Ereignis*. Heidegger wants to think beyond Being to that which lets Being happen or come to be. At this point there is a certain closure of metaphysics. And at this point, too, "Being" and "truth" in the metaphysical sense become something nonoriginary.

And it is here, too, that I see the point of contact between Heidegger and Derrida. For, in this delimitation of Being in favor of that which gives/produces

Being, Being and truth become "effects" in Derrida's sense. Although Derrida's earlier discussions of Heidegger tend to miss this point and to treat Heidegger as if he were straightforwardly engaged in a discourse about (instead of beyond) Being, his treatments from *Spurs* on do not. In *Spurs*, as we have seen, Derrida points out that there is a certain breach of the rule of Being and truth in Heidegger's thought, a certain dehiscence, or bursting forth, beyond them. "Each time that Heidegger refers the question of Being to the question of the property *(propre)*, of propriate, of propriation *(eigen, eignen, ereignen, Ereignis* especially), this dehiscence bursts forth anew" (*Spurs* 115–17).

To think the *Ereignis* is to think *beyond* Being to that which gives or grants Being (and truth) and makes of it an effect. And this, Derrida rightly points out is already there, in *Being and Time:* "Its irruption here does not mark a rupture or turning point in the order of Heidegger's thought." But then Derrida throws himself off the track: "For already in *Sein und Zeit* the opposition of *Eigentlichkeit* and *Uneigentlichkeit* was organizing the existential analytic" (*Spurs* 117). For it is not what organizes the existential analytic but what organizes, nourishes, and directs the understanding of Being *(Seinsver-ständnis)* that matters, and that is the *Woraufhin*, the "upon which" of the projection. Derrida allows his preoccupation with the delimitation of the proper, his critique of authenticity, to waylay him here and miss the point which he himself opens up. I want to stay on this track, however, to follow up this point, in order to present a more radical version of Heidegger, beyond onto-hermeneutics, beyond the eschatological circle. Derrida criticizes Heidegger's "nostalgia" and "the myth of a purely maternal or paternal language, a lost or native country of thought" (*Marg.* 29/27), so let us call this more radical Heidegger a "Heidegger demythologized." Only then will it be possible to situate Heidegger and Derrida vis-à-vis each other. In chapter 3, I underlined the distinction which is made in *Being and Time* between Being and the *meaning* of Being, which as I pointed out turns on an easily missed distinction between a "primary" and "secondary" projection. In the first place, Heidegger says, the being is projected upon its Being; this is a preliminary, primary projection. It is projected in its *Vorhandensein*, or *Zuhandensein*, or Dasein. Then it is projected again and more decisively in terms of the "meaning" of that Being. Let us read again the pertinent text from *Being and Time:*

> What does *"meaning"* signify? . . . [M]eaning is that wherein the understandability [*Verstehbarkeit*] of something maintains itself—even that of something which does not come into view explicitly and thematically. (SZ 323–4/BT 370–71)

Meaning is not exactly the object of understanding, *what* is understood by the understanding, but that *in which* what is understood is suspended, held up *(hält sich)*. It is not a *quod* but a *quo*. Meaning sustains what is understood, giving it a pivot around which its understandability can organize itself. Hence,

" 'Meaning' signifies the 'upon-which' *[das Woraufhin]* of a primary projection in terms of which something can be conceived in its possibility as that which it is" (SZ 324/BT 371). It is because the being is projected in its Being in the first place—the "primary" projection—that it is something understood. But it is because we point to a certain center of reference, a certain pivot or organizing point *in* this primary projection (the "upon-which" of the primary projection), that we can lay claim to knowing the "meaning" of what is understood. The meaning makes the projection-of-Being possible, which in turn makes the appearance of the being possible. Meaning always has to do with making possible (SZ 324/371). There are not two projections but two phases of one and the same projective undertaking: the first, in which the being is projected upon its Being; the second, in which we determine the lines of force in that projection which sustain and hold it together.

Heidegger is at work on formulating not a binary Being/being pair but a ternary, tripartite articulation in terms of (1) the being which is to be understood (projected); (2) the *Being* of that being, which provides it with its horizonal frame; (3) the *meaning* of the Being of that Being, the *upon-which* of the projection of the being-in-its-Being. Heidegger is thus distinguishing beings/ Being/meaning; the projected/its projection/the upon-which of the projection.

The problem with the history of metaphysics, then, is not that it has no theories of Being—indeed, that is all one ever finds there—but that it neglects to take the second step. Metaphysics fails to realize that the step-back is a two-step—first, from beings to Being and, then, from Being to the upon-which of its projection. Hence, metaphysics functions naively, missing the hidden upon-which, even though that is what the understanding of Being feeds and nourishes itself upon *(sich nährt)*:

> All ontical experience of entities . . . is based upon projections of the Being of the corresponding entities—projections which in every case are more or less transparent. But in these projections there lies hidden the "upon which" of the projection; and on this, as it were, the understanding of Being nourishes itself. (SZ 324/ BT 371)

The "understanding of Being" is more or less obvious, but what is not so obvious, and what needs to be worked up, is the "upon-which" that nourishes the understanding of Being. And so the "hermeneutic" task of *Being and Time*, which is the question of the "meaning" of Being, is not to come up with a new projection of Being but to find the hidden upon-which in terms of which the various metaphysical projections of Being are organized. The hermeneutic question is not intra-ontological but meta-ontological, as Heidegger says in the last Marburg lectures:[11] it is already *about* metaphysics and the projections of Being one finds *in* metaphysics.

It is therefore not Heidegger's point, although he sometimes suggests that it is (and when he does, that is the Heidegger who is still within metaphysics), to offer a competing Being/beings distinction. He does not propose a superior theory-of-Being which will surpass its competitors just because they invariably speak of beings and hence never succeed in crossing the line, the slash, between Being/beings. On the contrary, he is after the slash itself, the way the line is drawn in metaphysics between Being and beings, the rule which all metaphysics follows in distinguishing Being/beings. Heidegger does not want to get into the fray, to enter a names-of-Being contest with the latest and best news about "Being." That is precisely the onto-hermeneutic project which Derrida rightly criticizes and which I want to demythologize. Heidegger wants to move quietly and inconspicuously around the edges of these debates and to pick out the rule which organizes the various entries in the contest.

He is interested not in the "message" (the projection) but in the nature of the delivery service (the upon-which). He does not seek the "meaning of Being" in the conventional sense. For, in the conventional sense, "meaning" refers to the primary projection, to determinations like *Zuhandensein* and *Vorhandensein*. And that is just what populates the history of metaphysics—like the various "world views" (*Weltanschauungen*) described in *Basic Problems of Phenomenology*. Rather, Heidegger's horizonal-hermeneutical gesture is meant to put its finger on what sustains *(hält)* and maintains in subsistence *(nährt)* all such projects. Heidegger has already dropped out of metaphysical competition in *Being and Time*. He is already asking about metaphysics, which is to ask beyond it. He is already on his way, *unterwegs*, not toward Being but *beyond* it, as he says in *Basic Problems* (GA 24 399–400/BP 282).

That means that the word "hermeneutics" in *Being and Time* is easily misunderstood. For, in its straightforward sense, it suggests the onto-hermeneutical project, namely, that *Being and Time* is going to make a breakthrough and come up with the one true "meaning" (in the conventional sense) of Being that has eluded the history of metaphysics heretofore. The aim of *Being and Time* thus construed would be to hit upon the "meaning" of Being that everyone else has missed (where "meaning" has the sense of the inherent essence or configuration of Being, i.e., the primary projection). On that reading, everyone wants to know what is the big hermeneutical secret which Heidegger knows and everybody else has missed, and Heidegger is criticized for failing to come up with it or for saying that there is no language for saying the secret which he knows. Onto-hermeneutics is crypto-hermeneutics.

But, in fact, meaning, and consequently hermeneutics, has the different, quite technical, and unusual sense of the "*Woraufhin*," the meaning maker or producer which organizes meanings or horizons and shapes them up. It is not *itself* a meaning in the conventional sense (a *quod*) but a kind of meta-meaning which sets up meaning (a *quo*) in the straightforward sense. And to the extent that Heidegger was concerned with "meaning" in this sense, he was well on the way beyond the "meaning" of Being in the metaphysical sense.

The four "theses" about Being in the *Grundprobleme* were meanings in the metaphysical, onto-hermeneutical sense, variously determining Being as essence/existence, position, etc. Heidegger was simply interested in arraying these theses, displaying them on a grid, and rooting through them to see what *organized* their conception of Being. It was not his point to develop a *fifth* thesis. When he said that time is the meaning of Being, this was not supposed to be a competing thesis, Heidegger's own thesis about the metaphysical meaning of Being; it was a meta-thesis about how metaphysical theories take shape and are organized, namely, in virtue of time determinations where the now is privileged.

From this point of view, the distinction between authenticity and inauthenticity is not what is important in the existential analytic. Derrida's attack on this distinction, although correct as far as it goes (in pointing out that the distinction is couched in the language of self-presence), turns out in the long run to be largely irrelevant.[12] Above all, Derrida is wrong to think that it organizes the existential analytic (*Spurs* 117). What is important about the authentic/inauthentic distinction is that it is a temporal distinction, that it gets articulated in terms of, or organized around, time. This is to say that its *meaning* is temporal. The only way one can articulate it is in terms of two different ways that Dasein temporalizes itself. The distinction serves to point out that the "meaning" of the Being of Dasein is temporality: its various ways to be are ways of temporalizing. The question of valorizing one over the other, of treating one as proper and the other as not, is just not to the point. In *Being and Time*, authenticity and inauthenticity are modes of temporalization, that is, "effects" of the way Dasein temporalizes. They are both displaced as effects of Dasein's "meaning," i.e., of Dasein's temporalizing. That is a point which Derrida misses, but it is also a point one can see in *Being and Time* only because of this demythologized reading of Heidegger which is opened up in the first place by Derrida.

Metaphysics is in the architectural business of drawing up Being/beings proposals, making drafts of how the Being/beings blueprint should look. It draws ontological grids, with the aim of framing things out, securing them, organizing them around a solid center, grounding them on sure foundations. It is not Heidegger's point to get into that business with a rival grid of his own but to question beyond it and see what is going on in all such undertakings.

Heidegger's intention slowly became clearer over the years, even though the onto-hermeneutical Heidegger kept intervening, keeping the ambiguity of the text alive. We were never quite sure whether "hermeneutics" had the onto-hermeneutical sense of deciphering the meaning of Being in the way that metaphysics does, learning the secret which would put all other metaphysical schemes to shame, or whether it had this demythologized, deconstructionist, meta-ontological sense of trying to catch on to the way views-of-Being take shape and get organized. We were never sure whether hermenetics meant a feat of deciphering which would outdo all the others or a more austere project— withdrawn from all onto-hermeneutical competition—of seeing what was going on in metaphysics. And it was no wonder that the latter sense, which was quite unusual and original, was so easily missed.

After the Marburg period, Heidegger gave up speaking of the "meaning" of Being, because that word belonged too irrevocably to the transcendental-phenomenological tradition, despite the innovativeness of his own usage. But when he began speaking of the "truth of Being"—in a gesture meant to turn away from subjectivism—he complicated things in a different way. For the "truth of Being" suggested the onto-hermeneutical fallacy even more forcefully, albeit nonsubjectivistically. For it seemed to say that there is (or was) one surefire, luminous disclosure of Being that descended on the early Greeks and has since dropped out of view, leaving the rest of us waiting for its second coming in an onto-hermeneutical revisitation. The "truth of Being" suggests that the other views—not exactly world views but views of Being, *Seins-anschauungen*—did not have the "truth" but something less ("correctness"), that they did not know the secret, that they dealt with concealments, coverings over, whereas Heidegger, with his hot line from Todnauberg to the early Greeks (in those pictures of the *Hütte* we can see the swath cut in the mountains for the power lines), knew something nobody else knew.

But then there are the numerous marginalia in the *Gesamtausgabe*, which gloss "Being" as *Ereignis* and the "truth" of Being as *a-letheia*, stressing the *lethe*, the coming-to-pass of a sphere of manifestness from ineradicable conceal-ment.[13] Here, in my view, the post-eschatological, the post-postal Heidegger, glosses the eschato-hermeneutical Heidegger. Here is the meta-ontological hermeneutics which rewrites the onto-hermeneutics.

Consider the import of Heidegger's refusal, in the end, to translate *a-letheia* as "truth" *(Wahrheit)*. Truth is the shape of things within an epoch, the experienced look or configuration of beings in their Being. It is the phenomenal manifestness which is written all over things in an age. When Heidegger distinguishes the truth of beings, as ontic truth, from the truth of Being, as ontological truth, that suggests even more strongly an onto-hermeneutics which wants to get a look at the face of Being itself, not just beings, which wants to decipher the secret meaning of Being. But *a-letheia*—with the hyphen—points beyond this ontological hermeneutics to something else, something more de-constructive. *A-letheia* means the process by which things (beings) emerge into presence (Being), the on-going happening of that process, from the Greeks to the medievals to the moderns. There were numerous "truths" (in the sense of

Wahrheit) over the epochs, all of them truth-events, events of *a-letheia*, ways that *a-letheia* happens, truths as "effects" of *a-letheia*, to give it a Derridean twist. Truth as the unconcealment of beings in their Being, the unconcealment of the Being of beings, is an intra-metaphysical event made possible by *a-letheia*. Indeed, far from getting beyond metaphysics, the truth of Being is what constitutes metaphysics.[14]

When Thomas Aquinas determined Being in terms of *esse*, that was the shape that truth (as *Wahrheit*) took for Aquinas, the way it happened in the thirteenth century. Aquinas certainly knew the Being/beings distinction and got to the truth of Being (as *esse*). But he did not think *a-letheia;* he did not see what was happening, did not see what he said as the way things come to pass, come to presence *(wesen* in the verbal sense) in his time. He had no sense that the Greek and the patristic and the medieval determinations of Being were so many ways that *a-letheia* unfolds, so many ways that beings spring into manifestness and assume a particular vocabulary and language.[15]

Understood in this way, truth and the truth of Being ("die Wahrheit des Seins") are effects, derivative sendings of *a-letheia*. It is not the truth of Being in this sense which is the *Sache* for Heidegger but *a-letheia*. The question of the truth of Being is still intra-metaphysical, like stopping with the "primary projection" of Being in *Being and Time*. But what is *a-letheia?* Whatever it is, it cannot be translated as truth without seriously misleading everybody, just the way that "meaning" in *Being and Time* is not meaning in the conventional sense that it was taken to have. *A-letheia* means the ongoing, historical, epochal process by which things emerge from concealment into unconcealment, in various shapes and ways, in various configurations and historical stampings, without *a-letheia* itself bearing one of those stamps. It is not peculiar to, not locatable in, any one of the epochs. That would make no sense at all. For the epochs are effects of it, and it is the process by which the epochs spring up or happen. It is not one of the dispatches but the postal service at large. It is not any particular secret or hidden truth, except that it is so disconcertingly close to us that we keep missing it, so inconspicuous by its nearness, which I suggest is a notion of nearness that has nothing to do with the metaphysics of presence, *pace* Derrida.

So truth and even the Greek experience of *aletheia* (if one does not hyphenate it and just treats it as the Greek word for truth rather than as a provocative and highly unusual term, like *woraufhin)* were susceptible to this same confusion, between the onto-hermeneutic sense of a hidden secret and the deconstructive-hermeneutic sense of that which renders the various "truths of Being" possible. The "truth of Being" sounds like the hermeneutic secret, the hidden truth we have all been waiting for. But *a-letheia* means to get beyond all such hidden secrets and long-awaited master names in order to name that process in virtue of which the array of epochal names of Being take shape and are named with master names like *ousia, esse,* and the rest of the ontological thesaurus.

And once we see that about *a-letheia,* we see that Derrida had in mind only the first sense of "truth" in *Spurs* when he spoke of Heidegggger's onto-hermeneutics and his being deceived by the Dionysiac woman. That is all quite true of *Wahrheit* and the unconcealedness of Being. But it is assuredly not true of *a-letheia* as this truth-process, this sheer springing up of the epochal shapes of truth, in a "play" of which we will have more to say later. By *a-letheia* Heidegger meant that there are many truths, as many as the epochs required, not too few but too many, a surfeit of them. By his use of *a-letheia,* he did not hold out in his hand the long-awaited truth of Being but only pointed to the matrix from which these many truths spring, in a way to which Derrida's account of a kind of protowriting which produces various metaphysical effects is comparable.

But it is to Derrida's credit that he knew that something else was afoot in Heidegger's text, that there was a certain delimitation of truth in terms of *Ereignis.* It is unfortunate that he allowed his preoccupation with *le propre* to get in the way of following this up and, in fact, to throw him off. *Ereignis* does not mean appropriation in the sense of the hotbed and seat of all propriety and ownness. It means *producing* ownness, sending things into their own, their proper shape in the various epochs, giving things (the Being-of-beings) the tenuous identity that is never insulated from difference, which they enjoy for a while in the epoch. It itself is beyond the distinction between proper and improper, identity and difference, because it grants these and all distinctions. It gives ownness and unownedness—and hence might be translated as "en-owning," endowing with ownness—just the way Dasein's "temporalizing" *gives* both authenticity and inauthenticity in *Being and Time,* grants them as effects. In my view, Derrida opens up this reading of Heidegger but then misses it himself.

All of this comes to a head in the question of "difference." In the Marburg period, the "ontological difference" sounded like a straightforward onto-hermeneutical project. The history of metaphysics is the story of so many failures to get beyond beings and to see the difference between Being and beings. Every time metaphysics takes a stab at determining "Being," it comes up with some sort of being (substance, form, will, mind, etc.). But in *Being and Time,* work was begun to come up with the determination of the meaning of Being which will really hit the mark, which will truly get beyond entities, which will succeed in determining Being *as Being* and not as some entity or another. It is all a matter of onto-hermeneutic penetration, of getting beyond the sphere which heretofore has held metaphysicians captive, in order to get access to the Being which is truly *different* from beings.

But, as Heidegger's thought progressed, it became clear that that was *not* his project, that this onto-hermeneutic project was not the *Sache*. He was not interested in getting beyond beings to their Being, to the Being which is not-a-being, which is different from beings. That is what metaphysics is always doing. All the great metaphysicians have Being/beings distinctions, in some cases quite explicitly, as did Aquinas who distinguished *esse* and *ens*. It would be ludicrous to suggest that Aquinas did not know the ontological difference, that he did not think *esse* as *esse* and as distinct or different from *ens;* he did it all the time. And that is just what the Thomists who read Heidegger immediately respond.

But that was not what Heidegger was looking out for. He was concerned with the difference between Being and beings *as a difference*, with the "and" in the difference, with how the difference gets opened up in the various metaphysical epochs. He wanted to think the process by which Being and beings dif-fer, how they are spread out in any given epoch, thereby opening up the clearing which characterizes that age, the shape that things take in that epoch, the way things are differentiated. At one point he spoke of the *Aus-trag*, which literally translates the Greek *dia-phorein* and means bearing across or over. He used the expression "auseinander-zueinander-tragen," of which *Aus-trag* is a kind of shorthand, meaning carrying outside of each other and toward each other. *Aus-trag* thus is that power of dif-fering which bears Being and beings outside of each other and holds them apart, even while it bears them toward each other and so holds them together. In so doing, *Austrag* opens up the differential spread which characterizes the arrangement that entities are given in that epoch. And there are, of course, many such differential spreads, and it is not Heidegger's business *(Sache)* to come up with the latest and best one. His work is to think that spreading process, that process of differentiation which he was searching to name with words like *Unter-Schied* and *Aus-trag* (even as in *Being and Time* he spoke so strangely of the "upon-which" that "holds" or sustains the projection of the Being of beings).[16]

He was looking for a word which would do for him what *différance* does for Derrida, that is, distinguish a primary, originary difference from the difference which belongs to the identity/difference binary opposition, that is, difference as an effect. His "difference" did not mean any ontic difference between entities, *or even* the ontological difference between Being and beings, but that which *opens up* the ontological difference, the dif-fering in the difference. Heidegger thus had no interest in an onto-hermeneutical difference which would have outdone all the others that metaphysics had up to then devised. His concern was with a deconstructive hermeneutic of dif-fering itself which could explain how ontologies and the ontological differences they turn on were so many effects of *Austrag* or *Unter-Schied*.

That is why, in the conversation with the Japanese, after saying that he has given up on the word "hermeneutics," Heidegger points out that the one way to preserve the word is to think it in terms of difference. At this point Heidegger is saying that his concern is not with the actual messages that Hermes delivers— the many "truths" of Being that Hermes has been shuttling back and forth from Anaximander to the present. The deconstructed version of hermeneutics is not bent on reading off the actual content of the messages that Hermes bears. Rather, it consists in a certain hermeneutic relation to the "two-fold," in an attentiveness to the way the two—Being/beings, Presence/present—fold out, thinking the two-fold as a two-fold, preserving it as such (US 122–26, 136/OWL 30–33, 40; see chap. 4, above). The hermeneutic relation does not have to do with the "message" *(Botschaft)* in the straightforward sense but with the message sending or message making (even as in *Being and Time* meaning does not have the straightforward sense but the sense of the meaning-making work of the *Woraufhin*). And that is what Derrida's critique of onto-hermeneutics misses (and opens up): that side of the hermeneutic relation which is directed not at the message but at the medium, the messaging, the sending, the two-fold, the difference as such.

Occasionally this post-onto-hermeneutical, this post-postal Heidegger, breaks out into the clear in Heidegger's text, making it plain that there is no privileged meaning or "truth" of Being, that no sending enjoys any rights over any other; there is no secret letter being sent special delivery to Freiburg. There can be, he says, no assessing of progress in the history of the Western epochs.

> Not only do we lack any criterion which would permit us to evaluate the perfection of an epoch of metaphysics as compared with any other epoch, the *right* to this kind of evaluation does not exist. Plato's thinking is no more perfect than Parmenides'. Hegel's philosophy is no more perfect than Kant's. Each epoch of philosophy has its own necessity. We simply have to acknowledge that a philosophy is the way it is. (SD 62–63/TB 56)

And even as early as 1938 he was warning us not to try to rank Aristotelian and Newtonian physics, that each enjoyed its own epochal necessity and integrity and that such comparisons trade in incommensurables and are as foolish as ranking the poetry of Aeschylus and Shakespeare (HW 76–77/QCT 117–18). The history of Being unfolds as it does. That is all one can say. *Eidos, ousia, actualitas, res cogitans et extensa, Geist, Wille-zur-Macht*—these are so many master names that have been put forth, so many ways "Being" as an effect has been projected, so many dispatches that have been sent. There is no question of preferring one to the other or of ranking them, no question either of waiting for the delivery of the letter which holds the secret, the master name. It is a question only of attentiveness to the giving and the sending which is at work throughout the postal epochs, the epochal-postal system itself: "das Ereignis ereignet."

This is made clear above all in "Time and Being," where Heidegger warns us against taking *Ereignis* as a master name.

> "Being as *Ereignis*": Formerly, philosophy thought Being in terms of beings as *idea, energeia, actualitas,* will—and now, one might think, as *Ereignis.* Understood in this way, *Ereignis* means a transformed interpretation *(Auslegung)* of being [= an onto-hermeneutics], which, if it is correct, represents a continuation of metaphysics. (SD 22/TB 21)

Ereignis would then be reduced to the level of an *Auslegung,* an interpretation of Being, Heidegger's entry in the hermeneutical, metaphysical contest for the master name of Being; indeed, he would be the aletheological winner. But his point is to extricate himself from this onto-hermeneutical contest, to put an "end" to this ongoing onto-hermeneutic naming, by marking off its closure. The *truth* of Being would then be that there is no truth, no privileged sense of Being, and hence no privileged epoch either. There is just *a-letheia,* the incessant giving and taking of presence over the epochs, the incessant repetition, or playing out again and again, of one metaphysical scheme after another.

But then what can it possibly mean to overcome the "oblivion of Being" for Heidegger? That turns out to be a certain "awakening" to this state of affairs, a certain Socratic realization that there is no master name, master language, or master epoch. The only release *from* the oblivion is to awaken *to* the oblivion.

> The thinking that begins with *Being and Time* is thus, on the one hand, an awakening from the oblivion of Being—an awakening which must be understood as a recollection of something which never has been thought—but on the other hand, as this awakening, not an extinguishing of the oblivion of Being, but placing oneself in it and standing within it. Thus the awakening from the oblivion of Being to the oblivion of Being is the awakening into *Ereignis.* (SD 32/TB 29–30)

This "awakening" is the demythologized version of the "new dawn" to which we would awaken in the eschatological, apocalyptic Heidegger. We do not awaken to a new day, to the brightness of the dawn of a new epoch beyond the *Gestell:* rather, our eyes are opened to the fact that we live in one of the names of Being, a grant*ed,* giv*en,* contingent, historical configuration, and that the history of the West is nothing but the constellation of such dispatches. And that is all there is. We do not displace the night of the *Abend-Land* but awaken to it, awaken in the midst of the night.

> . . . [T]he withdrawal which characterized metaphysics in the form of the oblivion of Being now shows itself as the dimension of concealment itself. But now this concealment does not conceal itself. Rather the attention of thinking is concerned with it. (SD 44/TB 41)

It is not withdrawal which is overcome—that indeed is how any epoch and corresponding metaphysics happens; it is what constitutes the history of Being—but the withdrawal of that withdrawal. Now the withdrawal itself is recognized for what it is. The only "truth" which remains is *a-letheia*, the recognition of the truth/untruth process from epoch to epoch.

The truth of Being is demythologized. The history of Being turns out to be a set of dispatches of Being.

> Metaphysics is the history of the way Being is stamped *(Seinsprägungen)*, that is, seen from the *Ereignis*, the history of the withdrawing of the *sender* in favor of the dispatches *(schickungen, envois)* which were sent along, of the current letting-presence of the present. (SD 44/TB 41)

Being is packaged in the form of presence—which lets beings be present—and the matter for thought is to think that which lets presence itself be. The thing is to get beyond all the presents/gifts, which can be poison *(Spurs* 121) if they obscure the thought of what sends presence out as a gift and an effect into the various epochs—that is, if they obscure the whole postal process which remains in concealment behind the packages we receive in the mail.

On this more austere, more deconstructive reading of Heidegger, it is now clear that the whole project of "eschatology," so well encapsulated in the introductory paragraphs of the Anaximander essay, belongs to the project of onto-hermeneutics and privileges a certain epoch, a given dispatch, what Derrida calls the myth of the native land of thought. Eschatology suffers from a metaphysical-hermeneutic illusion that there is a *meaning* of Being or *truth* of Being in the metaphysical sense, that it was once granted to us in a privileged epoch, that it has since dissipated, and that it is the task of thought to restore and recover it. It turns on a metaphysical circle and a metaphysical conception of repetition as having to turn back and recapture a lost primordiality and on a metaphysical presupposition about the necessary unity of the destining, the *legein* of the *Geschicke*. But on Heidegger's own terms there can never have been a primordial epoch, a privileged meaning or truth of Being.

No form of *Wahrheit* has any rights or privileges over any other. We lack the standpoint and the right to make such a judgment. What concerns thinking is the *a-letheia* process, the springing up of the epochs in intermittent periods of manifestness from a deep-set *lethe*, to which no one has the master-her-meneutic key. There is no master name of Being which has been forgotten and which *Denken* can find. Instead of a master name we have the un-name of *a-letheia* (the hyphen breaks up its nominal unity, functioning like Derrida's *a*) which cannot be translated into any language and is no more Greek than *différance* is merely French. *A-letheia* means to be an un-name which points to that from which all of the metaphysical master names, the names which pretend to have mastered beings, issue *(aus-tragen)*. And that goes for the Greeks; they have no master names either. How could they? Did they not exist in time, with determinate views and institutions, and did they not have an arrangement of things, a grid, upon which they laid things out, and is that not all granted by *a-letheia*? They never said *a-letheia*, never hyphenated it, never made it an un-word, never wrote it the way Heidegger, our meta-hermeneutical Heidegger, tried to write it.

Thus, the end of metaphysics means the end of privileging the Greeks (and of Greek privileging). The Greeks, too, inevitably treated *a-letheia* as *orthotes*.

> The natural concept of truth does not mean unconcealment, *not in the philoso-phy of the Greeks either*. It is often and justifiably pointed out that the word *alethes* is already used by Homer only in the *verba dicendi*, in statement, and thus in the sense of correctness and reliability, not in the sense of unconcealment. . . .
>
> In the scope of this question we must acknowledge the fact that *aletheia*, unconcealment in the sense of the opening of presence, was originally only experi-enced as *orthotes*, as the correctness of representation and statements. But then the assertion about the essential transformation of truth, that is, from unconceal-ment to correctness is also untenable. (SD 78/TB 70)

And even if what the Greeks experienced had a particular phenomenal glow, a shining, phainesthetic radiance, a pre-objectivizing unconcealedness (US 132/OWL 38), still they, too, like everybody else, lived in what was given and granted.

> Only what *aletheia* as opening grants is experienced and thought, not what it is as such. (SD 78/TB 71).

> This unconcealedness comes about in the unconcealment as a clearing; but this clearing itself, as *Ereignis*, remains unthought in every respect. To enter into thinking this unthought *(Ereignis)* means: to pursue more originally what the Greeks have thought, to see it in the source of its reality. To see it so is in its own way Greek, and yet in respect of what it sees is no longer Greek, is never again, Greek. (US 134–35/OWL 39)

But the failure to think the clearing, to move beyond what is given to the giving itself, is no human fault, for "self-concealing, concealment, *lethe* belongs to *a-letheia*," not as a mere addition but as the very heart of *aletheia* (SD 78/TB 71). *Lethe* belongs so primordially to *a-letheia* that *a-letheia* remained unthought by the Greeks themselves, including their word *aletheia*. The Greeks, too, are caught up in epochal withdrawal, and, contrary to *Plato's Doctrine of Truth*, we cannot pin any special blame on Plato. *A-letheia* is always and already with-drawn from view. Hence, it is necessary to experience "*a-letheia*" in a way which moves "over and beyond the Greeks" ("über das Griechische hinaus"). Not only do we have to get beyond Being, we have to get beyond the Greeks. And with that admission we get beyond the eschatological Heidegger.

What does *ratio, nous, noein,* perceiving *(Vernunft-vernehmen)* mean? What does ground and principle and especially principle of all principles mean? Can this ever be sufficiently determined unless we experience *aletheia* in a Greek manner as unconcealment and then, above and beyond the Greeks, think it as the opening of self-concealing? (SD 79/TB 71)

Notice the two-step: first we think *aletheia* in a Greek manner; we start with the Greek experience of truth as manifest unconcealment, with the Greeks' phainesthetic experience, which is their particular experience of *Wahrheit.* Then we exploit a feature of the Greek language which is peculiar to it: the letter alpha here *can be* rendered as an alpha-privative—who is to stop us? We recognize no language police—and hence the whole word can be repeated/ altered as *a-letheia,* un-concealment. We radicalize the word, beyond any claim about etymology or philology, into a thought of the process of *a-letheia,* reaching something which is in its own way Greek yet never was or will be Greek.

Our demythologized Heidegger does not privilege the Greek epoch, does not declare it less an *epoché,* but exploits a suggestive peculiarity of the Greek language to make a point which is no longer Greek. And Heidegger does that with the Greeks because he finds their language so suggestive, so ripe, because he is especially good at repeating Greek words in interesting and innovative ways, just as others are good at repeating the words of the Scriptures or Plato or the *Tao.* The same thing could be done in other ways, with Meister Eckhart's German, e.g., or with James Joyce. There is no privileged native land or native language of thought. In the same way, *différance* exploits a peculiarity of the French language which suggests the protowriting that Derrida is after. Other natural languages must find their own ways, exploit their own peculiarities. Kierkegaard appears to have made considerable progress beyond metaphysics with Danish. And Heidegger does it all the time with German. One of the things that make Kierkegaard, Heidegger, and Derrida stand out is their ability to do this sort of thing with their own languages, instead of just talking about it, as do the rest of us.

Heidegger finds in the Greek word *aletheia* a fold which he can unfold, a peculiarity which helps him to say something which no Greek ever thought or said. *A-letheia,* rewritten by Heidegger, is no longer a Greek word, no longer endemic to any epoch, and hence does not give the Greeks any special rights or privileges, no more than Heidegger's German or Derrida's French gives them any privileges.

There just is no special onto-hermeneutical meaning or truth of Being, no special natural language to say it in, no special epoch in which it all happened long ago, no Camelot, and accordingly no reason to believe that there is a coming epoch in which it will all come again. Eschatology is metaphysics, not plain old metaphysics but quite a wonderful and alluring metaphysics, a tale told by a genius which mesmerizes us. But when we awaken, we catch it with its coattail stuck in the door, trying to sneak out the rear exit of *physis* and *kinesis*.

To that extent Heidegger *is* the best metaphysician yet. If I had to choose among all of the metaphysical schemes from *eidos* and *ousia* to *Gestell*, if I had to pick a place to live and make my dwelling, I would choose the *Geviert* which the mythological early Greeks first thought and which is coming again, if we are lucky, in the second coming (Come! *Viens!*). Derrida is right: the *Geviert* is the most beautiful postcard Heidegger ever sent (CP 74). But I will take my Heidegger demythologized, if you please.

Postal metaphysics breaks down. There is no longer a question of recovering an original message which gets sent across the ages. Teleology and eschatology differ only in the means they use to deliver the mail. Teleology uses regular lines and has regular deliveries, and we know when to expect the postman. Eschatology is more wanton, more playful, and we know neither the day nor the hour when the mail will be delivered. But in both cases there is a primordial dispatch to be carried across the epochs, a unified destiny sending a unique message. This second, more radical Heidegger knows that the message is that there is no message, no privileged sense-of-Being, no special instructions coming from Milesia. The point is to give up the postal expectation, to get beyond waiting for the mailman, to cease waiting for the envelope with the winning name, the master name for Being. We are brought before the matter for thought just at that point when we surrender the illusion that Being has a privileged meaning or truth, when that illusion crashes. That is our thunderstorm.

Heidegger says that *lethe* is the heart of *a-letheia. Lethe* means the self-concealing of the origin, but in that self-concealing *(sich verbergen)* there lies a sheltering *(bergen)* and preserving *(verwahren)* (SD 78/TB 79). Concealment keeps safe, provides a place of safekeeping. The task of thinking then is to protect this lethic recess from the harsh and destructive lights of metaphysics, to preserve the withdrawal in its mystery. Metaphysics launches an all-out assault upon things; it is a power play on the part of human conceptuality, and the critique of humanism was meant to counter its pretentiousness and will-to-power. The history of metaphysics is the story of so many attempts on the part of metaphysics to capture things in its net, to see to it that things are subdued by the will-to-know, by power-knowledge. And, if the eschatological Heidegger tried to get beyond metaphysics by the retrieval of a lost Ionian radiance, the post-eschatological Heidegger came to a more sober realization about the essential, radical concealment of things—that all there is, is dispatches from who knows where *(lethe)*.

The truth is there is no truth. But, for Heidegger, this is the occasion for a certain reverence and respect for the mystery, for openness to what holds itself back, all of which is what he means to name in the word *Gelassenheit.* The upshot of Heidegger's work is a deepened appreciation for the intransigence of things, the refusal of truth in the sense that teleology and eschatology demand. Thinking for him means retiring these metaphysical ambitions and admitting ourselves into the free play of *a-letheia*.

The saving message is that there is no saving message. This is the apocalypse without truth or revelation, an apocalypse that is just a set of dispatches and that looks like a catastrophe *(Fins* 477/94); at the least it is a danger. And here, at this point of the apocalypse without apocalypse, we mark the point at which Heidegger and Derrida are joined and intertwined.

But it is also the point where the two ways swing off. For Derrida, this moment is experienced as one of liberation and affirmation, in a metaphorics of Dionysiac celebration and the free play of repetition. If there is no truth in the sense demanded by metaphysics, if metaphysical truth is dead, then the signifier has been emancipated, set free into its essential element beyond grammar and logic and onto-theo-logic. But, for Heidegger, this moment is experienced in a metaphorics of reverence, openness, and *Gelassenheit.* In both cases letting-be: in one, the letting-be of the trace, the mark, the signifier, a breaking down in order to free up discourse of every type; in the other, the letting-be of that which itself lets presence be, letting the epochs spring up. In both cases, play: the play of *différance,* the play of the Heraclitean child-king who plays with the epochs without why. Thus, even if, as Derrida conjectures in *Spurs,* Heidegger is alert to the Dionysiac woman, this vigilance issues in a different, non-Dionysiac metaphorics, indeed a metaphorics of meditative still-ness (which Constantin and all who want to think with the flux find alarming). And so our project of double-crossing Heidegger and Derrida is still unfinished.

SEVEN

Cold Hermeneutics: Heidegger/ Derrida

COLD HERMENEUTICS

We have slipped Derrida into Heidegger's corporation. We have let Derrida's deconstructive analysis loose on Heidegger's eschatology—on the myth of the early Greeks as a great beginning, an epoch of radiant gods and gleaming temples, and on the story of the second coming. We have left Heidegger demythologized, deeschatologized. Up to now Derrida has had his way. But now the logic of the double cross sets in. Derrida the infiltrator get infiltrated; the deconstruction of hermeneutics is exposed to the hermeneutics of deconstruction: a cata-strophic reversal.

What has all this deconstructive energy done? What has been accomplished by this delimitation of Being and truth? Derrida's answer must be: nothing— what did you want? What are we to do now, after the end not only of metaphysics but even of Heideggerian eschatology? Nothing—whatever you like. This is not nihilism, and it is not unheard of. We have heard it from a bishop. St. Augustine said it first, "Dilige, et quod vis fac." This is all by way of a warning not to conceive of deconstruction as if it were a philosophical program which intended to produce determinate results in a series of ordered steps, as if it were a new world view. It is a warning about the danger of all such programming. Deconstruction does not mean to set itself up as the latest metaphysics for us to settle into. On the contrary, it means to throw us out into the cold, to divest us of the comforts of philosophy, to let the whole tremble, to restore the difficulty of things. We relinquish any claim to finding a competing metaphysics, or anti-metaphysics, in Derrida. We give up the need to land on our feet after a go-around with *différance*.

So far, Derrida has gotten everything. We have let him think that Heidegger has been thoroughly infiltrated. But all of this was part of a plot to snag him on a Heideggerian hook, a quasi-hermeneutic hook. The more we give him, the deeper we let him penetrate Heidegger's corporation, the more we draw him in. We give Derrida everything: the abyss; the mirror-play of signifiers; the delimitation of Being, meaning, truth, and the proper; undecidability; dissemination; solicitation (especially solicitation). But Derrida will see this as *le coup de don.*

Now what has become of us? What is left of "we" and "us," after they are disseminated? That is undecidable. It produces not a definite effect but one which keeps shifting, ambiguous, impossible to decipher, unyielding to a *hermeneuein* which wants to fix its essence. This must be the end of hermeneutics. Indeed it is—if hermeneutics requires a fixed matter of investigation, fixed meaning. "We" have been divested of that; the self is in question. We do not know where to turn next in the matter of "interpreting us" *(Marg.* 147 ff./123ff.). But the bishop said this, too: "Quaestio mihi factus sum."

What is all this undecidability doing? Instead of answering our questions, it keeps them astir, which is after all the work questions are cut out to do, their "proper" kind of *kinesis.* Undecidability is the way to keep questions in question. Questioning is thought's movement, *kinesis,* the work *(ergon)* of a thinking which cannot rest ("just insofar as it can not rest," Aristotle would add). Questioning is a way of staying under way. Undecidability keeps us in motion, keeps us faithful to the flux, in *physis,* closes off the escapes routes, does not permit us to climb through the window (meta-*physis*). Undecidability consigns us to the *doxa,* wandering two-headed in a maze of differential interweavings, with no footing, on constantly shifting, slipping grounds. It keeps us off balance, in the *ébranler,* the trembling.

What is to become of us? Wie befinden-Sie sich? Martin would ask, How are we doing, we who have become an enigma to ourselves? One imagines the effect that Socrates produced in those he cross-examined. First of all, outrage and indignation at someone who is so disruptive, impudent, impious. But then, in an unguarded moment, after the noise and bustle of the hours in the *agora* had subsided, a cold shiver of recognition. After all, he is right. We do not really know what piety is, we who talk about it all the time and accuse Socrates of violating it. Or justice, though we cry out against injustice. We do not know how to define a good state, or how to bring one about. Socrates must have been terribly difficult to have around. He kept telling the "truth" on the Athenians in an apocalypse without apocalypse, kept embarrassing them. He kept disconcerting them, producing a work of dis-concertion wherever he found the concerted efforts of a few to run the state to their own advantage, to produce the effect of knowledge or of virtue where there was none. Discomfort, disconcertion, being shaken by a cold hermeneutic shiver, *sollicitare.* That was Socrates' work, the effect he produced.

Wie befinden-Sie sich? Disconcerted, decentered, *ängstlich.* If you were stung by Socrates, what did that do to you? It left you unable to decide between what came by nature and what was acquired, between piety and impiety, a good state and a bad, justice and power, and even between Socrates and the Sophists.[1] It threw you into undecidability, divested you of your comforts, and robbed you of your sleep.

Now it is in just this Socratic effect, in this cold shiver of recognition that Socrates has the goods on us, that I locate a certain hermeneutic effect, a hermeneutic element, one which links Kierkegaard and Nietzsche, Heidegger and Derrida. It is the effect that is produced when someone goes around telling the truth—that truth is a Dionysiac, that truth herself partakes of the vine, the truth that there is no truth. Unlike the narcotic truth by which metaphysics hopes to induce sweet dreams, this one keeps you up at night. It is the effect produced when someone is loose who is not trying to arrest the play, to still the flux, to tell a bedtime story so we can sleep a little better—someone trying to make life difficult. These Christian-Platonists are always worried about their sleep, Zarathustra said. Christian-Platonism, meta-physics: getting beyond the *kinesis* and the *physis*, getting a good night's sleep. Who can sleep with all this turmoil and commotion? *Aufhebung* is a noiseless hush, Constantin said, but repetition makes a racket. Johannes Climacus said that most people would give up Christianity in a wink because of all it demands from them, except for the fact that it makes for such a comforting way to die. More good sleep.

Cold hermeneutics does not believe in "Truth"—it renounces all such capitalization—something hidden by and stored up in a tradition which is groaning to deliver it to us. It has lost its innocence about that and is tossed about by the flux, by the play, by the slippage. It understands that meaning is an effect. This is not a hermeneutic we seek but one which is visited upon us against our will, against our *vouloir-dire*, which we would just as soon do without. It catches us off guard, in an unsuspecting moment, just when we were beginning to think all was well and the tremors had passed. Derrida's effect is to keep us *Angstbereit*, ready-for-the-*ébranler*, ready for the difficulty and the flux. We keep a stage-coach horn on our desk, like Constantin. Just when the metaphysics of presence is about to convince us that being clings to being, that truth is a well-rounded whole, a hermeneutical or eschatological circle, cold hermeneutics opens up an abyss. Heidegger's hyphen punches a whole in truth's well-rounded sphere.

One can speak of a certain hermeneutic truth here, I daresay—if instead of capitalizing *aletheia* we hyphenate it. This is the truth of which Nietzsche said that too much of it would kill you, that the strength of a spirit could be measured by the degree to which one needed the truth "attenuated, veiled, sweetened, blunted and falsified." What cold hermeneutics knows is like the knowledge which Nietzsche attributes to the sufferers, whom he calls the "elect of knowledge," who are almost sacrificed by their knowledge, which carries them into "distant, terrible worlds."[2]

Of course, speaking of the end of the apocalyptic tone and a truth which kills generates a heroic and apocalyptic tone of its own. That is why Derrida himself will not say what we say, does not write what we write, about the hermeneutic truth and cold hermeneutics (although he does speculate about Freud/*froid*, CP 407). He is alert to the dangers of an apocalyptic-hermeneutic tone. His daimon is always prohibitive, his dialectic always negative, his praxis always disruptive. Derrida, the philosopher of *kinesis*, always stays on the move, remains a moving target, roaming the streets, suspicious of every attempt, such as ours, to take stock of where all of this is getting us. He has to travel light, does not want to have possessions to protect, does not want to speak with authority, to have views to enforce, to suppress dissent. He does not want to stop the perpetual motion of the mail. Socrates must outdrink everyone. We cannot get him drunk and then wring from him just what he thinks justice really is. *In vino veritas* remains within the metaphysics of truth. So we must take the risk of saying it for him— and then commend our sayings to the flux.

In this cold hermeneutics, this hermeneutics of the shiver which issues from the *ébranler*, we see Heidegger peering over the shoulders of Derrida, whispering in his ear. Heidegger infiltrates this operation, striking this Socratic conversationalist with the taciturnity of thought, finding a quiet hermeneutic element in the storm of dissemination. Under Heidegger's subversive influence, the *abime*, the uncontrollable mirror-play of signifiers, is confronted by an *Abgrund*, a dark abyss in a moment in which we are struck dumb. Derrida sets about the deconstruction of all mystagogues and rationalists, of all who have claimed to see the light. Heidegger whispers in his ear that putting all metaphysics under the sign of suspicion is a way of sheltering what conceals itself, protecting it from harsh lights, be they the lights of the *Aufklärers* or of *Schwärmerei*.

Heidegger infiltrates Derrida with a hermeneutic moment—an apophatic, not a cataphatic, hermeneutics—a moment in which we concede the play in which we are caught up, a moment of openness to the mystery which everywhere invades us. It is this dark and mysterious play which we systematically attempt to avoid, to arrest, to dominate, to "attenuate, veil, sweeten, blunt and falsify" with an arsenal of explanatory-hermeneutic devices, the instruments of comfort devised by cataphatic hermeneutics, the maker-of-veils, hermeneutics as *Schleier-machen*, veil making. Cold hermeneutics pierces the veil with its stylus tip, knocks the wind out of its sails (*Spurs* 127, 139). Hermeneutics as Schleiermachean, Diltheyan, Gadamerian veil making; cold hermeneutics as un-veiling, not the *Wahrheit* but the abyss, *a-letheia* itself.

To put the trick Heidegger plays on Derrida as pointedly as possible, what Heidegger whispers in Derrida's ear after the breakdown of the postal principle is "die Sache selbst." But is that not the transcendental signified, the packaged goods, the *ousia*, which the postal principle claims to deliver? Not at all. With the breakdown of the postal principle we experience the power of the *Sache in* its slipping away, its power to elude all such manipulative devices, every technique designed to package and deliver it, every attempt to dominate it. In the free circulation of postcards we see the very coming to pass of the *Ereignis*, of postal dispatching. The *Sache* for Heidegger is not Being, as in metaphysics, not the stored up riches of the tradition, as with Gadamer. It is not even—and here we write with Heidegger against Heidegger—it cannot be the eschatological turning but only the very movement of the *Ereignis* itself, its *kinesis*, the open in which the epochs unfold. The *Sache* is no thing, no supremely present something, no dispatch long flown whose return we await. It is the movement of sending which is never itself one of its own dispatches, the very process in which one master name after another flies up like sparks and then dissipates. And it is the power of that movement to draw us in, in a moment of *Eingenommentheit*, of being taken in, so that we come under the spell of one of the master names or of an *Aufhebung* of all of them or of one of their opposites and are drawn into the contest. Freedom and letting-be for Heidegger mean to awaken to that, to that process which keeps unfolding in Western language and metaphysics and keeps drawing us in.

But have we not learned that the thing itself slips away (VPh 117/SP 104)? Yes and no. There is no *Sinn* or *Bedeutung*, no objectivity or ideality, no Being or beings outside the incessant labor of the signifier. There is nothing—i.e., we have no access to anything—outside the textual chain which links us to things. Reference is always already infiltrated by de-ference, caught in its skids, skewed badly enough to convince us that we have no naked contact, no raw presence-to-presence immediacy. Without the signifier, the thing itself slips away altogether, right down the drain. But with it, we remain in tenuous contact with it, never sure of ourselves. When Derrida says, against Husserl, that the thing itself always slips away, he is at once deconstructing the dream of naked presence and opening up a kind of grammatological phenomenology and a new reading of Husserl. Derrida argues not that nothing is present but that what is present is produced by a repetition which itself requires the labor of signs. Indeed, *were* there no signs, there would be no retention and then indeed would things slip away. The thing itself—naked presence—slips away. And good riddance. That is said against Husserl. But the thing itself, the world delivered by signs, always hangs around—this is said with him. Signs both mediate and block, refer and defer, and they do so in one tangled, textual operation, so that at one and the same time they skew our contact with things and put us in touch with the "other" in a way that cannot be replaced. The thing itself—a sheer, seamless presence—sinks away in favor of a textured product.

But that means that Derrida's remarks come to the same point as Stefan George's saying: "Where the word fails, no thing may be" ("Kein Ding sei, wo das Wort gebricht"). For failing the word, i.e., lacking the play of signifiers, the thing itself slips away indeed. It is the "word," Heidegger says, which "sustains" *(hält)* the "relation" *(Verhältnis)* between things and words, which lets them be (US 176–77/OWL 73). Words give things their maintenance—*Unterhaltung:* read Derrida's *maintenant* (US 187–88/ OWL 82). In the junctures of *Sprache*, things emerge, linger for a while, and recede. The thing itself always steals away—if signs are useless. Where the word fails, the thing itself always slips away.

So the point of the Derridean stylus is not to dismember the theory of intentionality but to deflect Husserl's intentional arrow just a bit, to let us know that it does not travel across a void which offers it no resistance but is skewed and blown about by the winds of the withdrawal. There is only one way to hit the mark and many ways to miss it (*Ethica Nic.* 1106 b 28ff.) Intentional marksmanship, like virtue, is hard, and the point of deconstruction is to restore the difficulty both to life and to intentionality.[3]

The point of all this—the Derridean, Heideggerian, Kierkegaardian, neo-Husserlian point—is to concede the elusiveness of the thing itself, to catch on to its play, not to jettison it (whatever that would mean). That is the cold, hermeneutic truth, the truth that there is no truth, no master name which holds things captive.

But, as we have said, this same cold truth issues in different metaphorics in Derrida and Heidegger. In Derrida, it takes an emancipatory form; in Heidegger, a meditative one. Derridean emancipation means celebration, actively joining in the dance and enjoying the play into which all things are put. Moreover, Derrida carries his deconstruction of metaphysics into the marketplace, into the *agora,* gives it an ethicopolitical cutting edge, makes of it a *praxis* of protest. It is in the name of onto-hermeneutical truth that the postal police do their work, within the University and without. Every good delivery service has its armed guards, its security force, to protect their goods, their secrets, their valuable packages, their packaged values. Derrida is good at disrupting the claims of the powers that be, at disputing their authority, at confounding their claims and putting them into play. He stays in the city and practices a metaphorics of celebration and liberation.

Heidegger never saw the ethicopolitical cutting edge of the delimitation of metaphysics. He was never a good Socrates, and he stayed out of the city and its *agora* as much as possible. Heidegger practiced his cold hermeneutic on the country path, in a metaphorics of taciturnity, stillness, and splendor.

But, even if it is possible to separate out the strands in this interwoven fabric, this doubled crossing of Derridean and Heideggerian threads, what I mean by radical hermeneutics keeps them in undecidable complicity and confusion. I do not want to insulate either from the other, lest one start believing in its own authority.

DECONSTRUCTION IN THE MARKETPLACE

In *Positions,* Derrida refers to his work as a "unique and differentiated textual 'operation.'" He also describes it as an "unfinished movement" (*Pos.* 11/3).

Deconstruction is ongoing, always unfinished work, not a position but a praxis, not a theoretical outlook or standpoint but an activity which is always *in actu exercitu*. For Derrida, speech and writing alike are acts, speech acts and literary acts, designed to produce an incessant perlocutionary effect. Deconstruction is an exercise in disruption which displaces whatever tends to settle in place. Now, if I have felt the effect of this textual operation, the thrust of this stylus tip, I would say that the whole thing is a work of emancipation, a strategy or praxis of liberation. It is not a theoretical discourse about freedom but a textual operation performed in the name of liberation. The emancipation of the signifier from the rule of a priori grammar begun in the Husserl essays is generalized into an emancipatory project which seeks liberation from all oppressive, regularizing, normalizing, and exclusionary discourses. It means to issue in free writing, free speech, free literature, and free science, freedom in the academy and freedom outside.

Like Foucault, like a good many philosophers today, Derrida is concerned with power, its effects, its use and abuse, its delimitation. He is interested in what he calls *pouvoir-écrire*, the power of writing, writing power, the discourse of power and the power of discourse, its capacity to exclude, to declare abnormal, to repress, to standardize, to devalorize and degrade.[4] The work of deconstructive analysis is aimed at concentrations of power which are above all the targets of decentering and dissemination.

It starts out as a way of liberating the reading of literature and philosophy—one which criticizes, among other things, the disciplinary separation of philosophy and literature which is enforced by the University. Thus, it is possessed of an institutional consciousness from the start. It is part of the naiveté and the natural attitude of traditional philosophy to think the institutionalization of philosophy is something neutral, an innocuous setting within which philosophy operates without intervention. Derrida, in "The Ends of Man," begins by saying, "Every philosophical colloquium necessarily has a political significance" (*Marg*. 131/111). It is part of the grammatological reduction to throw the naive belief in the neutrality of the University setting into doubt. From there, deconstructive analysis spreads out into a generalized analysis of the power structure of all institutions, even if it preserves a special interest in the University. It is concerned with concentrations of power wherever they are found: in the dominant categories and oppositional schemes of Western metaphysics and literary criticism; in the educational institutions which house metaphysics and literature; in the institutions of society at large which house the University.[5]

Derrida is probably best known, in this connection, as a leading voice in GREPH (Groupe de recherches sur l'enseignement philosophique) which is dedicated to maintaining the place of philosophy in French education. GREPH successfully fought off a proposal introduced under the Giscard administration in 1975 to eliminate philosophy from the final year of the lycée (the Haby project). Indeed, GREPH sought to extend the role of philosophy in the curriculum and pursued the idea of philosophy on the elementary school level. For the entrenched powers, philosophy is dangerous and subversive criticism. It serves no evident purpose in a social system geared to producing results. The elimination of philosophy removes an obstacle to the rule of a uniform discourse, free of dissent and disruption. In a state educational system whose aim is to produce trained and efficient professionals and specialists, philosophy has no use. Without philosophical criticism, Derrida thinks, the rule of a uniform political and technical power will be unbroken. On this point, he has a definite conception of the *Gestell* as the current dispatch.[6]

That is why Derrida is also quite interested in promoting philosophy in the public media. As the principal speaker at a meeting held at the Sorbonne in 1979 ("Les Etats generaux de la philosophie") which he had helped organize, Derrida spoke of the need for philosophy and the humanities to be involved in the new communications technologies. It is necessary to come to grips with "the power of the media" to disseminate a public culture, one which is filled with uncritical philosophical content. The humanities have insulated themselves from these developments and hence have all but eliminated their influence on public affairs and unwittingly allowed a repressive power structure to extend its influence over modern life.[7]

As a result of his work with GREPH, Derrida was invited to form in 1983 the College Internationale de philosophie, whose aim is to establish a forum for discussion of central social and political issues across disciplinary lines and professional specializations. Derrida wants to delimit the artificial divisions of the disciplines, the systematic exclusions which the "disciplines" enforce and in which academic institutions cooperate—the exclusion of one discipline from interference with another, the exclusionary character of professional standardization, the exclusion of the nonprofessional altogether. Part of the irreverence and iconoclasm of deconstruction is precisely to defy the regulating discipline which has turned the disciplines in upon themselves and isolated them from one another and from society at large. The College will address a wide-ranging series of problems which concern the "rights of man" (*pace* the critique of humanism!). It will scrutinize "totalitarianism, physical and psychical torture, organ transplants and genetic engineering, human rights, the relationships between politics and religion" and other issues which "solicit" philosophy today and make it "tremble" (*ébranlements*).[8] Militarism, sexism, totalitarianism, torture, ethnocentrism, racism, the academic establishment—these are the concrete targets of deconstructive analysis, the concrete embodiments of the "metaphysics of presence."

Derrida is a great and gifted critic of established authority, of the "powers that be," as we say in English. And that is a revealing expression, suggesting as it does the powers that proceed (or which pretend to proceed) from Being as presence. Derrida is exceptionally good at showing that these are powers that only pretend to be, appear to be, and that they are, from the ground (which they lack) up, subject to *kinesis*. They are the powers that *become,* that have *come* to be and that will sooner or later come to grief, to kingdom come. Derrida wants systematically to show that every such established authority is an effect, a product, that it has not fallen from the sky. He wants to show the "destructibility of the world," to borrow Husserl's phrase, in the sense of encrusted social-political power structures.

That is why I favor the Socratic analogy when dealing with Derrida: the practitioner of disruptive strategies whose point—whose style/stylus—is to unmask pretension, to foil the claim to knowledge. And as Socrates did not avoid the semblance of sophism, neither does Derrida avoid the semblance of a wanton aestheticism and anarchism. Like Socrates, Derrida's daimon is not positive. We do not need encouragement to construct schemes, to lay things out in a political program, in a metaphysical panorama or a bureaucratic flow chart. Indeed, it is always in the name of these totalizing views that the police do their work. Blood is usually shed in the name of Being, God, or truth, even and especially when it is shed in the name of "country." Pro deo et patria. The constructions of metaphysics, like the poor, are always with us. But it is the Socratic role to keep us honest about these schemes, to remind us of their contingency and alterability, to make the police think twice, or perhaps think in the first place.

Furthermore, it will do no good to propose revolutionary schemes which are then formulated in the terms of the ruling discourse. For they thereby are already assimilated and declawed. The task of deconstruction is to keep the ruling discourse in question, to expose its vulnerability and the tensions by which it is torn.

From this point of view, from the point of view of Socratic praxis, of a strategy of disrupting any and every entrenched authority which wants to insulate itself from critique, of an analysis which means to be also a critique of institutions, Derrida's thought has a distinct advantage over Heidegger's *Denken* which, left to its own devices, is at a loss to explain its political implications. One need only read *Der Spiegel's* 1966 interview with Heidegger to get a sense of the frustration one experiences in trying to wring from Heidegger the social or political consequences of "thought."

> *Spiegel:* . . . We politicians, semi-politicians, citizens, journalists, etc., we constantly have to make decisions of one kind or another. We must try to adapt to the system we live in, we must attempt to change it, must look for the small opportunity of reform and the still smaller one of revolution. We expect help from the philosopher, if only indirect help, help in a roundabout way. And now we hear: I cannot help you.
> Heidegger: And I cannot.

Now that is not a corner into which Derrida paints himself. Rather, he turns Heidegger's critique of metaphysical constructionism, which necessarily includes the construction of political programs, into a deconstructive *strategy*. Heidegger says to *Der Spiegel*:[9]

> So far as I can see, an individual is not, because of thought, in a position to grasp the world as a whole so that he could give practical instructions, particularly in the face of the problem of finding a basis for thinking itself. So long as it takes itself seriously vis-à-vis the great tradition it would be asking too much of thinking to have it set about giving instructions. By what authority could this take place? In the realm of thinking there are no authoritative assertions.

To be sure. But, for Derrida, this is the point of departure for a deconstructive strategy, a critical-Socratic praxis whose point is to expose the limitations, to delimit the authority, of every assertion which does set itself up as authoritative. And this is because Derrida thinks not that there are no authorities but that there are no absolute authorities, that authorities are always suspect, that they are only as good as the results they produce, that authorities are contingent "effects" whose tenure must not survive their utility.

One usually describes such critical enterprises as Derrida's as "parasitic." But the point of Derridean criticism is precisely to show the derived and secondary character of everything which proclaims itself as host and living substance (Marg. 382–90/321–27). I take it from Derrida that there is a kind of unresolved dialectic, a rhythmic alternation, between tentative schemes and their disruption. The former are necessary fictions, pragmatic necessities—which we may be sure will be forthcoming from those who are not reluctant to offer their definition of justice—and the latter (the disruptions) keep them honest. I take it that, while Derrida provides no *criteria* for what makes for better or worse fictions, he does describe the *conditions* under which decisions should be reached. He thinks that things get worked out in a way which is very much like what Rorty (following Oakeshott) calls the conversation of mankind (but with no Rortian illusions about the charms of bourgeois liberalism)[10]—by a kind of ongoing debate in which the forces of rhetoric clash and settle into a consensus of whose contingency it is the role of the Socratics and Derrideans to remind us, to the point of distraction and infuriation. Courses are decided by the most appealing insights available, the most persuasive arguments, sometimes by those who have experience and sometimes by those who have new ideas, sometimes well and sometimes disastrously. That is always how it has been.

The upshot of Derrida's critical praxis is not confusion and anarchy, as is often claimed, but free and open debate. A good deal of Derrida's goal is to make the debate fair by exposing the dismissive and exclusionary gestures that tend to characterize the ruling discourse. Students, women, blacks, gays, the retarded, minorities of all sorts, "amateurs" (= lovers), nonprofessionals, nonexperts,

Jews, Catholics, atheists, scientists—all have in various ways and at various times been simply deprived of participation in "normalized" discourse. Debate is conceived in advance to be possible only among those who conform to the ruling paradigm. Opinions are serious only if they are held by people whose opinions we are prepared to respect to begin with. Deconstruction is extremely good at showing how the dice are loaded, how the game is fixed, how the play has been arrested before it starts. Deconstruction aims to keep the play in play, to keep the play fair. If it is not fair and free, play is not play but a thinly disguised form of necessity.

Derrida shows the contingency of every discourse and every practice, the capacity of any discourse to repress and exclude, the reformability of anything which claims to be authoritative. It will, of course, be pointed out at once that this leaves us with the problem of deciding which among the indefinite variety of discourses and practices we should settle upon. For Derrida that decision is to be reached in open debate, in the public forum, in the *agora*. He does not offer decision procedures and criteria of decidability. Such criteria are banal, after the fact, wooden, or, even worse, repressive and in any case have nothing to do with real choice or discovery. On the contrary, he offers a Socratic warning about the coefficient of undecidability which attaches to whatever we decide upon and a praxis for upsetting unfair, exclusionary discourses. He does not provide criteria but the conditions for a fair game. He argues for a kind of cross-insemination, in which matters will be settled by a debate without profession-alized authorities and authoritarian specialists, by a cross-fertilizing dialogue among many different points of view which is one of the foremost aims of the College. He argues against protecting generic, disciplinary purity, against method, and against professional jealousies in reaching decisions on matters of public importance. The insistence upon "scientific rigor" and "strict method" in deciding matters of public policy is an open door to a professional, authoritarian elite and the waylaying of responsible participatory decision making.

Thus, as I hope to show in the next chapter, the sense of the play in which all things are caught up has nothing to do with irrationalism. On the contrary, I do not see how a sensible view of reason can be developed apart from a recognition of this play.

Hence, the great advantage of Derrida over Heidegger, which stems from the fact that he is a Parisian intellectual, not a *Schwarzwalder*, is to produce a liberating effect. Heidegger has unnecessarily shortened the reach, the de-constructive effect, of "thought." The implications of "thought" ought to be not the helplessness conveyed by the *Spiegel* interview but the incisiveness, the in-cisions, of deconstructive critique practiced by Derrida. The critique of meta-physics can be exercised not only on the level of the epochal vocabularies of Being but also on the level of the concrete political and institutional vocabul-aries. It ought to be put to the test of the analysis of institutions and practices. It ought to be able to demonstrate the alterability of all existing arrangements. Every existing *polis* requires, and deserves, the gadfly, the Socratic sting of deconstructive analysis, whether it likes it or not.[11]

HERMENEUTICS ON A COUNTRY PATH

But, if Heidegger has shortened the reach of his critique of metaphysics and Derrida has brought it into the marketplace and even put it on television, this is not to say that we ought to pave over the country path and replace it with an interstate highway. I am always interested in the double-cross: subverting Heidegger by means of Derrida, subverting Derrida by means of Heidegger, and always by means of pressing their point of intersection—the delimitation of Being and truth *(Wahrheit)* as effects. That delimitation, I say, produces two different results—one typically Derridean, deconstructive, disruptive and celebrative; the other typically Heideggerian, deconstructive but meditative—but both are profoundly, if differently, emancipatory. I say that neither result can be insulated from the other, that the thinker must be dragged into the *agora*, and Socrates must be made to leave the city, if only on weekends.

To delimit Being and truth as effects, as structures which evolve and pass, which are granted, linger for a while, and go under, is to recognize the flux, the play in which all things are caught, and the temporary and contingent character of the forms that are traced in it. For Derrida, this issues in a metaphorics of dance and free play, of free signifiers, both in the Univesity and without. Heidegger develops another side of it, which he calls the "high and dangerous play"—let us say, the deep play—in a metaphorics of stillness and simplicity. In neither case is it a question of arresting the play. In both cases one wants to keep the play in play, but the metaphorics of the play, the resonances and resoundings of the play, are different. It is my intention not to join each to the other in a moment of *Aufhebung* but to see to it that each subverts the other just at the moment when one tends to dominate, when one starts to take itself seriously, when one becomes exclusionary of the other. Instead of an *Aufhebung*, I want to keep these two after each other, giving each other no rest, each keeping the other in play. And, if this is to be described as a dialectic, let it be a negative dialectic whose point is to give no comfort or place to hide. In this way one raises the tension and deepens the resonance of what I call here radical hermeneutics.

What I mean by hermeneutics in its radicalized mode has all along been this willingness to stay in play, to stay with the flux, without bailing out at the last moment. Radical hermeneutics, on my reading, is the philosophy of *kinesis*. It is ironic that in his critique of Heidegger's notion of authenticity, Derrida thinks he has to defend Aristotelian *kinesis* against Heidegger (*Marg.* 66–72/57–62). He points out, quite rightly, that in Aristotle's conception of time as the measure of motion, motion is peculiarly resistant to the binary presence/ absence schema of metaphysics. Motion is the act of a being in potency while it is still in potency. The being in motion neither is (what it is in motion toward) nor is not (what it was at the point of departure of the motion). Aristotelian time and motion escape the categories of metaphysics, slip through its cracks (*Marg.* 70–72/61–62). Now Heidegger got his first professorship (at Marburg, in 1924) precisely because of the brilliance with which he developed that point (see GA 61). And, as we have seen, this was also a favorite point of Kierkegaard's: the one place where ancient ontology does not try to suppress the flux but to reach an honest formulation of it is Aristotle's definition of motion. The one crack in the front which Greek meta-physics puts up against the *physis* is Aristotelian *kinesis.*

And, far from undoing what Heidegger means by "authenticity" in *Being and Time* (and here we join forces with the reading of Heidegger which Thomas Sheehan has been putting forward for some time now),[12] Derrida is actually just explaining it. Authenticity is Dasein's attempt to keep itself in motion, despite the pressure of present business to grind its existential movement to a halt. Instead of taking up with what is pressingly present all around it, Dasein stays with its Being as *possibility, Seinskönnen.* When Heidegger says that in Being-toward-death Dasein must cultivate the possibility of death *as a possibility* (SZ/ BT, §52), he is simply paraphrasing Aristotle's definition of motion: the act of a being in potency (temporalizing, thrown, and projected), insofar as it stays in potency, insofar as it temporalizes. Death cannot be grasped as something which has actually happened but only inasmuch as we are in movement toward it. More generally, the Being of Dasein cannot be grasped by means of the categories of presence and absence but only by taking Dasein in its being-possible, its ability to be *(sein-können).* Death as a futural possibility is not present or absent—which are the only categories the metaphysics of *Vorhandensein* has at its disposal—but what wavers in indefinite possibility. And authenticity consists in keeping alive that indefiniteness, that possible-who-knows-when, maybe-soon, maybe-now, that sense of walking on thin ice, without assurance, keeping the play in play, keeping the exposure to the abyss in play, without arresting and tranquilizing it. Being-toward-death means staying open to the possible just insofar as it is a possible; it means staying in motion.

So like it or not—and it is Derrida who insists that we take no account of the *vouloir-dire* and that includes Derrida's *vouloir-dire*—by his attempt to keep the play in play, to keep *kinesis* in motion, Derrida is involved in a project of "authenticity" in the only sense that Heidegger ever meant it. He has not razed the project of authenticity but rewritten it so that it means not *le propre* (the properly self-present, stable, and self-identical) but the work of *kinesis*, of keeping underway, of keeping on the move, of not allowing movement and play to atrophy. He calls it *ébranler*, solicitude, making the whole tremble. And let us point out—by invoking a "note from *Being and Time*" and thus repeating as subversively as possible a Derridean gesture—that "care" means *sollicitudo*. In a note to the *cura* fable Heidegger reports: "Even as early as the Stoics, *merimna* was a firmly established term, and it recurs in the New Testament, becoming 'sollicitudo' in the Vulgate" (SZ 199 n.vii/BT 492 n.vii). And then Heidegger tells us that he developed the idea of care by reading Augustine in the light of Aristotle! Authenticity means unrest, disquiet, uneasiness, agitation, keeping off balance (even as running is a constant falling forward), resisting the illusion of stability and solid foundations. Authenticity means *vor-laufen*, running forth, keeping Dasein on the run. Indeed, and here is more Derridean subversion, sollicitare judicium donis means to bribe, to "shake down" a judge! And that is what our double cross of Derrida amounts to, a shakedown which makes him tremble with a hermeneutic moment.

But then do not call it authenticity, which is spoken in the language of metaphysics. Call it instead a kinetics, an arché-kinetics. In this arché-kinetics, I say, there is a hermeneutic moment in which we recover, discover, retrieve the movement by which we are transfixed. In this moment a shudder of recognition—which is the echo of the *ébranler*—resonates through our(non)selves, leaving us temporarily speechless, suffering from another bout with *Un-heimlichkeit* and a Kierkegaardian trembling. It is in this shudder, this trembling, that I locate a cold and comfortless hermeneutics which I think it is the special virtue of Heidegger and Kierkegaard to have expounded.

Heidegger's later writings preserve this trembling and readiness for the shudder, not, to be sure, in the existentialist accents of *Being and Time*, but in the terms of the history of Being and the play of the epochs. And I have always found *Der Satz vom Grund* (1957)—the same text which Derrida uses to address the question of the University (n.11)—a particularly apt text for this side of Heidegger. [13] Here Heidegger says that the movement of Being—let us gloss this for Heidegger as *Ereignis*—resists any higher rule. Elsewhere he wrote that *Ereignis* cannot be accounted for, cannot be rationalized or grounded. "What remains to be said? Only this: *Ereignis* comes to pass as *Ereignis*" ("das Ereignis ereignet," SD 24/TB 24). Every notion or semblance of "ground" (*Grund*) remains foreign (*weg und ab*) to it (SG 185). And so he speaks of Being as the *Ab-grund*, the abyss. This is not to say, however, that thinking is thereby cast into an empty void (*völlige Leere*). On the contrary, it is brought into correspondence with Being as such (with that which gives Being), i.e., with Being as play, with the play of Being. And the groundlessness of that play resonates in man himself who, caught up in that play, finds his own being at stake (SG 186). But what is play and how are we to think it? We have very little preparation for thinking of play in terms of its "mystery." We tend instead to think of play, as in German idealism, e.g., in terms of the dialectic of freedom and necessity and hence still within the framework of metaphysics. But to think play without assimilating it to the categories of metaphysics is to seek the sense of the *Ereignis* itself, of its historical movements of concealment and unconcealment, closure and dis-closure, the way *a-letheia* plays itself out. This is the play of the sequence of epochs which constitutes the history of the West, in which we are caught up and at stake. This cannot be fathomed by some rational rule, by a calculus which can describe and predict its movements—and let us add, with and against Heidegger, by any eschatology which thinks it knows its circular law. It can only be addressed by "mortals," by those who "dwell in the nearness of death" (SG 186–87). And so we are brought back to the problematics of death, described once, too metaphysically, as the problem of authenticity, now rewritten as arché-kinetics. The way to keep the play in play is to keep death in play, to keep mortality, to keep the movement toward death in motion ("to cultivate death as a possibility"). But what can that mean?

It means, in part, to concede that we have hit a dead end when it comes to mastering and dominating *Ereignis* and its play and reducing it to rule. We get to be mortals when we experience this dying out of our metaphysical wits. According to Heidegger, being mortal also means—and this you get on the country path, not a paved street—a heightened sense of being earthly, of arising from, depending upon, and returning to the "earth." And that indeed is why we are called "humans," according to the fable on *cura* which we just cited (SZ/BT §42: "And because there is now a dispute among you as to its [= man's] name, let it be called 'homo,' for it is made out of *humus* (earth)."

Death alone can take the measure of the immeasurable, of the play. That is not to say that death has mastery over the play but just the opposite, that in the experience of mortality you understand that nobody has mastery over the play, that the play is immeasurable, unfathomable, that we are caught up in the extraordinarily complex texture of textuality which we cannot unravel. In Derrida's terms, the experience of being unable to dominate a text, to get control of everything that is happening in it, is part of being "mortal" in this sense. And that is why Heidegger talks about "the mystery of the play."

Now "mystery" is one of those words which Derrida always ducks (*Diss.* 300–301,n.56/268–9,n.67). He does not want the disseminative play to become a negative theology,[14] to be treated as a symptom of a hidden Being, to have us all falling on one another's breast. He does not want to center dissemination on a mysterious, absent *Sache selbst* and hence to arrest its play after all by making it spin in place. And I agree. I am not trying to get Socrates drunk to find out what he really thinks. I am not trying to domesticate Derrida for the house of Being.

But suppose the mystery is the mystery of the play itself, of *a-letheia*, of the concealment and un-concealment which plays itself out in the history of the West, if the mystery is not the *deus absconditus* but the history of the high and dangerous play in which the essence of man is caught up? This play follows neither a linear-teleological nor a circular-eschatological rule. It plays without why, just plays. Es spielet, weil es spielet. It gives no comfort; indeed, it is the source of the most unsettling danger. There can be no question of a metaphysics of presence but only of a play which plays itself out in the history of metaphysics. Commenting on a fragment from Heraclitus—the philosopher of the flux par excellence and a hidden hero for Kierkegaard, Nietzsche, Heidegger, and Derrida—Heidegger writes (in a text whose importance deserves a full citation):

> The destiny of Being *(Seinsgeschick)*: that is a child playing, playing a board game; the kingdom—i.e., the *arché*, the creative, governing grounding, the Being of beings—belongs to a child. The destiny of Being: a child which plays.
>
> Accordingly there are also great children. The greatest and, through the mildness of his play, the kingly child is that mystery of play into which man and his lifetime are brought, on which his essence is staked.
>
> Why does the child play, the great child of the world-play caught sight of by Heraclitus in the *aion?*
>
> The "why" sinks into the play. The play is without "why." It plays for the while that it plays. There remains only play: the highest and the deepest.
>
> But this "only" is all, one, unique.
>
> Nothing *is* without *ground*. Being and ground: the same. Being as grounding has no ground, but plays as the abyss that game which as destiny plays up to us Being and ground.
>
> The question remains, whether and how, hearing the movements of this play, we play along with and join in the play. (SG 188)

Being and ground—and truth *(Wahrheit)* and the proper—are like balls being played to us, sent our way by a playful *Ereignis* (Derrida calls this an "effect"). The diverse *archai* that metaphysics is always delivering to us—*ousia, eidos, esse,* etc.—are the playthings of a child, his scribblings, drawings, toys. Metaphysics is the effect produced by a child-king. There are no hidden comforts, no hidden assurances, no steadfast guarantees concealed in this play. The play has the improbability of a child at play and an uncertainty which is marked by the question with which the passage concludes. But there is something at stake in this play, something at issue, so that the game is high and dangerous. What is at issue is who and what we are—we who are put into play, we who have been deprived of the metaphysical resources to "interpret us"— and whether and how we will join in the movements of this play, whether we will repress it by means of solemn metaphysical assurances, attempt to subdue it by means of the technological will-to-power, or, as Heidegger here says, learn to play along with it, keep it in play, deny it rest and arrest.

Heidegger does not speak of the "dissemination" of meaning but he has an equally nonmetaphysical counterpart called "groundlessness." The history of metaphysics is the history of the formation of so many guiding and ruling meanings, so many master names around which entities are centered, given an *arché,* and so hierarchized. The formation of historical meaning is governed not

by some Hegelian necessity or by caprice but by an epochal play of concealment and unconcealment. "Meaning" in the metaphysical sense, the ontological "truth of Being," the "proper" meaning which It gives these
foundational words, is the effect, the history of the effects, of *a-letheia*. The
history of Being for Heidegger is the historical play of certain elemental words,
names of elemental power, "master names"—like *logos, eidos, energeia, actus,
Gegenständlichkeit*, etc.—of which Heidegger says:

> Citing these moments remains a mere enumerative remark, far removed from the
> insight into the respective epochs of the full destiny of Being and into the manner
> in which these epochs spring up suddenly, like buds. The epochs can never be
> derived from one another and forced into the course of a continuous process. Still
> there is a tradition from epoch to epoch. But the tradition does not run through
> these epochs like a strand which ties them together; rather the tradition emerges
> each time from the concealment of the destiny, just as from the same source
> different streamlets emerge, nourishing one stream which is everywhere and
> nowhere. (SG 154)

The epochs spring up suddenly and just as suddenly give way. What is common
to them is the "full destiny of Being" *(volles Seinsgeschick)* from which they
emerge, not the bond of a logically derivable course. They arise—like buds on a
branch, unpredictably but yet with a certain naturalness—and they pervade
their time, indeed constituting and defining the age, and then they are
eclipsed. There is no grounding of these elemental words. Even while they give
themselves out to be *archai, principia*, grounds, and foundations, they are but
touchstones and points of organization around which Being is understood in a
particular epoch, around which, as Foucault would say, a certain *episteme* takes
shape. But they do not escape the epochal play, the play of transformation and
alteration, of epochal repetition, which is at work in the history of metaphysics.
They cannot lay claim to anything more than a certain historical aptness,
ripeness.

What is the "full destiny" of which Heidegger speaks? This has for Heidegger
ultimately an eschatological sense and obeys the rule of the eschatological
circle. He thinks that it is the same destiny which has sent itself out first, in the
early Greeks, and is destined—perhaps, the play is dark and uncertain—to
return, according to the dynamics of an eschatological parturition and repetition, in a renewal of the *Geschick*, a momentous reversal in which the end into
which we have been driven will turn itself around and issue in a new beginning.
And, although I take eschatology to be a neometaphysical conception, which
privileges the metaphysical circle and the effect of unity, it remains true that
"there is" always the "same" in this sense, namely, the *Ereignis*, sending Being,
ground, and truth, sending one *arché* after another, according to neither
necessity nor caprice. The *Ereignis* plays with a free play, without why. The rule
of the circle is a "why," the last "why" which Heidegger himself tried to impose

upon it, the last bit of nostalgia and hope, as Derrida says. To let the epochs play without why is to release them even from the circle, the circular destiny of eschatology, and simply to let the epochs happen in a kind of free repetition. Then the "full destiny" means "fully in play."

The matter to be thought will be not these configurations of historical meaning, each of which constitutes the "truth of Being" in its own day, not the diverse letters that the *Seinsgeschick* has been sending our way throughout the history of the West, but the process by which they are sent. The matter for thought is that process, a fully released sending and destining—where destining is indeed extricated from any sense of fated necessity—of Being. The matter for thought is the *Seinsgeschick*, *Ereignis*, *play*: the play of the sendings, the open, *a-letheia*. Thinking is to think this play as a play, to come into play with this play. The task of thinking is not to be taken in by any particular historical configuration but to make the step *back*, to see in any particular historical meaning a giving of that which withdraws and hence to experience that giving-withdrawing itself, to experience it as such.

That is the moment of the highest vigilance for Heidegger. It is that moment of "awakening" discussed in the "Seminar" to "Time and Being" (SD 32/TB 30), the moment when one experiences the contingency of any historical configuration and one is alerted to a deeper movement, the movement of *Ereignis/a-letheia*. Then, and only then, does one appreciate the fragility and precariousness of the hold which conceptual-representational thinking has upon things. To take conceptual thinking seriously, to suppose it exempt from the play, is to suffer the illusion of *con-cipere (capere)*, *be-greifen*, which thinks it has a hold on the play just when the play has a hold on it and which thinks that it can dominate texts, epochs, and mortals themselves.

And that realization is what Heidegger calls releasement *(Gelassenheit)*, which means at once to be released *from* the illusions of representationalism and willfulness and released *to* the mystery of the play, the holding sway of the withdrawal. For Heidegger, releasement toward things is always openness to the mystery.[15] The mystery is what withdraws beneath, behind, beyond the grip of concepts, the range of historical meanings and conceptualities. The mystery is what eludes the cunning of rationality, of technology, ontology, theology (and even eschatology). And, because he experiences this play as mystery, not as slippage, Heidegger's response to it is in the tones of humility, silence, simplicity, of a certain profound taking stock of our mortality.

So I read Heidegger's recourse to the neomythology of the fourfold, his beautiful postcard, not as the recollection of a lost epoch or as the anticipation of a new destiny and a new commencement or as the description of a first beginning or new beginning. We know that every beginning is already a repetition and always infiltrated with *lethe*. Rather, his recourse to the fourfold is the experience one has once one finds oneself in the play, once one realizes that there is nothing but the play of the epochs. The life of "mortals"—on the "earth," implicated in the play of world-time, which is likewise our own life-time—is Heidegger's highest hermeneutic achievement, the highest, or perhaps the deepest, moment of hermeneutics. The thing is not to get drawn into locating this time in some privileged age which had it once or in an age which may be coming any day now. Heidegger's recourse to the fourfold is instead a moment of vigilance, of alertness to the contingency of historical meanings, and of openness toward the mystery which withdraws, to the open in which the epochs form.

Gelassenheit is a certain transgression of the ruling power plays which dominate our world. It is the point where one awakens to the manifold efforts which are everywhere in place to hold things in the grip of one system of power or another—both metaphysical and sociopolitical systems. *Gelassenheit* is a certain intervention in these power systems which releases their grip and lets things be and lets mortals be, lets them go. *Gelassenheit* is freedom. It is not the privilege of some ancient golden age nor a promise held out for the future. It is a quiet intervention, here and there, which denies the ruling power systems their authority. *Gelassenheit* is possible, Heidegger says when he is not thinking eschatologically, for all of us, in one way or another, to a greater or lesser extent (G 15–16/DT 46–47). It is a small intervention which opens things up for us, giving us a taste of a nonmetaphysical experience of things—and one another (Heidegger keeps missing this second point, about one another). And maybe it will catch on. Maybe others will catch the spirit of the thing. Maybe a small crack can become a breach which can make a whole system come undone—if the word spreads. And maybe television and advanced forms of electronic communications will spread the message (would Heidegger be horrified at that?), the message of the apocalypse without truth and revelation. Maybe a little transgression here and there will spread. Maybe not.

Mortals are ones who understand the *kinesis*, who have no illusions about a lasting city, who have let go of their constant constancy, who do not cling obstinately to being and presence. They have acquired a little gentleness which comes of appreciating their limits, a little thankfulness which comes of appreciating the time that has been portioned and sent their way. They have a sense of the rhythm of birth and death, of falling ill and growing well, of the passages from childhood to maturity to old age, of day and night, of the transitions of the seasons, of the movement of the years—all of which comes of living close to time. They understand the limits of their reach, the fragility of their hold on life,[16] the unpredictability of events, the fallibility of judgment. They appreciate that we are all siblings of the same night, bound together by our mortality (though this is not a point which Heidegger exploits.) They understand—where that means to stand under, to expose oneself to, to awaken to—the groundlessness of things: that everything is caught up in a certain fortuitousness which Heidegger, with his affection for the Greeks, calls a play of concealment and unconcealment.

The groundlessness of mortals means that we live in the sweep of the epochs—from *eidos* and *actus* to *Gegenständlichkeit* and *Technik*—which tell a story which could have been otherwise. We keep our distance from the illusion of treating these epochal principles with finality, of taking their pretensions seriously, of regarding their hold as fixed. We learn the play of their movement, the movement of their play, the giving and withdrawal at play in them. We learn above all that we are part of a movement which we did not initiate, that we depend upon forces which we do not dominate, that we draw our life from powers we do not fathom. We learn openness—which means at once graciousness, for one knows that has always to do with gifts and giving—and we learn a sense of transiency, for one knows the powers of withdrawal. Someone, something, the Lord or not, always giveth and taketh away. There is always giving and taking-again *(gjen-tagelse)*. We learn to come to grips with *kinesis*, with coming to be and passing away, and with the mysterious powers which govern that movement.

Derrida will not talk like this. He distrusts all talk of understanding however it is hyphenated and subjected to catastrophic inversion. He fears domesticating his work, making it safe, removing its Socratic sting. And that is as it should be in a deconstructive strategy. Were he to try to take such meditative stock of things, deconstruction would become the latest metaphysics, and it would have something to defend. That is why one must formulate this hermeneutic moment with care (solicitude). One must insist that it is a hermeneutic of trembling, without comfort, that it is an understanding from which one suffers, that we are trying not to be helpful but to make things difficult.

Derrida's deconstructive work issues in a grammatological exuberance which celebrates diversity, repetition, alteration. Heidegger's deconstructive work issues in a meditative stillness, which could not be more alert to the play in which all things are swept, but it is stunned by the power of its sweep and culminates in a deep sense of the play in which mortals play out their allotted time.

And what I call radical hermeneutics will not let either the Heideggerian or the Derridean gestures win the day, will not entrust full authority to either, but in a conniving way—and it is said that Hermes was also a conniver, and we know that solicitude means making bribes—keeps subverting one with the other. Just when thinking is lost in solemn stillness, when it is beginning to take itself seriously, dissemination bursts upon the scene with its disruptive laughter. Even so, thinking follows dissemination home, after the singing and dancing is over, through the city streets, to see if it ever takes off its mask.

PART 3

The Hermeneutic Project

EIGHT

Toward a Postmetaphysical Rationality

COPING WITH THE FLUX AND THE HERMENEUTIC PROJECT

What are we to do now, after the "end" of metaphysics? How does one go about one's business after giving Heidegger and Derrida so much? How are the sciences possible if one talks in terms of a child-king and the foundering of principles? And what guidelines can there be for action if the *archai* are so many sendings, if there are no "metaphysical foundations"? If there is no master name, if there are too many truths, what has become of science and ethics, thought and action, theory and practice (provided we can make such distinctions)? If the flux is all, and linguistic, historical structures are nothing more than writings in the sand which we manage to inscribe in between tides, what then? What can we know? What ought we to do? What can we hope for? Who are we, we who cannot say "we," we who are divided from ourselves, our (non)selves?

Radical hermeneutics cultivates an acute sense of the contingency of all social, historical, linguistic structures, an appreciation of their constituted character, their character as effects. And so the question which presses in upon us now is whether in such a conception we are thrown to the wolves, whether we must simply abandon the notion of "rationality" as another case of metaphysical seriousness, whether anything and everything goes—in science, ethics, human affairs generally.

I want to argue in the concluding chapters of this study that, although there is no way to get rid of the wolves (exposure to such perils is part of the human condition), there is no reason we need be consumed by them. We are trying to restore the difficulty in life, not to make it impossible. Far from undermining the idea of "reason," this radical hermeneutic issues in a postmetaphysical rationality which is, I think, a far more reasonable reason than metaphysics has been proffering for some time now. Reason is not undone by the foundering of metaphysics but liberated, emancipated from metaphysical prejudices which tended to make of it something less than it is and which in fact turned it into something considerably more dangerous than wolves. I want then to repeat, or to write differently, what "reason" means, to redescribe it, not to jettison it. I want to show that it is not the personal invention of those who speak in its name. "Reason" has had a fortune not unlike "God" and "country": some of the worst violence is committed in its name. And I am no more interested in irrationalism than I am in atheism (except insofar as the latter is an effective strategy in the logic of displacing onto-theo-logic).

The work of redescribing what "reason" means and of liberating it from metaphysics and dogmatism is beginning to catch on. Husserl wanted to liberate rationality from the deductive model that had come to dominate all discussions of reason from Descartes on and to replace it with an intuitive model. Reason for him is an evidential system, an interconnectedness of experiences with intuitive credentials which makes up the ordered panorama of the sciences and their foundation in transcendental life (*Ideas I*, Part IV). Transcendental phenomenology is everything that reason and metaphysics want, but without the idle constructs of groundless theorizing (*Cartesian Meditations*, §64). Eventually, however, Husserl's liberation ended up in a new subjugation of reason to intuition which tied the hands of reason in a new way, by demanding a transcendental self-justification of it (Heidegger's objection) and by precluding the free manipulation of signs which do not require intuitive redemption (Derrida's objection).

This liberation took a more distinctively hermeneutic turn with Gadamer's attempt to rethink rationality along the lines of Aristotelian *phronesis*.[1] In Gadamer, reason is emancipated from the rule of method and becomes a more plastic, flexible, and spontaneous faculty of application or, perhaps better, appropriation of norms which are at best only general schemata for new and idiosyncratic situations which cannot be anticipated in advance. No longer bound to the rule of fixed technique (more Cartesianism), reason is reconceived along the more classical models of *sensus communis*, practical wisdom, and good judgment, of that acuity which someone has who "knows his way around," whose judgment has been sharpened by making decisions in the concrete. There are no manuals to guide such judgments, and such manuals as can be written are no more than lifeless distillations of the mobile intelligence of concrete investigators, treatises on method which are left speechless before a new turn of events.

The originality of Gadamer's conception lies in his insistence that both practical reason and scientific reason need to be understood in terms of *phronesis*. This point is exploited in a particularly fruitful way in Bernstein's *Beyond Objectivism and Relativism* where it is put to work organizing the insights of postempiricist philosophies of science from Kuhn to the present. But there are definite limitations to such a project from the point of view of a radical hermeneutic. The hermeneutic conception of *phronesis* presupposes an existing schema, a world already in place. It is the virtue of applying or appropriating a preexisting paradigm. But what happens at that point where the schema is in crisis, where worlds founder, where the epochal fluctuations of which Heidegger speaks come about? Then *phronesis* itself is put in crisis. For then it is not a question of having the skill to apply but of knowing what to apply. Then we find ourselves brought up short. The whole "founders" (Constantin), is "solicited" (Derrida). Now it is just at that point that we need to describe what it would be like to be "rational," for it is just at that point that we no longer have *phronesis* to fall back upon and that we need a notion of rationality beyond *phronesis*. Craft and skill and a sense of what the situation demands all founder at that point when the situation as a totality is not organized, when the horizons are skewed, when the whole trembles, when things are ruptured, decentered, disseminated, as they say in Paris. Then one enters uncharted waters, unmarked ways. All there is, is the way, making-one's-way, the *Be-weg-ung*, the movement, as they say in the *Schwarzwald*. (Aristotle just called it *kinesis*.)

Heidegger said that the play is at once the "deepest"—for structures are but inscribed upon the flux—and the "highest"—for joining in the play is a free, productive release, the highest and best wisdom, the last and best stand one can make (SG 188). The one god that Nietzsche could tolerate was one that laughed and danced, and some of Heidegger's best pages have to do with the play of the fourfold and with finding a God before whom one can sing and dance. The difficulty, however, is that the world places little confidence in the play of things and a great deal of reliance on constraints, authority, and institutional structures, and that is why we are overrun with creeds and criteria, rules of life and rules of method. The fact is that the advocates of free play meet resistance at every step. They are suspected of anarchism, nihilism, of intellectual, social, and moral irresponsibility. Those who would dance and play before their God have constantly to dodge the theological bullets aimed their way by the defenders of the true faith. The free play of the faculties is checked by the demand for aesthetic standards. No matter how much or how well we are counseled to enjoy the play, there are always those who are threatened by such emancipation and who insist on knowing what the "criteria" are for determining exactly what that is.

I want to argue in what follows for a notion of "reason" which begins by acknowledging the uncircumventable futility involved in trying to nail things down. In the end, I want to say, science, action, art, and religious belief make their way by a free and creative movement whose dynamics baffle the various discourses on method. But I do not treat that as a negative start, as a kind of despair in reason, but as the only really sensible, or reasonable, view of reason. The problem with reason today is that it has become an instrument of discipline, not a mark of freedom, and that, when it is put to work, it is taken out of play.

According to Feyerabend's argument "against method," the basic "principle" *(arché)* which should guide scientific research is "anything goes," i.e., the suspension of principle and *arché* in an "anarchistic epistemology." (Feyerabend understood quite well that the first step in deconstruction is a strategy of reversal, of standing the prevailing orthodoxy on its head.) And, since anarchy sometimes means violence, he reformulates his position as "Dadaist."[2]

> A Dadaist would not hurt a fly—let alone a human being. A Dadaist is utterly unimpressed by any serious enterprise and he smells a rat whenever people stop smiling and assume that attitude and those facial expressions which indicate that something important is about to be said. A Dadaist is convinced that a worthwhile life will arise only when we start taking things *lightly* and when we remove from our speech the profound but already putrid meanings it has accumulated over the centuries ("search for truth"; "defense of justice"; "passionate concern"; etc. etc.) A Dadaist is prepared to initiate joyful experiments even in those domains where change and experimentation seem to be out of the question (example: the basic functions of language). I hope that having read the pamphlet the reader will remember me as a flippant Dadaist and *not* as a serious anarchist.

Is this Dada or Derrida (Derri-dada?)? It is hard to see the difference. Or is it Nietzsche? Do not "joyful experiments" belong in a "joyful science" *(fröhliche Wissenschaft)?* In any case, Feyerabend supplies the right touch at this point. But the flippancy and inflammatory delivery of writers like Feyerabend and Derrida are easy to misunderstand. There are more circumspect ways to put their point—though circumspection is not always the best strategy—as in the Augustinian version: "dilige, et quod vis fac," that is, love and do what you will.[3] (No one has ever accused Augustine of anarchism.) Augustine meant that, if the heart is so filled with love that everything one does issues from love, then it is both unnecessary and impossible to spell out in detail just what it is one should or should not do. Indeed, once one has to spell out obligations between lovers, the love is gone.

Now I think that Feyerabend's "quod vis fac" ("anything goes") is prefaced by a "dilige scientiam," love science (then anything goes). Search everywhere, question everything, entertain any hypothesis, leave no stone unturned in search of good science. Above all, do not be blinded and hamstrung by wooden maxims and methodological constraints when what the matter—*die Sache*—requires is plasticity, inventiveness, suppleness, the ability to play along with the matter. Doing what you will always proceeds from an overarching sense of the "way" *(odos)*, of what is underway, and it issues everywhere in similar results—the freedom of the children of God, of Heraclitus's child-king, of Nietzsche's child, and even of the children of scientific searching and researching.

The real obstacle to understanding human affairs lies in the tendency to believe that what we do—whether in building scientific theories or in concrete ethical life—admits of formulation in hard and irrevocable rules. It is precisely this claim that human life is rule-governed which brings hermeneutics—of both sorts, in its "first essence" and of the more radical sort—out of its corner and into the fight. Hermeneutics pits itself against the notion that human affairs can finally be formalized into explicit rules which can or should function as a decision-procedure, whether in scientific theory building or in ethics. An important part of the hermeneutics of play is to deconstruct, to undo that myth.

But it is just as important to show that such a view does not throw us back into anarchy and chaos—although sometimes a little chaos is a good strategy, and that, I think, is what motivates Feyerabend and Derrida. But ultimately reversal gives way to displacement. To take a stand against methodologism is to get beyond the rationalist/irrationalist controversy and to liberate a more reasonable notion of reason. Our preoccupation with methodology needs to be replaced with a deeper appreciation of *methodos, meta-odos,* which is "the way in which we pursue a matter *(Sache)*" (SG 111), the way we make our way toward the *Sache*. The concern with "method" so characteristic of modern science—or we should say philosophers of science?—makes science subservient to method (US 178/74), so that method rules instead of serving, constrains instead of liberating, and fails conspicuously to let science be!

In its best sense, i.e., in its "retrieved" Heideggerian sense, method is the suppleness by which thinking is able to pursue the matter at hand; it is an acuity which knows its way about, even and especially when the way cannot be laid out beforehand, when it cannot be formulated in explicit rules. *Meta-odos* is a way of keeping underway, in motion, even when it seems there is no way to go—the repetition which repeats forward. The methodologist, on the other hand, thinks that, if science, art, ethics, and religion are not rule-governed, they can only be matters of mere caprice. He is a sworn enemy of what is in principle unpredictable; he distrusts those who play and those who advise us to love and do what we will. So it devolves upon us to show, at the conclusion of our study, that this hermeneutics of play provides for a more sensible understanding of human affairs than do the misguided aspirations of the methodologists. By divesting us of the illusion of pure abiding presence and of a spelled-out treatise on method which will assure our mastery over things, radical hermeneutics does not leave us in the lurch but rather gives us some room to stretch our intellectual limbs.

In the following three chapters of this study, I want to try to spell out what that means, to show how we "cope with the flux"—in the concrete, so to speak. To do this I want to address the areas in which the demand for rules and criteria is particularly pressing and where our own thoughts on the flux seem the most likely to lead to disaster: science and ethics, where I argue for what I call here a postmodern conception of rationality (chapter 8) and an ethics of dissemination (chapter 9). Finally, I will try to encapsulate my idea of "radical hermeneutics" by way of what Heidegger calls "openness to the mystery," toward which, it will turn out, our reflections on science and ethics have in fact all along been oriented (chapter 10). In so doing we will have addressed Kant's three questions: What can I know? What ought I to do? For what can I hope?

Like all authors, I want to create the illusion that I am the master of this text, that there is a certain progress in these three chapters, that they are edging toward a conclusion. For they move in the direction of the "unencompassable," which means that sphere which eludes, which outplays, any effort to hold it captive. Before the world is stabilized as the object of scientific construction, and hence given a certain metaphysical status, it is more primordially *physis*, the flux, which cannot be restrained or contained or encompassed within the limits of scientific constructions. Before ethical life is bound up by a net of rules of conduct, there is the prior mystery of other persons, who outstrip whatever we think we know of them and command our respect. Finally, we come up against the mystery itself, the unencompassable depth in both things and our (non)selves. And then we are brought up short. That it seems to me is where hermeneutics leads us: not to a conclusion which gives comfort but to a thunderstorm, not to a closure but to a dis-closure, an openness toward what cannot be encompassed, where we lose our breath and are stopped in our tracks, at least momentarily, for it always belongs to our condition to remain on the way.

SCIENCE, RATIONALITY, AND PLAY

The hard case is science, particularly the natural sciences. For it is here that talk of the play and the flux is most likely to lead to trouble, most likely to look irresponsible. Yet it seems to me precisely here that one can make the best case for putting the play back into reason and against a hard-line, rule-governed notion of rationality. Indeed, I would say that the great breakthrough in the emergence of a postmetaphysical conception of rationality is to be found in the delimitation of the positivist conception of scientific reason which was provoked by the publication of Thomas Kuhn's *The Structure of Scientific Revolutions* in 1962. This book is the central document in a body of literature which has reshaped the terms in which we think of science, a body which stretches back to the work of Karl Popper, which includes the work of figures such as Feyerabend, Lakatos, and Michael Polanyi, although Polanyi was not part of this school and worked quite independently of it.[4]

Philosophers in the continental tradition who have followed these developments have realized that the concept of reason which these thinkers shaped was importantly like, and indeed helped explain, the undeveloped notion of rationality in *Being and Time* and in Merleau-Ponty's *Phenomenology of Perception*. Interesting comparisons of Heidegger and postempiricist philosophers of science have begun to appear.[5] The most interesting document in this regard is

Bernstein's *Beyond Objectivism and Rationalism*. Written by a philosopher who moves with ease between continental and Anglo-American philosophy and philosophy of science, Bernstein's book, which uses Gadamer's hermeneutics as its point of reference to the continental tradition, is an impressive statement of the way in which these separate developments have tended to converge.

I want in the present chapter to continue that discussion, not in terms of Gadamer and the hermeneutics inspired by *Being and Time*, which is Bernstein's strategy, but in terms of the more "radical" hermeneutics inspired by the later Heidegger and Derrida which I have been working out in these pages. Like Bernstein, like nearly everyone else, my point of departure is *The Structure of Scientific Revolutions*, which has set the terms for the current debate. This remarkable book, which has set off a revolution of its own, is an apt vehicle for posing the question of reason vis-à-vis a philosophy of the flux. For everything that Kuhn wants to say turns on the distinction between "normal" science and "revolutionary" science or, to give it a deconstructive twist, between normalization and transgression, between a settled disciplinary frame and the violation of that frame, between normalized authority (authoritative normality) and its disruption.

Kuhn's book raises the question of the extent to which any challenge to the prevailing mode of thought is inevitably regarded as "irrational" or, conversely, the extent to which "rationality" is anything more than the prevailing mode of thinking. And he shows that science makes no progress, does not stay in motion, does not make its way along the way, unless such challenges are not only periodically issued to the prevailing normality but in fact succeed in their palace coup. Now the political metaphor here is not just a metaphor (nothing ever is). The palace in question is the political framework of the ruling authority, namely, the university and the scientific "profession." Thus, one of the more interesting features of Kuhn's work is its sensitivity to the political and institutional conditions under which "reason" and "science" labor, which also interest Derrida and (even more so) Foucault.

One of the more commonplace and prevalent misunderstandings of the nature of scientific activity, Kuhn thinks, is the Baconian notion of a random collecting of facts in a theory-free and "unprejudiced" manner, from which a theory slowly emerges. But that sort of fact gathering is most likely to produce a morass, not to move science forward (SSR 16). Fact gathering proceeds in the most efficient and productive manner when it is guided beforehand by a theory, by a certain conception of the way things are. Theory leads science to generate facts of which it had not the slightest suspicion and which, outside the theory, appear to be of no significance whatever. Facts are arti-facts. They become facts only within the "network of theory" to which they belong, as when Heidegger says that, because an entity is what it is only within the horizon of the understanding of Being within which it is understood, there can be no "bare facts" (SZ 363/BT 414). It is interesting that, while the Anglo-American world had to suffer through a dark ages of positivism before reaching this realization, the interpreted character of perception has been a basic staple of continental thought since Husserl's *Logical Investigations*.

In speaking of a "paradigm," Kuhn meant to emphasize the business of science as an activity organized around certain model or exemplary exercises in problem solving (like Heidegger's point that science and theory always have their praxis). Science trains its initiates by presenting them with model cases of problem solving, and the best of the new scientists are the ones who are the most skillful in applying and amplifying these exemplars. They excel in a praxis rather than in a grasp of theoretical concepts (SSR 47), so that their (arti-)facts are the issue of an art. For Kuhn, then, the body of fundamental concepts, the network of theory, is embedded or implicit in the paradigm; it is not laid out (*ausgelegt*) or explicitly worked out. Paradigms "embody" theory (SSR 109). Thus, what Heidegger calls a "horizonal projection" of "fundamental concepts" is for Kuhn embedded in a paradigmatic exercise so that the scientist has more a working mastery of these concepts than a reflective grasp of them. This demands a certain insight into the demands of concrete problems, which resist formulation into explicit rules. It is never possible to spell out in advance the rules by which paradigms can be applied to concrete problems, that is, to "rationalize" the paradigms by reducing them to rules. And that is why Kuhn thinks that Polanyi has "brilliantly developed" the notion that "the scientist's success depends upon 'tacit knowledge,' that is upon knowledge that is acquired through practice and that cannot be articulated explicitly" (SSR 44, n. 1).

But it is also possible to put this in terms of Gadamer's development of *phronesis* as knowing how to apply, which is the point around which Bernstein's argument is organized. *Phronesis* is knowledge which is impoverished in the abstract—if you try to formulate it in a rule, it sounds anemic, like saying of courage that it consists in being neither rash nor cowardly—and acquires texture only in the application, which "knows" the difference between the two in the concrete. And it can even be formulated in terms of Derrida's theory of repetition: a paradigm forms when a particular experimental practice begins to catch on, to get passed along, and reenacted over and over again, with an ever-accumulating sophistication, alteration, and extension, until a community of practitioners, of those who know to repeat the practice, is built up.

The really interesting case for radical hermeneutics, however, is not normalized but transgressive, i.e., "revolutionary," science, namely, those points in the history of science when all of the skill—let us say, all of the *phronesis*—of the practicing scientist will not do, when, despite his best efforts, certain puzzles simply resist solution so obstinately that the scientist begins to blame the paradigm instead of herself. Now this is a conservative process, Kuhn thinks, and it is well that it is, lest science be victimized by every passing fancy. Scientists are properly very loath to question their paradigms, because experience has shown that most puzzles usually do succumb to the powers of the paradigm. Kuhn is so insistent on this point, I might add, that one is astonished to see the charges of irrationalism that are thrown up against him.[6] But occasionally the scientist faces a puzzle which is not just a puzzle but a genuine anomaly, a counterexample, an unexpected result which simply cannot be accounted for by the paradigm. This is a moment of "crisis" for the science, and the crisis lasts until a new paradigm is proposed which covers the anomaly. In *Being and Time*, Heidegger said that the level a science has reached is measured by how much stomach it has for such crises (SZ 9/BT 29). In other words, normal science is and needs to be shaken by periods of revolution, if science is to have any "movement."

The question is: what is it like to live in these revolutionary periods? This is the point at which I think *phronesis* has its thunderstorm.[7] *Phronesis* functions only within an existing framework, an established paradigm. It is a fundamentally conservative notion in the best sense of that word, that is, it knows how to keep something alive, to renew it in changing circumstances but always within the compass of an established order. It requires a stable paradigm, a more or less fixed order. Aristotle conceived of the functioning of *phronesis* within a fundamentally stable *polis*, not within a period of revolutionary conflict. *Phronesis* is the virtue which enables us to apply courage, e.g., to a new situation. It is acquired slowly, by practice, by imitating the moves of the prudent man. But suppose the *polis* is divided among itself, torn into competing factions, each of which has its own ideas about the prudent man. Suppose the *polis* is decentered, ruptured, in conflict? Suppose it is a mixed *polis*, populated with Athenian democrats and Spartan warriors (and Chinese wise men), each of whom speaks of loving the gods and the city and of doing one's civic duty but each of whom has entirely different ideas and practices, so that one does not know whether it is courage which is called for? *Phronesis* cannot function if there is a conflict about who the prudent man is. The young men (sic!) of the *polis* will not make progress in *phronesis* if they do not know which prudent man to follow, if there are too many prudent men. And the state of revolutionary science, of the conflict of paradigms, is like not knowing who the prudent man is.

When Kuhn used the term "incommensurability" to describe this state of affairs, he was visited by a thunderstorm of his own. He meant that competing paradigms lack a common, external measure, a neutral third party to which they could both appeal and whose authority they would respect. Paradigms range over a field which they themselves have opened up (like "projections"), so that they are loosely (not strictly) self-validating, i.e., they tend to confirm themselves, to generate data that confirm their own power, to solve problems that they are equipped to solve and to avoid the ones that they are not. The advocates of a new paradigm, on the other hand, have learned to see the world in different terms, to situate things in a new framework—of which the Copernican "paradigm-shift" is the most intuitively clear example. Heidegger would say they have effected a "change-over" (*Umschlag*, SZ/BT §69b) in their mode of projection. There is no common meta-theory to which the advocates of both paradigms can appeal, since their views affect the whole network of scientific theory. Nor are there any common, neutral facts to which they can appeal, since, as we have seen, facts are always arti-facts of the theory in which they belong. Hence, the debate between the advocates of the paradigms is at cross-purposes. Each has its own standards of what constitutes good science, and each holds equally "reasonable" views. Enter the wolves.[8]

Now one might think that there are certain meta-paradigmatic criteria in terms of which paradigms can be judged and directly compared with each other—like accuracy, consistency, scope, simplicity, and fruitfulness.[9] But, although everybody is willing to accept these "criteria," Kuhn argues, they are utterly ineffective in resolving conflicts. Indeed, they conflict with one another, so that we can get accuracy only by sacrificing fruitfulness, or conversely. One paradigm is better in one regard but not in another. In the end, scientists have to choose which criteria are more important to them and where they want to concentrate their labors. These criteria, it turns out, are not hard and fast rules but very high-altitude scientific "values" which are of no practical use. Everybody can agree about them without agreeing about what to do.

Now on the face of it, this looks like another situation in which *phronesis* can help out; it appears to be a matter of knowing how to apply these higher-level values, as Bernstein suggests.[10] But that I do not accept. For these values do not have the determinacy of an Aristotelian virtue. They are quite vacuous generalizations, much more like slogans about loving the gods, which men of very different persuasions would repeat in our hypothetical mixed *polis*, than like the relatively determinate schemata of the virtues. Having recourse to these values in science as a decision procedure for solving a dispute is like telling a young Greek to be a good citizen, when his problem is whether that means he should be more like an Athenian democrat or a Spartan warrior or a Chinese sage.

Even the appeal to "evidence" is skewed ("in slippage," they would say in Paris), for a new paradigm is not adopted purely on the weight of the evidence. Evidence is not a "given" (the principle of all principles never *works!*), for what is important evidence in one view is not important in another. Furthermore, the evidence which supports a new and promising and suggestive hypothesis is usually much slimmer than the evidence supporting the prevailing view. What is afoot in such radical shifts in the views of scientists are the instincts, the tacit knowledge, the faith of the scientists who advocate the new way of seeing things. All of their working acumen as practicing scientists tells them that the old paradigm is spent, that the future lies in a new direction, that there is more and promising research and work forthcoming from the new paradigm than from the old. Conclusive evidence for the new paradigm is brought forth only afterward, after it has become the received view and the guide of normal science.

The defenders of the true faith were fast to descend upon Kuhn for all of this, for throwing science to the wolves, making it a matter of irrational choice. But I would say that he has described a situation in which reason is put to its best test, when it must show what it is made of, when it is thrown back upon its own resources and insights, when it must make its way without the guidance of a discourse on method or by applying and appropriating an established way. The way is not established here but in the making. Reason is forced here to cut its own path, to break with established habits, to *think* in a radical, ground-breaking way. I would say that at this point reason is put *in play* with the matter at hand, that it moves along the way *(Weg)*, is put effectively in motion *(Be-weg-ung)*. At this point, where no established way has been charted, there is a certain free play of scientific rationality, a free repetition of possibilities which the old system harbored, a creative transformation of old signs—let us even say, a releasing of the signs which make up the old system. We reach a point where the old paradigm is made to tremble, and a new configuration arises out of its shaking, its *ébranler*. Let us call this paradigm shift a repetition which alters, a creative, productive repeating. (Derrida should write about science.)

In normal science, the initiate skillfully applies the paradigm to the day-to-day problems of scientific work. In revolutionary science, the paradigm trembles, and what it means to do science is in question. There are no guidelines, other than to pursue what seems to be best for science itself, for fruitful research and problem solving. There are no rules to fall back upon; what is at stake is not only a particular paradigm but science itself. "What is at stake"—that is the language of play and of the game.[11] The most creative moments in the history of science occur precisely when scientific stereotypes "loosen"—in times of crisis, anomaly, of "human idiosyncrasy, error and confusion" (SSR 138).

> . . . [T]he new paradigm emerges all at once, sometimes in the middle of the night, in the mind of a man deeply immersed in crisis. What the nature of that final stage is—how an individual invents (or finds he has invented) a new way of giving order to data now all assembled—must here remain inscrutable and may be permanently so. (SSR 90)

The one generalization Kuhn does offer is that such insights ordinarily occur in a young scientist or one new to the profession, for such individuals, "being little committed by prior practice to the traditional rules of normal science, are particularly likely to see that those rules no longer define a playable game and to conceive another set that can replace them" (SSR 90).

Now whatever this inscrutable, midnight decision making is, it is not Aristotelian *phronesis*. *Phronesis* is the virtue of older men, and young men have only the beginnings of it. *Phronesis* is a process of deliberation and not the product of a midnight visitation, of a breakthrough to a new way of seeing things which is most likely to occur in the young and inexperienced. *Phronesis* does not come in a flash but is slowly nurtured through years of training. Times of scientific crisis are times of a certain free play, when the regular business of science is in jeopardy, when the best minds are loose, in play with the play of the issues before them, on their own. Incommensurability occurs at the interstices between scientific epochs, in moments of epochal play (Heidegger), points of Foucaultian rupture.

According to Kuhn, part of the explanation of the success of science is the enormous authority it exercises over its initiates. The young scientist is guided not so much by rational evidence, as we like to think, as by the authority of his teachers and the textbooks (SSR 80). And these teachers present not evidence for their laws but models to be faithfully imitated and applied via textbooks which rewrite the past in their own image (SSR 136–43). And that means that the revolutionary scientist has to deal with a considerable amount of repression, professional rejection, and fear of subversion (SSR 5). This is perhaps Kuhn's most Parisian moment: normal science flourishes because of its authoritarian practices. But that is not an objection to normal science for Kuhn or Derrida. Il faut la verité. Science flourishes because of the violence with which it enforces its paradigm (which is a Parisian way of saying that the scientific community is organized around a paradigm which it believes in) and because of the violence that the paradigm inflicts on the world (a Parisian way of saying a conceptual framework, a way of seeing things). But Derrida would likewise insist that all such violence must be seen *as* violence, that every paradigm is a fiction, a contingency, a way of laying things out which cannot claim absolute status or immunity from reform. Science, too, is an interpretation, Nietzsche said. And so there must always be room in science for iconoclasm, for scientific paradigm breakers, for those who resist the received view, who suspect "normalcy." That is what Rorty likes about Derrida and why he tends to see Derrida, Kuhn, and Heidegger in the same light. Subversiveness is structurally necessary to normalcy, that is, whatever has been normalized is only a certain contingent arrangement of signs whose efficaciousness is responsible for its success but which is so marked by contingency that it is always vulnerable to subversion.

On this point, about the subversion of normalcy, Derrida is closer to Feyerabend than to Kuhn. Feyerabend defends what he calls counterinductionism, the claim that everything which is not suggested by the data, every contrary and perverse assumption, must be entertained, precisely in order to test the strength of the received view, and that includes myths, popular superstitions, ancient religions, witchcraft, and voodoo. That indeed is why Feyerabend thinks that normal science is a myth; science never degenerates into such a totalitarian condition—a view which is also suggested by Derrida's notions of dissemination and decentering. If Kuhn thinks that there actually is a time when "normal science" is peacefully settled into place and has the faith of everyone, then a Derridean would suspect that that is a simplification (just as he would suspect Heidegger's epochal units). If, on the other hand, Kuhn thinks that normal science is honored more in the breach than in the observance, then Derrida would not object to the idea.[12]

Kuhn's willingness to read the history of science without the optics of metaphysics even shows up in his attitude toward "truth." The shift from one paradigm to the next does not represent an increase in rationality for Kuhn, since it would be good science to defend either paradigm. The rationality of each position is different, not better or worse. Then how does science make progress? Not by gradually approximating the "truth," if that means that the match between scientific theories and the real world grows tighter and tighter.

> There is, I think, no theory-independent way to reconstruct phrases like "really there"; the notion of a match between the ontology of a theory and its "real" counterpart in nature now seems to me illusive in principle. Besides, as a historian, I am impressed with the implausibility of the view. I do not doubt, for example, that Newton's mechanics improves on Aristotle's, and that Einstein's improves on Newton's as instrument for puzzle-solving. But I can see in their succession no coherent direction of ontological development. (SSR 206)

The validity of scientific theories is their power to solve the puzzles with which nature presents us, their power to control and predict phenomena. The shift from one paradigm to another does not stem from a deeper insight into nature but from a shift of strategy in coping with the puzzles faced by the scientist, in coping with the flux.[13] Il faut le paradigme.

Oddly enough, Heidegger holds a more conservative point of view about scientific truth than does Kuhn. Heidegger thinks that any projective interpretation which is not "free-floating," that is, capriciously devised, has a "disclosive" force, that is, it illuminates and frees up the things themselves. He does not take truth to be social consensus or a pragmatic will-to-power but disclosure, effecting a clearing. Consequently, there is a streak of scientific realism in *Being and Time*. The *Umschlag* by which the scientist shifts into gear is not a capricious turn of fancy but a genuine projectedness onto nature *as* the being which is understood in the natural sciences. The world can be projectively understood in any number of ways, beginning with the primordial engagement of Dasein with the world in circumspective concern and extending out to the most abstract constructions of the theoretical sciences. The air is thinner and "less primordial" in the sphere of theoretical-scientific projections, but this is not to say that such projections are fictions, as Derrida and Rorty openly claim and as Kuhn intimates. Even later on, in his less innocent and more deconstructive hermeneutic of the history of Being, when Heidegger becomes more severe about science, he never intends to deny science its truth within its own proper domain but only to delimit its pretension and its will-to-power which blinds us to the simple event of the *Ereignis*, which is the real matter for thought.

In sum, any adequate account of scientific rationality must see that in its finest hours—in moments of crisis and discovery, of revolution and progress—reason requires a moment of free play and intellectual legroom *(Spielraum)*. We do not destroy the reputation of reason with this talk of the play; we just tell a more reasonable story about it.

THE PLAY OF REASON AND THE PRINCIPLE OF REASON

But reason is a serious matter. Leibniz gave it the form of a great principle: nothing is without reason; nothing is without sufficient reason; nothing is unless a sufficient reason is rendered for it. And no less an authority than Heidegger has taken the principle of reason very seriously, devoting a lifetime to the question of reason and ground, of founding and grounding. He even criticized his own first attempts to get at the essence of reason *(Wesen des Grundes)*, pointing out that you do not get at what is coming to presence *(wesen, in the verbal sense)* in reason until you hear it as a "principle of reason" *(Satz vom Grund)* (SG 48).[14] For Heidegger, the principle of reason was a serious concern *(Sache)*. And with good reason. For the "principle of reason" is all around us today. As a principle, reason is an *arché*, a *princeps*, a prince, which like all royalty makes its presence felt everywhere. It has an enormous sphere of influence *(Machtbereich)*, leaving nothing out, no entity untouched by the claim it makes. It demands reasons, sufficiency, the rendering of a sufficient reason, for everything. So how can we speak of the play of reason if reason is a deadly serious principle?

Let us hear more from Heidegger. The principle of reason is very "high and mighty" *(grossmächtig, SG 42–43)*. It has us all in its grips, makes a claim *(Anspruch)* upon us (who are its "subjects"), demanding of us that we ground and found, render reason, render homage to the *arché*/king. Heidegger said that it is no merely human voice which sounds in this saying (*Spruch*) but the voice of Being itself. To live within the sphere of influence of this principle, to be claimed by this claim, is the fate of those who live in the last epoch of metaphysics, the age of the atom, the nuclear age. That is where this high and mighty principle makes a particular show of strength. For the atomic age marks the epoch of the final and most extreme instance of treating entities—and Being itself—in terms of reason, as matters for rational control, the raw material of reason's will to power.

This final, most extreme extension of reason's might, of its demands for rational grounds, is the age of *Gestell*, which means the *collected (Ge-)* energy, the accumulating momentum under which man is *put (stellen)*, all of the power of the impulse by which man is driven to put things under the rule of reason, to reduce things to rational rule. There is a double *stellen* in *Ge-stell*. For the way man sets upon (*stellen*) the earth is itself a function of the way he is "put upon" by the force of the epochal sendings. The power which man exerts upon things is itself due to the power under which he himself lives. The rule of the principle of reason, of the reason/prince, of the *arché*, is granted by the *Ereignis*, which sends the age of *Technik*, sends the Being of beings as the technical-calculable world. *Technik* is the master name in the present age for Being as presence, as *Bestand*, as the presence which stands in reserve, available for use. It is because Being sets upon man with such a fury that we are ourselves caught up in pushing things around.

So now it is clear. Heidegger took reason seriously because, in the nuclear age, when reason takes the form of a principle, all the play has been removed from reason and reason has become deadly serious. The play of reason has hardened into an authoritative principle. And so Heidegger set himself the task (SG) to delimit reason, to set forth the historical-epochal limits of reason as a creature of modernity and of the Cartesian subject and so to break up the deadly hold which the principle of reason has on us.

The "subject" demands that a "reason" be brought forth for the "object" only because the subject has long since ceased to let the being be in its own ground (SG 53–54). And if no reason (*ratio*) is forthcoming (*reddere*), the being is declared null and void, no being at all (*nihil*), a mere phantom of the subject. Whence whatever claims citizenship in the domain over which reason rules needs to show its papers, to give a reason to the subject, which is the agent of the king, acting on his behalf, collecting the tax due. But Heidegger wants to know if there are any entities which defy the authority of reason, which elude the sphere of influence of the *arché*/king. Can there be a suspension of reason's relentless search for the "reason why," respite from its relentless teleological and archaeological demands? He gets help from a renegade mystical poet:[15]

The rose is without why; it blooms because it blooms;
It cares not for itself, asks not if it's seen.

The poet is obviously a subversive, an outlaw, an enemy of the state and the king, one of those apocalyptic voices which are bent on stirring every one up. The law says that nothing is without reason, but the outlaw poet says that the rose is without why.

Notice though that the poet does not say that the rose is without reason or ground, but without *why*. The mystical rose then does not exactly contravene the principle so much as it ignores it and takes no part in its seeking and asking for reasons. The rose breaks with the *reddere* rather than with the *ratio*—in order to subsist, rest, linger, in its *own grounds*. The poet lets the rose be, lets it rise up and linger for a while in its own emergent *physis*. But letting-be is what *legein* and *logos* mean, and *ratio* is the Romanized, de-cadent, fallen off, derivative sense of the original Greek experience, which gives it a treacherous twist that sets in motion the medieval scholastic and early modern Latinization of *logos*, which leads to Leibniz (SG 67ff.) Another powerful Heideggerian tale!

Heidegger thus exposes the rule of the principle of reason to its *other*, to the thinking which has the boldness and the audacity not to demand reasons—rather the way one learns to float only by surrendering every attempt to swim and by remaining perfectly still. That takes practice and a bit of courage; it is simple but hard. Poetic thinking is like that. It achieves a relationship with the world which is more simple and primordial than reason; it is in touch with things long before the demand for reason arises and, indeed, is so deeply tuned to things that the need for reasons never arises.

Now I daresay there is no more radical or wonderful delimitation of the principle of reason than that. Another stunning postcard from Freiburg. And I mean that seriously. This delimitation of the principle of reason is referred to by Heidegger himself, somewhat playfully I must say, as the "leap" from the ground: the *Satz*—for leaping is one of the senses of *setzen*—from the *Grund*; a leap right off the firm ground into who-knows-what (SG 95). This is the leap in virtue of which we take leave of the domain and the dominion of the principle of reason, of the reason/prince. And if we land in a place, it is that place or *topos* where there is no giving or taking of reasons, no propositional discourse at all, for it is the "propositions" or "claims" issued by the subject which require reasons and grounds. If we leap from the ground, then we must land in an abyss, an *Ab-grund*, a sphere of groundlessness. We take a leap off the stability of the ground, the solidity of presence—terra firma—and we land in the flux! The flux is that sphere of groundlessness which Heidegger calls the *Spiel*, the play which plays without why, according to the outlaw poet. And so Heidegger delimits the principle of reason and makes room for the play by locating the region where the play is to be found outside the reach of the principle.

Indeed. The play is all (SG 188). Beneath, behind, around, to the side of all grounding and founding, in the ground's cracks and crevices and interstices, is the play. That is the first, last, and constant thought of this study. The one great danger, the most perilous condition of all—and here I ask to be pardoned if I temporarily adopt a serious and apocalyptic tone, it will soon pass—is to take reason too seriously. But we have just said that Heidegger took reason seriously all his life. True, but now we can see that he did that in order to make a leap out of its domain into the play. He took reason seriously just long enough to show that there is a sphere of play outside the reach of the principle of reason, outside the reach of the long arm of the law. There is a sphere of poetizing and thinking which forever eludes rationalization, reason giving, rendering reasons. Heidegger shows us that reason is one of the powers which only *pretend* to be, and that we ought not to take its pretensions to universal jurisdiction seriously.

And Heidegger had an excellent reason for saying this. For the fact is that the *arché*/king, let us say, the emperor, has no clothes. It is one of the most embarrassing things in the history of metaphysics. If we ask the principle of reason for its own reason, if we ask what is the reason for the principle of reason, if we ask about the reasonableness of reason, we get no answer. The silence is very embarrassing. Under pain of infinite regress, the buck of reason stops with the principle of reason itself. The principle cannot itself have a reason (SG 27–28). It must be its own authority, speak with its own voice. It cannot call the police; it is the police.

And so there is a certain groundlessness in the principle of ground, a certain hollowness in the voice which is making such unlimited claim upon us and which we do well to listen for. There is a point where we must call the king's bluff, delimit his claim and authority, deny him universal and unqualified authority. The principle of reason has no reason but wants us to take its word for it that *everything* requires a reason. But we must not lose our nerve. We must just defy the king, refuse to pay such an exorbitant tax. For there are always thinkers like Heidegger and Angelus Silesius—and others, too, a long list of people (early Greeks and German poets do not have a corner on the market)—who simply defy the principle of reason, who have delimited its sphere of influence *(Machtbereich)*. They invoke other possibilities, other ways to think. They "write differently," and they seem to be no worse off for it. On the contrary, they are better off; they have made their way into the domain of play.

Still, Johannes Climacus used to say that he was worried about those who took the "speculative leap" (in the Hegelian sense), for, though that may all be very well for them, they leave the rest of us behind to face the worst. If Heidegger and Silesius have found their way *beyond* the range of the principle of reason, have opened up a different way to think, one that I for one want to cherish and nourish (the range of the play itself) that does not mean that we should let the principle of reason have its way in its own sphere, that its power should not be checked even within its own sphere of influence, that we should let it be a wholly unreasonable tyrant in its own domain. Heidegger found a reason not to take reason seriously by finding a sphere of play outside of reason. But I want to let play infiltrate reason itself. I do not want to leave the country but, remaining within its borders, to insist upon the play of reason itself. I want to say that just because reason is serious business, we must keep it in play and give up the thought of escaping across its borders.

And that is what I have been arguing in this chapter and particularly in my discussion of Kuhn. I think it is a serious mistake to think that reason is always a dead serious affair of rule-governed procedures, of fixed techniques. If Heidegger has delimited reason in one way, by finding another way of thinking in another sphere outside the sphere of influence of reason itself, there is also another way to delimit reason and check its authority, and that is to infiltrate its corporation, plant secret agents in its system, and put reason itself, in its own sphere of influence, into play. We want to establish a *Spielraum* for reason. We want to give it some space, as we say today, give it some free play, some room to move around. For it is my view that reason itself, not just mystical poetry and Silesius's rose, cannot be understood for what it is apart from the play. When the chips are down, reason finds itself without the help of established rules, on its own, in free play, in motion, in *kinesis*. When the guard rails which science devises for its comfort and guidance fail it, when it is thrown on its own, when it has nothing to fall back on but its own ingenuity, then reason is fully at work, which means fully in play.

I resist the notion that the life of reason can be *formalized*, reduced to a rule of law. I am betting against the artificial intelligence industry, e.g., at least against its deep project, which is to reduce all of the fluidity, the ambiance, the free play which marks human intelligence to the rule of law. I like the disruptive raids which Hubert Dreyfus has made on its camp, showing the staggering complexity which is involved in so simple a matter as being able to read handwriting, to recognize the "same" character no matter how badly scribbled and scrawled, and to hear the human voice in all of its variations of accent, intonation, emphasis, etc. The work of artificial intelligence can only make its way so far into the flux, and then it hits the blur of the pure flow, the fluidity, the play. I think that Dreyfus is right, that, if one day we are able to synthesize human intelligence, that will only be because we have found a way to clone a human being or otherwise to reproduce the human body. And, when that happens, we will have made another human being, but we will certainly not have reconstituted human intelligence by means of a digital processor. And that is because we do not process isolated bits of information. Rather, in a way which has been felicitously described by Gestaltists and phenomenologists, we organize, interpret, read, alter, and configure patterns in amazingly swift, adroit, and complex ways. We do not pass through a series of ordered steps; we do not run through all the combinatorial possibilities. We are not presence/absence machines, electronic switchboards with one switch on and one switch off, but rather some kind of fluid movement which is all too messy for AI research to master. Writers like Dreyfus are like Heideggerian secret agents who work their way into the computer industry and effect a work of disruption within *Technik*, delimiting its claims locally, not globally, as Heidegger, and most of us, are content to do.[16]

And what the phenomenologists showed about human perception and intelligence, which is perhaps best encapsulated by Merleau-Ponty's notion of "ambiguity," has been pushed even further by Derrida and the "(non-)principle" of "undecidability."[17] Derrida is delighted by the *graphic* structure of the computer revolution, by all the talk of pro-gramming, of a new way of writing, of the displacement of the book by the screen, etc. But no one has shown better than Derrida the limits of the AI project—not by any theoretical arguments against it, to be sure, but by his own practice of writing. For, if the digital processor can capture the work of signs, it cannot capture its play. If it can reenact the formalizable and structural features of signs, its a priori grammar, it cannot reenact the play of signs, cannot exploit the phonic, graphic, semantic linkages, cannot learn the slippage, the disseminative drift, the free play. We can teach the computer to work but not to play (it can only play rule-governed games). We can teach it anything that is rule-governed, any logic. We can teach it *ratio* as calculative thinking. We could teach it onto-theo-logic, but we could never teach it how to read *Glas* (or write *Glas*).

This is all a way of saying that we should defend the play of reason against the principle of reason, that we should not reduce reason to the principle of reason, that we should not give away the word "reason" to those who have in mind only rule-governed processes and fixed decision-procedures. That is a very unreasonable view of reason, one which takes the play out of reason, which reduces reason to dead seriousness. That is the one thing I have against Heidegger's leap into another region. For I do not want to leave reason behind in the hands of *Technik*, like a retreating army abandoning its comrades to the enemy.

Strategically it is a bad idea to allow one's opponents to say that they speak in the name of reason. That puts one in quite a bad light. For, even if there is nothing irrational about the rose which is without why, it certainly makes it look like there is. It is much better to infiltrate the corporation of reason, to write about science in the way that Kuhn and Polanyi do and the whole generation of philosophers of science which they inspired (and also, we should not forget, in the way that Heidegger started out in *Being and Time*). We should write about computers in the way that Dreyfus does, produce essays in literary criticism and anthropology, in the whole spread of the "sciences"—natural, social, and human—essays which show the play which is in play within reason.[18] And it is not just a matter of writing but maybe even of getting on television.

There is a moment in the life of reason when reason is cut adrift, when it is not buoyed up by fixed guidelines. The function of reason is to make a cut into the flux, to reach a certain configurational resolution of a perceptual flow or of the flow of a problem, when it reorganizes the model, the paradigm, tinkers with its system of signs, begins to write differently. It is in such moments that reason starts a revolution—in physics or economics or theology—and revitalizes an entire generation of very serious researchers. We are not in the position of having either to make the leap out of reason into another sphere or to remain confined within it. The idea is to emancipate those who live within reason's sphere of influence, to introduce liberal reforms into its laws, to reinsert the play which informs even calculative thought. The best sort of calculation is done not by calculators but by calculative minds in free flight, in play. If things are as we say, in flux, in undecidable drift and slippage, and if reason is to respond to things, to keep up a correspondence with them (according even to the most classical demand of the metaphysics of truth), reason must play it loose, be capable of unexpected moves, of paradigm switches, of following up unorthodox suggestions. The most reasonable view of reason denies that you can write a handbook about the way reason works. You have to learn to play the game. Thinking is a hands-on process, which is an interesting way to rewrite what Heidegger says in *What Is Called Thinking?*—that only beings with hands can think (WHD 49–50/WCT 14–15).

But one point more remains to be made about the free play of reason, and that concerns the necessity of keeping the game fair, i.e., the politics of reason. All this talk about unorthodox views and revolutions is likely to make the politicians and university administrators nervous, and they would just as soon put a stop to it. Kings have always had a way of dealing with revolutions and palace coups.

THE INSTITUTIONALIZATION OF REASON

Reason today has been institutionalized. It is not allowed to roam the streets freely. That suggests that it is mad, or ill, and that we have had to put it away (or maybe the opposite, that it is mad or ill because we have put it away). I have not been authorized to exclude these suggestions, to ban these associations. I am just trying to propose that today reason is housed within the framework of an institution, like the university, that it functions within an administrative setting. After all, we can hardly avoid institutional forms of life. And we ought to be wary of a clean and decidable opposition between a confined reason and a reason set free. Do we not require both? Do we not require a kind of undecidable fluctuating between reason's institutional and noninstitutional forms, a kind of double agent which is able to slip back and forth without being noticed between both forms of life? In any case, it is impossible to have a reasonable discussion about reason if we do not recognize that it has been institutionalized. And that is what we mean to do here.

Kant spoke of "pure" reason and the "autonomy" of reason. But that is a dangerous abstraction, for reason is always already embedded in systems of power. To a great extent what "reason" means is a function of the system of power which is currently in place, and what is irrational is what is out of power. Indeed, it is of the essence of the power which institutionalized reason exerts that it is able to define what is out of power as "irrational." Those who dissent from the ruling standards of reason are often declared irrational in much the same way that those who dissent from the current administration in Washington are declared unpatriotic. One enlists the authority of the institution in the service of one's own ideas. And those who dissent have to show that they are not against reason or the country—that they are not mad or traitorous—when they are only against the ideas which currently prevail.

Both Heidegger and Kuhn have alerted us to the hollowness of a pure "logic of science" which prescinds from the institutional circumstances in which scientific ideas are generated and debated. Heidegger warned against the growing consolidation of the "institutional character of the sciences," which is wiping out the difference between the natural scientist and the humanist, who is gradually disappearing.

> He is succeeded by the research man who is engaged in research projects. These, rather than the cultivating of erudition, lend to his works its atmosphere of incisiveness. The research man no longer needs a library at home. Moreover, he is constantly on the move. He negotiates at meetings and collects information at congresses. He contracts for commissions with publishers. The latter now determine along with him which books must be written. (HW 85/QCT 125)

And Kuhn, to the dismay of many, showed how "professionalism" and the authority of the scientific old guard had more to do with the work of science than philosophers of science wanted to admit. One way to deal with something new, Kuhn shows, is to outlaw it, to brand it a nonopinion and nonprofessional, to say that it just does not register on a professional scale. One simply excludes it and deprives it of a voice. And to a certain extent, he says, the ruling generation of scholars is never persuaded by the logic of a new paradigm but simply outlived by its younger proponents.

No account of reason can prescind from the institutionalization of reason in the university. Debates about reason are debates conducted by university professors in journals and books, at symposia and public lectures, by men and women who aspire to tenure, promotion, and support for more research. What is rational and what is not are very often a function of the powers that be within the academy, of those who hold the senior faculty positions in a more or less identifiable number of elite institutions. It is they who set the style and tone of the discourse in the profession. They define the "right questions" and the right way to go about addressing these questions. They set the standards for, and determine the selection of, the kinds of articles that can be published in the journals, the sorts of books that the best university presses publish, the kinds of proposals that can be supported by the foundations. They review one another's books, discuss one another's articles, invite one another to the colloquia and seminars they sponsor, recommend one another for foundational support, hire one another's doctoral students, invite one another to serve as visiting professors, nominate one another for distinguished chairs and lectureships and offices in professional societies—in a self-validating, self-congratulating circle which controls the profession.

All of this has the effect of defining what is or is not "rational discourse" in the profession. Those who do not debate these issues, and/or who employ a different sort of discourse, relegate themselves to publishing—if at all—in marginal journals and presses, to teaching—if at all—in secondary and tertiary institutions, and to getting along without the help of foundational support of their work. In American philosophy it is only respectable in certain places to cite twentieth-century French and German philosophers, and readers of Heidegger and Derrida are still more likely to be found outside the philosophy departments in most elite universities. Thus, with an irony that would make Kierkegaard jealous, philosophers who have spilled not a little ink in debates about "rationality" enforce extraordinarily ethnocentric and exclusionary standards about what reason means and how one is supposed to conduct debates about rationality.

But the power exerted *within* the university is dwarfed by the power exerted *upon* the university from without. For the university belongs to a technico-political power structure.[19] It is part of a social system which has increasingly technical and pragmatic expectations of the university and, hence, of what is "rational." This social system is more and more under the sway of the "principle" of reason. The university is looked upon accordingly to supply the technical and professional needs of society—its needs for scientists, engineers, accountants, computer specialists, nurses, physicians, lawyers. The university even provides a pool of talent and a training ground for professional sports teams. It is expected to train future citizens, to make good Americans (or Frenchmen, or whatever one needs). The university is put more and more to work by the society to which it belongs, and it has less and less time for the free play of ideas whose ground, reason, and practical purpose cannot be easily or directly shown. And the disciplines in which one hopes to find such free play, to the extent that they are not themselves overrun by the "principle of reason" and subjected to technical purposes, are retained almost as ornaments or quaint tokens of a bygone age and because of the extreme embarrassment that would result if one simply dropped them.

The play of reason is arrested by the principle of reason; the free movement of reason within the university is checked by its institutionalization in the university. The energies of reason and the university are channeled into career preparation, submitted to constant monitoring by the principle of reason. The university becomes an instrument of normalization, of reenforcing and resupplying the existing order, and of the exclusion of those who dissent from it. It becomes a center where everything is centered on a national purpose, a vocational purpose, a technical purpose, where absolutely nothing is "without why" and where everything decentering and in free play is held suspect or dangerous, even though it is essential to reason, indeed is what reason is. Even the "humanities" are "legitimized" pragmatically, by offering a "rationale" for their inclusion in the curriculum, which is to provide for more upright and articulate leaders in the professions, leaders who know how to write and speak and analyze, who have "values" along with skills, and who can "communicate effectively." The humanities, too, obey the principle of reason—effective communication: *ratio sufficiens, ratio efficiens.*

And there is another, perhaps better, rationale for the humanities. For they provide a useful place to house those who speak, write, and think differently, who are given to subversive, decentering thoughts, who raise high-level criticisms of the existing order. We keep them off the streets, out of the marketplace where the effect of their dangerous discourse can be contained. And on this point, Derrida thinks, even Marxism has institutional respectability and remains an "intra-institutional" force.[20] It has adopted the respectable style of the university discourse and hence can be both assimilated and contained by the university. Marxists circulate mostly within the the borders of the campus.

Ultimately, the university is called upon to lend a hand in the preparation for war. It must supply the brainpower for the will-to-power. It supplies the physics, the engineering, and the computer technology which the nation needs in order to maintain and increase its arsenal of nuclear weaponry—and nowadays perhaps to build an elaborate and dangerous laser defense system which will extend the nuclear race into outer space. The tallest, most impressive, and newest buildings on the campus are financed by and dedicated to the defense effort. Government-controlled grants see to it that the national purpose is always served. Nothing is without reason, particularly research which leads to more and more dangerous weapons. After that comes research into a cure for cancer, instead of an exposé of the industrial powers which are furiously pumping carcinogens into the atmosphere and food supplies. And, as the free play is taken out of the university, no one dissents. No one even knows what is going on in other parts of the university.

The question of reason cannot be discussed apart from the *Gestell*, which is the frame which frames us in, which frames the university in, which frames reason into a principle of reason. It is the *Gestell* which makes the institutionalization of reason so dangerous. In *Being and Time*, Heidegger made some acute and suggestive remarks toward a hermeneutics of science: that even in its most theoretical moments, it remains a praxis; that it is guided by a certain way of projecting the Being of entities; that it is periodically shaken by fundamental revolutions in its conceptual horizons; that any "logic" of science can only limp along lamely after the fact, etc. In his later writings, Heidegger lost his patience with such work. And that is no wonder. It is as if he was seized by the urgency of an increasingly more dangerous situation. After 1945 all the terms of the debate about *Technik* changed dramatically. The nuclear arms race was launched; the power of the atom was unleashed as a weapon and had already seared human flesh. The idea of war had undergone a sea change. A quarter of a century later a man would walk on the moon, which frightened Heidegger half to death.[21] And today, with the advent of electronic miniaturization, the power of the computer has been expanded into the smallest corners of our "factical life," increasing immeasurably the powers of normalization and the rule of "information."

It is no wonder that Heidegger's voice became more shrill, more apocalyptic. Here is one of the cases where apocalypticism serves a purpose, when it is a voice of protest in a world where messages are under the systematic control of a powerful postmaster, where the only message sent out across public lines is the principle of reason. The later writings became an attempt to interrupt the message of that high and mighty principle, to point out the danger of an expanding technology which was transforming the world and man's relationship to the world, transforming our ideas of art and man and of the city, the *polis* and its institutions. Things are endangered even if the bomb is not dropped, he said, endangered in their "essence," in the way they come to presence, namely, as the raw material of technical power. Things are put upon by man because man is himself put upon by the way technology comes to presence, by its essence as *Gestell*.

Thus, the sober hermeneutic analyses, suffused with the technical vocabulary of phenomenology, gave way to the voice of protest. The hermeneutic determination of the essence of science was displaced by a deconstructive critique of the Wesen of technology, of what is coming to pass, what is coming about, in a technological world.[22] Heidegger is no longer concerned with a logic of science—not even an existential or hermeneutic logic, a genea-logic. Science belongs together with technology as inseparable forms of the will-to-power as knowledge, of the will-to-know, the will to dominate and manipulate, of what Foucault calls "power-knowledge." The metaphysics of the will-to-power stamps our age, marks our epoch, dominating all the phenomena of our time— political and social, scientific and artistic. We are in danger of being swept up in an enormous totalitarian and totalizing movement which aims to bring every individual, every institution, every human practice under its sway. He is not concerned with science and technology themselves but with the preoccupation with control, manipulation, and power which they induce. He thinks they have a common essence, that science cannot be purified of technology, that science is driven by a desire for control and mastery, that science is the will-to-power as knowledge. They spring from a common metaphysics which articulates the guiding conceptions of modern technological civilization, the ontology of technology.

All problems—political, social, personal—are conceived as technological problems for which an appropriate technology of behavior is required. The world has become the raw material for the various technologies of power— political technologies which manipulate and control public opinion and policy; social technologies which set standards of conduct; educational technologies which insure the normalization and regulation of schools and children. It is not only nature which must submit to our control but education, sexuality, the political process, the arts—in short, the whole sphere of human practices. Nuclear power and bio-power; power/knowledge; the will-to-know and knowing as willing. This is what is coming to pass *(wesen)* in science and technology, in the sense that this is the frame of mind of a culture dominated by the success and prestige of science and technology. And the university bends slowly under the power of the principle of reason.

Heidegger's meditations on play and Derrida's exuberant demonstrations of textual play are emancipatory acts of protest against the momentum of the growing forces of control and the concentrations of power. Foucault and Adorno, Kuhn and Feyerabend, Heidegger and Derrida represent important delimitations of normalization, regulation, and manipulation, ways to check the rule of the police. They speak in the name of letting-be, of letting earth and sky, mortals and the gods, literature and science, the university and the city be, of letting all be, which is an old and difficult art. If what is called reason is always exercised within networks of power, then any really reasonable idea of reason must include a vigilance about power. It should proceed from an acute sense of letting-be, which lets reason play itself out, which listens to dissent, continually exposing what is called reason at any time to its other, exposing the ground to what it takes to be groundlessness and abyss.

It is thus essential to what Kant might call "the interests of reason" that we preserve the life of protest, dissent, and free play, the skill in writing differently and thinking differently, of debating openly. There may be no such thing as pure and disinterested reason, but there is no reason why competing interests cannot compete fairly. To protest against the reduction of reason to a principle is not to protest against reason but to argue for its expansion and for restoring it to its full scope. It is to sound an alarm about the institutionalization of reason, for we have put reason away, put it in a safe place, confined it in closed quarters in order both to keep it safe and to keep the existing order safe from it. And that is why Kierkegaard and Nietzsche are more important figures in this regard than Husserl or Heidegger. For they do not bend their knee to what the university calls reason. They reject the etiquette, the style, the discourse, the good manners of the university which keep everything safe, which preserve decorum at all costs, including the cost of repressing dissent. Kierkegaard, Derrida says, is "one of those thinkers who are foreign, even hostile to the university, [but] who gives us more to think about, with respect to the essence of the university, than academic reflections themselves."[23] Neither Kierkegaard nor Nietzsche could have survived, could have written as they did, could have created as they did, could have *taught* as they did within the university.

We have draped reason with institutional authority. We have made it a *princeps*, an *arché*/king, not only by turning it into a rigorous technique and fixed method but by giving it political authority, by creating a rationality-caste, a guild of specialists and professional practitioners of reason. The original Enlightenment idea of reason—as a protest against entrenched authority—has so withered away that what nowadays calls itself reason is the latest and most dangerous authority of all. What we call reason today is a central power tightly circled by bands of military, technical, and industrial authorities which together make up the administered society.

That is why a philosophy of decentering, dissemination, and undecidability set on the deconstruction of the metaphysics of unity and presence, a philosophy which speaks in the name of play, is widely perceived to be not only subversive—which it is; it means to be that—but also irrational, which it is not. In fact, it speaks in the name of reason, by reminding us that reason is always already embedded in systems of power in which it is inevitably caught up. Deconstruction protests the dangerous illusions of pure reason and pure logic which lull us to sleep about the real interests by which reason is always subverted. It speaks against the "principle" of reason, against a technical conception of reason and an *arché* of unrestricted authority. It speaks in the name of freedom—of speech and writing and action—and of keeping the game fair. It warns against a rationality which declares its other irrational and seeks its exclusion, like the leper, or its confinement, like the mad.

Heidegger said that the principle of reason is exposed to an abyss, that the desire for rationale is itself without ground, that the ground cannot fill up the abyss. If the political system of the university is infatuated with this principle, then the role of "thought" is to expose it to the abyss which reason wants to repress, which means, Derrida writes:

> . . . preparing oneself thereby to transform the modes of writing, approaches to pedagogy, the procedures of academic exchange, the relation to language, to other disciplines, to the institution in general, to its inside and its outside. Those who venture forth along this path, it seems to me, need not set themselves up in opposition to the principle of reason, nor need they give way to "irrationalism." They may continue to assume *within* the university, along with its memory and tradition, the imperative of professional rigor and competence. There is a double gesture here, a double postulation: to insure professional competence and the most serious tradition of the university even while going as far as possible, theoretically and practically, in the most directly underground thinking about the abyss beneath the university. . . . It is this double gesture that appears unsituatable and thus unbearable to certain university professionals in every country who join ranks to foreclose or to censure it by all available means.[24]

And so here is the answer to the question that I posed at the beginning of this discussion, about the distinction between a confined, institutionalized reason and the free play of reason. It is not a question of choosing between these alternatives. We cannot do without one or the other. Institutions are the way things get done, *and* they are prone to violence. They are inextricably, undecidably, pharmacologically both things at once. Nothing is innocent. And so it is a question of vigilance about that and, hence, of exercising a certain double agency, a critique exercised from within, of assuming the role of a treacherous and wily Hermes who subverts, who does an "inside job" on the institution. One needs to operate within the university, to prove oneself according to its standards, in order to expose it to its other, to the abyss, to keep its standards and its preconceived notions of rationality in play, to keep reason in play and to keep the play in reason.

Consider the alternative. Suppose the university is reduced to nothing more than an instrument of war, and the manufacturers of armaments are awarded all the contracts they seek, and the counselors of war win the day and our (whose?) first-strike capability becomes so great that it provokes a "preemptive strike." Let us make it simpler. Let us suppose, in keeping with the philosophy of play, that an error in a computer chip in a nuclear command post somewhere sets off an irreversible chain of events in a network of computers that has been designed with staggering technical perfection (*ratio sufficiens, ratio efficiens, ratio perficiens*) which culminates in a nuclear conflagration. The planet, denuded of most of its living species, will nonetheless continue to repeat its solar orbit until, its energy spent, it falls back lifelessly into the sun. Then all things will be returned to the flux. The principle of reason will sound no more. Repetition, as for Constantin, will have proven too much for us. The play will be all, after all.

NINE

Toward an Ethics of Dissemination

THE IDEA OF A POSTMETAPHYSICAL ETHICS

The withdrawal of foundations described by radical hermeneutics, the difficulties it throws in life's way, is no less troublesome for the question of action than for the question of rationality. We are faced with the problem not only of what we can know but also of what we are to do. If moral "principles" are also the playthings of a child, if the "foundation of morals" is the *arché*/child, what then? How are we to act? Where does action find its guidelines? The critique of metaphysics includes within its sweep every metaphysical ethics. And that poses the question of the possibility of an ethics *after* metaphysics, of a postmetaphysical ethics.

Consider the case of Heidegger and ethics. Heidegger put metaphysical ethics in its place. He produced a searching critique of it as an ethics of "values," which arises precisely from the metaphysics of subjectivity. He showed the barrenness of any idea of Being which stands in need of supplementation by "value" and the hollowness of any imperative which is issued not by Being but by the "subject." When Being is reduced to an object, values are made the issue of the subject. It would be a considerable mistake, however, to think that Heidegger thereby simply washed his hands of ethics. On the contrary, he put in the place of this impoverished ethics of values a deeper thinking of what he called "originary *ethos*." When pressed about this point he explained that everything that he said about the "truth of Being" had direct ethical import (GA 9 356–7/BW 235). For the truth of Being means nothing less than the way a historical people "dwells" *(wohnen)*, that is, the constellation of art, science, and political arrangements within which they live out their lives (cf. EM 117, 146/IM 128, 160). The truth of Being means the way a historical people settles into an understanding of the world, of the gods, and of themselves. And so he rightly insisted that his "thinking" is a more originary ethics, which is better prepared to think what is all around us today than any bankrupt "theory of values."

The relationship between what he calls the truth of Being and *Wohnen/ethos* goes all the way down. Talk about the truth of Being constitutes a more radical,

236

originary *(ursprünglicher)* ethical discourse. It cuts across the differences between competing schools of ethics and ethical points of view in order to name
the basic shape of life in an epoch, the fundamental form according to which
human practices are organized from epoch to epoch. Thus, the difference
between the *techné* of the early Greeks and the *Gestell* of late modernity is not
just a difference between two ontologies or interpretations of the meaning of
Being. It is also the difference between two ways that human life is lived out,
two attitudes toward human life and human institutions—one marked by a
gentle letting-be and the other by a ruinous control. In the one, human life is
experienced as the life of "mortals" who move in rhythm with and in response to
the powers of the cosmos and in the other as the raw material of further control,
of genetic engineering and behavioral technologies.

Techné and *Gestell* provide the ontological setting for the endless ethical
debates of philosophers and theologians, and nowadays of professionals of all
sorts—health care professionals, lawyers, engineers, business managers, etc.
Techné and *Gestell* are rich in ethical import; they constitute a kind of meta-
ethical or deep-ethical constellation within which any historical "ethics" in the
narrower sense takes shape. Particular ethical debates always occur within this
constellation and hence are a step removed from the level on which Heidegger
is thinking (WHD 34/WCT 89). Debates about the ethical use of life-supporting
technologies, e.g., or about artificial insemination and abortion, take place
within the framework of the hitherto unsuspected power to control human life
which is granted by *Gestell*, and the resolution of these debates reflects the
attitude that one takes to controlling life. And this more originary thinking in
terms of the history of Being, which thinks the *Gestell* which dominates
contemporary man, penetrates more deeply into the question of *ethos* than any
possible "value thinking."

Thus, in the place of the displaced ethics of modernity, the ethics of values,
Heidegger puts his own "originary" ethics. Originary ethics is an important
delimitation of value theory which stands value theory on its head. Directives
are issued by Being itself, not man, whose task is to become responsive to the
nomos sent his way, not to be a legislator of universal imperatives. But from the
point of view of radical deconstructive work, reversal is but an opening move, an
initial gesture on the way to a more radical displacement. As the reversal of the
ethics of values, originary ethics remains within the sphere of influence of the
metaphysics of truth. Heidegger's more originary *ethos* is a higher version, an
eschatological version, of metaphysics. For it tells the story of the primordial
ethos and the great beginning, prior to the subject-object split, and looks ahead
to a new dawn, which is to be an eschatological repetition and renewal of what
began in the early Greeks, before metaphysics and all metaphysical ethics. But
I have my doubts about primordial epochs and new dawns. I am inclined to
think that "great beginnings" are a mixed blessing, that ancient greatness looks

better at a distance and is the result of blurring the *différance* by which it is inhabited, that every epoch is equally an epoch of withdrawal and *lethe*, which is indeed what *epoché* (suspension/withdrawal) means.

I have made this argument up to now largely in terms of the question of the "meaning" or "truth" of Being, but the argument also plays itself out in ethics. For everything that Heidegger says about the truth of Being, about the poetic "dwelling" of the early Greeks, and about the *Gestell* has the deepest ethical import (in this originary but quite real sense of ethics). The standard criticism of Heidegger—that Heidegger has no ethics—is a quite superficial charge and is blind to the more pertinent point, namely, the ethics that he has. In my view, Heidegger's ethics is marked by the same eschatological structure which characterizes everything that he says about the *Seinsgeschick*. My difficulty with Heidegger is not that he has no ethics but that his ethics is eschatological, and it is eschatology which causes all the trouble.

The question of a postmetaphysical ethics, thus, must be approached in connection with the delimitation of eschatological metaphysics which we have been pursuing. This delimitation lands us squarely in the play and in the dissemination of the manifold senses of Being. On this deconstructive rereading, Heidegger's most uncircumventable thought lies in the *Ereignis*, which is not "the truth of Being" ("Being as *Ereignis*") but that which gives Being, gives the manifold meanings or truths of Being. The truth of Being is that there are many truths of Being. And, if the truth of Being means the primordial *ethos*, then in the end there is no primordial *ethos* but only the manifold senses of *ethos*, the array of historical differences. Thus, I want to consider here the import of the dissemination of the truth of Being for the question of dwelling. Where are we to turn if, after the deconstruction of metaphysical ethics, we likewise want to undo Heidegger's eschatological ethics? Where are we to turn, whence are we to get guidance and direction, if "originary ethics" (*ursprüngliche Ethik*) also founders, if the letters delivered by Hermes are scattered to the four winds?

My argument will be that action today takes its point of departure not from fixed points of reference and steady principles (as in a metaphysical ethics) and not from the *nomos* issued by a primordial *ethos* (as in eschatological ethics) but precisely from the dissemination of principles and primordial epochs. It is precisely from the breakdown of standpoints and resting points of all sorts that we begin to act. If radical hermeneutics wants to expose us to the flux, then I want to show that this does not therefore leave us in the lurch. On the contrary, I will argue that this in fact liberates action—from subjugation to metaphysical principles on the one hand and eschatological dreaming on the other hand. I want to show, to put it as flippantly as possible, that there is an ethics of dissemination—which is also, I will argue, an ethics of *Gelassenheit*—an ethics which arises, not in spite of but precisely because of the foundering of metaphysical and eschatological ethics. I want to defend an ethics which arises from cold hermeneutics, the hermeneutics without comfort, which issues from the salutary interplay of Heidegger and Derrida.

I am thus continuing in the present chapter what I began in chapter 8, namely, a set of reflections aimed at "coping with the flux," at learning to get along in the concrete without the guardrails of metaphysics. In the previous chapter I argued that the project of radical hermeneutics produces what might be called a certain "displacement effect." That is to say, the displacement of metaphysics does not remove the old names—science, ethics, art, religion, to name the most famous—from the scene but produces a certain rebound effect on them so that they remain operating, but without metaphysical certification. The exposure of scientific rationality to the abyss does not, and is not meant to, raze somehow the project of science itself (I do not even know what that would mean), but to deprive it of metaphysical prestige and hence also liberate it from metaphysical domination. Radical hermeneutics does not shift us altogether from one world into another, from the world of technology and the *Gestell*, let us say, to that of Heideggerian jugs and bridges. On the contrary, it leaves us standing, if slightly off balance, in the same world, the only world of which we have any experience. And it was in that sense that we spoke of a postmetaphysical conception of rationality, one which, having extricated itself from the various attempts to "ground" the sciences and bring them under the rule of a metaphysically inspired "method," releases science to be what it is, releasing the element of play at play in all scientific work. Having exposed the life of reason at large to a certain "groundlessness," radical hermeneutics throws it onto its own so that it is not the puppet of some method but is forced to make its own way without metaphysical, methodological assurances. Science and reason remain displaced, kept slightly off balance, robbed of their security—but liberated and put back into play.

Now I want to make much the same argument in terms of ethical action. The thought of the flux does not leave action behind, does not let us enter a new world, make a leap into a different sphere where there is no longer any need to act. The thought of the flux remains always and already in the same sphere, faced with the demand to act but now with a transformed relationship to action. We act not with the security of metaphysical foundations but with a raised awareness of the insecurity to which we are exposed. We act not on the basis of unshakable grounds but in order to do what we can, taking what action as seems wise, and not without misgivings (Kierkegaard called it "fear and trembling"). We act, but we understand that we are not situated safely above the flux, that we have not secured any transcendental high ground, that we do not have a view of the whole. We act, but we act with a heightened sense of the delimitation of subjectivity, not sure of this "we" or of who or what acts within us or what deeper impulses are at work on us. We act with fear and trembling, with a deep sense of the *ébranler,* whose tremors are all around us. We act because something has to be done. We act not on the basis of metaphysical schemes or on the more subtle basis of eschatological dreams but on the margins of metaphysics and eschatology, "after" they have foundered, in the midst of *(inter-esse),* a condition of dissemination which is also a condition of liberation.

The course I want to pursue in the present chapter, then, is as follows. (1) I begin with the eschatological reversal of metaphysical ethics, with the critique which eschatology makes of the ethics of values. (2) Then I make a critique of eschatological ethics and of the primordial *ethos.* Finally, I make some proposals about what I am calling here an ethics of dissemination (3) and *Gelassenheit* (4). In short, I move from the dissemination of ethics to the ethics of dissemination, from a metaphysical to a postmetaphysical ethics.

ESCHATOLOGICAL ETHICS: WAITING FOR A GOD—OR ST. BENEDICT

I begin with an eschatological story in ethics. In the beginning is *Sittlichkeit,* the primordial ethical community, a deep cultural and sociological solidarity, the togetherness of a people bound by shared goals and goods. The members of such societies have a common understanding of their ethos which they express in tales and sagas about their heroes. Embedded in those sagas is the structure of the way Being is granted to them, the way it is given them to dwell. Discussions about this common *ethos* take the form of a descriptive phenomenology of what everyone understands—some more articulately than others—to be proper and fitting. Strife and disagreements occur only within the framework of a common possession. But at a certain critical point, when scientific and objectifying thinking makes an appearance, the ground gives way beneath this cultural solidarity. Competing "world views" and "ethical theories" emerge, each scrambling for primacy. The scrambling grows worse and not better, the disagreements spread and positions harden, resulting in deep and irresoluble ethical conflicts. The authority of the old view is undermined, but nothing new takes its place. The result is the emergence of the theory of "values." The old idea of a shared "good" or the common ethos is replaced by a marketplace of competing values posited by a plurality of competing subjects. Being and the Good are separated, as Being is reduced to "factuality" and the Good becomes a "value." The oblivion of Being and ethos sets in. A philosopher appears who presides over this chaos, who understands that the old world is dead, and who speaks the most eloquently in the name of values. But his very critique of nihilism (the old values have lost their force) in the name of new, life-preserving values (the old values must be transvalued) is itself the deepest, most extreme form of nihilism, the *eschaton.*

Still, there is a way out. It is always darkest before the dawn. In the danger is the saving. In this most extreme oblivion of the primordial *Sittlichkeit* there lies the possibility, nourished by historical *An-denken*, by a memorial recollective thinking, to find again, to repeat, what has been lost. Looking backward is the best way to look ahead. But the recuperation of the past possibility, of the lost solidarity, is not anything within our power. The emergence of reintegrated social bonds, the restoration of a community characterized by this primordial solidarity, is a goal lying effectively beyond anyone's reach. We need outside help. For "ethical" paradigms cut deeper than scientific ones. Primordial *Sittlichkeit* cannot be instituted, like a scientific revolution, merely by an exercise in scientific inventiveness, by the genius of a young scientist who sees things anew. Rather it represents a deep-set form of life, a historical solidarity, which it is not within the power of some individual or group to bring about.

That is why the only way out of the current morass in this view is to wait for a fundamental shift, a new day. One philosopher is waiting for a god to save us, while, on the other side of the sea, another keeps watch for a new, doubtless very different, St. Benedict to steer us through the new dark ages of the present *eschaton*. On either account, we are waiting for a new growth of *Sittlichkeit* to close the crisis and reinstate a new tradition of "virtue" or of "original *ethos*" (which are, I think, pretty much the same thing). Eschatology always leaves us hanging, waiting for some notable with salvific gifts to bail us out of this extreme, eschatological peril.

That I think is a fair, if slightly flippant, digest of the eschatological story. And it is pretty much the same story told both by Heidegger and by MacIntyre, who, although they are otherwise unlikely bedfellows, agree in all the essentials: the great beginning in the Greeks, the terrible decline in modernity, the hope in a new beginning; nostalgia, antimodernism. They both look to antiquity for light and a time of original solidarity; they both point their finger at the theory of "values," and specifically at Nietzsche, as the heart of the modern ethical malaise; and they both leave us dreaming of a new dawn (while the forces of oppression ravage the land).

Now however alluring such a story may be, however much it makes for good reading—and who can resist a good yarn?—it requires, in my view, deconstructive, genealogical disruption, a vigilance in Derrida's and Foucault's unmistakably postmodern styles. (It comes down to whether the critique of modernity should be waged under the flag of antimodernism or postmodernism.) For eschatological stories always come to grief. They plant the seeds of our discontent so deeply—in the loss of the ancient world, in a fall from primordiality— that nothing short of a miraculous renewal can save us. And, since miracles are beyond our individual or collective reach, they leave us dreaming of a new dawn, a wondrous transformation, even while they remain oblivious to the possibilities of the present.

MacIntyre, of course, is an outsider to the story I have been telling from

Kierkegaard to Derrida, and he has no interest in the deconstruction of meta-physics or the overcoming of metaphysical humanism or in any other continen-tal exotica. Indeed, he prides himself on his Anglo-American "clarity" and freedom from continental vice, particularly from the dark sayings of a Geman *Seinsdenker*. Presumably he will not take it as a favor that I have put him together with Heidegger here. Still he fits so nicely into the point I am making about eschatological ethics that I cannot resist pointing out a few things about his work.

Like all eschatologists, MacIntyre begins with the loss; that is Constantin's law, the law of all nostalgia. We cannot miss the eschatological ring of the "after" in "after virtue." We "latecomers" are after virtue, too late for it, too late for medieval Aristotelianism and too early for a new wave of *Sittlichkeit*. But in the danger is the saving: just by thinking through the modern demise, by telling a story on it, perhaps we will find the means to get the Christian-medieval tradition back on its feet and go after virtue again. So the story starts with a fascinating allegory of a catastrophe in the natural sciences, which is meant to tell the story on us, about how we have fallen into a condition of irresoluble ethical conflict and incommensurability after the dissemination of the old *ethos*. The catastrophe is the Enlightenment and its project of carving out a space for the "moral" as opposed to the "legal" or "theological," each of which then needs "justification." (In Heidegger, the Enlightenment begins with "too little," with the "epistemological subject"; in Heidegger/Gadamer, it carves out the "aes-thetic.") But it is already too late. Just by posing such questions—about how to get from facts to values, from the subject to the object—the scandal has already been given; the seal of *Sittlichkeit* has already been breached beyond repair. What has gone dead is the bond between the individual and the *polis*. (The modern idea of an autonomous individual appears in antiquity only in the form of madness or exile.) In the Greco-medieval world, what is expected of one is to be discerned by insight and a kind of knowledge *(phronesis)*, not justified or enforced with rules. At the point at which rules and arguments are required, the *polis* is finished. True, there were differences in the old world. There are large gaps between the courage of a Homeric warrior, the civility of an Athenian democrat, the humility of a medieval nun, the *caritas* of St. Francis. MacIntyre fills the screen with such portraits (AV 121ff.), which are brilliantly carried out, like ethical analogues to Heidegger's *Seinsgeschicke*. But all of these differences are contained (was there ever a time when they were not?) within the overarch-ing unity of a shared conviction about doing one's part for the *telos* and liking it. And that is the nerve of MacIntyre's argument, for, if the disputes in antiquity cut as deeply as do ours, then their differences, too, are ultimately "incommen-surable," their debates irrational, and the classical world has no advantage over the modern.[1] For the trouble today is that the *telos* has withered away, has been replaced by a sea of competing *teloi*, a conflict of wills, a war of willing subjects, the will-to-power. That means that what has gone wrong with ethics (as a science) today is rooted more deeply in our sociology, in the way we live; we lack a paradigm in the science of ethics because our concrete social practices have deteriorated. And so the trouble we are in cuts deep. We need a change in the very substance of our lives, and that is a task which is evidently beyond the means of any individual or group to carry out. But, if that is so, what are we to do now?

Now for the eschatological conclusion, the second sense of "after," and another saga. We began with the loss, so we end with hope in the new day. Our times resemble that dark moment when, as the barbarians stood ready to overrun the Roman empire, certain small communities formed to preserve civility and learning and a nobler way of life.

> This time however the barbarians are not waiting beyond the frontiers; they have already been governing us for quite some time. And it is our lack of consciousness of this that constitutes part of our predicament. We are waiting not for a Godot, but for another—doubtless very different—St. Benedict. (AV 263)

It is an irony, a kind of *felix culpa*, in MacIntyre's argument that, at the point where he is most given to eschatological yearning, he renounces it. For instead of surrendering entirely to his own version of the *Übermensch*, a new St. Benedict, MacIntyre does have some advice about what to do between now and the second coming of a new growth of *Sittlichkeit*. And that is to go under-ground, through the formation of small subcultures and communities—health and educational institutions, for example, where the good life can be practiced while we await the parousia, where we can save ourselves while the others are consumed by acquisitiveness. Turning his back on modernity, MacIntyre re-pairs to his small communities to practice his Aristotelian insights, modernity and its liberal individualism notwithstanding. But how far is that, in fact, from retreating from the public in order to nourish one's virtue in private, and how far is that from what he calls emotivism raised to the scale of small commu-nities? As a matter of fact, it is even reminiscent of the sort of advice Derrida and Foucault give about pursuing local, not global, reform.

The problem with eschatological stories is that they always end just where the story begins, which is the complaint Judge Wilhelm lodged against Johannes the Seducer about romantic love stories. After one finishes denouncing fate and the Enlightenment, one has only gotten as far as the beginning. The state of ethics after the catastrophe, after virtue, is what Derrida calls the *ébranler*, the diaspora, the dissemination of metaphysical guardrails and social solidarity. That is indeed a good way to pose the question of ethics, and it is one of the strong points of MacIntyre's argument. But MacIntyre does not make a single step forward, which is what repetition demands, but makes instead an elegant, erudite recollective slide backward. For, as I hope to show in what follows, eschatology always blinds itself to the *différance* and violence in the old world, like that optical illusion Constantin pointed out: seen from far enough away, even a square tower looks round. Eschatology fails to see that nothing is innocent, that it is only a question of different forms of difference and violence. MacIntyre urges us to replace one form of violence with another. The catastrophe is always and already in place. There never was perception, presence—or virtue.

In Heidegger, who is the protagonist in our account, the eschatological story has a Being-historical twist. Heidegger, of course, wants to undo metaphysical, humanistic ethics. Modernity is for him, too, an *Abfall*, *de-cadere*, a decay, but one which has eaten into the very movement of the history of Being. So Heidegger's tale speeds along at a much higher altitude than does MacIntyre's. And his critique of ethics is much more radical, because he seeks no succor from the *Nichomachean Ethics* as a treatise on "ethics" (let alone from medieval Aristotelianism) or from any metaphysical project. He thinks all the trouble started when Plato and Aristotle launched the project of a philosophical ethics, for that led, in a line which Heidegger tries to draw, straight to modern subjectivism, value theory, and Nietzsche, i.e., the end of ethics. The trouble starts not with the Enlightenment but as soon as philosophy opens its door and begins unloading its conceptualizing tools. The decline, the *Abfall*, actually sets in with philosophy itself, so the primordial *ethos* can be preserved only by poetic thinking, not by a restoration of the classical notion of ethical rationality. So MacIntyre really swings to the right of Heidegger and actually looks a lot more like Gadamer than Heidegger. Indeed, if he could get over identifying continental thought with *Being and Nothingness* (the standard Anglo-American orthodoxy before Rorty, which represents a level of insight comparable to identifying Anglo-American thought with logical positivism), he would find Gadamer a companionable thinker. Perhaps he would find no consolation in that either.

Heidegger began with a radical rereading of Aristotle in which he tried to read the ethics out of the *Nichomachean Ethics* and the metaphysics out of the *Metaphysics* and in which he headed straightaway for the overcoming of metaphysics. For him the history of ethics launched by Plato and Aristotle issues ultimately in the Cartesian project of value theory. In *Being and Time*, the issue of the "moral subject" and its "obligations" is utterly displaced because it depends upon the notion of a worldless, isolated subject, which *Being and Time* treats quite mercilessly. We are no more in the fix of having to establish and justify Dasein's bonds with other persons than we are of proving the existence of the world. The scandal is that modernity has become so moribund as even to pose these problems. The matter for the existential analytic is to do a hermeneutic phenomenology of resolve (which retrieves Aristotle's *phronesis*) and then to round resolve off in §74 with a hermeneutics of historicity which says that *what* factical, resolute Dasein has to resolve upon (which a more decadent time would calls its "duties") is a function of the historical world to which it belongs—which is not all that far from the MacIntyre/Gadamer line.[2]

All this gets radicalized in the later, quite incisive critique of value theory. Being is conceived in too impoverished a manner to begin with if it needs to be supplemented with "value."[3] The notion of value arises only if man has been uprooted, cut off from things which speak for themselves, and forced to prove the existence and binding power of values, even as he is forced to prove the existence of the external world (EM 149-52/IM 164–67). Originally, *axioma* meant that which emerges into appearance with a clarity which commands our respect, that which is held in the highest regard because of its own commanding appearance (aspect, look; SG 34). And, since Being means *physis*, that which emerges into presence, and *axioma* means what emerges into presence with a commanding brilliance, it is clear that *physis* and *axioma*, Being and that which commands our respect, belong together. Thus, the opposition between "fact" and "value" is a corruption, a falling out of what originally belongs together.[4]

While the breach between Being and value came to the fore in modernity, it was prepared for by the Platonic gesture of locating *agathon* above being. It was furthered along by Descartes, for whom everything is a function of the *ego cogito*. As the spatiotemporal world is an object for the thinking subject, value is an object of the willing subject. That in turn set the stage for Nietzsche, who saw in the clearest terms that values are wholly the product of the valuing, willing subject, which he called the will-to-power.[5] The debate about the *objectivity* of values was pointless for Nietzsche; the only issue is to *hierarchize* them in terms of their ability to serve life, to replace the debate about objective and subjective values with one about healthy or sick values. But "the attempt to revalue all values," the subtitle of *The Will to Power*, to displace life-denying with life-affirming values, is, for Heidegger, Nietzsche's most severe limitation (EM 151–2/IM 166–67). For even a transvaluation of Christian-Platonic values remains entangled within the metaphysical net of value thinking:

> . . . in metaphysics, Being has debased itself to a value. Herein lies the testimony that Being has not been accepted and acknowledged as Being. . . . If, however, value does not let Being be, does not let it be what it is as being itself, then this supposed overcoming is above all the consummation of nihilism. (GA 5 259/QCT 104)

Thus, for Heidegger, the death of God does not mean what it means for Nietzsche, that God as the highest value *(summum bonum)* has lost all value. It means rather that Being itself has been reduced to a value and so negated in its truth. It does not mean that men no longer believe in God but rather that those who do, the theologians, regard Him as a value, as an object for a valuing subject, which is a blasphemy and a subversive atheism of its own. Hence, it is the humanism of "the last three and a half centuries of European history," in which "man has risen up into the I-ness of the *ego cogito*," which has wiped away the horizon of Being (death of God). "The horizon no longer emits light of itself" (GA 5 261/QCT 107). Metaphysical thinking is what is truly murderous. Nihilism means that Being itself is destroyed in the self-assertion of the subject. Epistemology and axiology are of a piece with the modern ontology of subjectivity.

To find a better day one must go back to the time prior to Plato and Aristotle. The very project of a philosophical ethics, such as we find in Plato and Aristotle, is a sign that thinking is waning and scientific, disciplinary distinctions are becoming entrenched: "The tragedies of Sophocles—provided such a comparison is at all permissible—preserve the *ethos* in their sagas more primordially than Aristotle's lectures on 'ethics'" (GA 9 354/BW 232–33).

Ethics as a scientific discipline is already a falling out of the originary thought of *ethos*. But what is originary *ethos?*

> If the name "ethics," in keeping with the basic meaning of the word *ethos*, should now say that "ethics" ponders the abode of man, then that thinking which thinks the truth of Being as the primordial element of man, as one who eksists, is in itself the original ethics. (GA 9 356/BW 234–35)

There is then a more originary thinking of the dwelling of man, a more originary thinking of *ethos*, than any metaphysical ethics can attain. This originary *ethos* refers to the primordial world in which mortals dwell, the world of the fourfold, of the heavens and the earth, of the gods and mortals themselves. Here man lives in a primordial bond with the world. In such a world there is no opposition between *physis* and *nomos;* rather, man takes his bidding from physis, from Being.

> Only so far as man, eksisting into the truth of Being, belongs to Being can there come from Being itself the assignment of those directions that must become law and rule for man. In Greek to assign is *nemein. Nomos* is not only law but more originally the assignment contained in the dispensation *(Schickung)* of Being. (GA 9 360–61/BW 238)

Nomos means not only rule *(Gesetz)* but also *Zuweisung*, what is assigned or allotted to us. And this allotment is contained in *die Schickung des Seins*, the way Being has been destined, dispensed, sent, apportioned—or allotted—to us. *Ethos* means, therefore, the particular shape which one's historical *(Geschick, Geschichte)* existence takes, the historical mode of Being-in-the-world to which each of us is assigned by the movement of Being itself, and the demands which such historical existence puts upon us. The most primordial bond to which each of us is subject is thus the bond we each have to the historical form of life which has been sent our way by Hermes.

Otherwise all law remains merely something fabricated by human reason. More essential than instituting rules is that man find the way to his abode in the truth of Being. This abode first yields the experience of something we can hold on to. The truth of Being offers a hold for all conduct. (GA 9 361/BW 238–39)

There is no greater "hold" on human conduct than that of Being itself, i.e., the epoch or historical constellation of Being in which we find ourselves, the historical setting into which one has been put. That is a bond which is not instituted by man—by a social contract or the legislation of pure reason—but in which man finds himself always and already situated. And the most primordial thinking on the *ethos*, on the way man dwells historically, is what Heidegger calls "originary ethics" *(ursprüngliche Ethik),*[6] which is our only hope for living as anything more than mere creatures of human reason. If the directives by which man is guided do not have their roots in something more than man, then they are "merely something fabricated by human reason"—which in the end leads to Nietzschean "values" as products of the will to power.

To act is to act within a historical community with historical goals and aspirations. The force of the *nomos* lies in the historical demand which is placed upon the individual to assume his place within that society (MacIntyre), to answer the call of Being in his time (Heidegger). I wonder if there is any cash value difference between these views. In both cases it means moving in harmony with the rhythm of the primordial historical community, experiencing its world, its gods, its art, its social matrix. The only difference is that MacIntyre thinks that all these things intersect, not only in the Greek temple but in a medieval Benedictine abbey as well (in fact better). And both think that the trouble starts when this kind of historical solidarity is disrupted, which Heidegger thinks commenced with philosophical thinking itself but which MacIntyre situates in modern philosophy and science.

Once the "hold" of the history of Being on the historical individual is broken, it cannot be restored. Both modern ethics and modern epistemology begin with too little. The isolated epistemological subject is no less a fiction than the notion of an isolated moral subject, looking helplessly about with the eyes of pure reason for rules of conduct and ethical criteria. Such an uprooted de-historicized search—that is to say, the project of Enlightenment ethics—is as doomed to fail as is the Cartesian project of proving the existence of the world. If one has reached the point where the foundationalist question in ethics has to be raised, then it is already *too late*. In originary thinking, the only question is to discern what one's *ethos* demands, never to found or rationalize it.

Unlike MacIntyre, Heidegger thinks that the primordial *ethos* cannot be assimilated by philosophy at all; as soon as the philosophical tradition begins to treat of it, it ends up mistreating it. There is already at work, even in the *Nichomachean Ethics* itself, the process that leads to the Enlightenment project

and the philosophy of values. Value philosophy is the upshot of the philosophical discipline of "ethics." It inevitably waylays original ethics, setting in motion
the distinctions, debates, and scholastic disputes which culminate in the contemporary diaspora, the nihilism of value theory, the time of need.

MacIntyre, on the other hand, takes classical ethical theory to be the legitimate spokesman of the ancient *ethos*, adequately reflecting it and providing it
with a rational voice. Heidegger does not seek a rational voice for it but a poetic
one, because he thinks that the primordiality of this *ethos* is disrupted by the
very rationality of the voice, the tone of disinterested and disengaged reason.
He wants instead the voice of song which sings of our engagement with the
world and which makes no pretense of holding court over it.

Whether the classical *ethos* broke up after the sixth century B.C. or the
thirteenth century A.D., the point is that originary *ethos* (or *Sittlichkeit* or
ethical solidarity) is a deep historical formation which it is not within the power
of any individual or group to restore. Its renewal would require a thoroughgoing
change in the *Seinsgeschick* which would transform us and our mode of dwelling. That is why the *Der Spiegel* interview with Heidegger ends up where it
does, invoking the prospect of a god who will save us, that is, of a thoroughgoing
change in the *Seinsgeschick*, for that alone will suffice in this "time of need."[7]

> *Heidegger:* . . . philosophy will not be able to effect an immediate transformation of
> the present condition of the world. That is not only true of philosophy but of all
> merely human thought and endeavor. Only a god can save us. The sole possibility
> that is left for us is to prepare a sort of readiness, through thinking and poetizing,
> for the appearance of the god or for the absence of the god in the time of foundering
> *(Untergang)*; for in the face of the god who is absent, we founder.

We are left hoping for an eschatological flip, for a turning in things which no
mere mortal is capable of producing. Be it a new god or a new St. Benedict, the
solution to the ethical dilemma in which we are caught up lies beyond our
reach. What has gone wrong with our ethical lives cuts deeper than human
resolves to do better can reach. It has to do with the breakup of an ethical
solidarity which it is simply not possible to restore by means of some sort of
reform movement. Our ethical undoing reaches all the way down to the
epochal-historical substance of our lives. We have lost something which cannot
be restored by even the most heroic of efforts. There is, or so it seems, nothing
to do but wait and hope.

THE DECONSTRUCTION OF ESCHATOLOGICAL ETHICS

But we have tried to cast a suspicious, Parisian eye over all these eschatologies,
to take a long deconstructive look, because we have second thoughts about the
"truth of Being." And that entails the breakdown of a privileged *ethos* and a

release of the play of ethnological diversity, of the "manifold sense" of *ethos*. Deprived of any primordial, uncontaminated mode of dwelling, every epoch is equally a mode of withdrawal, finitized by its very structure as an "epoch." Every epoch is but a particular way we are granted to be and to dwell. The age of the early Greeks, of medieval towns and abbeys, of modernity—none can be privileged. Each has its own hazards. Each is inhabited in its own way by *différance* and *Unter-Schied*.

Visions of primordial solidarity are usually blind to deeper disruption, to the rent in the garment of the originary community. The ancient city is no homogenous and gleaming city on a hill or in a "rock-cleft valley," innocent and without violence. Or better—since it is not homogenous, since nothing is unambiguously and decidably what it is, since everything is marked with conflicting tendencies—the ancient city is not *only* that. For its exemplary qualities are always already compromised, infiltrated by their opposites, which it tries systematically to exclude. Even so, the modern world, the epoch of technology and subjectivism, is not unambiguously what Heidegger and MacIntyre say it is. It too is a-lethic, torn by conflicting tendencies, with virtues to match its vices, a liberation from antiquity as well as a degeneration of it. The whole thing is just much more pharmacological than eschatology is willing to grant, much more of a poison/remedy. A-lethic epochality and undecidability go hand in hand. We do not say that the ancient world was not what MacIntyre and Heidegger—and Hegel and Hölderlin—say it was. But that it was not only that, that it is more, and that it is in contradiction with itself. And we say that there is more to modernity than they allow. Eschatological tales are too simple; they try to make things too easy. And the function of the deconstruction of metaphysics—which is comfortable only with simple essences—is to complicate things, to restore life to its original difficulty, to show that things never *are* what we say they are, that they do not have pure and unambiguous presence.

The tale that Heidegger tells about the classical world is more involuted and "textualized" than he lets on. Consider Heidegger's Parmenides. This Parmenides is a marvelous creation, a winged and airy thing not too different from the goddess whose poem he is passing on (we have another one of those beautiful postcards from Greece, bearing a Todnauberg postmark). He is a poetic thinker whose poem sings of the inner harmony and belonging-together of Being and thought. In his poem we learn that the matter for thought (*die Sache des Denkens*) is Being, not beings, is indeed the two-fold itself, and that the way along which thought travels (*Denkweg, meta-odos*) is poetic, not logical or philosophical. Parmenides is not the first of the philosophers, the herald of rigorous logic, but the last of the poetic thinkers—not a less than philosophical anticipator of philosophy but a more than philosophical thinker before thinking goes into decline.[8]

Now that is a rewriting of Parmenides for which I have a taste; it is an extraordinarily creative repetition which opens up that text and gives joy, releasing the text into a play of which generations of plodding scholars have been utterly innocent. No one with a feel for the Greeks can be unmoved. This is not to say that Heidegger could not go toe-to-toe with any "Greek scholar" who wanted to give him an argument. He is as capable of playing the conventional, university game as anyone else, including all those who resent his capacity for opening up another field of play altogether.

I have neither the will nor the wit to dismiss Heidegger's Parmenides. I only want to complicate the picture, to say that Parmenides is all that and much else besides, that the text is complex, that it unfolds in many ways. I want to complicate by implicating, by showing complicity, by showing that Parmenides' poem has loose ends stretching in many directions, that Heidegger cannot draw clean margins around it by "situating" (er-örteren) it neatly within poetic thinking. By this I do not only mean that Parmenides' text is also in complicity with the tradition of logical, unpoetic thinking which follows in its wake, that it is caught in the web of metaphysics even "before" metaphysics, that it virtually invented the metaphysics of presence which Heidegger protests, that the idea of the poem is to fold up the two-fold into an unfoldable, self-present One. I do mean that, too. But what I have in mind in particular here is Heidegger's exclusion of the *political* Parmenides.

By this I have in mind in part that Parmenides was an eminently political man, a man of action and political prominence. The ancient town of Elea was a large and prosperous city on the Mediterranean coast of southern Italy ("magna Graecia"), a crossroads for Greek shipping. And Parmenides was its governor. And, according to Diogenes Laertius and Plutarch, he was the author of a constitution, of a set of "admirable laws" for Elea.[9] When he encountered the young Socrates in Athens, he was very likely there on political business. Had there been an ancient "press" and had there been interviews of prominent personalities such as Parmenides, one would not likely have heard from Parmenides the hesitancies of the *Der Spiegel* interview but the astute judgments of a man of the world. His would-be interviewers would have likely had a hard time preventing him from reading his entire constitution into the interview.

I do not want to deprive Parmenides of his poetic gifts. I want to say he is more like Meister Eckhart than Heidegger lets on. Eckhart was one of the most gifted preachers and mystics of medieval Europe. He was also the provincial general of the German Dominicans and for a time ran both the German and the French provinces. He also preferred Martha to Mary. Mary he said, had only one gift: contemplation. Martha had two: contemplation *and* action.[10] Parmenides and Eckhart (and Martha) illustrate part of my point against Heidegger. Heidegger leaves the thinker mute in the face of the ethicopolitical. He cuts short the reach of the deconstruction of metaphysics; he never exploits its ethicopolitical cutting edge. He has isolated thinking from the *agora* and driven it up into the mountains. He sees clearly the illusion of totalizing schemes which purport to know how to run everything. He is a master at the delimitation of metaphysical principles and of the danger of the *Gestell*. But he does not let thinking takes its place in the political sphere; he does not let it assume its political facticity. He does not point out that the sociological equivalent of the destruction of the history of ontology is the critique of political systems. That is what his own notion of *ethos* commits him to, but he never delivers, whereas it never entered the head of Parmenides or Eckhart that their lofty work of thought was in the slightest way incongruous with their situatedness in the *polis*.

Now that gets us closer to the point I am making about Heidegger's exclusion of the political. The same ancient "thinking" which Heidegger celebrates is inextricably interwoven with ancient politics, ethics, economics, and the rest. There is no clean break between primordial *ethos* and ethics, between the primordial *polis* and politics. There is no clear and decidable difference between them such as Heidegger wants to enforce. It is not possible to sanitize early Greek thinking or wash its hands of its sociopolitical setting. The political structure of the ancient world belongs as much to its *Seinsgeschick* as do the tragedies of Sophocles or the thinking (be it poetic or rational) of Parmenides. Each is entangled and interwoven with the other, and together they all contribute to the textuality of the same *Seinsgeschick*. Why are we to privilege one over the other? Would not the voice of Being speak as robustly in "the laws of Parmenides" (Plutarch), if we had preserved them, as in Parmenides' poem? Parmenides is logician, politician, poetic thinker. He is all of these things, and we love them all. We do not want to repress any of them. We want to enjoy the free play of all of the things that Parmenides is and can be and is not yet. Is not the *Seinsgeschick* of the Greeks delivered to us just as much in their political institutions as in their poetic thinking and their temples? Does it make any sense to try to separate them?

The most telling feature of the point I am trying to make against Heidegger— that the Greek *polis* is as much the place of the clearing of Being among the Greeks as the tragedies of Sophocles or the poem of Parmenides—is that Heidegger himself has already made this point. Heidegger knows this. He saw it once and said it once, quite clearly, in 1935. And then, perhaps for reasons interwoven with his own biography, he backed off and let it drop. Heidegger is discussing nothing other than Parmenides saying that Being and thinking are the same. The saying is dark, Heidegger says, and so for light on the passage he recommends a reading of the first chorus from the *Antigone* of Sophocles. In line 370 of that passage, the poet refers to the *polis*. And upon this Heidegger comments:

It [the passage] speaks not of *poros* but of *polis;* not of the paths to all the realms of beings but of the foundation and scene of man's being-there, the point at which all these paths meet, the *polis. Polis* is usually translated as city or city-state. This does not capture the full meaning. *Polis* means, rather, the place, the there, wherein and as which historical Dasein is. The *polis* is the historical place, the there *in* which, *out of* which, and *for* which history happens. To this place and scene of history belong the gods, the temples, the priests, the festivals, the games, the poets, the thinkers, the ruler, the council of elders, the assembly of the people, the army and the fleet. (EM 117/IM 128)

The thinkers and the poets and the temple are situated by Heidegger within the *polis*. All of the paths of Greek life intersect there, in this scene of history, where all of the work of the poets and thinkers and statesmen are preserved (EM 146/IM 160). Thinking and doing the work of the *polis* belong together in the unity of the same *Seinsgeschick*. The *Seinsgeschick* is given shape in the *polis* just as much as in the poet or thinker. Indeed, inasmuch as it provides a place for and preserves poet, thinker, and temple, one could even argue for a certain primacy of the *polis*, of the political.

The Greek temple sits in the rock-cleft valley, or on the hilltop, facing the east, overlooking the sea. The sun glimmers on its stone. It provides a space in which the open itself opens up, in which sun and stone, sea and sky, gods and mortals are what they are. The temple "fits together and at the same time gathers around itself the unity of those paths and relations in which birth and death, disaster and blessing, victory and disgrace, endurance and decline acquire the shape of destiny for the human being." In the expanse which the temple opens up lies "the world of this historical people" (GA 9 28/BW 168).

But that includes the socioeconomic system to which the temple belongs. It includes the slaves who dragged the stone up the hill. It includes "free man and slave, male and female, Greek and non-Greek"—entities which should be added to the catalogue of binary oppositions whose paths intersect in the temple. Slaves, non-Greeks, and women are also the place where the truth of the Greek world happens. Their exclusion from the primordial community and the solidarity of the originary *ethos* are part of that world's "clearing." The mode of dwelling granted to them is part of the open. (What share in the "open" do they have who are excluded?) The systematic exclusivity and repressiveness of the Greek democracy "intersects" in the Greek temple just as much as does the fourfold. They *all* intersect there—not only poets and thinkers but also slaves and women. The slaves and those charged with running the household must be inserted into Heidegger's rhapsodic accounts of Greek *techne*.

And, furthermore, this is so on Heidegger's own terms, by his own account of the strife of *lethe* and *a-letheia, Heil* and *Un-heil*. The primordial *ethos* is not innocent, unambiguous, untouched by *lethe* and "the evil" *(das Böse)* which, we have it from Heidegger himself, simultaneously appears in the clearing of

Being, along with the holy (GA 9 358/BW 237). Is the primordial *ethos* innocent of "the malice of rage" ("das Bösartige des Grimmes"), of "the compulsion to the unholy" ("Andrang zum Unheil") (GA 9 360/BW 268)? How could that be, on Heidegger's own terms? And, if not, then why must we bend our knee at the mention of the early Greeks, except for the illusion induced by looking on at a distance and the charm of a good eschatological yarn? On Heidegger's own terms, and by the very structure of *a-letheia*, every "epoch" is defined by the withdrawal which makes it possible and so none can be privileged—whether the epoch lies at the beginning (Heidegger), the middle (MacIntyre) or the "end" (scientism). By the very structure of *a-letheia*, epochs are all caught up in the play.

A good part of the kinship that I detect in the positions of Heidegger and MacIntyre is that they both provoke the same objection. For MacIntyre's critique of the Enlightenment project and his privileging of medieval Aristotelianism suffers from very much the same defect. The tradition of "virtue" was indeed, as MacIntyre argues, rooted in an essentially teleological conception of society. As such it was also a rigorously hierarchical system and so bound to the binary oppositions of higher and lower, of means and end, which governed the relationships between male and female, lord and serf, sacred and secular, aristocrat and *hoi polloi*, Greek and non-Greek, Christian and Jew—the relationships of the classical world. It is precisely on hierarchico-teleological grounds that Aristotle justifies slavery: slaves are "living instruments" useful for running a household *(Pol.* I, 4), whose merely passive reason serves the purposes of those who possess the full presence of reason. In a teleological scheme, woe unto to them who are a means to the *telos*, who get ground up by the teeth of the *telos*.

Aristotle, the rational voice of the best Athenians (AV 148), wondered aloud to what extent women and slaves participated in the rational principle and hence could be said to have virtue at all *(Pol.* I,13). Christian knights and inquisitors practiced the profession of slaughtering those who did not share their faith. St. Thomas endorsed the idea of civil punishment for religious dissent *(Summa Theol.*, IIa-IIae, Q. 11, a.3). And in general one had a much better chance of participating in medieval social solidarity and Christian *caritas* if one were not a Jew. It did not occur to anyone to condemn capital punishment, including burning people at the stake if they happened not to hold the preferred theological views, or to insist on the right of people to govern themselves, have their own religious faith or none at all, and so on. No small amount of blood was shed in the name of medieval *Sittlichkeit*.

Now, as Bernstein points out,[11] MacIntyre knows this as well as anybody, but he thinks he can simply stitch over the Aristotelian view with an Enlightenment patch—so that no one is to be excluded in principle from the *polis*. He thinks that we are rightly "affronted" by the exclusion of non-Greeks, barbarians, and slaves (and women, Bernstein adds) from political rationality and that we should be of a more generous nature ourselves (AV 158–59). But the point is that this kind of exclusion and repression was not merely a minor flaw in the classical world, an unfortunate blind spot, which we can mend. Exclusion and repression were built into the structure of a hierarchico-teleological system. The ancients thought in terms of binary oppositions—between reality and appearance, truth and opinion, those who know and those who are ignorant, those who should lead and those who should serve and follow, believers and infidels, etc. (In Derrida's terms, it was a good example of a presence/absence system.) Hence, to try to patch this over is not simply to make an adjustment in the classical view but to undo the whole scheme and to swing off in the Kantian-Enlightenment direction of universalization. It is to make a shift to an entirely different *Seinsgeschick,* or sociology, which claims that no one is a means, that every one is an end-in-itself, and which does not define people "functionally." In tele-ological schemes, people are used to meet ends. Teleological communities are inevitably hierarchical communities. Such communities have solidarity, it is true, but it matters a lot where one is consolidated in the system of means and ends.

The Enlightenment clearly means more than one thing. It is rightly taken to task by Heidegger and MacIntyre, indeed by phenomenologists and late Witt-gensteinians at large, for its foundationalist projects in ethics and epistemology. But by asserting the spurious autonomy of subjectivity—whether ethical or epistemological—from the historical world in which the individual is inextrica-bly embedded, the Enlightenment *also* discovered the legitimate aspirations of the individual, of every individual, to be *included* in the common good. It does both things at once, and I wonder how it could have done one without the other. I wonder how the discovery of the individual, of conscience, of the force of dissent, of freedom could have happened otherwise. Is this not another case of the *pharmakon* in which it is difficult to sort out the remedy and the poison?

Nor need we confuse the pseudo-individualism and the spurious autonomy to which the Enlightenment gave rise with its egalitarianism. Egalitarianism does not commit us to the fiction of the isolated individual. It is the expression of the desire to *share* in the community and its common good, the recognition that this is a universal aspiration which is not confined to a few best. The goal of universal freedom—encapsulated in the Hegelian schematic "one is free, some are free, all are free"—is essentially an Enlightenment achievement. This discovery of the individual is not at odds with a genuine sense of the community but essential to its very idea. For what is a community if it does not recognize the rights of *all*, without exception, to belong to the community and not to be excluded? And did not the old *polis* fail to be a true community by its exclusionary practices?

The ancient city was hierarchized and centered. Its sense of teleology went hand in hand with a metaphysical chain of being stretching from god to the world. It was founded on hierarchical oppositions between creator and created, sovereign and subject, free man and slave, male and female—the sociological embodiments of Derrida's binary, meta-physical presence/absence oppositions. And such a world deserved the undoing it received at the hands of the Enlightenment—and does not deserve to be revisited. Even if they are dead ends as foundationalist projects, the Cartesian experiment and the categorical imperative paid off in lessons about universal freedom. If there is something to object to in the notion of autonomous reason, there is at least as much to object to in hierarchizing human worth in terms of gold, silver, and brass, or of occurrences along a divided line, or of freeman and slave, believer and infidel, and the rest of that intolerant, intolerable world. Nothing is innocent.

The lesson we learn from the ancient city and its metaphysics is that deep solidarity can only be achieved on a limited scale, and that, wherever it is found, it has drawn a line around itself and become exclusionary. Friendship is a good beyond measure, but it seems to mete itself out in measured amounts. If friendship is the bond of a community in the classical sense, the modern nation cannot be that sort of community but another sort. Perhaps it can be a community defined not by its convergence upon one, as in a metaphysics of presence and unity, but, in a postmetaphysical way, by its high threshold for tolerating dissent and respect for differences. In the same way that, in the previous chapter, I argued that there is no advantage in giving the word "reason" away, here I argue that there is nothing to be gained by giving the word "community" away.

The strongest part of MacIntyre's argument, curiously enough, is that he recognizes this perfectly. Having said that the sociology which corresponds to classical ethics has dissipated, that history has turned a few corners since then, he quite rightly points out that what survives of the Aristotelian ideal can be put to work today in small communities which work together for a common good— like the university or the hospital or certain surviving ethnic communities. That I think is his soundest advice, but such recommendations should always be read in conjunction with Foucault's and Derrida's critique of the "normalizing" use of power that such communities exert, a point which we discussed in the previous chapter in connection with the university. The mistake is to start sounding eschatological about all of this, to indulge in comparisons with the decline of the Roman empire, and to look wistfully for a charismatic, eschatological figure to see us through the dark night as we huddle together around our Aristotelian (or Heraclitean) fires waiting for a new dawn.

MacIntyre is also quite right, in my view, to argue for the essentially historical character of ethical thinking and to insist that to every ethics there is a corresponding sociology, by which he means rather the same thing that Heidegger claimed about the convergence of the "truth of Being" and the primordial *ethos*. An ethic is an essentially historical affair. It does not proceed by way of ahistorical norms, but it belongs to each historical people, to each epoch and culture, to sort things out for itself and to reach an articulation of Being and *ethos* which meets its needs.

And that means that an essential part of addressing the question of ethics today is to get our sociology right, to learn to think our *Seinsgeschick*. And I think that MacIntyre and Heidegger are particularly adept at this, at describing *our* sociology, that is, the way Being and dwelling are delivered to us these days. In fact, I have argued, they tend to have very much the same conception of our present *ethos*, which is the sociology that our ethics must address.

MacIntyre sees our sociology as a Weber/Nietzsche split, a vicious dichotomizing of a well-oiled Weberian bureaucracy (reason reduced to instrumental reason), on the one hand, and an anarchy of subjective values, on the other hand (no reason at all): increasing powers of external control along with inner anarchy. In short, a vicious object/subject, power/license split. I think Heidegger sees very much the same state of affairs.

> Certainly the modern age has, as a consequence of the liberation of man, introduced subjectivism and individualism. But it remains just as certain that no age before this one has produced a comparable objectivism and that in no age before this has the non-individual, in the form of the collective, come to acceptance as having worth. Essential here is the necessary interplay between subjectivism and objectivism. It is precisely this reciprocal conditioning of one by the other that points back to events more profound. (GA 5 87–88/QCT 127–28)

The Enlightenment means liberation, but this liberation is part of the metaphysics of subjectivity and objectivity. We have replaced the teleological schema of antiquity, which confined individuals to assigned places within the system, with a new complex of evils, of subjective individualism on the one hand and a spreading objectivism on the other.

But Heidegger takes this a step further than MacIntyre.

> In the planetary imperialism of technologically organized man, the subjectivism of man attains its acme, from which point it will descend to the level of organized uniformity and then firmly establish itself. This uniformity becomes the surest instrument of total, i.e., technological, rule over the earth. The modern freedom of subjectivity vanishes totally in the objectivity commensurate with it. (GA 5 111/ QCT 152–3)

In other words, for Heidegger, the Weberian/Nietzsche dichotomy is not a stable system. The will-to-power of instrumental, technological reason will end up extinguishing whatever is left of "man" in the modern "subject," culminating in the unchallenged rule of the *Gestell*. A power has been unleashed which will undo the gains of modernity and its sense of the freedom of all—a power which tends of itself toward control and manipulation, toward Foucault's "disciplinary society." We are endangered by a system of controls which is as ominous as the one enforced by the ancient teleology.

Now in my view Heidegger and MacIntyre have taken an important step toward writing the sociology within which a postmetaphysical ethics is to be articulated. But it is not a question of looking back wistfully in nostalgia at a lost world, which is recollection, the melancholy repetition which repeats backward, but of beginning where we are and pushing ahead, which is the repetition which repeats forward. What we require now is an ethics which corresponds to the sociology of the *Gestell*, the ethics for what Heidegger calls "the time of need," the time of ever-increasing powers of objective control which go hand in hand with the consignment of what is not technico-objective to caprice. And it is to address that need that I want to speak of an ethics of dissemination.

AN ETHICS OF DISSEMINATION

But what could an ethics within radical hermeneutics be like? How can there be a morals without a metaphysics of morals? I want to press the case that an ethics, albeit a radical ethics, arises not in spite of the foundering of metaphysics and eschatology but precisely because of it. It is precisely the fact that metaphysics comes to grief, its pretensions exposed, its claims delimited, that gives rise to ethics and some idea about how to dwell with one another. With Heidegger and Derrida, I have argued that the history of metaphysics is the story of so many attempts to still the flux, to contain its course, to arrest its play. Radical hermeneutics resists the consolations of philosophy and tries to get ready for the worst—that the history of the West has too many meanings, that there are too many truths of Being. For us, *a-letheia* means the scene across which a tireless troupe of historical actors continually passes, coming and going, reciting their lines and then vanishing into the dark.

Now to say there is only the flux, the *kinesis*, the ceaseless happening of *a-letheia* is not to claim a privileged insight, to have broken the code, which is hermeneutics in the metaphysical sense. It is not a claim but a concession that, like Socrates, hermeneutics lacks a master key and does not know the master name. It roams the streets of philosophy, listening to all who claim to have the key, who say that all is ruled by *nous*, while finding only explanations in terms of joints and sinews. Finally, it dawns on us what the muse means: that ignorance is the highest wisdom, that the delimitation of metaphysics is the best meta-ontology, that it is better to confess the inadequacy of our accounts than to put too much stock in them. It is better to concede that the creatures of metaphysics, the plurality of metaphysical schemes, are so much scaffolding stretched across the flux and are only as good as the results they produce, the degree to which they let life flourish, let the gods and mortals, the skies and the earth flourish, only as good as the measure of play they mete out. The one mistake that Socrates found among the politicians, craftsmen, and artists was that they took themselves and their opinions seriously—always a deadly flaw, putting an end to the play, an end to the discussion, so that any disagreement after this, after we get serious, will draw blood.

Radical hermeneutics is a lesson in humility; it comes away chastened from its struggle with the flux. It has wrestled with the angels of darkness and has not gotten the better of them. It understands the power of the flux to wash away the best-laid schemes of metaphysics. It takes the constructs of metaphysics to be temporary cloud formations which, from a distance, create the appearance of shape and substance but which pass through our fingers upon contact. *Eidos, ousia, esse, res cogitans* and the rest are so many meteorological illusions, inducing our belief in their permanence and brilliant form yet given to constant dissipation and reformation. And no matter how wantonly they are skewed across the skies there are always hermeneuts who claim to detect a shape, an *eidos* in the clouds—a bear here, a man with a long nose there. There are always those who claim they can read the clouds and find a pattern and a meaning.

Now it is not the function of radical hermeneutics to put an end to these games, like a cold-blooded, demythologizing scientist who insists that the clouds are but random collections of particles of water. That, too, is the spirit of seriousness. Its function is to keep the games in play, to awaken us to the play, to keep us on the alert that we draw forms in the sand, we read clouds in the sky, but we do not capture deep essences or find the *arché*. If there is anything that we learn in radical hermeneutics it is that we never get the better of the flux; we never make a deep cut into its lethic makeup.

Now to say that radical hermeneutics is a lesson in *humility* is to slip into the ethical mode. The moral of radical hermeneutics for morals itself is to sharpen our sense of the contingency of our schemes, of the dissolubility of the meta-physical world. The moral for morals is that none of us occupies a privileged place of insight, none of us has access to a god (or a goddess) who passes on to us any hermeneutic secrets. Being nothing more than mortals ourselves, and lacking divine informers, we have little choice but to confess that we do not know the master name. "Authenticity" *(Eigentlichkeit)* in radical hermeneutics means *owning up* to that embarrassment. There is nothing to do but face the worst, the play of the epochs, of the temporary constellations within which we live out our historical lives, to wade into the flux and try not to drown. And owning up to that, I say, has the salutary (we need another word than "saving," salvific, which is the language of eschatology) effect of inducing us to proceed with caution. We ought to produce our schemes and our programs for dealing with the flux—and we shall certainly continue to do that, we cannot avoid it, we have to act and plan and direct and teach. Like someone charged with disarm-ing a bomb, one has to do something, but, being the only one around, one stands a good chance of being scattered to the four winds. That inspires caution.

It makes one proceed in such a way as to keep as many options open as possible. It deflates pretension and divests us of too great a confidence in our schemes, from pressing them to the last detail, from being willing to draw blood on their behalf.

Such authenticity, which means owning up to our shortcomings, inspires moreover a certain compassion. We are, after all, all siblings of the same flux, brothers and sisters in the same dark night. We all have our midnight fears, a common mortality. After Socrates put down the pretensions of the politicians, craftsmen, and poets, he might have reflected that all of the pretension arises from a deep hermeneutic fear, which nobody wants to face, that we do not know the answers to the questions he puts. We are all unsettled by such thoughts and fears. Radical hermeneuts always succeed in making things difficult.

And so I envisage, as the moral upshot of all this, a "community of mortals," bound together by their common fears and lack of metaphysical grounds, sharing a common fate at the hands of the flux, sent by a *Geschick* which will not disclose its name, which does not have a name. Both "mortals" *and* a "community"—not solitary Dasein, stripped down to its own naked being-towards-death (although there is always something to that, too). We huddle together for warmth in the night of this cold hermeneutics, shaken by the same trembling, by the same *ébranler*. A cautious humility and compassion are the first "virtues" which the flux breeds, the first bit of rewriting of the old tables which it permits. *Virtus* in Latin has the sense of strength, the hardness which can take a beating, which can get along without comfort, which understands what Aristotle said when he said that it is hard to hit the mark. Nietzsche thought that the good news was bad news, that the truth is the flux, and that we need the strength of the *Übermensch* to cope with it, to bear the un-truth of *a-letheia*. That, it seems to me, is the distilled essence of all his talk about the hard virtues and being tough-minded. And Nietzsche condemned pity, for pity is making things easy while the truth is difficult, refusing to face the worst, throwing metaphysical dust in our eyes. But pity, as Nietzsche himself will grant, is not the same as compassion. Compassion arises precisely from the sense of a common fate, from suffering *(passio)* a common *(com)* comfortlessness. Compassion is the sense of togetherness which mortals share who understand the finitude of the cut they make into things.

We do not, after all, know who we are. Questio mihi factus sum. A bishop said that. That is not the metaphysical foundation of a new morals but the lack of foundation which inspires trepidation about all of our schemes and compassion for all of us who must in any case take action. And it is from the standpoint of Socratic ignorance that I speak of a radical ethics, or an ethics of dissemination and of *Gelassenheit*. The thought of the flux, it seems to me, makes us wary of power, of the will to impose a scheme which we know to be no more than a fiction, at times a useful fiction, at times a dangerous one. The thought of the flux puts us on the alert to the exercise of power and sensitizes us to all those who are ground up by schemes and principles and metaphysical *archai,* none of which is anything more than a more or less alluring formation of clouds. And so, by an ethics of dissemination, I mean an ethics bent on dispersing power clusters, constellations of power which grind us all under.

If, as MacIntyre and Heidegger alike agree, there can be no meaningful talk about ethics apart from the present sociology or current truth of Being and if, further, that historicality is to be described in terms of the metaphysics of power, control, and objectification, then it seems to me that the ethics which addresses the present time of need—the age of the *Gestell*—is an ethics of dissemination. Such an ethics addresses the sociology which is everywhere around us today, which instantiates the binary oppositional schemes of Western metaphysics: higher and lower, ruler and ruled, cause and effect, science and opinion, master and slave, same and different, male and female, rich and poor, privileged and unprivileged.

Proceeding from a salutary deconstructionist mistrust of all such binary schemes, in which the privileged term represses and excludes its opposite, its other, an ethics of dissemination is an ethics of otherness, an ethics aimed at giving what is other as big a break as possible. The binary oppositional schemes into which deconstruction likes to sink its teeth, and which turn on the guiding distinction between presence and absence, are ripe with sociological equivalents. The powers that be, the men (sic) of substance, of *ousia,* the man of means, are all sociological instantiations of the metaphysics of presence and, like all such structures, secretly depend upon, and are the effects of, the opposite which they suppress. Hence, the ethics of dissemination begins by systematically reversing these oppositional schemes, reversing the discrimination strategically, in order finally to displace oppositional arrangements in favor of the open and nonexclusionary.

Dissemination is directed at constellations of power, centers of control and manipulation, which systematically dominate, regulate, exclude. Its model is the Socratic work of showing up the contingency of every scheme. It delimits the authority of all programmers, planners, managers, and controllers of all sorts. It compromises the prestige of the expert, releases all the loose ends in every system, exposes the systematic violence of any tightly organized structure (university, church, hospital, government, etc.) And it does all this not by any show of strength of its own but by letting the system itself unravel, letting the play in the system loose. If Aristotle was trying to extend the natural bonds of family and friendship to the larger scale of a polity so that a cultural life both larger and grander than the life of the clan would be possible *(Pol.,* I, 2), we have the opposite problem. For us the powers of organization and manipulation have grown so vast that they threaten to run out of control. The alliance of capitalism (or of socialism) and technology results in an accumulating momentum which is about to overrun us all.

The task of a radical ethics is to disrupt that momentum, to assert difference, to preserve the right to dissent, to allow the idiosyncratic its rights. Given MacIntyre's irresoluble conflict of wills—let us say of "undecidables"—the alternative is not to dream of a new St. Benedict or to wait upon a flip in the *Seinsgeschick* but rather to provide for the conditions of a free and nonmanipulated public debate in which competing viewpoints can be adjudicated. But *how* are we to adjudicate them? By blind emotivist outbursts or even by a cultivated and articulate emotivism? "Emotivism" is a metaphysical notion which turns on the illusory distinction between pure reason and pathology. Reason is always already motivated, moved, interested, even as emotion is never blind (SZ, §31). Whatever progress we make depends on the ambiguous mix of what meta-physics tries vainly to separate. In a radical ethics our own concern is to keep the conversation moving, mobile, and to trust the dynamics of the *agora*. We do everything we can to see to it that the debate is fair, that no one's voice is excluded or demeaned, and that the vested interests of the powerful who usually end up having their way are restrained as much as possible.

This is not merely a hermeneutic problem in the Gadamerian sense. There is no question here of applying an agreed-upon standard, and Gadamer tends to ignore the subversion of hermeneutic *phronesis* by a diversity of power plays. It is rather a deconstructive problem which requires vigilance about the subversion of discourse by a priori metaphysical schemes, by exclusionary practices, by a rhetoric systematically bent on sustaining the prevailing order. It requires a Socratic vigilance which insists on keeping the game fair.

But what will *guide* the deliberations in the *agora?* By what standards and criteria will that judgment be formed and informed, given that we lack the paradigmatic prudent man to whom Aristotle could point? I think it is futile and wrong-headed to press this question. For the question arises, in my view, from a foundationalist compulsion, a Cartesian anxiety. The likelihood that we could actually get direction from such a principle (provided that it is something more than banal to begin with) is no greater than the likelihood that it will blind and bind us, repress something (or someone), cut off possibilities, make us miss a chance to make a fresh cut into the complexity of the situation we face.

We can ask for nothing more than the free assembly of diverse points of view in which men and women with mixed motives and with uneven intellectual and rhetorical abilities will hammer out solutions for this problem or that, with more or less successful or disastrous results. I would say that the notion of free play is never more valuable than here, that what is required above all is the free play of ethicopolitical discourse, a kind of public debate in which we allow ethicopolitical reason to play itself out. Political and ethical rationality seems to me essentially a matter of fair play. And, if it is objected that that is a metaphor, I would press the case of how one is to distinguish proper and metaphoric. We have always to do with metaphors. The crucial distinction is not between literal and metaphoric but between good metaphors and bad, and I am arguing that the flux and free play are good metaphors.

Faced with the more or less idiosyncratic situations which constitute our day-to-day problems, reason can at best take a first cut, hammer out a more or less adequate and temporary solution. It is always a question of wading into the flux and doing the best one can not to drown. The essential thing, on this view, is to delimit the power of powerful interests and metaphysical ideologies to dominate the talk and arrest the play. The point is always to keep the play in play. In the ethicopolitical sphere, the notion of play does not mean that we abandon reason and let the chaos wash over us. It means that we keep the debate fair and free from manipulative interests.

The great mistake of meta-physics is to think that we have to come up with a pure, interest-free rationality. We have begun this study with Kierkegaard's delimitation of that fiction. Metaphysics is launched on the myth of disinterested reason, even as it founders on the inevitability of interest, of being always and already embedded in some situation or another, always already being betwixt and between—*inter-esse*—this interest or that. Otherwise reason would not "care" what the solution is. Socio-ethicopolitical discourse does not require a transcendental rationality which transcends local interests—if it does, we are finished—but simply the keeping of competing interests in play in a fair game, letting the dynamics of the *agora* play itself out in a fair competition. Nor does it require a community founded on friendship, for friendship is local and exclusionary. It just requires a fair competition and respect for all the passionately interested competitors the game attracts.

And, if we can get that far, then it might turn out that we are not entirely bankrupt in the matter of a paradigmatic exemplar after all. This postparadigmatic diaspora, this postmetaphysical lack of foundations, generates a new morality of civility and fair play. And that would send us searching for a scarce commodity these days, that is, one who plays a game for the love of it (love and play are without why, Meister Eckhart said), and who plays fairly, without steroids or calling a strike because he is not satisfied with his base contract. If we have "lost" agreement about the practice of virtue within a single paradigm, there remains the virtue of dealing with that loss—for that loss is our sociology in the time of need. Moreover, that "loss" is also—by reason of the undecidability which infiltrates everything—a gain, particularly if you were a slave or a woman or a Jew in the old sociology, if fate had assigned you a humble spot in the old teleological scheme. If the Aristotelian *polis* demanded *phronesis*, that is, the skill to apply the agreed-upon paradigm, the modern mega-*polis* requires civility, which is a kind of meta-*phronesis*, which means the skill to cope with competing paradigms. Civility is the virtue of knowing how to like and live with the dissemination of *ethos*.

The ethics of dissemination proceeds by way of a great distrust of everyone who wants to save us or give us foundations. It distrusts all schemes and programs, all metaphysical and eschatological visions. It proceeds on the assumption that every such program harbors within it an exclusionary gesture, a repressive act, a movement of normalization and leveling. It suspects that after a certain point every good idea becomes inflexible and repressive, that schemes cling tenaciously to life and presence long after they have spent their capital and done their work. But it is not opposed to institutional organization or the notion of community. It requires rather the hardiness *(virtus)* of repetition to keep all such institutions free, to keep them mobile, in motion, flexible, in flux, reformable, repeating forward. It does not deny that institutional organization is usually the way to get things done, that we tend by a natural momentum to organize our practices along systematic lines. The role of an ethics of dissemination is only to keep such organizations honest, to stay on the alert to their equally "natural" tendency, once established, to resist alteration, to suppress and normalize, to persist in place, in keeping with the metaphysics of presence. That is just what injustice means according to Heidegger's reading of the Anaximander fragment: when things cling tenaciously to presence (GA 5 356/ EGT 42–43). Institutions are a good example of the sociology which corresponds to the metaphysics of presence and Anaximander's *adikia:* they claim to have dropped from the sky, to be part of the powers that *be*—instead of the powers that have *become*. And the ethics of dissemination is a genealogy of suspicion which insists that institutions have come to be partly through prudence and partly through power politics, partly by the cunning of reason and partly by raw cunning.

If Gadamer thinks that institutions are solely the product of accumulated prudence and the refinements that have been introduced by human reason over the ages, I think that is metaphysical nostalgia. They have as much to do with power as with prudence. But, if Foucault thinks they are solely the products of power, that is metaphysical reductionism. The debate between power and prudence is a debate between competing ideologies, between metaphysicians who believe in binary oppositions, who think that there are clear and decidable differences between things and who cannot tolerate the ambiguity of the flux.

The function of an ethics of dissemination is not to try to level all institutional arrangements or discourage the formation of new ones—we have seen Derrida's interest in the university—but to *intervene* in ongoing processes, to keep institutions in process, to keep the *forms* of life from eliminating the *life*-form they are supposed to house. It means to disrupt hardened shells, to practice the Socratic art, to be a gadfly and sting ray—but always in the *polis*. There is no human life outside the *polis* or in a solitary, free subject (the sociological equivalent to Descartes's epistemological subject). The ethics of dissemination operates only in a community and in the ongoing conversation of mankind.[12]

It offers no overall strategies, no total schemes or master plans, but only local strategies for local action.[13] It practices local strategies in this institution or that, in this political struggle or that. Its function is to keep the system in play wherever it has become inflexible, wherever anyone is overcome with the spirit of seriousness, wherever it finds the grim countenance of someone bent on saving us. It takes its stand with those for whom the system was *not* designed— women, children, the mad, the ill, the poor, blacks, the religious and moral minorities—those who are being excluded by the system. It assumes that all systems represent the will of the most powerful as well as of the most reasonable, and it operates on behalf of those who lack power, those who are situated on the short end of any binary oppositional scheme. It does not speak in the name of a master plan; it speaks only of a series of contingent, ad hoc, local plans devised here and now to offset the exclusionary character of the prevailing system. Its role is to break up clusters of power, constellations of ruling interests, to put them on the run, to keep them in play. It bears no name beyond its disclaimer not to know the master name.

Now it can be objected that all of this evades the real question: just what systems in particular are crushing us? Do not systems which seem to hurt now in the long run liberate? And how do we intervene when we want to? But my whole point has been to deny that there are such general formulae and to take the steam out of the heady pursuits which they inspire. I distrust the whole idea of "the answer," and I take it that I have already said enough to put "the answer" into question. If I have argued anything, it is that addressing our sociology is ultimately a matter of getting down to cases, of getting a lot of heads together— specialists and nonspecialists, perpetrators and victims, dreamers and pragmatists, professionals and amateurs (which means lovers)—and letting them hammer something out for the time being, which may even last quite a while— to their surprise.

My point in all of this has not been to lay out a master plan but to put such plans into question and thereby to show that those of us who speak in terms of free play and the flux, of deconstruction and dissemination, are not bound to the muteness of the Der Spiegel interview, that we are not without our ethico-sociopolitical two cents. The talk of the flux does not leave us ethically bankrupt. On the contrary, it sharpens our suspicion of anyone bent on accumulating capital.

AN ETHICS OF *GELASSENHEIT*

But this ethics of dissemination is also an ethics of *Gelassenheit*—and here we are again letting Derrida draw Heidegger into the *agora*—which means an ethics of letting be, of letting gods and mortals, earth and sky be and be in play. For what more reasonable outcome can be expected of the delimitation of metaphysics and of its transcendental-horizonal scheming, of thinking as willing, than "releasing" or letting be? Letting the play be is the best advice radical hermeneutics has. And on that point, as I said, it has a bishop on its side: dilige, et quod vis fac.

The ethics of dissemination belongs together with the positive discovery of *Gelassenheit*. Systems that subordinate one individual or group to another in the name of a *telos* are trying to put the play out of play, trying to arrest the play (and often enough to arrest people and put them out of play), whereas *Gelassenheit* means letting-be. Now this is a slightly more difficult notion to develop than dissemination, and to do so adequately will carry us over into the next chapter. So it is the point on which I both conclude this chapter and move on to the next, and concluding, chapter.

I take the idea of *Gelassenheit* to be not merely an old mystical idea (for which I must say I have considerable affection) but also quite a modern idea, perhaps even postmodern, too. And that can be shown by singling out the three sources of the idea of an ethics of *Gelassenheit:* Meister Eckhart, Kant, and Heidegger (in chronological order).

For Meister Eckhart, *Gelassenheit* means living "without why," by which he means something quite interesting.[14] The soul's relationship to God should be "without why" (Angelus Silesius was a reader of Eckhart). That means that the soul should not act on the basis of demonstrated or even revealed truths *about* God, or for the sake of what it wants to gain *from* God, for these are both "why's"—bases and grounds and expectations—and as such treat God as some exterior principle. Living without why, with *Gelassenheit*, means seeking nothing exterior or outside—or, better, not seeking at all—but simply letting God's life well up in us and flow through us as an inner principle of life. We should love God as we love life, Eckhart said, for Himself, not as we love our cow, that is, for its milk. *Gelassenheit* means then a certain splendid releasing of life which Eckhart identifies with love—for Eckhart the highest and clearest case of *Gelassenheit* is love—which lets life rise up and flow over, which puts away the machinery of metaphysics and the mean desires of egoism in order to let the truly divine God flow in Himself, in the world, and in others. He spoke of the "life" of God, which is love itself, as a *bullitio* and *e-bullitio*, a welling-up and flowing-over, and in terms which look a lot like Heidegger's rewriting of *physis*.

Here then was a principle of *caritas* with some teeth in it, a *caritas* put forward by a Christian which had a "revolutionary" twist to it. (And that is why I think this old mystical idea is also very contemporary.) Eckhart saw the life and love of God to be ubiquitous, not confined to just a few privileged souls—not just to priests, e.g., which made the churchmen of his day uneasy, or to males (he preached to women and told them that they all had the divine spark, the *Seelenfünklein*), which made the church*men* uneasy, or even just to Christians, which made nearly all Christendom uneasy. Furthermore, he did not think that the presence of God was confined to churches and sanctuaries, or that God necessarily preferred the Latin language, but that the German vernacular in which he preached would do just fine. And that is why the Reformation took a liking to him and why the papal inquisitors gave him a hard time. Although a high-level Dominican administrator himself, Eckhart was starting to disseminate power clusters in medieval Christendom, and for that he earned the wrath of the Curia and felt the sting of its institutional power.

Eckhart stood at the head of a German mystical tradition which made its way into modernity in a number of ways, including the Reformation and German idealism, which led Nietzsche to quip that the father of German philosophy is the Lutheran minister. That makes Eckhart its grandfather. Now I think that Kant's moral philosophy is one of the fields fertilized by this stream. Everybody knows that a good deal of the inspiration of Kant's ethics is his own personal experience in his pietist home and the deep impression made upon him by the simple men and women who led lives of common and unadorned decency without the aid of metaphysics. At the heart of Kant's philosophy is the notion of "respect" for each and everyone, from the lowliest workmen to the noblest lord, a respect which treats each person as an "end in itself."

There is no denying that Kant nearly buried this experience under an avalanche of metaphysical dualism and that he badly misstated his case by treating each individual as an instance of the law, so that it is the law—which the individual both authors and instantiates—which endows each individual with his worthiness for respect. He would, of course, have done better to say that it belongs to his experience and ours that persons of themselves inspire and command respect (with the aid of Heidegger's phenomenology of *axioma*, SG 34), that we do not treat them or ourselves as means to an end. But, in terms of Kant's foundationalist anxieties, that would have given morals an empirical rather than a rational footing.

Even so, I would say that in Kant's notion of a kingdom of ends, of the worthiness of all of us to be included in the community, the old idea of *Gelassenheit* is merged with the modern idea of liberation. The idea is to honor the divine spark within us all, or the law, or whatever superstructure one wants to invoke, in order to name the life which flows in and through others and us, to let all of us be the being which we are, to release us all from manipulation and control and treat "the beings which we ourselves are" with respect. [15]

Now, in addition to commenting on Kant's phenomenology of respect (GA 24/ BP §13b), Heidegger also returns quite explicitly to Eckhart and invokes the very expression *Gelassenheit* to name the sort of relationship we require in order to deal with earth and sky and the gods, in order to let them be and thereby to let ourselves be, as "mortals." The one point I would urge in dealing with Heidegger, however, is that he tends to be a little more interested in letting jugs and bridges be and to let it go at that, and he never quite gets around to letting *others* be, to our being-with others as mortals, to the fellowship or community of mortals which I mentioned above. I do not think there is anything in what he says which excludes his doing this. He just never does. So we will do it for him and, by doing so, restore to *Gelassenheit* its ethical context. For remember that in Eckhart, to whom we owe this idea, *Gelassenheit*, letting-be, meant love, *caritas*. That is why the ethics of dissemination belongs together with an ethics of *Gelassenheit*, and both are united in the Augustinian formula "dilige, et quod vis fac."

One of the finer things Heidegger has to say about *Gelassenheit* occurs in his short address to the people of Messkirch when he remarks that *Gelassenheit* means "openness to the mystery" (G 25–26/DT 54–55). As usual, he is speaking about Gelassenheit toward things *(Dinge)* and the mystery of the play of the world. But here, in our postmetaphysical ethics, we want to think *Gelassenheit* toward others, the sense of respect or reverence the other commands, which arises from the fact that we know that here we are dealing with deep waters. Other persons are places in the flux where the waters whirl about in a particularly bewildering way, where the woods are particularly dark and deep, where the cloud formations are mysterious, perplexing, inviting, even frightening.

It is to this notion of the mystery that I now want to turn. In the end, radical hermeneutics does not lead us back to safe shores and terra firma; it leaves us twisting slowly in the wind. It leaves us exposed and without grounds, exposed to the groundlessness of the mystery. It is the play of the mystery which metaphysics is intent upon arresting, and it is in order to reopen that play, to get the police off its back, that we undertake radical thinking. This intractable mystery is the final difficulty that hermeneutics is bent on restoring. And it is upon this note, of openness to the mystery, that I want to "conclude" this study and thus complete the illusion that we have here a "book," with a beginning, a middle, and an end.

TEN

Openness to the Mystery

ON THE GROUND OF THE SOUL

One of the background heroes of the present study is Meister Eckhart. Kierkegaard and Husserl, Heidegger and Derrida have been given prominent roles to play in our script, while Eckhart makes only passing appearances. Still, Eckhart belongs to our pantheon. He is one of the great masters of disruption, of thinking through and thinking against the grain of everyday conceptions. He is adept at throwing the guardians of Being and presence (and of their version of the "true faith") into confusion and consternation. If you think the master name of God is Being, he would say that God is a "pure Nothing," without even a little bit of Being. And if you took him at his word, and called God pure Nothing, then he would show you that God is pure Being. The more anyone would talk about God, the more he would pray God to rid him of "God." When anyone praised the transcendence of God, he would say that God and the soul are one. Eventually the Curia made him pay for that sort of thing, but not before he was able to cut into the garment of medieval onto-theo-logic, disrupt the mail of the medieval *Seinsgeschick* and set it spinning.

Now I want to go back to Eckhart one more time. Eckhart said that, beneath the busy work of conceptualizing and willing, down at the base of the soul—or, alternately, out on the tip or the fine point of the soul—there is a certain deep spot, which he called the "ground of the soul," where the soul was able to establish contact with God in a way which broke through all the *Gerede* about God which the theologians and preachers kept plowing up and down the landscape of medieval Christendom. Heidegger called it the "heart's core" (*Herzengrund*, WHD 157/WCT 144). There was a point, in short, of what Eckhart called "breakthrough" (*Durchbruch*), where one got to understand the utter intractability of God to what theologians, priests, and common sense said was "God." At that point, he said, we have the sense not of being flooded with light but of having fallen into an abyss (*Abgrund*), where all the familiar conceptions we have devised about God collapse, all the comforting reassurances we have been giving one another about what God is simply turn to dust. We are confronted then with the truly divine God *(der göttliche Gott)* who refuses to submit to this human nonsense.[1]

Durchbruch meant breaking through to another, altogether more strange and forbidding region where, embarrassed by the clumsiness of the things we say about God and the meanness of our desires to get what we can from God, we are finally led to break off all such human pettiness and to appreciate the sheer transcendence of God, his utter resistance to this kind of mortal folly. Only then, when one started to appreciate that dimension of God—which in Eckhart's vocabulary was called the Godhead in God—did one begin to make headway. Here, in these deep waters, in this strange, uncanny, and uncomfortable sphere, the soul was initiated into a chastened sense of the mystery of the Godhead. The "breakthrough" must have felt a lot like a "breakdown"—of everything familiar and comforting—and that indeed was a big part of it. Although Eckhart meant that the breakthrough was the place where God broke loose, he sometimes described it as if it were the place where all hell broke loose. It sounds a lot like the realm of what Heidegger calls the "uncanny" *(Unheimlich)*, where we are deprived of all the familiar creature comforts of home *(Heim)*.

Now I think that radical hermeneutics leads to rather the same sort of result. For whether or not one believes in God or mystics, one can still speak of something like a ground or fine point of the soul, a certain deep spot in the mind where the constructions of science grow dim and the cunning of common sense and the agility of *phronesis* go limp, where they wither away and lose their power. (Even in Aristotle there was something beyond *phronesis*, which was the divine element in the soul.[2]) Whether one is a Dominican friar or not, there is a fine point in the mind where one is brought up short, a moment of midnight reckoning where the ground gives way and one also has the distinct sense of falling into an abyss. It is found in Kierkegaard when he talks about fear and trembling, in Heidegger quite pervasively (in the *Nichts*, the *Unheimlich*, the abyssal play, etc.), in Derrida's talk of the *ébranler,* and even, I would say, if you read it carefully, in Husserl, in the description of the annihilability of the world, its vulnerability in principle to decompose, deconstitute, deconstruct, leaving nothing behind but the pure time-flux.

Put in terms of one of the ruling images of the present study, I would say that in the thin membranes of structures which we stretch across the flux, in the thin fabric we weave over it, there are certain spots where the surface wears through and acquires a transparency which exposes the flux beneath. There are certain breaking points, let us say, in the habits and practices, the works and days, of our mundane existence where the flux is exposed, where the whole trembles and the play irrupts. Then we know we are in trouble. The abyss, the play, the uncanny—in short, all hell—breaks loose, and the card castles of everydayness come tumbling down. Something breaks through because the constraints we impose upon things break down. So there is an experience in radical hermeneutics which is a distant cousin, an analogue perhaps, of what Eckhart called *Durchbruch*. It is of just this sort of thing that Heidegger was speaking when he wrote about "openness to the mystery."

What breaks down in the breakthrough is the spell of conceptuality, the illusion that we have somehow or another managed to close our conceptual fists around the nerve of things, that we have grasped the world round about, circumscribed and encompassed it. Breakthrough is the countermetaphorics to the metaphorics of the concept: *be-greifen, con-capere, con-ceptus*. This is not to say, of course, that we no longer have to do with conceptual thinking, that the work of science and ethics and of institutional arrangements of all sorts are brought down. We have been through all that in the previous chapters. Nor do I mean that this is some sort of after-hours pastime, something which we might entertain after dinner, just before we nod off. I would say, rather, that it inhabits the margins and fringes and interstices of everydayness and keeps turning up on us disturbingly, unexpectedly, only to vanish again—just as in those films which keep flashing back to past episodes in the lives of their protagonists and then resume the narrative where they left off.

At the end of an interesting essay entitled "Science and Reflection"—*Besinnung* means a kind of meditative reflectiveness—Heidegger spoke of what he called the "unencompassable" *(das Unumgängliche)*, the thing (no-thing?) we cannot get around, both in the sense of something we cannot avoid running into somewhere along the way and in the sense of something we cannot surround, circumscribe, or encompass with our concepts. It is what is left over, the radical hermeneutical residuum which conceptual thinking and planning can never exhaust, include, assimilate (VA 64/QCT 175–76). It is the moment of withdrawal *(Ent-zug)* which inhabits everything which is "given," the absence *(Ab-wesen, ab-esse)* in everything which we try to summon into presence *(An-wesen, prae-esse)*. But not just the absence but the play of presence and absence, the unsettled, unsettling fluctuation between the two, so that we can never lay hands on a fixed structure or a stable stuff.

We are trying here to get as far as Heidegger's notion of *a-letheia*, thought in all its radicalness, where *a-letheia* is no longer even a Greek word but a concession on the part of thought of the ineradicable *lethe* from which all things spring up and to which they return. Physics, Heidegger says, cannot penetrate *physis*, nor history the movements of the *Geschick*, nor linguistics the heart of language. The sciences are so many straw huts which we erect against the winds of the withdrawal. Prior to their objectification in the sciences, which would reduce them to transparency, *physis, Geschick* and *Sprache* are a-lethic movements, movements of emergence from and return to *lethe,* by which they are both concealed and hidden from the glaring lights of metaphysics—the same point Eckhart would make about the "Godhead"—and also sheltered and preserved from its grasping network of concepts. Heidegger's first, last, and constant thought, in my view, is that thinking is in the end directed at that lethic dimension, that the de-limitation of conceptual thinking issues in a *Gelassenheit* toward the *lethe,* the concealed heart of *a-letheia,* the mystery which withdraws, which never hands itself over in a form we can trust.

Now what I have called here radical hermeneutics tries, if not to live constantly in that element, at least to spend some time there, to make an occasional excursion into that desert. It exposes itself to the twilight world of ambiguous and undecidable figures which populate that shadowy sphere. Its role is not so much to "come to grips" with it—that is the metaphorics of grasping, and we have insisted on its ability to elude our grip—as it is to cope with it or, best of all, to stay in play with it. I would even say, though here we must be careful, its role is to "construe" it. By construal, I hasten to add, I do not intend to return us to a more traditional hermeneutic, bent on interpretive projection and finding meaning. I have already said that radical hermeneutics arises only at the point of the breakdown and loss of meaning, the withdrawal and dissemination of meaning—in short, the thunderstorm. By construal, then, I have in mind coming to deal with this loss of meaning by confronting the meaning of the loss, of the withdrawal, of the *lethe* itself. By construal I mean the particular way one has found of remaining open to the mystery and venturing out into the flux.

And that is why I like the talk of the ground of the soul. For I think that all of us—even if we are not early Greeks or German mystics and have no *Hütte* in the Black Forest—to some extent or another, to a greater or lesser degree, more or less implicitly do reach some sort of an accommodation with the flux in a deep corner of our soul, make a kind of deep construal of the flux and learn to live with it. I am not sure if it really matters *how* one does this, that is to say, what sort of accommodation one reaches, so much as it matters *that* one does it, that is, that one hit a point of breakdown, breakthrough, breaking out. To each is granted his own way. And if it is true that this is a possibility for all of us, it is also true that some of us are especially adept at repressing and excluding the flux and trying to arrest its play. We have all acquired considerable skill at taking the easy way out the back door of the flux.

And so, by way of a conclusion to this study, I want to pick out one of those spots where I think that the surface wears thin and the flux shows through, one of the interstices and joints which are prone to leak. In so doing I am offering up an additional piece of evidence, or testimony, for the whole project of radical hermeneutics, for what it is and what good it does us. I think there are many such places of opening and breakthrough. Heidegger mentions four such places in "Science and Reflection"—language, nature, history, and man. Or one could take the work of art, which is one of Heidegger's favorite moves, or one could follow up one of Heidegger's more egalitarian suggestions, for example, that the possibility of this deep experience is constantly presenting itself to us in even the most simple and commonplace experiences of everyday life (G 15–16/DT 46–47).

I have chosen instead to take another route, one which not only has been systematically omitted by Heidegger but has been developed at length by one of his sharpest critics, Emmanuel Levinas.[3] I take my point of departure from the human face, the surface of the face, the face as sur-face over the flux (and so in a sense I am continuing to unfold the project of a radical ethics). Flickering in the twilight of presence/absence, the face is a mysterious (Heidegger) and undecidable (Derrida) form. We catch a glimpse momentarily, *augenblicklich*, in the blink of an eye, of a light in the eye of the other, which leaves us wondering, puzzled, provoked. It is the "face" as the most conspicuous point of access, the outermost surface of our body, which opens the way to the recess, the "ground" of the soul, its most hidden chambers.

In particular I want to say a word about suffering and the face, about the "face of suffering." Now at that point I will have to be careful. I am not unaware that suffering is a topic which is particularly apt to inspire apocalyptic and eschatological deliverances which represent a kind of swearing which I have tried to swear off. But it is nonetheless a topic which cuts deeply and is extremely good, I think, at delimiting the pretenses of the metaphysics of presence—and at exposing the flux below. So I will try to address this issue with a minimum of salvific pronouncements.

The analysis of suffering will carry us off simultaneously in two different and opposite directions—in the direction of the religious on the one hand and, let us say, the "tragic" on the other. It will provide at one and the same time—and this is the essence of its ambiguity and undecidability and the reason why I single it out here—the genealogy of religious attitude, the pre-creedal soil from which religion springs, and the genealogy of the antireligious, tragic view, of what Gabriel Marcel once called "the refusal to be saved."[4] It swings off toward both Augustine and Nietzsche, both the saving hand of the Father and a wild cosmic play. And it will do both things at once with the both/and of the *pharmakon*. Now the interest of radical hermeneutics in all this will be not to resolve this dispute, to close this issue, but to cultivate the open space, the distance which opens up between the feuding parties. For that opening puts flesh and bones on the abyssal play of which we have been speaking.

So the present chapter rounds off the project begun in chapter 8 of showing that all this talk of the flux and the play does not abandon us to the wolves. It does not deprive us of science or ethics but, if anything, provides us with a more sensible accounting of them. And now I want to say that neither is it inimical to the notion of a more chastened, postmetaphysical notion of religious faith. Indeed, I think that, without this notion of the flux, faith becomes a dangerous dogmatism. And, since that is just what faith too often is, not every true believer will look with favor upon the story which follows.

The aim is always to avoid the illusion that our institutions and practices, that our reason and our faith, that we ourselves have dropped from the sky. Radical hermeneutics is a sustained attempt to write from below, without celestial, transcendental justifications. It is an attempt to stay with the flow of *physis* without bailing out when the going gets rough, which is what that fateful "*meta-*" has always done. Dissemination does not throw reason, morals, and faith to the four winds; it simply gives a more humble account of their provenance. I do not deny that it makes us feel like someone who has just been exposed for lying about his family background, so that now it is a matter of public knowledge that he does not come from wealth at all. But that is just one more chilling effect of the cold truth.

THE FACE OF SUFFERING

The face is a shadowy place, a flickering region where we cannot always trust our eyes. And my interest lies not in reducing this ambiguity but in exploiting it. There is a lot of what Derrida calls undecidability and dissemination written all over the face, which is a tricky place, full of ambiguous signals and conflicting messages. We speak of something being true or false "on its face" (*super-faciem*, sur-face), and that means in an entirely manifest way, with nothing hidden, left behind, concealed. But of course the human face is anything but that. It is, on the contrary, a hall of mirrors, a play of reflections, a place of dissemblance and dissimulation, sometimes a place which we manipulate in order to produce an effect, sometimes a place where the truth gets out of the bag on us against our will. Sometimes our face betrays us, and sometimes we give the lie to others by putting on a convincing face. The human face is anything but simple and unambiguous, anything but just surface. It is streaked with hidden depths and concealed motives.

Indeed, it is hard to imagine a better example of the a-lethic makeup of things than the face (which is why Heidegger and Levinas ought not to be pitted against each other so uncompromisingly). What better example of the play of concealment and un-concealment, of closure and dis-closure, than the play of the face? It conceals what we want to hide and un-conceals what we were trying to keep under wraps. And that is because the face is the setting for language, the place where Heidegger's famous *Sprache* or *legein* makes its home and without which *différance* would not get a word in edgewise. Language is *lingua*, tongue, but also lips, mouth, eyes, the whole ensemble of facial accompaniment, orchestration, and expression. Husserl barred the face from linguistic status on the very grounds that make it interesting—that is, the realm of the non-intentional, the pre-conceptual.[5]

But consider the phenomena which Husserl cuts off. The cold look with which the words are calmly delivered discloses an even greater anger than angry words. The look of hurt says more than the words which say it does not matter. The look of love which says nothing at all says more than any words; routine words of love are betrayed by eyes which show that love has gone dead. A smile, a slightly arched eyebrow can give away everything; one's whole being-in-the-world gets out from under one's conscious control—for better or for worse. The look of fear betrays the brave words; the look of eagerness mocks the cool words; the look of love tells the truth on the words of indifference. Despite the polite greeting, we suspect we are not welcome at all. In short, the body and the face lend discourse a spontaneous support that it is hard to produce consciously, even as they betray us when we are out to keep our feelings hidden.

We are not sure what signals we are sending; we are not sure of the signs which others send us. We are not sure if the other is not just an adept actor who can make us believe anything, who has acquired the diabolic art of getting those spontaneous and preconceptual bodily powers under control, so that by manipulating them he can manipulate us. Often the signs the other sends us are uncertain and confused, not only to us but to himself. He does not know what he wants. As often as not, we do not know what to make of the gestural life which streams toward us from the other just because the other is himself in a state of wavering and uncertainty. And sometimes we know better than he what he is groping for. Who is speaking here? Not just an "I myself," which is a fiction of meta-physics, but a complex of repressed desires, the structure of a discourse, a set of historical presuppositions, an unconscious—all of these and who knows what else. The flux flows through these words and inhabits the gestures of this speaker and curls itself up into the enigmatic knot which is the face. The face is a complex, fluctuating, wavering spot in the flux, a good example of the *da*—in *Da-Sein*, of a place where the dynamics of closure and dis-closure plays itself out palpably—a clearing indeed but an a-lethic one which is not neat and unambiguous.

In short, the face is one of those places of opening (Heidegger) and break-through (Eckhart), where the bottom drops out, where the surface opens up, where shadowy formations replace the rock-hard identities of being and presence (Derrida). One begins to sense the abyss within, the unmanageable flow which inhabits it, that one has to do here with deep waters and with who knows what.

The face instantiates *a-letheia*. Contrary to the standard version of Parmenides, Heidegger said that *a-letheia* is not a well-rounded whole in which being clings to itself but a hyphenated, fluctuating play in which things are never reducible to what they are. The look of the other draws us into the mystery, shakes our naive belief in surfaces, shapes, and cloud formations, in self-identity and the steadiness of presence. The eyes of the other lure us into mystery and confusion, shadows and dark recesses; they are not windows of the soul but a house of mirrors. They are soft spots where the ground gives out beneath us and we plunge downward, unable to touch bottom, black holes trapping light. Who is speaking here? What looks out upon us from these eyes? What strange powers inhabit this look? In the face the mystery makes itself felt, produces its effects. In the face we feel the power of the *Ent-zug*, the withdrawal, and we are drawn into and along with that draft (WHD 5–6/WCT 9), drawn down shadowy corridors and a dizzying hall of mirrors. *Physis* loves to hide, not only in the consciously controlled hiding of one bent on dissimulation but even more importantly in the self-concealment of the self from itself which makes the very idea of self questionable. Questio mihi factus sum. The mystery consists not in a self-transparent Cartesian ego hiding behind the cloak of the body but in the mystery that the other is to himself, that all of us are to ourselves. The face exposes the self-confoundment which envelops us all.

Now it is precisely in this a-lethic, mysterious structure of the face, which is the point where all of the bodily and gestural life of the other converges, that I think Kant should have located the origin of "respect." As it was, Kant was a keen phenomenological observer of respect. He quite rightly insisted that respect has to do with something which humbles us, brings us up short, stops us in our tracks, something surpassing which inspires a mix of fear and awe and admiration, something which both strikes us down and draws us near. That, as Heidegger pointed out, is good phenomenological work (GA 24 189/BP 133). But of course Kant "read" all this in terms of the "law," whereas I take that to be a rationalist mythology, a certain way the Enlightenment had of stabilizing the flux (which is not to say that I think there is some demythologized way of stating the hard truth). What moved Kant, as we said above, was the experience he had of those decent people with whom he grew up, the lives of virtue they led, the humbling experience he had of living with people who were not consumed with meanness and self-interest. In short, the faces that filled his young world.

So I would not say that the person is an instance of the law but rather that the law is a way of writing the person with capital letters, giving the person a louder voice. In my view, the second and third versions of the "categorical imperative," about respecting others and the kingdom of ends (it is only the first formulation which is barren), do not issue from the voice of pure reason, or the pure rational will, which is just a way that meta-physics has of trying to make everything safe and transparent. These versions give words, rather, on my accounting, to the powers which stir in the look of the other, which emanate from his face and bodily life. To respect others is to come under their spell, to feel their influence; it is more like entering a field of energy than meeting up with another empirical object. That is why we say some people just "fill the room" with their presence (otherwise that would be a commentary on their weight). I do not think that Kant was wrong but that he had recourse to the wrong organon. He needed to replace his logical table of judgments with a phenomenological account of the origin of the feeling of respect. He needed a phenomenology of the face, not a metaphysics of morals, to give his ethics the sort of punch he wanted it to have, to give it force and to protect the sphere of ethics from the destructive effects he perceived in Newtonian physics (a good phenomenology would also have forced a different philosophy of science out of Kant).[6]

One could then run the whole of Kant's ethics, and Kant's examples of ethical issues, through this phenomenological propaedeutic rather than running universalization tests on them, which ends up ruining them. To some extent I think this is what Levinas has done. It is the face of the other which issues the command not to kill and indeed, as Levinas insists, which makes murder impossible (not physically, to be sure, but ethically), which makes murder a radical disturbance of the peace, so that the face of the victim lives on to haunt the murderer. Why do we cover the face of the one to be executed and the face of the executioner? Who is being protected against whom? Suppose we insisted that all of this be carried out face to face, eye to eye? That would be a gamble, because it would either stop it altogether or radicalize the brutality even further. Were the executioners at Auschwitz watching the faces?

It is clear that the face of the other is not a value posited by the will but an intervention from without, a command issued from the hidden depths of the other. Here is a deconstruction of "value" back into *axio* which Heidegger never tried (SG 34). It is the look of the other which commands respect; aspect and respect belong together preeminently in the face. Something, someone stirs here, over which we have no control. There are powers and gods here which e-lude our domination. Something, who knows what, is at work, *en-ergon*—in play—here which we cannot bring within the horizon of our familiar constructs and convenient systems of placing. We are dis-comforted, dis-concerted, de-centered, dis-placed. Stable structures shake loose, the whole trembles, the abyss opens up. We are brought tripping before the mystery.

In an a-lethic view, whatever shows itself, whatever comes forth, issues from hidden depths. We know we cannot touch bottom here, that we cannot squeeze what stirs here between our conceptual hands, cannot get it within our grip, cannot seize it round about. The mystery is self-withdrawing, self-sheltering. And that is what gives rise to respect. Husserl said that the transcendence of a thing is proven by the adumbrative character of our apprehension of it (*Ideas I*, §41–44). Were we able to make absolute contact with it, know it through and through, make it utterly transparent, then it would no longer be other; it would be our own conscious stream, would be us. What is other is always transcendent, e-lusive, given only adumbratively, in shades and shadowings. Respect arises from the withdrawal and transcendence of others. They work their magic on us by exploiting the power of the unknown, of the withdrawal, by an action at a distance, shadowing forth the forces that stir within but never delivering them as a whole (either to us or to themselves). The respect the other commands plays on the mystery of depths we cannot fathom. When we drop our metaphysical plumb lines we never hear them touch bottom. We know that we have to do here with a system we cannot dominate, a puzzle we cannot decipher.

And so it is not the "presence" of others which "fills the room" but their absence. And not just absence but the interplay of presence and absence, of the self-giving which is also self-withdrawing, of the look in someone's eyes which leaves us provoked, solicited. It is the *lethe* at play in *a-letheia* which inspires the mix of awe, fear, and admiration which Kant calls respect—and which Heidegger calls letting-be. There are gods here, too, not just in Heidegger's jugs and bridges, and not just in Heraclitus' stove, but in the visitors who come to see Heraclitus, in others, and even in condescending old Heraclitus, too.[7]

But it is the face of suffering which puts teeth into the mystery and prevents us from confusing the mystery with an object of poetic reverie or from using it as the occasion for a recollective leap out of existence, which only leaves the rest of us to face the worst. Suffering is first of all a modification of the face, one of the faces the face can assume, one of the ways it can be and come to presence, as when we speak of a face distorted by suffering. Now if the face of the other commands respect, if it is the seat of a power which emanates from the other, then what strikes us above all about suffering is that it is a violation, that it has no regard for human life (and not only for human life, for the suffering of animals has become more and more a concern of late) that it invades the sphere of the other, deals recklessly with what demands respect and warrants reverence. If there is something "inviolable" about the other, something which demands that we treat him or her with dignity, suffering is more like a wanton marauder which violates at will. Suffering is violence: human violence, when it is the suffering which human beings inflict on one another; the violence of the cosmos itself, when suffering is inflicted by a natural disaster or a disease which strikes without warning. Wherever it originates, the effect is always the same. All the pressing matters of our everyday concerns are suspended; something intervenes which supervenes them, some sort of vandal has entered the scene and has knocked over the tables and chairs of everyday existence and made a ruin of life.

Suffering creates an inverted world. A disease strikes down the important and the famous, who moved only in circles of authority, and makes them dependent on a hospital aide. It wrenches a person out of a busy life and puts in its place long empty hours of lying in a bed. It takes a person of dignity—of bearing and grace, of wit and good humor—and reduces her to a listless and melancholy shadow of her former self. An accident robs a strong and swift athlete of her legs, the pianist of her hands, the painter of her eyes.[8] Mental disorders shatter the soundness of a mind, torment it with groundless fears and anxiety, haunt it with repressed desire, inflicting pain of a different but no less real sort. And poverty robs a child of nourishment and parents of their dignity. Suffering diminishes our being, impoverishes our mind and wills and bodily energy.

The vandalism of suffering is indiscriminate; it does not *respect* anything: age, virtue, power. It does not respect what commands respect, does not honor that sphere of inviolability which the body of the other opens up. The body of the other is not a material object but a field of influence which we do not enter or approach lightly. We do not get too close to another unless we know we have been invited. We do not stare brazenly at a mark on another's face, or go over and poke at it curiously as if it were a mark on a window. We are even embarrassed if we brush closely up against a stranger. But suffering shatters all those good manners, that sphere of inviolability, invades that privacy, treats the body savagely—maiming, enervating, and distorting it, withering its powers, wasting its life.

Suffering exposes the vulnerability of human existence, its lack of defense against the play of the flux. It takes a good earthquake to make a scholar appreciate the contingency of things, Johannes Climacus said (even though he writes well about modal logic). Suffering is the best refutation of what Heidegger calls subjectivism and metaphysical humanism, for nothing demonstrates more forcefully the limitation of the "conscious subject" and human powers than blind and fortuitous violence. Our lives are conducted along a narrow line, on either side of which lies the chaos—of a breakdown in our biological integrity, a chance mishap, the wanton violence of the streets, the volatility of political upheaval, and, nowadays, the specter of a nuclear accident or a nuclear holocaust which sends us all hastily back into the flux.

In the face of suffering the constructs of onto-theo-logic are exposed for what they are, the confidence of common sense is refuted, the acuity of science and the agility of *phronesis* are reduced to silence (which is why Aristotle added good luck to wisdom in his recipe for happiness). It is the best "testimony" (we are, after all, outside the realm where arguments and counterarguments settle anything definitively) for the flux which swirls all around us. The look of one whose powers are withering, of a young life being wasted, the look of hunger—it is always the faces of the children which the relief agencies show us—put us in touch with a sphere which everydayness tries systematically to repress. The familiar structures of our practices and everyday beliefs shatter, breaking down and breaking open. Breaking down gives way to breaking open, so long as we take the occasion to let ourselves be instructed by the abyss, to let the abyss be, to let it play itself out, not in a passive gesture of surrender to destruction but in the sense of what Heidegger calls openness to the mystery.

THE GENEALOGY OF THE RELIGIOUS

It is at this point that I want to insert a radical hermeneutic, a radically interpretive gesture, which consists not in finding meaning but in dealing with the breakdown of meaning, the shattering and foundering of meaning. It is not a hermeneutic which finally fixes meaning and truth once and for all but a hermeneutic fired by the dissemination and trembling of meaning and truth. It is a hermeneutic of the *ébranler*, possible only when the whole trembles. It is not a hermeneutic which gives comfort but a hermeneutic which is ready for the worst, which has been thrown out into the cold. It is here that I think that things swing off into the extremes which I am calling the religious and the tragic and that we get a flesh and blood idea of what we have been calling the flux and the play.

I begin with the religious. There is a momentum in the analysis of suffering which bears us toward a religious hermeneutic. From the standpoint of radical hermeneutics, the religious spirit has looked down the dark well of human suffering and found there a loving power which takes the side of suffering. He hears the voice of God in the rumble of the flux, feels the hand of God in its tremors. So if we speak of the "eyes of faith," we do not mean that a special light shines on the believer which is withheld from the rest of us but rather that he has a certain facility to construe the darkness, to grope in the dark. Such eyes are accustomed to the lack of evidence and to living without assurances. I reject all forms of privileged positions above the flux and binary oppositional schemes. I am always arguing that we get the best results from facing up to the flux itself, without throwing dust in our eyes. I write a genealogy of religion from below, and I ask all who do otherwise how they acquired their elevated position. The eyes of faith mean that the believer is good at making his way through the dark, at keeping on the tracks of the divine. Far from being able to see God everywhere, the believer has perhaps the sharpest sense of all of the withdrawal of God, His absence from the world. His faith consists precisely in bending in the direction of the God who withdraws.

But this is not to be construed eschatologically. I do not mean that the age of faith is over and that the believer looks for the signs of a new age of the gods. That puts us right back into the *Der Spiegel* interview, waiting for a God to save us and a new flip in the *Seinsgeschick* while romanticizing bygone epochs. I mean that, for a radical hermeneutic, God is always and everywhere, in all the epochs, essentially withdrawn from the world, even as faith says He is omnipresent. His very self-giving is self-withdrawing, a-lethic. God is never *given* in some sheer excess of presence or plenitude. If we had walked the streets of Galilee with Jesus, Kierkegaard said, we would not have seen the divinity without the "condition" (faith).[9] God is always self-deferring, even when he reveals himself. His presence is deferred even as it is revealed in "the world of the Greeks, in prophetic Judaism, in the preaching of Jesus" (VA 183/PLT 184). He defers His presence wherever He addresses us. The very nature of faith is to deal with things which appear not. So true is this that in an age of faith like the Christian Middle Ages, when everyone was talking about God, it was necessary for a figure like Eckhart to insist on the self-deferral of God behind all this onto-theo-logic (not to mention all the ecclesiastical power plays), lest there be nothing to revere. God's presence is always caught up in the play of presence and absence. The faith of the believer consists in staying in play with that play, which involves maximum risk and uncertainty. Far from having magical powers, the eyes of faith suffer systematic strain from having always to do with shadowy forms and twilight figures.

The genealogy of the religious is found in a hermeneutic of suffering. The religious is a response to what gives itself and withdraws in suffering. Suffering presents itself to the religious mind as a fundamental moral outrage, a violence with no rights which wastes life. Thus, the religious attitude arises precisely as a *protest* against suffering. It is essentially defiant, protesting, protestant— against a violation of life which must not go unanswered—and catholic, because it speaks on behalf of all who suffer. I do not think that religion accepts suffering as God's will or as a punishment for sin or as a means of sanctification, at least not in its most robust and healthy form, but that it protests suffering in the name of life and that it affirms God in order to make its protest on behalf of life heard, to write its protest in capital letters. I do not think it begins from above, with God, as if it dropped from the sky, and then explains suffering in a downward movement as God's will or as part of a redemptive scheme. Rather, it begins from below, by grappling with the flux, with suffering, and then affirms God in an upward movement, as a response to suffering and an expression of its outrage. The genealogy of religion in suffering means that the affirmation of God is implicated in the affirmation of life and the protest against suffering. Religion arises as an expression of solidarity with the suffering.

Religion, accordingly, is fundamentally a defiant gesture. It speaks in the name of life and against the powers that demean and degrade life. It does not arise negatively, from a rejection, but affirmatively, from an affirmation of life, from the momentum and energy of life itself. In this framework, the very idea of "God" means He who stands always and necessarily on the side of those who suffer, He who intervenes on behalf of the sufferer. Religion has both a fiduciary quality,[10] a certain trust in a loving hand which supports those who suffer, and a defiant quality, which is neither passive nor acceptive of suffering. In the face of suffering, the believer is compelled to think, as one who believes in life and refuses to allow it to be wasted, that God stands with those who suffer, that that indeed is what it means for there to be a God.

That is why religion, on this conception, is politically subversive, with a subversion which cuts across the ideologies of right and left. Liberation theology flourishes in Latin America where Catholic priests and nuns are called Marxists because they stand by the poor and oppressed, the starving and excluded. And in Poland, where the priests also stand with the poor and those who have no voice, the church is called counterrevolutionary, when all that means is that the church here, too, is engaged in a work of liberation, of disrupting constellations of power, of standing on the side of those who are systematically deprived of their dignity and even of their lives.

The political theologian Johann Baptist Metz says that religion speaks *ex memoria passionis*, from the memory of suffering.[11] Christianity, he writes, "tries to keep alive the memory of the crucified Lord, this specific *memoria passionis*, as a dangerous memory of freedom in the social systems of our technological civilization." That puts some teeth into the idea of memory which Heidegger linked with the heart's core, when he was speaking of Meister Eckhart (WHD 91ff./WCT 138ff.) Instead of just remembering the Greek temples and jugs, we need to remember suffering. This memory is dangerously liberating and disrupts the prevailing order which allows a few to prosper from the sufferings of many. It is not a comforting memory, which filters the past through a screen of nostalgia (not "recollection"), but a disturbing and dangerous memory which makes a demand upon us ("repetition"). It is a deconstructive memory which will not let us forget, will not let us settle down into the complacency of well-fed presence. "Every rebellion against suffering," Metz says, "is fed by the subversive power of remembered suffering." And that is why Metz has had enough of the history of presence, of metaphysical histories of the victorious and dominant, and puts a word in for a deconstructive (we are supplying this word for him because I think that deconstruction always has a political exchange value) and subversive history of the defeated, forgotten, and excluded, a "history of the vanquished," which proceeds by telling dangerous and liberative stories. This kind of memory prevents the "privatization" of suffering which excludes its political dimension. It is not surprising that the most powerful religious images in the Judeo-Christian tradition—the Exodus and the Crucifixion—are images of injustice and liberation.

So when religion betrays its work of liberation—as it does over and over again—we wonder what has gone wrong. Religion is a way of coming to grips with the flux, a struggle with the powers of darkness, which is "authentic" only so long as it "owns up" to the contingency of its symbols. Faith makes its way in the dark, seeing through a glass darkly, and it is genuine only to the extent that it acknowledges the abyss in which we are all situated, the undecidability and ambiguity which engulfs us all. We do not know who we are, not if we are honest, or whether or not we believe in God: that is the point of departure for any genuine faith. We do not know what fears or aspirations give rise to faith. The believer is not someone who has been visited from on high by a supervenient grace but someone who, like the rest of us, does what he can to construe the darkness, to follow the sequence of shadows across the cave, to cope with the flux. To invoke a grace from on high is just one more familiar way of bailing out on the flux—just when we are needed the most. It is one more way to say that one has gained an exemption from the human condition, that God has privileged a few with a lifeline that He has not thrown out to others—which would be comic were it not so dangerous.

Now it is just then—when religion starts to think in terms of a gift of grace given only to a chosen people—that religion begins to degenerate into a factional power and a force of oppression. It starts to lose its protestant (protesting) quality as soon as it ceases to be catholic (universal), as soon as it fails to see that it is committed in principle to universal liberation. It becomes metaphysical and starts dividing the world into the binary opposition of believer and infidel, as if believers have a hot line to Hermes which has been withheld from the in-fidels, those whom we define in terms of their lack of the gift of presence which we have been granted. Then religion sits down to the table with the powers that be, just when it ought otherwise to have been committed to their disruption. What Johannes Climacus says about discoursing with a Hegelian—that we must first wring from him the concession that he is a human being and not speculative philosophy in the abstract—also goes for believers. Faith is not magic. It is only worth its salt if it functions in continual exposure to its own deconstruction.

THE GENEALOGY OF THE TRAGIC AND THE DIMENSIONS OF THE ABYSS

So just when the case for the religious view was starting to build up a head of steam, it springs a leak. Just when we were considering returning to the faith of our youth, radical hermeneutics upsets our plans. Radical hermeneutics is trying to describe a situation in which we never get any rest, in which things are never secured against their opposite. We can never build a shelter against the winds of the flux. Nor indeed is that our desire. For we have insisted all along that we get better results by owning up to the flux. The religious response to suffering cannot be insulated against its opposite, because suffering is an undecidable, a wavering trickster, a-lethic. Religion coexists in continual exposure to an opposite and contradictory genealogy, one which condemns religion on its own terms, that is to say, precisely because it begins by affirming its solidarity with the suffering. I have let religion begin with its best punch, but it is precisely that punch which the "tragic" means to absorb and to counter with a contradictory reading.

In the tragic view, suffering is *not* a violation, not a vandal which comes crashing into life, destroying and undoing life. It is, on the contrary, part of life, a moment in its total output of energy, a phase of its movement, part of its overall momentum. Suffering belongs integrally to life and cannot be excluded. Consequently there is no question of protesting suffering, for that would be to protest life itself. Life is always already incised by suffering, and that is a condition of its vitality. Suffering does indeed have its rights; it is part of the overall "justice" of life. Suffering is not guilty but innocent. Suffering belongs within the sphere of Anaximander's *dike*, part of its balance of forces.

Religion does not begin with God but with suffering, and it invokes God to make its protest heard. In the same way, the tragic view does not begin with atheism but by affirming the whole wheel of life and suffering, and it denies God in order to make its affirmation heard. Religion affirms God in order to protest the injustice of suffering; the tragic denies God in order to affirm the justice of suffering. Genealogically speaking, the distinction between the religious and the tragic is not, first of all, a distinction between theism and atheism but a distinction in the stand they take about suffering.

Nietzsche—the great spokesman for a tragic hermeneutic in our time, indeed in any time—criticizes a selective affirmation of life which tries to exclude suffering, to say that it is not part of the whole. One cannot make a vow with life which, like a faint-hearted bridegroom, takes life for better but not for worse. One cannot swear a partial allegiance to life which takes one part but not another. If one affirms life, one must affirm the whole, the "going-under" as well as the "going over," the pain as well as the pleasure, the midnight as well as the high noon. Zarathustra's pre-Copernican sun moves in a circle around us, going over and going under, and that is the movement of life itself, the relentless rhythm of the flux. Affirmation must embrace the whole circle, the entire circulation of the flux, without discrimination, without exclusion, without rejecting the lower and baser parts:[12]

> *My New Path to a "Yes."*—Philosophy . . . is a voluntary quest for even the most detested and notorious sides of existence. . . . [T]he *hidden* history of philosophy, the psychology of its great names, came to light for me. "How much truth can a spirit *endure*, how much truth does a spirit *dare?*" . . . [T]his does not mean that [such a philosophy] must halt at a negation, a No, a will to negation. It wants rather to cross over to the opposite of this—to a Dionysian affirmation of the world as it is, without subtraction, exception, or selection—it wants the eternal circulation: the same things, the same logic and illogic of entanglements.

This highest, most Dionysian relation to existence is called *amor fati*. It takes life as it stands, unpurged of its harsher aspects. It does not hierarchize life into binary oppositions of higher and lower, systematically affirming only one side, as if either side were not inevitably entangled with its opposite. All things are entangled, ensnared, interwoven, "textualized." Hence, it is not enough to tolerate or accept suffering: one must affirm it, indeed love it, love the whole, the entire ring-dance in which all things are caught up. We cannot get away with saying that we will endure it "just this once." We cannot incorporate temporary provisos and conditions into the contract with life. We must enter into an unconditional agreement, with no hidden clauses or covenants. To affirm life is to affirm it all and to affirm it over and over again, raising the pitch of the affirmation of existence to infinity—which is the sense of eternal return. Was that life? Well, then, once more! All joy wants eternity, wants to recur, to increase, to perpetuate itself into infinity. It wants to turn the wheel again and again, which means both to ache with pain and to pulsate with pleasure, for these are entangled with each other in the tension of a Heraclitean bow.

Thus, in one of the last entries in *The Will to Power*, Nietzsche opposes the symbol of the crucified Christ—by religion's own accounting, the symbol of solidarity with those who suffer—to the symbol of the martyred Dionysus. Both are martyred, suffering gods, but the difference lies in "the meaning of suffering" each bears:[13]

> In the former case [Christ], it is supposed to be the path to a holy existence; in the latter case, being is counted as *holy enough* to justify even a monstrous amount of suffering. The tragic man affirms even the harshest suffering: he is sufficiently strong, rich and capable of deifying to do so. The Christian denies even the happiest lot on earth: he is sufficiently weak, poor, disinherited to suffer from life in whatever form he meets it. The god on the cross is a curse on life, a signpost to seek redemption from life; Dionysus cut to pieces is a *promise* of life: it will be eternally reborn and return again from destruction.

Suffering is integral to life, and life is innocent. The innocence of becoming implies the innocence of suffering. Suffering is but a phase of the flux, a moment of the becoming, as innocent as driving winds or cascading waters. In the tragic vision, suffering is worked into the very texture of life, entangled with it, not dialectically—in order to produce a higher resolution—but, in the manner of Heraclitus, as part of the natural movement of the flux and its system of tensions and strife. War is the father of all: the strife between things, the tensions within life are what drive life on.

The religious spirit has divided life into parts, hierarchized it into the bearable and the unbearable, true life and the enemy of life, guilty and innocent. His soul is weak and timid, and everything which touches him causes him pain. For him, life is refuted by suffering; his soul is sent reeling toward the after-worldly, the meta-physical, by pain and torment. He has been waylaid by suffering, the movement of his soul has been broken, his upward ascent reversed, and he sinks back into a melancholy longing for release. The genealogy of religion from suffering means that religion turns on the assumption that "all those who suffer from life as from an illness are in the right."

To this religious type, Nietzsche opposes those for whom suffering is a condition of life, the fire in which life is steeled, who grow strong from their suffering, whose life is enhanced and promoted by suffering. Suffering raises the tension of the bow, organizes all of the powers of the organism, hardens, strengthens. It is thus the capacity for suffering which is the true measure of the will to power. " . . . [H]ow deeply human beings can suffer almost determines their order of rank. . . . " Suffering ennobles, sets the best over the worst, creates a spiritual ordering among men so that Nietzsche can speak of "this spiritual, silent haughtiness of the sufferer, this pride of the elect of knowledge."[14] Sufferers suffer from what they know, from the almost unbearable and hard knowledge that the flux is all.

The capacity to suffer "almost" determines the order of rank. Why "almost"? Because enduring great suffering is not enough. Ascetics know how to suffer. But they do not know how to affirm, to laugh. Tragic suffering is caught up in a deeper affirmation and love of fate; it issues from a deeper source, a deep and resonating laughter:[15]

> *The Olympian vice.*—. . . I would go so far as to venture an order of rank among philosophers according to the rank of their laughter—rising to those capable of *golden* laughter. And if gods too philosophize . . . I do not doubt that while doing so they also know how to laugh in a new and superhuman way—and at the expense of all serious things. Gods are fond of mockery; it seems they cannot refrain from laughter even when sacraments are in progress.

The ultimate affirmation of life, of the circle of joy and suffering, takes the form of laughter, a Dionysiac exuberance which sings and dances, which affirms and exults in the totality of life. "The most suffering animal on earth invented for itself—laughter."[16] The young shepherd laughs with a more than human laughter, the laughter of overcoming, of the *Übermensch*, the laughter for which Zarathustra longs. The face of suffering for Nietzsche is transformed by laughter. The tragic actor wears a comic mask. The cry of suffering is drowned out by the laughter of Zarathustra, singing and dancing even as he goes under.

The real difference between the religious and the tragic is that, in the tragic view, suffering is not a violation, not an injustice, not an intruder without rights. Life is not unfair. It is as innocent as the wind. Life and suffering are intertwined and entangled in a Heraclitean balance so that there is no question of choosing one or the other but only of the affirmation of both or of neither. Were there to be here a phenomenology of respect, it would be of an entirely different sort—one which would speak in terms of the noble *(vornehm)*, that which sustains suffering as part of the total compact between the individual and life.

I know of no way to adjudicate between these incommensurables, nor is that my wish. I prefer to keep the debate open, which is why I do not think that the religious voice is drowned out by Zarathustra's dithyrambs. I think that all this Nietzschean exuberance has some accounting to do. For despite its talk of Heraclitean play, the tragic does not allow suffering its play, which is to cut into and waste life. The tragic view, against its own rhetoric, is in fact not hard enough: it accepts, embraces, and makes light of just what it should resist. It is tolerant of that against which it should raise its voice in protest. It accepts just what it should defy. It lets violence off too easily. Its notion of the justice of strife is that of a weak-willed judge. It has no nerve for a real fight, which means to resist the wasteful effects of suffering.

The tragic view assimilates suffering into a pure cosmology of forces which does not let suffering be suffering. It makes good sense if one is speaking of natural disasters: the hurricane is innocent. If one is speaking of the lamb and the bird of prey, the falcon is innocent. If one is speaking of the natural inevitability of death, old age, and disease, the virus is innocent. But it makes no sense at all if the natural disaster is precipitated by the greed of industrialists who misuse natural resources; if the disease is caused by industrial pollutants dumped indiscriminately into the atmosphere, if the aging is premature because the body of the peasant has been broken and exploited by the landowner, if death is caused by an act of state terrorism against a dissenter.

From the point of view of a religious *memoria passionis*, the tragic view has a short memory and is a pawn in the hands of those who know how to play the game of power. It is the religious view which is radical and liberating, while the tragic view is the laughing gas of the suffering. It asks them to love their exploitation and affirm it in a Dionysian dance. Suffering is not innocent, not when there is systematic exclusion and oppression all around. If the religious view is politically subversive and stands on the side of the oppressed, the tragic view is politically naive and must explain why it does not counsel the exploited, the poor, and the excluded to love their oppression as the play of forces, which is just what the powers that be have been telling them to do for some time now. Can "the innocence of becoming" be stretched far enough to include those who repress, exploit, and take away life?

We get a sense, then, of the "dimensions" of this "abyss." In the one case, a purely cosmic view of existence, a ring-dance of forces playing itself out, a philosophy of Heraclitean play and of acceptance. In the other case, a deeply ethicoreligious view of existence which hears the voice of the oppressed crying in the midst of that world rumble. What is calling to us from that abyss? Whose voice is it? Or is it no voice at all but the rumble of the cosmos in its endless transformations, the washing of the Heraclitean river against its shores. In the one case, an innocent, joyful ring-dance of the elements, of fiery ether, water, and earth, as they change places with one another, each living the death of the other. In the other case, an abyss resonating with the voice of those whose chance for life has been aborted by concentrations of power bent on holding them in check. In one case, an indiscriminate affirmation of the play of all things; in the other case, a protest on behalf of just those places where the play has been arrested and life taken away.

In the one case, a purely cosmological Heraclitus who affirms the play of forces; Heraclitus the intoxicated extramoralist. In the other case, the Heraclitus for whom the play has to be balanced and fair, for whom the *logos* means a proportion, a fair share, so that no element can dominate, for whom the soul must be dry and moderate. For the one, the Crucified as the symbol of the refutation of life and, for the other, as the symbol of solidarity with the suffering which wastes life. For the one, a philosophy of the play of forces which incorporates suffering into the play; for the other, a protest against suffering in the name of the play and precisely a way to keep the play in play.

Both views invoke the same powers and speak in the name of the same gods: life, love, affirmation, free play. The incommensurability of their conflict signifies not only the lack of a common measure but of any measure at all. The dimensions of the conflict mark off the measurelessness of the abyss.

Is suffering violent or innocent? Does it speak with a moral or an extramoral voice? Does it summon us to resistance and protest and subversion of the powers which inflict it or to a Dionysian embrace? Is the rumble of the world-flux a purely cosmic dance, or does the voice of God call out to us obscurely in all that chaos, leading us down the labyrinthine way? Is it God calling? Or the world? Or are we just hearing things? Should we set all these acoustics aside as illusions with which we should not trouble ourselves, not while the pressing business of our quotidian lives is all around us?[17]

What—or who—is speaking to us here? What signs does it send us? The tragic and the religious are markers of the abyss which is always the issue for radical hermeneutics—conflicting messages from Hermes, enigmatic letters coming in a disturbing delivery service. The very distance between the messages coming in from "Dionysus" and "Christ" charts the open space of this abyss, marks the chasm which spreads out before us. The issue between them, the gap that opens up as each goes out *(ex-ire, aus-tragen)* from the other, pointing in its own direction, opening up its own distance, constitutes the dimensions of the abyss, the space of its play. The wavering between them illustrates our abandonment to the measureless, our lack of a fixed point from which to take its measure.

Suffering makes the whole tremble. Suffering is not merely suffering. It bursts asunder and opens us up to eternal things (eternal recurrence? an eternally loving hand touching our lives in a mysterious manner?). It transforms itself before our eyes, metamorphoses from an intraworldly and mundane event into an opening onto the whole. It is one of the places where the grip of everyday concerns is broken, where the spell of the quotidian loses its hold. The thin surface of existence gives way, and, like Alice, we fall down a long dark well. In suffering we are provoked, solicited, opened. It is as if Husserl's thesis about the destructibility of the world actually came to pass, and the world of the natural attitude suddenly came undone, leaving us to survey the chaos, the undoing, the deconstitution, the de-construction. On the one side, suffering is merely that, a self-identical empirical fact, but, on the other side, it surpasses itself and spins off into the abyss, pulling the ground from under us. The face of the one who suffers is itself, but it is also essentially more. And it is the sense of this "more" which radical hermeneutics wants to cultivate.

I do not think that anyone ever really succeeds in getting to one side or the other of this undecidable rift, that one really "is" or "is not" religious, wholly Augustinian or wholly Nietzschean. There never really was an Augustine or a

Nietzsche who instantiated those texts, not if that means to have consolidated oneself entirely on one side or the other of this divide, to "be" religious or irreligious, decidably, without doubt. That, too, is the metaphysics of presence and identity. I do not think that we know whether we believe in God or not, not if we face the cold truth. On the contrary, I think we spend a good deal of time slipping back and forth between the two, between Abraham and Zarathustra, Augustine and Nietzsche, trying to find out what we think.

Questio mihi factus sum. We do not know who we are, not if we are honest.

The mystery withdraws. The mystery is the withdrawal. *Lethe* is the unshakable heart of *a-letheia*.

The task of thinking, which is conducted in the ground of the soul, is to keep open to the mystery, to keep the play in play.

GELASSENHEIT AND PER-SONA: THE MYSTERY OF THE PERSON

We will not be taken in by the Dionysiac woman/truth. We are on to her game. No one is granted a seat above the flux from which to survey the whole—be it the whole history of Being or the whole history of morals—and to pronounce on the meaning of suffering. And it is for that reason that we have constant recourse to the ethics of dissemination. We are all bound together by the mystery of our mortality and by midnight shadows. We constitute a community of unknowers who, precisely in virtue of their helplessness, require *(brauchen)* one another. It is precisely the uncertainty of things which links us indissolubly, which commits us to the dispersal of power structures which think they have the final word. We are as wary of tragic aristocracy as of religious theocracy. The only rule we have come to respect is the rule of lethe and of the powers of withdrawal.

But we can at least learn something from all this. We can be educated—led out, *e-ducatum*—by the withdrawal, instructed in the lesson of the *lethe*, that the withdrawal shelters hidden powers. (Is it the power of the world? of the soul? of God?) And in being thus educated, in this learned unknowing, there lies the motive of a universal letting-be, of a generalized *Gelassenheit* which lets be, which releases gods and mortals, earth and sky—and let us expand this Greco-Germanic catalogue to include male and female, Greek and Jew, East and West, weak and strong, healthy and sick, animal and human (and whatever else we have been inclined to subordinate, hierarchize, marginalize). In this generalized *Gelassenheit*, the task is to let all things be what and how they are. We learn to "think" in some deep sense (which is not a matter of acquiring knowledge), by letting the *lethe* in things resonate. And that is what we mean by an ethics of *Gelassenheit*—which is all at once an ethics of liberation, toleration, and solidarity. And so it is necessary to save Nietzsche from himself (even as Nietzsche tells us that we have to learn to lose him after we have found him),[18] to let the Dionysiac woman recoil on Nietzsche himself, to make of Nietzsche one more argument for the ethics of *Gelassenheit* and the community of mortals, to enlist him in a work of universal emancipation which he himself would have rejected as a project which smells too bad.

Now perhaps it is possible, at the end of this inquiry, to reconstitute a more radicalized notion of this being "which we ourselves are" without falling through the trap door of subjectivism. I once thought of entitling this book "The Recovery of Man."[19] But I rejected that notion because "recovery" is too strongly suggestive of "recollection" and because "man" smacks too much of humanism and sexism. But part of the agenda of this study has been to try to find some way of confronting this question—which is why I refused to give up on the word "hermeneutics." I have all along been looking for some account of human existence which has nothing to do with what the critique of humanism and subjectivism criticizes. If I can get that far, I will be satisfied.

It is clear that the word "self" will not do, because that is just the notion that the critique of metaphysics has most effectively delimited. The "self" is something which we define in terms of its self-identity. Yet what seems to characterize "us" above all is non-identity, difference, our power or, better, our vulnerability to spin off into the abyss. The self is precisely not that which always abides in itself, self-identically present to itself, but that which breaks under the strain, gives way to the pull of the flux, which is constantly being divested of its illusions, tormented by the unconscious, constantly being tricked by its history and its language. If we have learned anything in the last one hundred years of European thought, it is that the self is anything but what it pretends to be. And even to speak, as does Ricoeur, of a "wounded *cogito*" is to employ a euphemism which tries to contain and minimize the damage. The "self" is much more a place of disruption, irruption, solicitation.

By way of making a final stab at this question, I would like to dust off an old word which has the advantage of having been coined before the advent of the metaphysics of subjectivity and which is not as "logo-centric" as it seems: the old word *per-sona, per-sonare,* the person as sounding-through, resonating. This pre-Cartesian word does not name a seat of self-identity and has nothing to do with an egological metaphysics. On the contrary, it means to name a difference, to pick up the interplay between mask and voice, face and speech, look and language, *eidos* and *logos.* It means to open up and preserve the distance between the mask and the speaker and prevent their hasty identification. It means to preserve the non-identity of the speaker and the voice which resonates through the mask. Unlike the modern notion of the self-identical ego or self-present consciousness, the old sense of *per-sona* speaks in terms of difference and non-identity. It recognizes the mediation, the *per,* that nothing is immediately given or present here; far from being logo-centric, it aims at denying phonic immediacy. It is essentially the voice which does not keep silent, whose words are dispersed and disseminated and fall outside oneself, all over the stage, while the speaker remains concealed. It holds that whatever transpires on the face is echo, trace, sign, even dissemblance. It is a word for players, actors, the *theatricum philosophicum*. Unlike "ego" and "self," which belong to a metaphysics of identity, *per-sona* is embedded in the metaphorics of the flux. Everything deep loves the mask. *Per-sona:* the depths which rush under the surface, the deep resonance and rumble—of who knows what.[20]

The face of suffering is a mask through which something deeper resonates, leaving its echo behind. Who or what is speaking here, what voice sounds through the face? Is it the cry of the one who suffers, the breath of air he breathes, the spirit/breath (*spiritus, parole soufflé*)—is this the soul's a-spiration for God? What is stirring in these words? Whose voice speaks? What is the more than human "It" (*das "Es"*) which speaks whenever man speaks, which makes itself heard, if we are attentive enough, whenever human words are uttered? What abyss breaks through here? What is playing itself out here? Is it the voice of Zarathustra singing and dancing and, above all, laughing in tune with, attuned to, the rhythm of the cosmos, the movements of the flux, singing even as he goes under? Is it no human voice at all but simply the echo of the world-play as it plays itself out, the rush of its winds? Is the human breath but a share of this cosmic whirl? When we put our ear to the human mask, as to a shell we find on the seashore, what roar do we hear? "Is it the soul which is speaking?" Heidegger asks. "Is it the world? Is it God?"[21]

The task of a radical hermeneutics is not to decipher the speaker beneath the mask but to alert us to the distance which separates them—and then to preserve and keep it open. Its work is to keep open the Husserlian thought of the annihilability of the world, of the vulnerability of mundane formations, and the irreducibility of the flux—to keep open Constantin's project of finding a way through the flux, of pushing ahead in a repetition which produces as it repeats forward. Its work is the Derridean work of solicitation, of disarming the pretensions to presence and authority wherever they assert themselves, of keeping the play in play, of disrupting the attempt to arrest the play. Its work—and perhaps this is the least inadequate formulation of all—is openness to the mystery.

We—we who have become problematic to ourselves, we who cannot say "we," we non-selves who cannot call ourselves "man" and who have made "humanism" suspect—are the place where the abyss opens up, where the whole trembles, where the ground gives way. We: *per-sonà:* the opening through which the flux resonates.

LAUGHTER AND THE SPIRIT OF SERIOUSNESS

But all of this seriousness needs an antidote, lest we perish from it. For none of it is any excuse for losing our sense of humor. We ought to beware of letting these Heideggerian solemnities get a grip on us.

Indeed, it is an irony to me that, when Heidegger tried to exclude

Kierkegaard from the pantheon of "thinkers," he did so in the name of Nietzsche. The popular association of Nietzsche and Kierkegaard, Heidegger declared, is a mistake. (That was probably a shot at Jaspers.) Nietzsche moves in the same orbit as Aristotle, thinking the meaning of Being, in the Greco-Germanic chain of mountain tops communing with mountain tops. Kierkegaard is a merely regional writer, a religious author, covering a little corner down in the valley of the space marked off by Hegel (GA 5 249/QCT 94; cf. WHD 129/WCT 213).

In fact, Heidegger got not only Kierkegaard wrong but Nietzsche, too, and both for the same reason. For he never seemed to hear the booming laughter of Zarathustra or the cutting wit of Johannes Climacus. He never took account of the fact that these were anti-institutional figures who could not survive in the element of the university—irregular, incommensurable figures. He did not grasp the profoundly subversive character of Nietzsche's conception of truth or of Kierkegaard's whole project of disowning his books and ridiculing those who wrote metaphysical treatises. And he did not see that on this point both were deeply ex-orbitant thinkers, operating outside the orbit of metaphysics, on the other side of Aristotle's metaphysical project of calming the Heraclitean waters into the stability of *ousia*. Kierkegaard and Nietzsche were bent on letting the flux loose, letting it flow where it will. Their work began at that point where the metaphysical attempt to arrest the play founders. That is why Nietzsche himself took Aristotelianism to be an effete attempt to curb and moderate the great tragic passions.

Heidegger missed the wit and the cunning of the Dionysiac woman, as Derrida shows. And he took no account of the irony and cutting humor of Kierkegaard. Nowhere does Heidegger get stung by the tip of Kierkegaard's pen more sharply than in §74 of *Being and Time*, where the argument of the book reaches a crescendo in the boldface, italicized definition of *Wiederholung*. The problem is not only that Heidegger does not cite Kierkegaard, from whom the notion and the word were adapted, in accordance with the good manners of the university. Indeed, the missing footnote diverts us from the tip of the real point. For, were he to cite the book *Repetition*, which author would he cite? Who is the author of *Repetition*, Kierkegaard or Constantin (the first of whom puts the idea of authorship into question and the second of whom suffers from the disadvantage that he does not exist)? The notion that "repetition" is not a piece of academic architecture, that it does not belong at the end, indeed at the peak and dénouement, of a long and symmetrically organized book (with two parts, each of which has three divisions, with six chapters in each division), which was submitted for the sake of a professorship at Marburg—all of this is lost on Heidegger. The problem is not that Heidegger breaks a rule of the academic game but that Kierkegaard was playing another sort of game altogether.

Heidegger's long, italicized definition reminds us of nothing so much as the long-winded, puffed-up definition of truth which Johannes Climacus puts forth, tongue in cheek, in the *Postscript*. Climacus's definition is a joke. He is not seriously proposing a counterdefinition of truth to combat the Hegelian one—except strategically, humorously, ironically. The *Postscript* does not seriously propose to get into a metaphysical contest with Hegel, to counter Hegel's objectivistic metaphysics with Johannes Climacus's countermetaphysics of the existing subject, in a hand-to-hand metaphysical combat. The *Postscript* means to sink the ship of metaphysics—all metaphysics, objectivistic and subjectivistic—to let it crash against the reefs, to let it founder and come to grief. The *Postscript* means to be a booming laughter at metaphysics. It wants to put an end to all this metaphysical italicized chatter and to drag thinkers back into the streets of the flux.

That is why this book is an anti-book. It mocks the book, means to be un-book, the last book *(Concluding)* which is an un-book, altogether lacking in systematic control *(Unscientific)*, merely a piece of writing *(Postscript)*. It does not have a pretentious title *(Being and Time,* "On the Essence of Truth," or "Time and Being")*. If it had had to have a Heideggerian name at all, it would have been called "The End of Philosophy." Only when he started to talk like that, in his last writings, did Heidegger begin to catch up to Kierkegaard. But even then he did not hear the laughter. Though Heidegger is the great thinker of our time and even though the present work is in his debt on nearly every page, he remains vis-à-vis Kierkegaard in the acutely embarrassing situation of someone who does not get a joke—worse still, who does not even know that the speaker is joking at all—while everyone else is holding their sides. He missed the laughter in Kierkegaard and the woman/truth in Nietzsche, too, as Derrida shows. (Almost!)

Everything in Kierkegaard and Nietzsche turns on laughter—ironic laughter, exuberant laughter. Always the abyss but always the laughter. Nothing undoes the metaphysics of presence better than laughter. Nothing is more unsettling than laughter. Nothing heals like laughter. Nothing keeps us open like laughter. Nietzsche understood that the best and last resource for the tragic is laughter. The being which suffers the most, man, has invented laughter for itself. It is the power to laugh at oneself, one's fears, one's beliefs that liberates and keeps the flux in play, keeps us in movement with the flux, and keeps the openness to the mystery from becoming nostalgia and melancholy, malingering and moping. It is laughter which lets things be and extricates them from the traps which metaphysics lays for them.

Nietzsche makes the sound theological observation that the gods laugh even when sacraments are in progress and hence that we ought not to diminish religious life with the spirit of seriousness. That I take to be profoundly pertinent advice to religion for the free play of the religious spirit, for the liberation of the children of God, who are—as St. Paul said, when he was not

telling women to cover their heads in church or to obey their husbands—
neither Greek nor Jew, master nor slave, male nor female, who also affirm the
play of the world by seeing there a loving hand, even and especially when one
verges on the abyss. Suffering requires the mask of laughter. Laughter ennobles, strengthens, sees one through a bad time.

There is not a little Kierkegaardian/Nietzschean/Derridean wisdom in the
conclusion of Umberto Eco's *The Name of the Rose*, when it turns out that all
the blood was being spilled in an effort to keep Aristotle's missing book on
comedy under wraps and hence to repress the spirit of laughter. Old Jorge lived
in deadly fear of laughter, which he took to be the Prince of Darkness himself,
because he sensed its power to disrupt ecclesiastical authority and established
order, to liberate from fear, even the fear of death, to release the play of the
imagination. But, of course, as William (who stands with St. Francis) responds,
the face of the devil is more likely to be found in the grim countenance of a
"faith without smile and truth without doubt." That is what stokes the fires on
which human flesh is burned, what gives license to violence. That is the real
danger—if I may be permitted an apocalyptic moment. In the end, if the face of
one who believes, or one who struggles with injustice, or one who lays claim to
a solution or to a "scientific analysis" is not crossed by a smile, then he is getting
ready to save us with a metaphysical might from which, if we are lucky, we just
might escape with our lives.

And that goes for radical hermeneutics itself, which can claim no special
exemption from the spirit of seriousness. For all this talk about the abyss and
dark nights is not supposed to be a midnight metaphysics, or a *theologia
negativa*, but a way of awakening to the play of the flux and hence of staying in
play oneself. We have argued that thinking and acting, science and ethics are to
be understood in terms of the agility of one who knows how to cope with
shifting and elusive circumstances, which is more like the skill of a good dancer
than of a heavy-footed German metaphysician. We have argued that, in the end,
the best we can do, after "owning up" to the elusiveness which envelops us all,
is to let all things—gods, earth, and mortals—be. All this talk of the abyss and
openness to the mystery must be understood as the willingness to stay in play
with the play. The question always is whether and how, hearing the movements
of that play, we are able to join in it (SG 188). The play is all.

And what is playing in that play? Is it God? the soul? the world?

Dilige, et quod vis fac.

THE CONCLUSION OF THE BOOK

The book is an illusion. It pretends to have a definite beginning and a distinct
conclusion and to show the way from the one to the other. It claims to be able to
steer its way through the flux, which is why Heidegger preferred to speak of

detours, dead ends, and forest trails. This book has aimed at de-limiting such pretensions. And so it can claim here only to end, not to conclude. We do not aim at a conclusion but an opening. We do not seek a closure but an opening up.

When Kierkegaard described his *Unscientific Postscript* as "*Concluding*," he meant that he was giving up on writing books. He was promising that this would be the last time he would try such a foolish thing. He knew that the whole idea of the authorship of books was questionable and that no "finite existing spirit," as he put it, could ever wring a book out of the flux, could ever get a clean start in the rush of existence or ever top a book off with a conclusion. Of course he did not keep his word, and he slipped back into the same old bad habit— repeatedly. But at least he had the good sense not to sign his books—and to let Constantin and Climacus and all the others take the heat. Once he even wrote a review of *Either/Or* in his own name, which he satirically entitled "Who Is the Author of *Either/Or*?" Who, indeed?

List of Abbreviations

The following abbreviations are used in the body of the test to provide references to works in both the original language and, where available, the English translation; the latter is separated from the former by a slash. References to other works by these authors are to be found in the notes.

WORKS OF DERRIDA

Apoc. "Of an Apocalyptic Tone Recently Adopted in Philosophy," trans. John P. Leavey, *Semeia*, 23 (1982), 63–97.

CP *La Carte postale* (Paris: Flammarion, 1980).

Diss. *La Dissemination*, Collection "Tel Quel" (Paris: Editions du Seuil, 1972). Eng. trans. *Dissemination*, trans. Barbara Johnson (Chicago: University of Chicago Press, 1981).

ED *L'écriture et difference* (Paris: Editions du Seuil, 1967).

Fins *Les Fins de l'homme: A partir du travail de Jacques Derrida*, Colloque de Cerisy directed by P. Lacoue-Labarthe and Jean-Luc Nancy (Paris: Galilée, 1981).

Marg. *Marges de la Philosophie* (Paris: Editions de Minuit, 1972). Eng. trans. *Margins of Philosophy*, trans. A. Bass (Chicago: University of Chicago Press, 1982).

OrG *Edmund Husserl's L'origine de la géométrie*, translation and introduction by Jacques Derrida (Paris: Presses universitaires de France, 1962). Eng. trans. *Edmund Husserl's Origin of Geometry: An Introduction*, trans. John P. Leavy (Stony Brook, N.Y.: Nicholas Hays, 1978).

Pos. *Positions* (Paris: Editions de Minuit, 1972). Eng. trans. *Positions*, trans. Alan Bass (Chicago: University of Chicago Press, 1981).

SP *Speech and Phenomena*, trans. David Allison (Evanston: Northwestern University Press, 1972).

Spurs *Spurs: Nietzsche's Styles*, trans. Barbara Harlow (Chicago: University of Chicago Press, 1978).

VPh *La voix et le phénomene* (Paris: PUF, 1967).

WD *Writing and Difference*, trans. Alan Bass (Chicago: University of Chicago Press, 1978).

WORKS OF HEIDEGGER

BP *Basic Problems of Phenomenology*, trans. Albert Hofstadter (Bloomington: Indiana University Press, 1979).

BT *Being and Time*, trans. John Robinson and Edward MacQuarrie (New York: Harper and Row, 1962).

BW *Heidegger: Basic Writings*, ed. David Krell (New York: Harper and Row, 1977).

DT *Discourse on Thinking*, trans. Hans Freund and John Anderson (New York: Harper and Row, 1966).

EGT *Early Greek Thinking*, trans. Frank Capuzzi and David Krell (New York: Harper and Row, 1975).

EM Heidegger, *Einführung in die Metaphysik* (Tübingen: Niemeyer, 1953).

G Heidegger, *Gelassenheit*, 2 ed. (Pfullingen: Neske, 1960).

GA 1   *Gesamtausgabe*, vol. 1: *Frühe Schriften* (Frankfurt: Klostermann, 1978).
GA 5   *Gesamtausgabe*, vol. 5: *Holzwege* (Frankfurt: Klostermann, 1971).
GA 9   *Gesamtausgabe*, vol. 9: *Wegmarken* (Frankfurt: Klostermann, 1976).
GA 20   *Gesamtausgabe*, vol. 20: *Prolegomena zur Geschichte des Zeitbegriffs* (Frankfurt: Klostermann, 1979).
GA 21   *Gesamtausgabe*, vol. 21: *Logik: Die Frage nach der Wahrheit* (Frankfurt: Klostermann, 1976).
GA 24   *Gesamtausgabe*, B. 24, *Grundprobleme der Phänomenologie* (Frankfurt: Klostermann, 1975).
GA 45   *Gesamtausgabe*, vol. 45: *Grundfragen der Philosophie: Ausgewählte Probleme der Logik* (Frankfurt: Klostermann, 1984).
GA 61   *Gesamtausgabe*, vol. 61: *Phänomenologische Interpretationen zu Aristoteles: Einführung in die Phänomenologische Forschung* (Frankfurt: Klostermann, 1985).
IM   *An Introduction to Metaphysics*, trans. Ralph Mannheim (New York: Doubleday Anchor, 1961).
OWL   *On the Way to Language*, trans. Peter Hertz (New York: Harper and Row, 1971).
QCT   *The Question Concerning Technology and Other Essays*, trans. William Lovitt (New York: Harper and Row, 1977).
SD   *Zur Sache des Denkens* (Tübingen: Niemeyer, 1969).
SG   *Der Satz vom Grund*, 3d ed. (Pfullingen: Neske, 1965).
SZ   *Sein und Zeit*, 10th ed. (Tübingen: Niemeyer, 1962).
TB   *On Time and Being*, trans. Joan Stambaugh (New York: Harper and Row, 1972).
US   *Unterwegs zur Sprache* (Pfullingen: Neske, 1965).
VA   *Vorträge und Aufsätze* (Pfullingen: Neske, 1959).
WCT   *What Is Called Thinking?*, trans. J. Glenn Gray and Fred Wieck (New York: Harper and Row, 1968).
WHD   *Was Heisst Denken* (Tübingen: Niemeyer, 1961).

WORKS OF HUSSERL

Crisis   *The Crisis of European Sciences and Transcendental Phenomenology*, trans. David Carr (Evanston: Northwestern University Press, 1970).
CM   *Cartesian Meditations*, trans. Dorian Cairns (The Hague: Nijhoff, 1960).
Hua I   *Husserliana*, vol. I: *Cartesianische Meditationen und Pariser Vorträge*, 2d ed. (The Hague: Nijhoff, 1973).
Hua III.1 *Husserliana*, vol. III, book 1: *Ideen zu einer Reinen Phänomenologie und Phänomenologische Philosophie, Erstes Buch*, ed. Karl Schuhmann (The Hague: Nijhoff, 1976).
Hua VI   *Husserliana*, vol. VI: *Die Krisis der Europäischen Wissenschaften und die Transcendentale Phänomenologie*, 2d ed. (The Hague: Nijhoff, 1962).
Hua X   *Husserliana*, vol. X, *Zur Phänomenologie des Inneren Zeitbewusstseins* (The Hague: Nijhoff, 1966).
Ideas I *Ideas Pertaining to a Pure Phenomenology and to a Phenomenological Philosophy*, bk. 1B, trans. F. Kersten (The Hague: Nijhoff, 1983).
LU   Edmund Husserl, *Logische Untersuchungen*, vol. I, II/1, II/2. 5th ed. (Tübingen: Max Niemeyer, 1968).
LI   *Logical Investigations*, trans. John Findlay (New York: Humanities Press, 1970).
PIT   *The Phenomenology of Internal Time Consciousness*, trans. James Churchill (The Hague: Nijhoff, 1964).

WORKS OF KIERKEGAARD

CA   *Kierkegaard's Writings*, vol. VIII: *The Concept of Anxiety*, ed. and trans. Reidar Thomte and Albert Anderson (Princeton: Princeton University Press, 1980).

CUP   *Concluding Unscientific Postscript to the Philosophical Fragments*, trans. David Swenson and Walter Lowrie (Princeton: Princeton University Press, 1941).

E/O   *Either/Or*, trans. Walter Lowrie and Howard Johnson, 2 vols. (Princeton: Princeton University Press, 1959).

Pap.   *Soren Kierkegaards Papirer* (Copenhagen: Gyldendal, 1909–48).

PF   *Philosophical Fragments*, trans. David Swenson and Howard Hong (Princeton: Princeton University Press, 1962).

R: *Kierkegaard's Writings*, vol. VI: *"Fear and Trembling" and "Repetition,"* ed. and trans. Howard Hong and Edna Hong (Princeton: Princeton Universtiy Press, 1983).

SV   *Soren Kierkegaards Samlede Vaerker* (Copenhagen: Gyldendal, 1901–06).

OTHER WORKS

AV   Alasdair MacIntyre, *After Virtue*, 2d ed. (Notre Dame: Notre Dame University Press, 1984).

SSR   Thomas Kuhn, *The Structure of Scientific Revolutions*, 2d ed. (Chicago: University of Chicago Press, 1970).

W&M   Hans-Georg Gadamer, *Wahrheit und Method: Grundzüge einer philosophischen Hermeneutik*, 4th ed. (Tübingen: Mohr, 1975).

T&M   Hans-Georg Gadamer, *Truth and Method*, trans. G. Barden and J. Cumming (New York: Seabury, 1975).

Notes

INTRODUCTION

1. The title of my introduction is drawn from a stimulating paper on GA 61 that was given by Theodore Kisiel (Pennsylvania State University, July 1986). See his "On the Way to *Being and Time*," *Research in Phenomenology*, 15 (1985), 193–226.

2. In 1923 Heidegger gave a lecture course entitled "Ontology: Hermeneutics of Facticity."

3. Thomas Sheehan (chap. 7, n. 12 below) has been arguing the importance of Heidegger's readings of Aristotle for some time.

4. Richard Palmer, *Hermeneutics* (Evanston: Northwestern University Press, 1969); and Paul Ricoeur, "The Task of Hermeneutics," in *Hermeneutics and the Human Sciences*, ed. J. Thompson (Cambridge: Cambridge University Press, 1981), 43–62.

5. "Hermeneutics as the Recovery of Man," *Man and World*, 15 (1982): 343–67, reprinted in *Hermeneutics and Modern Philosophy*, ed. Brice Wachterhauser (Albany: State University of New York Press, 1986).

6. In chap. 10, below, the reader will see the continuity of the present work with my previous studies: *The Mystical Element in Heidegger's Thought* (Athens: Ohio University Press, 1978; reissued New York: Fordham University Press, 1986);*Heidegger and Aquinas: An Essay on Overcoming Metaphysics* (New York: Fordham University Press, 1982).

1. REPETITION AND *KINESIS*

1. Friedrich Nietzsche, *Twilight of the Idols and The Anti-Christ*, trans. R. J. Hollingdale (Baltimore: Penguin Classics, 1968), p. 35.

2. Nietzsche, *Twilight*, pp. 40–42.

3. "Founders," which appears in the old Lowrie translation (in Hong: "comes to grief"), is worth preserving. See Kierkegaard, *Repetition*, trans. W. Lowrie (Princeton: Princeton University Press, 1946), p. 34.

4. See the series edited by Mark Taylor, *Kierkegaard and Post-Modernism* (Florida State University Press).

5. Both Macquarrie and Robinson *(Being and Time)* and James Churchill *(Kant and the Problem of Metaphysics)* translate *Wiederholung* as "repetition" (without noting its Kierkegaardian origin), whereas Richardson uses "retrieve," rightly remarking that it is closer to the sense of *Wiederholung* in Heidegger himself. See Richardson, *Heidegger: Through Phenomenology to Thought* (The Hague: M. Nijhoff, 1962), p. 89, n. 181.

6. Kierkegaard, *Gesammelte Werke*, B. 3, *Wiederholung*, trans. H. Gottsched (Jena, 1909). Cf. Hans-Georg Gadamer, *Philosophical Hermeneutics*, trans. David Linge (Berkeley and Los Angeles: University of California Press, 1976), p. 214. See also Gadamer's remarks in his letter to Richard Bernstein in Bernstein, *Beyond Objectivism and Relativism* (Philadelphia: University of Pennsylvania Press, 1983), p. 265.

7. Heidegger's assessment of Kierkegaard is severe and precisely the one I contest in this chapter: "The comparison between Nietzsche and Kierkegaard that has become customary, but is no less questionable for that reason, fails to recognize, and indeed out of a misunderstanding of the essence of thinking, that Nietzsche as a metaphysical thinker preserves a closeness to Aristotle. Kierkegaard remains essentially remote from Aristotle, although he mentions him more often. For Kierkegaard is not a thinker but a religious writer, and indeed not just one among others, but the only one in accord with the destining belonging to his age. Therein lies his greatness, if to speak in this way is not already a misunderstanding." (GA 5, 249/QCT 9). Cf. WHD 129/WCT 213. To what

extent Kierkegaard had studied Aristotle directly is not clear. His reading of "to ti en einai" seems to have been based on G. Marbach, *Geschichte der Philosophie des Mittelalters* (Leipzig, 1841), par. 128, pp. 4–5, and of *kinesis* on W. G. Tennemann, *Geschichte der Philosophie* (Leipzig, 1798–1819), Ktl. 815–26, III, 125–28. I find Kierkegaard's interest in *kinesis* striking in the light of the work of Thomas Sheehan on Heidegger's interpretation of *kinesis*.

8. This is, of course, the remark of Heidegger. *The Question of Being*, trans. W. Kluback and J. Wilde, with the German text (London: Vision Press, 1959), pp. 90–91, which Derrida relates to a random note found among Nietzsche's papers in *Spurs*, 140–43.

9. On this passage from CUP, see J. Preston Cole, *The Problematic Self in Kierkegaard and Freud* (New Haven: Yale University Press, 1971), 150–55.

10. Calvin Schrag has long alerted us to the Kierkegaardian resonances in Heidegger; see his *Existence and Freedom* (Athens: Ohio University Press, 1960); and "Heidegger on Repetition and Historical Understanding," *Philosophy East and West*, 20 (1970), 287–96. Michael Zimmerman, *Eclipse of the Self: The Development of Heidegger's Concept of Authenticity* (Athens: Ohio University Press, 1981) is also very good on the Kierkgaard connection. Recently the connection between Heideggerian hermeneutics and Kierkegaard has been made by William Spanos, "Heidegger, Kierkegaard and the Hermeneutic Circle: Towards a Post-Modern Theory of Interpretation as Dis-closure," *Boundary* 2, 4 (1976), 455–88. Among French scholars, Jean Wahl established the general relationship between the early Heidegger and Kierkegaard; see "Heidegger et Kierkegaard," *Rescherches philosophiques*, 2 (1932–33), 349–70, and *Etudes Kierkegaardiennes* (Paris: Aubier, 1938). Alphonse de Waelhens regarded the notion of repetition in Kierkegaard as too obscure to allow a fruitful comparison with Heidegger; see *La philosophie de Martin Heidegger*, 4th ed. (Louvain: Publications universitaires, 1955), pp. 231, 352. I also think that Dan Magurshak has been doing a good job recently of settling the score between Kierkegaard and Heidegger; see his "*The Concept of Anxiety*: The Keystone of the Kierkegaard-Heidegger Relationship," forthcoming in *International Kierkegaard Commentary: The Concept of Anxiety*.

11. I treat the notion of repetition in Derrida in chap. 5 below, when I examine Derrida's critique of Husserl.

12. For an excellent study of repetition and mediation, see André Clar, "Médiation et Répétition: Le lieu de la dialectique Kierkegaardienne," *Revue des sciences philosophiques et théologiques*, 59 (1975), 38–78.

13. See Richard Popkin, "Kierkegaard and Scepticism," in *Kierkegaard: A Collection of Critical Essays*, ed. Josiah Thompson (Garden City: Doubleday Anchor Books, 1972), pp. 289–323.

14. Kierkegaardian repetition is thus the opposite of a repetition compulsion. See George Stack, "Repetition in Kierkegaard and Freud," *The Personalist*, 58 (1977), 249–61. Jacques Lacan is also interested in the connection between Kierkegaard and the repetition compulsion; see "The Unconscious and Repetition," in *The Four Fundamental Concepts of Psycho-Analysis*, trans. Alan Sheridan (New York: Norton, 1978); see also André Clar, p. 74, n. 78.

15. *Repetition* is subtitled "A Venture in Experimenting Psychology." See Hong's helpful explanation in R xxff.

16. At this point the original manuscript which Kierkegaard drafted breaks off. What follows is a rewrite done after Kierkegaard hears the news that Regine has married. We know, of course, that Kierkegaard has all along been addressing his abandoned Regine, whom he had left in Copenhagen, taking flight to Berlin. Considering that Job got his possessions back, that Abraham got Isaac back, that the young man expected to be made a fit husband, and that there is a thinly disguised bitterness in the remark about "feminine generosity" in the text announcing the girl's marriage, one has the distinct

sense that Kierkegaard thought that God would make him fit to be a husband, too. And we know that Kierkegaard, like the young man, once observed that had he more faith he would have married Regine.

17. Here and elsewhere in this chapter I give Derridean formulations to Kierkegaardian themes. For a Derridean reading of *Repetition*, see Louis Mackie, "Once More with Feeling: Kierkegaard's *Repetition*," in *Kierkegaard and Literature: Irony, Repetition and Criticism*, ed. R. Schleifer and R. Markley (Norman: University of Oklahoma Press, 1984), pp. 80–115; and Ronald Schleifer, "Irony, Identity and Repetition," *Substance*, no. 25 (1980), 44–54. Mackie's "Slouching Toward Bethlehem: Deconstructive Strategies in Theology," *Anglican Theological Review*, 65 (1983), 255–72, is the best Derridean treatment of Kierkegaard I have seen. Mackie reads Kierkegaard's denial that there can be an "immediate contemporaneity with Christ" as the self-deferring of the divine. In a similar vein, see Patrick Bigelow, "Kierkegaard and the Hermeneutic Circle," *Man and World*, 15 (1982), 67–82. I use this notion of the self-deferral of the object of faith in this chapter. Also see Sylviane Agacinski, *Aparté: Conceptions et morts de Sören Kierkegaard* (Paris: Aubier-Flammarion, 1977). Mark Taylor is preparing a collection of studies on *Fear and Trembling* to which Derrida is contributing; Taylor contributes a piece on Abraham as "Outlaw."

18. Both Kierkegaard and Derrida criticize the notion of the "first time" in the name of repetition: Kierkegaard, because he thinks it is aesthetically unrepeatable and ethically fragile and unproven; Derrida, perhaps more radically, because he thinks there never really is a first time. Derrida is speaking of Husserlian *Erstmaligkeit* (in "The Origin of Geometry"), which he treats as a transcendental illusion, a fiction which cannot be certified. See chap. 5 below.

19. Kierkegaard was already a critic of humanism, and on this point, his argument is more ontologically advanced than is Heidegger's in *Being and Time* (rather than ontologically naive, as Heidegger claimed), a point which Bultmann made against Heidegger as well. See Michael Zimmerman's discussion in *Eclipse of the Self*, pp. 144–45.

20. I allude to chap. 9 of *Writing and Difference*. For a suggestive expansion of an unrestricted economy in religious terms, see Mark Taylor, *Erring: A Postmodern A/theology* (Chicago: University Press, 1984), pp. 140–48.

21. For more on Kierkegaard's notion of repetition, see George E. and George R. Arbaugh, *Kierkegaard's Authorship* (London: George Allen and Unwin, 1968), pp. 94–105 (an illuminating commmentary); Robert P. Harrison, "Heresy and the Question of Repetition: Reading Kierkegaard's *Repetition*," in *Textual Analysis: Some Readers Reading*, ed. Mary Ann Caws (New York: Modern Language Association, 1986), pp. 281–88; George Stack, *Kierkegaard's Existential Ethics* (University Park: University of Alabama Press, 1977). See also the entries under "repetition" in *Soren Kierkegaard's Journals and Papers*, 5 vols., vol. 3, *L-R*, ed. and trans. Howard and Edna Hong (Bloomington: Indiana Unviersity Press, 1975). Cf. also "Strengthened in the Inner Man," in *Edifying Discourses*, 4 vols., trans. D. Swenson and L. Swenson (Minneapolis: Augsburg Publishing House, 1943), vol. 1, pp. 93–119.

22. See also *Johannes Climacus: or De omnibus dubitandum est, and a Sermon*, trans. T. H. Croxall (Stanford: Stanford University Press, 1958), pp. 151–52: "interest" means *inter-esse*, which has the twofold meaning of being-between and of being a matter of concern, clearly anticipating the notion that the Being of being-in-the-world *(in-der-Welt-sein)* is "care."

23. It is just this Kierkegaardian and Barthian project of sorting out the categories of Greek ontology from Christian reflection which Joseph O'Leary undertakes in *Questioning Back: Overcoming Metaphysics in Christian Tradition* (Minneapolis: Winston-Seabury Press, 1985).

24. It is precisely what I call here a hermeneutic—even if it be a cold and trembling hermeneutic—element in Kierkegaard which Gilles Deleuze opposes in the Kierkegaar-

dian notion of repetition. Deleuze sees clearly that the central point of repetiton in Kierkegaard is to oppose the fraudulent "movement" defended by Hegel and that on this point Kierkegaard is to be compared with Nietzsche. Something new happens in both these thinkers. They operate in the medium of the theatrical, not pure reflection. They are interested not in a conceptualization of movement but in inducing it: in Kierkegaard, the movement of the leap of faith; in Nietzsche, the movement of the dance. But Deleuze thinks that in the end Kierkegaard is not willing to "pay the price" for a philosophy of movement. Kierkegaardian repetition is always inward, spiritual, and recuperative "once and for all" of God and self. But Nietzsche's thought of becoming and movement is one of pure dispersal, earthly and natural, and needs to be affirmed again and again. Atheistic repetition is more radical than the repetition of faith. Cf. Gilles Deleuze, *Différence et Répetition* (Paris: PUF, 1981), pp. 12–20, especially 16–20, and 126–27, 377. Deleuze does indeed have more radical intentions than Kierkegaard. Deleuze wants to liberate difference, to defend a "pure" difference no longer sujected to identity, as it is in dialectics, where it is but a moment in the unfolding of identity. Liberated from identity, repetition means not the recurrence of the same but the occurrence of the new, always repeating with a difference. He defends profusion and "nomadic" dispersal which he somewhat misleadingly calls a new form of the "univocity" of Being (as opposed to that of Scotus and Spinoza). Being is not to be thought of as neatly differentiated and hierarchized into chains and categorial groups—which always manage to contain and constrict difference within the rule of identity—but rather as a pure acategorial profusion. Being thus is always, unremittingly, "univocally" different. Its difference keeps repeating itself; it is repeatedly different. It is always the same, viz., different. For a Kierkegaardian reaction, see André Clar, p. 77, n. 87. See Foucault's remarkable essay on Deleuze, "Theatricum philosophicum," *Language, Counter-memory, Practice*, trans. D. F. Bouchard (Ithaca: Cornell University Press, 1977), 165–96, especially 182–87, 192–96. Deleuze's more radical intentions, however, still fall under the influence of what I call here a radical hermeneutics. I will test this claim in Part II with another philosopher of difference and profusion, not Deleuze but Derrida. For a parallel treatment of Deleuze and Derrida as philosophers of difference, see Vincent Descombes, *Modern French Philosophy*, trans. L. Scott-Fox and J. M. Harding (Cambridge: Cambridge University Press, 1980), pp. 136–67.

2. REPETITION AND CONSTITUTION

1. This translation, suggested by Dorion Cairns, *Guide for Translating Husserl*, Phaenomenologica, no. 55 (The Hague: Martinus Nijhoff, 1973), p. 13, is used in the Nijhoff translations.

2. On the universality of the horizonal structure of intentional consciousness as a whole, see S. Stephen Hilmy, "The Scope of Husserl's Notion of Horizon," *The Modern Schoolman*, 59 (1981), 21–48. For more on horizons, see C. van Peursen, "The Horizon," in *Husserl: Expositions and Appraisals*, ed. P. McCormick and F. Elliston (South Bend: University of Notre Dame Press, 1977), pp. 182–201; and H. Pietersama, "The Concept of Horizon," *Analecta Husserliana*, 2 (1972), pp. 101–228.

3. See Robert Sokolowski, *The Formation of Husserl's Concept of Constitution* (The Hague: M. Nijhoff, 1970), p. 56, for a good account of this point. Graeme Nicholson seems to me to have missed the hermeneutic dimension of Husserl's theory of perception in his *Seeing and Reading* (New York: Humanities Press, 1985), a thoughtful rendering of Gadamerian hermeneutics. See my review of *Seeing and Reading* in *Research in Phenomenology*, 16 (1986).

4. See Merleau-Ponty, *The Phenomenology of Perception*, trans. Colin Smith (New York: Humanities Press, 1962), pp. 3–13.

5. Sokolowski, 60–61.

6. Paul Ricoeur explains this point quite well in his commentary on *Ideas I*. See the translator's notes to §§47–49 in *Idées directrices pour une phénomenologie* (Paris: Gallimard, 1950).

7. On this point Husserl would agree with Davidson on the myth of the framework. See Donald Davidson, "On the Very Idea of a Conceptual Scheme," *Proceedings of the American Philosophical Association*, 17 (1973–74), 5–20. See also Richard Rorty, "The World Well Lost," in *Consequences of Pragmatism* (Minneapolis: University of Minnesota Press, 1982), pp. 3–18.

8. In chap. 5, below, I discuss Derrida's interesting commentary on this text in VPh 94 n1/ SP 84–85.

9. Husserl also links his theory of preobjective predelineation and of explicative analysis to a theory of "actual and potential consciousness." See *Ideas I*, §35. In §115, Husserl expands the notion of an act to include a distinction between acts which are actually carried out *(vollzogener Akt)* and acts which are merely "stirring" *(Aktregung)*. The cogito in the proper sense is explicit intentionality, that in which the ego actually lives, but this is to be distinguished from acts which are alive before we know it (Hua III.1 263/*Ideas I* 273). The notion of conscious act must be broad enough to include nonexplicit, prethematic acts. And that of course is a significant expansion of the term, for it confirms what we have all along been saying. Husserl's commitment to intuition and the given has nothing to do with restricting us to the momentary, the actual, the present. Rather, it enjoins us to understand both object and act in the broadest sense and, hence, to take into account the potential, implicit, and tacit.

10. David Carr discusses this problem in his introduction to his translation of the *Crisis*, pp. xxxvi-vii.

11. In chap. 5, below, I take up Derrida's discussion of the dependence of the historical reduction on the theory of language in secs. VI and VII of OrG.

12. OrG 77.

13. W&M 240–56/T&M 225–40.

14. See Husserl's discussion of the "neutrality modification" in *Ideas I*, §§109ff.

15. The best critiques of the ontological presuppositions of Husserl's interpretation of consciousness by Heidegger are to be found in GA 20, §§10–13 and GA 21, §§6–10.

16. Husserl distinguishes two levels of consciousness, reflecting and reflected upon, in one and the same ego; he denies that there are two different selves; see *Cartesian Meditations*, §15.

17. Hans-Georg Gadamer, "The Hermeneutics of Suspicion," in *Philosophy and Hermeneutics*, ed. Shapiro and Sica, pp. 58–61. For a different view, see Richard Cobb-Stevens, "Hermeneutics without Relativism: Husserl's Theory of Mind," *Research in Phenomenology*, 12 (1982), 127–48.

18. In an interesting discussion of Husserl and hermeneutics Ricoeur writes, "But Husserl believed that self-knowledge could not be presumptive, because it does not proceed by 'sketches' or 'profiles.' Self-knowledge can, however, be presumptive for other reasons. Insofar as self-knowledge is a dialogue of the soul with itself, and insofar as the dialogue can be systematically distorted by violence and by the intrusion of structures of domination into those of communication, self-knowledge as internalised communication can be as doubtful as knowledge of the object, although for different and quite specific reasons." Paul Ricoeur, "Phenomenology and Hermeneutics," in *Hermeneutics and the Human Sciences*, ed. John Thompson (Cambridge: Cambridge University Press, 1981), pp. 109–10. Ricoeur's order of presentation is the opposite of ours, and his results differ from ours. After setting forth the limitations of what he calls Husserl's "idealism," he then proceeds to show the positive alliance of phenomenology and hermeneutics in two steps. (1) Hermeneutics presupposes a phenomenological moment because it is dedicated to the question of meaning, because it requires a critical moment supplied by the epoche, and finally because it shares phenomenology's view of the derivativeness of language. On this last point I believe Ricoeur is badly misled, for

the interpretive element in hermeneutics is embedded in language. If there were a prelinguistic sphere, interpretation would be a follow-up to pure givenness. (2) But conversely phenomenology implies a hermeneutic moment which can be seen by singling out the role of *Auslegung* in Husserl. Unlike the present discussion, Ricoeur sees *Auslegung* in terms of the problem of idealism, with which he began: egological *Auslegung* means the unfolding of the world out of the ego; we, on the contrary, see in *Auslegung* a sense much closer to Heidegger, and we align it with the *Vorstruktur* of understanding.

19. Michel Foucault, *The Order of Things: An Archaeology of the Human Sciences,* trans. Alan Sheridan (New York: Random House Vintage Books, 1973), pp. 318ff.

20. Merleau-Ponty, *Phenomenology of Perception,* p. xiv.

21. OrG, "Preface" and sec. I.

22. Foucault, *Order of Things,* p. 334. Taken on their own terms, of course, Foucault's remarks are directed against Husserl and Heidegger and aim at making both phenomenology and hermeneutics futile. This point is clearly expounded in Hubert Dreyfus and Paul Rabinow, *Michel Foucault: Beyond Structuralism and Hermeneutics,* 2d. ed. (Chicago: University of Chicago Press, 1983), pp. 34–41.

3. RETRIEVAL AND THE CIRCULAR BEING OF DASEIN

1. See chap. 1, n. 5, above.

2. As the young Heidegger said, over a decade earlier, in his *Habilitationsschrift,* ontology is the true optics of epistemology (GA 1 406).

3. In ontological matters, Heidegger says, all springing from, all originating *(Entspringen),* is de-generation (SZ 334/BT 383).

4. The project of destruction is not an innovation of *Being and Time* but a basic feature which marked Heidegger's interpretation of the phenomenological method throughout the 1920s. Indeed, the Duns Scotus book of 1916 already exerted a subtle and complex hermeneutic violence which made the medieval treatise *De modis significandi* speak in modern tones. For more on this point, see my "Phenomenology, Mysticism and the 'Grammatica speculativa': A Study of Heidegger's *Habilitationsschrift,*" *Journal of the British Society for Phenomenology,* 5 (1974), 101–17. The word itself first appeared as early as 1921—in Heidegger's review of Jasper's *Psychology of World-Views.* There Heidegger insists on the need for a "destruction of the tradition" aimed at explicating the primordial situations from which fundamental philosophical experiences originate, which are then subsequently given conceptual formulation in philosophy (GA 9, 3–4). There is a hermeneutic violence already in the early lectures on Christianity and St. Augustine (1920–21), in which Heidegger seeks to read the structure of the early Christian experience of time and contingency by way of a destructive *reading out* of the overlay of Neoplatonic ontology, which had infiltrated Augustine's formulation of his Christian experience. See Thomas Sheehan's excellent discussion in "Heidegger's 'Introduction to the Phenomenology of Religion, 1920–21,'" *The Personalist,* 60 (1979), 312–24; cf. chap. 1, n. 24, above.

5. For a commentary on this passage and a general account of "destruction" in Heidegger, see Samuel Ijsseling, "Heidegger and the Destruction of Ontology," *Man and World,* 15 (1982), 3–16.

6. Heidegger does not resist the comparison of this scheme to the Platonic theory of recollection (GA 24 463–5/BP 326–27).

7. I discuss Derrida's remark, which appears in "The Ends of Man," in *Margins,* in chap. 6, below.

8. It is also a Kierkegaardian logic. Kierkegaard was also worried about the way the individual's one-to-one relation to God could degenerate into something second-hand, indeed twenty-third hand, given all the *Gerede* (a notion which Heidegger also imported from Denmark) being passed around by ministers and metaphysicians. Heidegger thus

fused the Husserlian theory of language, as subject constantly to the threat of sedimentation and loss of original sense, with Kierkegaard's critique of idle chatter presented in
"The Present Age" (and shamelessly reproduced without citation in §§35–37 of *Being
and Time.)* See *Kierkegaard's Writings, volume 14, Two Ages,* ed. and trans. H. Hong
and E. Hong (Princeton: Princeton University Press, 1978), pp. 68–112, esp. pp. 97–102.

9. Lee Hardy argues that one requires, for such a self-recognition, the experience of
anxiety, which removes the distraction of the everyday world, the obstacle to self-
understanding. See his *"Angst* and Autonomy: Fundamental Ontology and the Idea of
Rigorous Science," *Anakainosis,* 2 (1979), 9–13.

10. I will have more to say about both the limits and the advantages of Gadamer's
appropriation of *Being and Time* in the next chapter and again in chaps. 8 and 9.

11. SZ 235/BT 494; 338/497; GA 9 249/QCT 94. See above, chap. 1 nn. 7, 10. George
J. Stack insists that Heidegger is indebted to Kierkegaard's conception of repetition and
that the conception is ontological in character. See his *Kierkegaard's Existential Ethics*
(University Park: University of Alabama Press, 1977), pp. 133–37. For reservations on
Stack's thesis, see Michael Zimmerman, *Eclipse of the Self* (Athens: Ohio University
Press, 1981), pp. 122–25.

12. *Kierkegaard's Writings,* volume 19, *The Sickness Unto Death,* trans. H. Hong and
E. Hong (Princeton: Princeton University Press, 1980), pp. 105ff.

13. This line of interpretation of Kierkegaard is pursued by Josiah Thompson,
Kierkegaard (New York: Alfred A. Knopf, 1973), and the contributors to his *Kierkegaard:
A Collection of Critical Essays.*

14. A pedestrian comparison: in athletics, it is said that a good team does not win
because it "gets the breaks" but because, by its aggressiveness and alertness, it "makes
its own breaks." Paul Ricoeur argues against the success of Heidegger's attempt to
balance the individual and the tradition in "Narrative Time," in *On Narrative,* ed. W. J.
T. Mitchell (Chicago: University of Chicago Press, 1981), pp. 165–86.

15. Hans-Georg Gadamer, *Philosophical Hermeneutics,* trans. D. Linge (Berkeley
and Los Angeles: University of California Press, 1976), pp. 201–202.

4. HERMENEUTICS AFTER *BEING AND TIME*

1. Gadamer and Derrida are in a sense "exemplary" figures of these three movements. In the broad strokes I am painting here, e.g., Ricoeur's position is a derivative of
Gadamer's and his criticisms of Gadamer only move hermeneutics closer to metaphysics.
Likewise Derrida is part of a broader group of recent French philosophers who have
made much the same argument against hermeneutics (e.g., Deleuze and, especially,
Foucault). I deal with Gadamer and Derrida in particular because both have a Heideggerian point of departure.

2. Theodore Kisiel, "Repetition in Gadamer's Hermeneutics," *Analecta Husserliana,* 2 (1972), 197; cf. W&M 370/354.

3. That is why Heidegger's later thought can be rightly ·called a "radical phenomenology," as it is in a recent volume. See *Radical Phenomenology,* ed. John Sallis
(Atlantic Highlands, N.J.: Humanities Press, 1978). Hannah Arendt's critique of
Gelassenheit in *The Life of the Mind* (one-volume ed.; New York: Harcourt, Brace,
Jovanovich, 1978), vol. 2, *Willing,* pp. 172–94, mistakenly seizes upon an expression—
"willing not to will"—which Heidegger introduces only to dismiss and supersede it as a
purely transitional stage.

4. *The Mystical Element in Heidegger's Thought,* pp. 223–40.

5. I have elaborated the question of the difference with some care in *Heidegger and
Aquinas,* pp. 147–84.

6. The expression "Aus der Erfarhung des Denkens" has exactly the same force.

7. Gadamer, *Philosophical Hermeneutics,* pp. 201–202. Cf. chap. 3, n. 15, above.

8. Aristotle, *Nichomachean Ethics* I.7 (1098a20-b10); II.2 (1103b25–1104a10). See

also my "Prudential Reasoning and Moral Insight," *Proceedings of the American Catholic Philosophical Association*, 58 (1984), 50–55; and Robert Henle, "Prudence and Insight in Moral and Legal Decisions," *Proceedings of the American Catholic Philosophical Association*, 56 (1982), 26–30.

9. I have learned a great deal on this point from Richard Bernstein, *Beyond Objectivism and Relativism: Science, Hermeneutics, Praxis* (Philadelphia: University of Pennsylvania Press, 1983). I discuss these issues in detail in chapter 8. See there the references to Kisiel's works in the philosophy of science.

10. I have the same argument against O'Leary, *Questioning Back*, who in the name of deconstruction gives us Gadamer.

11. I have the same objection against Nicholson, *Seeing and Reading*. See my review in *Research in Phenomenology*, 16 (1986).

12. Gadamer criticizes Heidegger in the converse terms—for abandoning history in favor of the *Seinsgeschick*. See *Hegel's Dialectic: Five Hermeneutical Studies*, trans. P. Christopher Smith (New Haven: Yale University Press, 1976), p. 109.

13. On this point I think Heidegger would side with Habermas's critique of the way Gadamer remains confined by the tradition, hammering on its walls from within, although he would hardly have any sympathy with Habermas's own recourse to a transcendental standpoint. Heidegger and Derrida adopt a critical, but nontranscendental, relationship to the tradition. See Habermas, "A Review of Gadamer's *Truth and Method*," in F. Dallmayr and T. McCarthy, eds., *Understanding and Social Inquiry* (Notre Dame: University of Notre Dame Press, 1977), 335–63.

14. "One must allow that such an historical self-consciousness as this is no less all-inclusive than Hegel's philosophy of the Absolute." *Hegel's Dialectic*, p. 110.

15. This is a perspective on Heidegger which requires a certain rereading of Heidegger in the light of Derrida and a critique of the notion of a "new beginning." See chapters 6–7.

16. For a good account of the rabbinic background of Derrida's work, see Susan Handelman, *The Slayers of Moses: The Emergence of Rabbinic Interpretation in Modern Literary Theory* (Albany: State University of New York Press, 1982), pp. 163–78.

17. It should be pointed out that Derrida does not think that there is a clean and decidable break between the two interpretations of interpretation, as he goes on to say in this passage (ED 428/WD 293). Hence, one cannot make a clean leap from one side to the other, leaving the first behind. Rather, one is always caught up in the system from which one seeks to extricate oneself and tossed between the two alternatives.

18. Writing, Roland Barthes says, "is an anti-theological activity . . . since to refuse to fix meaning is to refuse God and his hypostases— reason, science, law." *Image, Music, Text*, trans. S. Heath (New York: Hill & Wang, 1977), p. 147.

19. This is the argument that Derrida pursues against Heidegger in *Spurs*, pp. 52–53.

20. Nietzsche, "The Drunken Song," *Thus Spoke Zarathustra*, trans. W. Kaufmann (New York: Viking Press, 1966), pp. 317–24.

21. See the important use of *"presque"* in *Spurs*, pp. 114–15.

5. REPETITION AND THE EMANCIPATION OF SIGNS

1. Rodolphe Gasché is especially helpful in understanding Derrida's relationship to Husserl. See his *The Tain of the Mirror* (Cambridge: Harvard University Press, 1986); for other authors who highlight Derrida's reading of Husserl, see Irene Harvey, *Derrida and the Economy of Différance* (Bloomington: Indiana University Press, 1985); and John Llewelyn, *Derrida on the Threshold of Sense* (New York: St. Martin's Press, 1986). See my review of all three titles, "Derrida, A Kind of Philosopher," in *Research in Phenomenology*, 17 (1987).

2. I am importing here the imagery of *La carte postale*. In fact there is a premonition of this work in OrG 36/50.

3. This is my expression, not Derrida's. I do not mean to suggest that Derrida subscribes to this notion. For more on Derrida and Sartre, see Christina Howells, "Sartre and Derrida: Qui perd gagne," *Journal of the British Society for Phenomenology*, 13 (1982), 26–34.

4. In a well-known passage in the essay "Différance," Derrida explains that différance exploits both the spatial sense of differentiating and the temporal sense of deferral, in keeping with a plurivocity enjoyed by the French word différance but not the English word difference. See *Marg*. 3/3. In OrG 171/153, Derrida uses both différant and Différence, the capitalization of the conventional spelling.

5. Derrida uses this French expression, which literally means that which one wills or wants to say, as an apt expression for meaning as the intention of the individual subject, as opposed to what is constrained upon an author by the structure of the discourse which he employs. See *Marg*. 185ff./155ff.

6. I have examined this thesis in my "The Economy of Signs in Husserl and Derrida: From Uselessness to Full Employment," in *Deconstruction and Philosophy*, ed. John Sallis (Chicago: University of Chicago Press, 1987); I also argue there that deconstruction issues in a new, more semiotic version of phenomenology.

7. Derrida makes this plain in sec. (q) of "Limited Inc. a b c," *Glyph*, 2 (1977), 192–98. He is not in the business of denying intentionality or reference or self-consciousness but only the metaphysical claim that there is some kind of unmediated contact of the self with itself, with other selves, or with its object, apart from the work of signs. Accordingly, there is no escaping the vulnerability of these structures to mistake and misfire, which is built right into the very conditions which make them possible in the first place. Repetition is both an enabling and a limiting condition simultaneously. This exchange with Searle is interesting, both because it is thematically organized on the concept of repetition and because Derrida is rarely clearer and more judicious in the presentation of his views (which is not to mention the high play at work throughout the piece). Searle has added a recent rejoinder, "The World Turned Upside Down," *The New York Review of Books*, October 1983, pp. 74–79.

8. Husserl distinguished *Sinn* from *Bedeutung* in *Ideas I*, but not in *Logical Investigations*.

9. Derrida's point can be simply illustrated. Were one to invite a member of a fundamentally different ethno-linguistic group—say, Lévi-Strauss's Nambikwara Indians—to tabulate their basic categories of meaning (*Sinn*), we would no doubt find that, while their table of meaning would converge perfectly with their table of signification, it would be quite at odds with our own scheme of things. One is reminded of Borges's example from the Chinese encyclopedia, cited by Foucault, about which Foucault remarks upon "the stark impossibilty of thinking *that*." Foucault, *The Order of Things*, p. xv. But Husserl thought such differences could be transcended; see OrG, sec. VIII.

10. This is the point of the *Fourth Investigation*, on the idea of a pure grammar. It is interesting, too, that Heidegger's habilitation dissertation dealt with the *Fourth Investigation*. See my "Phenomenology, Mysticism and the 'Grammatica Speculativa': A Study of Heidegger's 'Habilitationsschrift,'" *Journal of the British Society for Phenomenology* 5 (1974), 101–17.

11. For a defense of Husserl against Derrida, see J. N. Mohanty, "On Husserl's Theory of Meaning," *Southwestern Journal of Philosophy*, 5 (1974), 238–44. See also his *Edmund Husserl's Theory of Meaning* (The Hague: Nijhoff, 1969), chap. 2.

12. That is why Derrida writes that he is not a sceptic, in the sense that he recognizes the Nietzschean and pragmatic *need* for truth as a necessary fiction. "We must have truth." ("Il faut la verité.") *Pos*. 79–80n23/104–5n32. The aporia which Robert Magliola poses for Derrida dissolves in the light of this fictionalism. See *Derrida on the Mend* (West Lafayette: Purdue University Press, 1984), part 1. For a sound appreciation of Derrida on this point, see Christopher Norris, *The Deconstructive Turn* (London & New York: Methuen, 1983).

13. Having an "intuition," Rorty says, is a matter of knowing how to play a language

game. Richard Rorty, *Philosophy and the Mirror of Nature* (Princeton: University Press, 1979).

14. Gregory Ulmer, *Applied Grammatology: Post(e)-Pedagogy from Jacques Derrida to Joseph Beuys* (Baltimore: Johns Hopkins University Press,1985).

15. See Rorty's "Philosophy as a Kind of Writing: An Essay on Derrida," in *Consequences of Pragmatism* (Minneapolis: University of Minnesota Press, 1982), pp. 90ff.

16. See the interview by Catherine David in *Le Nouvel Observateur,* September 9, 1983. Eng. trans. "An Interview with Jacques Derrida," *Graduate Faculty Philosophy Journal,* 10 (1984), 31–45.

17. For some key passages on repetition in *Dissemination,* see 140–41/123, 155–56/135–36, 165/143–44, 172/149, 194–97/168–71, 214–18/88–91, 324/292, 328/295, 405/365. For a more recent statement on repetition, see the interview with Derrida in Richard Kearney, *Dialogues with Contemporary Thinkers* (Manchester: University of Manchester Press, 1984), pp. 112–13.

6. HERMES AND THE DISPATCHES FROM BEING

1. I do not try to translate *Ereignis;* like Dasein, it is fast becoming an untranslatable technical term.

2. On two different occasions, when presenting his deconstructive critique of Heidegger, Derrida draws up short with this "almost," because he recognizes another motif in Heidegger's texts. Cf. *Marg.* 75/65; *Spurs* 115.

3. Nietzsche, *Beyond Good and Evil,* trans. R. J. Hollingdale (Baltimore: Penguin Classics, 1973), p. 12.

4. Derrida refers to *Twilight of the Idols,* trans. R. J. Hollingdale (Baltimore: Penguin, 1968), p. 40.

5. From the point of view of a Being-historical hermeneutics (onto-hermeneutics), Gadamerian hermeneutics remains within the sphere of influence of nineteenth-century hermeneutics. Gadamer does not try to think the destiny which is at work in the tradition, which is concealed by the tradition. He stays within the tradition and tries to savor what it has to offer.

6. In "Sending: On Representation," trans. P. Caws and M. Caws, *Social Research,* 49 (Summer, 1982), 322–23, Derrida says that, inasmuch as the later epochs are derivative, weakened, more concealed versions of the first epoch, they are in fact thought of as "representations" of an original presence. Heidegger thus employs the traditional metaphysical logic of "representational" thought from which he wants to dissociate himself.

7. See GA 45 for a fairly detailed account of the "two beginnings." In *Applied Grammatology,* Gregory Ulmer develops a reading of Derrida in terms of the problem of the new communication technologies.

8. "Sending," p. 321.

9. See "Le Retrait de la métaphore," *Poésie,* 6 (1979), 103–26; Eng. trans., *Enclitic,* 2 (1978), 5–34, in which Derrida analyzes the sense of metaphor in Heidegger in response to Paul Ricoeur's critique of "White Mythology" in *The Rule of Metaphor,* trans. Robert Szerny (Toronto: University of Toronto Press, 1977), pp. 280–95. This is one of Derrida's most sophisticated treatments of Heidegger, in which he singles out the notion of *Entzug* (with-drawal, *ent-ziehen, re-trahere, re-trait),* which is, it seems to me, the point in Heidegger's thought at which Being, truth and meaning are made to "founder," as I will argue below.

10. This is the argument also of "Sending," 318–26. For more on the *"Es gibt"* in Heidegger and Derrida, see *La Vérité en peinture* (Paris: Flammarion, 1978), pp. 313, 320–21, 391, 425; and my "Telling Left from Right: Hermeneutics, Deconstruction and the Work of Art," *Journal of Philosophy,* 83 (1986), 678–85.

11. GA 26, *Metaphysische Anfangsgründe der Logik* (Frankfurt: Klostermann, 1978), pp. 197–202.

12. Derrida argues that *Eigentlichkeit* is defined in terms of self-presence, self-

identity, self-possession, i.e., *le propre*, and that it depends upon a Platonic distinction between the primordial and the fallen (*Marg*. 33ff./31ff.) I will point out that, in fact, more carefully rewritten, it means *kinesis*.

13. See the marginalia to "The Anaximander Fragment" and "The Origin of the Work of Art" (among others) in GA 5. See also *Vier Seminare* (Frankfurt: Klostermann, 1977), pp. 73, 82–87, where Heidegger distinguishes three stages of his development in terms of the meaning of Being, the truth of Being, and finally the topology of Being, where the key word is *Ereignis* (which grants and so locates Being and truth).

14. Robert Bernasconi has a very helpful discussion of *aletheia* in *The Question of Language in Heidegger's History of Being* (Atlantic Highlands: Humanities Press, 1985), pp. 15–28.

15. I have worked this out in detail in my *Heidegger and Aquinas: An Essay on Overcoming Metaphysics*, esp. chap. 5.

16. ID 132–33/64–65; cf. US 25–26/202–203. And see *Heidegger and Aquinas*, pp. 147–58.

7. COLD HERMENEUTICS

1. That is why Derrida's criticism of Nietzsche in *The Ear of the Other*, ed. C. McDonald (New York: Schocken, 1985), pp. 28–29—that Nietzsche cannot be dissociated from the political effects he produces—can lead to trouble for Derrida, too, as Richard Bernstein has recently pointed out in "Serious Play: The Ethical-Political Horizon of Jacques Derrida" (unpublished). How can one free Derrida from some very sophistic effects that he has produced among his "followers"?

2. *Beyond Good and Evil*, no. 39, p. 50; no. 270, pp. 189–90. See also my "Three Transgressions: Nietzsche, Heidegger, Derrida," *Research in Phenomenology*, 15 (1985), 61–78.

3. Derrida corrects these misunderstandings of his work quite clearly in his interview with Richard Kearney, "Deconstruction and the Other," in *Dialogues with Contemporary Continental Thinkers*, ed. Richard Kearney (Manchester: University of Manchester Press, 1984), pp. 107–25. See also my "The Economy of Signs in Husserl and Derrida" in *Deconstruction and Philosophy*, ed. John Sallis (Chicago: University of Chicago Press, 1987).

4. "Scribble *(pouvoir/écrire)*," introduction to W. Wahrburton, *L'essai sur les hierglyphes* (Paris: Flammarion, 1978). Eng. trans., "Scribble (writing-power)," *Yale French Studies*, 58 (1979), 116–47.

5. These concerns are made clear in interviews, of course, but also in the texts themselves. The remark from "The Ends of Man" was delivered in New York in 1968 and was followed by a castigation of the then-current involvement of the United States in Vietnam (*Marg*., 131–35/111–14). The essays on Lacan and Freud contain a stringent critique of their sexism and "phal-logo-centrism." Derrida takes one of Lévi-Strauss's greatest accomplishments to be the delimitation of ethnocentrism and the exposure of Western Europe to its "other." In "White Mythology," he says that metaphysics and logocentrism are white not only because of their cold conceptuality but because they are European-white (*Marg*., 254/213). Part of the satire of *Limited Inc. a b c* is the call for the police to enforce normal discourse (*Lim Inc.*, 78–79/250–51). Derrida writes in an emancipatory rhetoric which is, I think, an allegory of his political agenda.

6. See the interview in *La nouvelle Observateur* (chap. 5, n. 17). For more on the institutional dimension of Derrida's work, see Jonathan Culler, *On Deconstruction: Theory and Criticism after Structuralism* (Ithaca: Cornell University Press, 1982), pp. 156–80. In *Marxism and Deconstruction* (Baltimore: Johns Hopkins University Press, 1982), Michael Ryan tries to enlist Derrida directly in a Marxist political program. But notice Derrida's caution about "Marxism" in *Pos*. 53ff./39ff. I would say that Derrida and Foucault belong to a non-Marxist left.

7. Jacques Derrida, "Philosophie des Etats Généraux de la philosophie," in *Etats Généraux de la Philosophie* (Paris, 1979); and Ulmer, *Applied Grammatology*, pp. 13–16.

8. The College was founded in October 1983 under the directorship of Derrida, assisted by Jean-Pierre Faye, Felix Guattari, and Michel Serres. See Charles Vial, "Paris, capitale de la philosophie," *Le monde*, 1983, pp. 9–10.

9. "Only a God Can Save Us: *Der Spiegel's* Interview with Martin Heidegger," trans. Maria Alter and John D. Caputo, *Philosophy Today*, 20 (1976), 279–80, 281, 283.

10. Rorty, *Philosophy and the Mirror of Nature*, pp. 389–94; cf. Michael Oakeshott, "The Voice of Poetry in the Conversation of Mankind," in *Rationalism and Politics* (New York: Methuen, 1975).

11. For recent examples of Derrida in the marketplace, see "The Principle of Reason: The University in the Eyes of Its Pupils," trans. C. Porter and P. Lewis, *Diacritics* (Fall 1983), 3–20; and "NO APOCALYPSE, NOT NOW (full speed ahead, seven missiles, seven missives)," trans. C. Porter and P. Lewis, *Diacritics* (Summer 1984), 20–31; and "Racism's Last Word," trans. P. Kampf, *Critical Inquiry*, 12 (1985), 290–98. See also Derrida's stinging rebuttal of two critics of "Racism's Last Word" in *Critical Inquiry*, 13 (1986), 140–70.

12. See the following ground-breaking essays by Thomas Sheehan, "Heidegger's 'Introduction to the Phenomenology of Religion,'" *The Personalist*, 60 (1979), 312–24; "Heidegger's Interpretation of Aristotle: *Dynamis* and *Ereignis*," *Philosophy Research Archives*, 4 (1978), 1–33; "Heidegger's Topic: Excess, Access, Recess," *Tijdschrift voor Philosophie*, 41 (1979), 615–35; "The 'Original Form' of *Sein und Zeit*: Heidegger's *Der Begriff der Zeit* (1924)," *Journal of the British Society for Phenomenology*, 10 (1979), 78–83; "On Movement and the Destruction of Ontology," *The Monist*, 64 (1981), 534–42; "On the Way to *Ereignis*: Heidegger's Interpretation of *Physis*," in *Continental Philosophy: Prize Essays*, vol. 1, ed. John Sallis (Pittsburgh: Duquesne University Press, 1983), pp. 131–64.

13. See, in particular, my *The Mystical Element in Heidegger's Thought*, pp. 47–96 and 245–54.

14. *Marg.* 6/6, 28/26–27; ED 217/WD 146. For a discussion of Derrida and negative theology, see my "Mysticism and Transgression: Derrida and Meister Eckhart," forthcoming in *Continental Philosophy*, 2 (1987).

15. "Die Gelassenheit zu den Dingen und die Offenheit für das Geheimnis gehören zusammen" (G 26/DT 55).

16. Part of the critique of humanism ought to be openness to all life, not just human life. In "APOCALYPSE NOW," Derrida remarks that it is not only the future of the human species which is endangered by the nuclear threat but also that of quite a few other species as well (p. 20). This kind of consideration has been recognized in the Christian tradition only in passing; St. Francis is the best example. The liberation theologian Leonardo Boff is also a Franciscan and the author of a study of St. Francis. See *Saint Francis: A Model for Human Liberation*, trans. J. Dierskmeier (New York: Crossroad/Continuum, 1984). Letting life be *(Gelassenheit)* extends across the spectrum of living things in a generalized *Gelassenheit*.

8. TOWARD A POSTMETAPHYSICAL RATIONALITY

1. In addition to *Truth and Method*, see "Hermeneutics as a Theoretical and Practical Task," in *Reason in the Age of Science*, trans. Frederick Lawrence (Cambridge, Mass.: MIT Press, 1981), pp. 113–38 and 47–48, 72, 91–92.

2. Paul Feyerabend, *Against Method: Outline of an Anarchistic Theory of Knowledge* (London: Verso, 1975, 1978), p. 21, n. 12.

3. For the source of this text and a commentary, see Etienne Gilson, *The Christian Philosophy of Saint Augustine*, trans. L. Lynch (London: Gollancz, 1961), pp. 140–41, including n. 50.

4. Bernstein's *Beyond Objectivism and Relativism* is the most pertinent and helpful account of this literature from my point of view. But see also W. H. Newton-Smith, *The Rationality of Science* (London: Routledge and Kegan Paul, 1981) for a nice account of the whole movement from Popper to the present. See also Polanyi's landmark *Personal Knowledge: Towards a Post-Critical Philosophy* (corrected ed.; Chicago: University of Chicago Press, 1962).

5. Theodore Kisiel, "Heidegger and the New Images of Science," *Research in Phenomenology*, 7 (1977), 162–81, "New Philosophies of Science in the USA: A Selective Survey," *Zeitschrift für allgemeine Wissenschaftstheorie*, 5 (1974), 138–91, "Scientific Discovery: Logical, Psychological or Hermeneutical?" *Explorations in Phenomenology*, ed. David Carr and Edward Casey (The Hague: Nijhoff, 1973), 263–84, and "The Rationality of Scientific Discovery" in *Rationality Today/La Rationalité Aujourdhui*, ed. Theodore Geraets (Ottawa: University of Ottawa Press, 1977), pp. 401–11. See also Joseph Kockelmans, *Heidegger and Science*, Current Continental Research, no. 207 (Washington: University Press of America, 1955); Joseph Rouse, "Kuhn, Heidegger and Scientific Realism," *Man and World*, 14 (1981), 269–90; and Robert Innis, "Heidegger's Model of Subjectivity: A Polanyi Critique," in *Heidegger: The Man and the Thinker*, ed. Thomas Sheehan (Chicago: Precedent Publishing Co., 1981), 117–30.

6. Imre Lakatos, "Falsification and the Methodology of Scientific Research Programmes," in *Criticism and the Growth of Knowledge*, ed. Imre Lakatos and Alan Musgrave (Cambridge: Cambridge University Press, 1970), p. 178. This volume contains a series of mostly critical responses to Kuhn (Popper, Toulmin, and Watkins), but Feyerabend "defends" Kuhn by saying that science is indeed at least and in fact even more irrational than Kuhn holds, a defense which Kuhn describes as "vaguely obscene" (p. 264) in his "Reflections on my Critics" at the end of the volume.

7. Bernstein offers a similar criticism of Gadamer; cf. *Beyond Objectivism and Relativism*, pp. 150–65. *Phronesis* presupposes that we have a community. But what are we to do if the *polis* is corrupt? Moreover, Gadamer never addresses the question of the exercise of power and domination which corrupts the city.

8. Rorty supplies a pointed example of this thesis in a rereading of the Bellarmine-Galileo case in which he denies that we can charge Bellarmine with acting irrationally. See *Philosophy and the Mirror of Nature* (Princeton: Princeton University Press, 1979), pp. 328–31.

9. "Objectivity, Value Judgment and Theory Choice," *The Essential Tension* (Chicago: University of Chicago Press, 1977), pp. 320–39. See p. 322–33.

10. Bernstein, *Beyond Objectivism and Relativism*, 54–55. Although Bernstein is sceptical of how much we can expect of *phronesis* (see note 7, above), he keeps pressing for more determinate criteria to provide the basis for decision making (155, 157–58). But just at that point I would insist that we must confess the play, for what causes *phronesis* to founder is just the unavailability of criteria. It is only after a free argument has played itself out that we can afterward, with a logic which limps along lamely after the fact, reconstruct what sorts of moves reason made which won the day. And it is only afterward, after the conditions for a new wave of normal science have been forged, that *phronesis* can again have a place—in the skillful application and extension of the new paradigm and in the training of young initiates.

11. ". . . [T]he central episodes in scientific advance—those which make the game worth playing and the play worth studying—are revolutions." Kuhn, "Reflections on My Critics," p. 241.

12. Feyerabend denies that there is such a thing as normal science, that science ever settles down into the totalitarian structure which Kuhn implies. Even during times of apparent agreement within the scientific community, there is a proliferation of competing and incommensurable paradigms. Normalcy and revolution are not successive but contemporaneous components in the ongoing upheaval which is the history of science. See Feyerabend's "Consolations for the Specialist," in *Criticism and the Growth of*

Knowledge, pp. 197ff., esp. pp. 207–14. On "counter-inductivism," see *Against Method,* chaps. 2–3. On the role of Feyerabend, Richard Rorty writes: "This anti-Kantian account of inquiry as coping is what Dewey offered us, and I think it is as good a story about the course of human inquiry as we are going to get. The 'anarchist' twist which Feyerabend gives it seems to me just idiosyncratic devilment, as does the nihilist twist which Derrida gives it. The Deweyan core seems to me perfectly sound." "A Reply to Dreyfus and Taylor," *Review of Metaphysics,* 34 (1980), 39–40.

13. On the other hand, Kuhn writes: "By the same token, no part of the argument here or in my book implies that scientists may choose any theory they like so long as they agree in their choice and therefore enforce it. Most of the puzzles of normal science are directly presented by nature, and all involve nature indirectly. Though different solutions have been received as valid at different times, nature cannot be forced into an arbitrary set of conceptual boxes. On the contrary, the history of proto-science shows that normal science is possible only with very special boxes. . . ." "Reflections on My Critics," p. 263. But some parts of his argument, namely, his views on truth, do raise this question, and it is not clear whether he thinks that paradigms do or do not seize upon something in nature.

14. For a discussion of Heidegger's self-criticism in SG, see my *Mystical Element in Heidegger's Thought,* pp. 89–96. For a general account of the argument of SG as a whole, see *op. cit.,* pp. 47–96.

15. A new translation of Angelus Silesius has recently appeared: *Angelus Silesius: The Cherubinic Wanderer,* trans. Maria Schrady (New York: Paulist, 1986). See p. 54.

16. Hubert Dreyfus, *What Computers Can't Do* (rev. ed.; New York: Harper, 1972, 1979). It would be amusing, were it not frightening, to see the outrage of the technologists at Dreyfus's treatment of their project. The reaction of the computer industry to this book is a good example of the political power any critic of the technological industry runs up against; one understands why Heidegger calls the principle of reason "high and mighty."

17. On the connection between Merleau-Ponty and Derrida on this point, see Rodolphe Gasché, "Deconstruction as Criticism," *Glyph,* 6 (1976), 177–215.

18. E.g., the hermeneutically oriented anthropology of Clifford Geertz, *The Interpretation of Culture* (New York: Basic Books, 1971,) and *Local Knowledge: Further Essays in Interpretive Anthropology* (New York: Basic Books, 1983). For more of the same, see *Interpretive Social Science: A Reader,* ed. Paul Rabinow and William Sullivan (Berkeley and Los Angeles: University of California Press, 1979); *Understanding and Social Inquiry,* ed. Fred Dallymayr and Thomas McCarthy (Notre Dame: University of Notre Dame Press, 1977); and *Social Science as Moral Inquiry,* ed. N. Haan *et al.* (New York: Columbia University Press, 1983). See also the excellent treatment of the social sciences in Bernstein, *Beyond Objectivism and Relativism,* 25ff., 93ff.

19. In the preceding section I used Heidegger's discussion of the principle of reason (SG) as a guide; in this section I use Derrida's "The Principle of Reason: The University in the Eyes of Its Pupils" (cf. chap. 7, n. 11).

20. Derrida, "The Principle of Reason," p. 16.

21. Heidegger, "Only a God Can Save Us," p. 277.

22. I have developed this point in my "Heidegger's Philosophy of Science: The Two Essences of Science," in *Rationality, Relativism, and the Human Sciences,* ed. Joseph Margolis *et al.* (The Hague: Martinus Nijhoff, 1986), pp. 43–60.

23. Derrida, "The Principle of Reason," p. 20.

24. Derrida, "The Principle of Reason," p. 17.

9. TOWARD AN ETHICS OF DISSEMINATION

1. In "Epistemological Crises, Dramatic Narrative, and the Philosophy of Science," in *Paradigms & Revolutions: Applications and Appraisals of Thomas Kuhn's Philosophy*

of Science, ed. Gary Gutting (Notre Dame: University of Notre Dame Press, 1980), pp. 54–74, MacIntyre criticizes the notion of incommensurability as irrational. Bernstein contests the success of MacIntyre's attempt to contain these differences in "Nietzsche or Aristotle? Reflections on Alasdair MacIntyre's *After Virtue*," in *Philosophical Profiles* (Philadelphia: University of Pennsylvania Press, 1986), pp. 115–40; Bernstein also points to Hegel's notion of *Sittlichkeit* as a model MacIntyre should embrace. See MacIntyre's response, "Bernstein's Distorting Mirrors: A Rejoinder," *Soundings*, 67 (1984), 30–41.

2. One may, with Ricoeur, complain of the "heroic" quality of Heidegger's rhetoric in §74. See Paul Ricoeur, "Narrative Time," in *On Narrative*, ed. W. J. T. Mitchell (Chicago: University of Chicago Press, 1980), 184–86. But it remains clear that Heidegger takes authentic action to be a matter of appropriating and extending one's historical tradition, not merely of achieving self-actualization.

3. Heidegger had been a critic of value theory ever since his earliest contact with it as a student of Heinrich Rickert at Freiburg. Rickert was a leading figure in the Baden school of Neo-Kantian value-theory. See David Krell's note in Heidegger, *Nietzsche*, volume 4, *Nihilism*, trans. D. Krell (New York: Harper and Row, 1982), p. 60n.

4. In his *History of Sexuality*, volume 2, *The Use of Pleasure*, trans. Robert Hurley (New York: Pantheon, 1985), Michel Foucault argues that for the Greeks the good life was an attempt to make oneself beautiful, to shine like a work of art; this puts Heidegger's *aletheia* to work in ethics.

5. Heidegger and MacIntyre have very similar views of Nietzsche. Cf. AV 109ff. and Heidegger's *Nietzsche*, B. II (Pfullingen: Neske, 1961), 141–256; Eng. trans., *Nietzsche*, volume 4, *Nihilism*, 96–197. See also GA 9 349/BW 228.

6. For more on Heidegger's ethics, see my *The Mystical Element in Heidegger's Thought*, pp. 254–58.

7. Heidegger, "Only a God Can Save Us," pp. 277–78.

8. Heidegger, *What Is Philosophy?* trans. W. Kluback and J. T. Wilde (bilingual text; Chicago: Regnery, 1967), pp. 52–53. For Heidegger's Parmenides, see ID, "The Principle of Identity"; "*Moira*," VA 231–56/EGT 79–101; EM, chap. 4; WHD/WCT, Part II, lec. 5ff.

9. For some basic information about Parmenides' life and the pertinent texts, see G. S. Kirk and J. E. Raven, *The Presocratic Philosophers* (Cambridge: Cambridge University Press, 1962), pp. 263–65.

10. I have treated Eckhart's reading of the story of Mary and Martha in *The Mystical Element in Heidegger's Thought*, pp. 137–39.

11. Bernstein, "Nietzsche or Aristotle," pp. 136–40.

12. I do like this expression which Rorty takes over from Michael Oakeshott in *Philosophy and the Mirror of Nature*, and I would today rewrite some of my "The Thought of Being and the Conversation of Mankind: The Case of Heidegger and Rorty," *The Review of Metaphysics*, 36 (1983), 661–85. I think this "conversation" is an excellent model for the ethics of dissemination.

13. See Foucault's distinction between "specific" intellectuals and "universal" intellectuals in "Truth and Power," in *Power/Knowledge*, ed. Colin Gordon (New York: Pantheon, 1980), pp. 125–33.

14. I have examined Meister Eckhart's idea of *Gelassenheit* with care in *The Mystical Element in Heidegger's Thought*, pp. 118–27, 173–83.

15. See my "Kant's Ethics in Phenomenological Perspective," in *Kant and Phenomenology*, ed. J. Kockelmans and T. Seebohm (Washington: University Press of America, 1984), pp. 129–46.

10. OPENNESS TO THE MYSTERY

1. See *Meister Eckhart: The Essential Sermons, Treatises, Commentaries and Defense*, trans. and ed. Bernard McGinn, The Classics of Western Spirituality (New York:

Paulist Press, 1981), especially sermon 52, pp. 199–203. For a treatment of these themes in Eckhart, see chapter 3 of my *The Mystical Element in Heidegger's Thought.*

2. The thoroughly Aristotelian notion of a state of mind beyond *phronesis*, having to do with a "divine" element in the soul, seems to me entirely missing from Gadamer (and Bernstein).

3. See *Totality and Infinity*, trans. A. Lingis (Pittsburgh: Duquesne University Press, 1969), esp. sec. 3. For an important critique of Levinas, see Derrida, "Violence and Metaphysics," ED 117ff./WD 79ff. Clearly nothing commits us either to the radical breach which Levinas sets up between individuals or to his sexist, patriarchal attitudes.

4. See Gabriel Marcel, *Homo Viator: Introduction to a Metaphysic of Hope*, trans. E. Craufurd (New York: Harper and Row, 1962), pp. 185ff.

5. See the *First Logical Investigation*, §5. In WHD 51/WCT 16, on the other hand, Heidegger gives preeminent significance to the gesture.

6. Heidegger contests Kant's view of science in *Die Frage nach dem Ding* (Tübingen: Niemeyer, 1962); and *What is a Thing?* trans. W. B. Barton and V. Deutsch (Chicago: Regnery, 1967).

7. See my "The Presence of Others: A Phenomenology of the Human Person," *Proceedings of the American Catholic Philosophical Association*, 53 (1979), 45–58.

8. I am guilty as sin when it comes to using the generic "he," "him," etc., which is a bad move on the part of one who would protest exclusionary gestures, so here I have reformed. One ought not to create the impression that it is "men" who deserve respect rather than humans. For a feminist critique of Kant's analysis of respect, incidentally, see Sarah Kofman, "The Economy of Respect: Kant and Respect for Women," *Social Research*, 49 (1982), 383–404.

9. Kierkegaard argues this in *Philosophical Fragments*. See Louis Mackey's superb discussion of this point in "Slouching Towards Bethlehem: Deconstructive Strategies in Theology," *Anglican Theological Review*, 65 (1983), 255–72.

10. I borrow this expression from Michael Polanyi, *Personal Knowledge: Towards a Post-Critical Philosophy* (Chicago: University of Chicago Press, 1962), pp. 264ff.

11. Johann B. Metz, *Faith in History and Society*, trans. D. Smith (New York: Crossroads, 1980), pp. 109–15; see generally pp. 88–118. Also see Edward Schillebeeckx, *Interim Report on the Books Jesus & Christ* (New York: Crossroads, 1981), pp. 55–63; and Matthew Lamb, *Solidarity with Victims* (New York: Crossroads, 1982).

12. Nietzsche, *The Will to Power*, trans. W. Kaufmann and R. J. Hollingdale (New York: Random House Vintage Books, 1968), no. 1041, p. 536.

13. Ibid., no. 1052, p. 543. See also the enthusiastic and illuminating commentary on this passage in Gilles Deleuze, *Nietzsche's Philosophy*, trans. Hugh Tomlinson (New York: Columbia University Press, 1984), pp. 14–25.

14. Nietzsche, *Beyond Good and Evil*, no. 270, pp. 189–90.

15. Ibid., no. 294, p. 199.

16. Nietzsche, *Will to Power*, no. 990, p. 517.

17. In the neo-pragmatic strategy of Richard Rorty, there is no deep question raised by suffering. The only thing worth bothering about is looking around for ways to minimize it. See "Method, Social Science and Social Hope" in *Consequences of Pragmatism*, 191–210.

18. See my "Three Transgressions: Nietzsche, Heidegger, Derrida," *Research in Phenomenology*, 15 (1985), 61–78.

19. "Hermeneutics as the Recovery of Man," *Man and World*, 15 (1982), 343–67.

20. Heidegger, too, seems prepared to admit this retrieval of the old word *persona*. "*Persona* means the actor's mask through which his dramatic tale is sounded. Since man is the percipient who perceives what is, we can think of him as the *persona*, the mask, of Being" (WHD 28/WCT 62). It is the voice of Being which sounds through the mask of the speaker, according to Heidegger.

21. *Der Feldweg* (3d ed; Frankfurt: Klostermann, 1962), p. 7. Eng. trans., "The Pathway," trans. T. F. O'Meara and T. Sheehan, *Listening*, 8 (1973), p. 39. The year before *Der Feldweg* was composed, Heidegger quoted this sentence from Nietzsche's *Nachlass*, written when Nietzsche was nineteen years old: "Thus man grows out of everything that once embraced him; he has no need to break the shackles—they fall away unforeseen, when a god bids them; and where is the ring that in the end still encircles him? Is it the world? Is it God?" (WHD 75/WCT 80).

Index

Actuality, 20, 34; actual experience, 44–45; and becoming, 33; and falling, 62; of intentional experience, 39

Adorno, Theodor, 233

Aesthetics: aesthetic object, 109; aesthetic repetition, 27, 29

Anaximander, 4, 159–61, 164–65, 180, 263, 283

Aquinas, Thomas: on *esse* and *ens*, 177, 179

Aristotle, 6, 12, 16, 18, 169, 200, 211, 216, 253, 255, 260, 261, 291; his doctrine of *kinesis*, 1, 3, 13, 17, 34, 41, 198–99; his ethics, 244, 246; on practical knowledge, 109; on time, 198–99; *Metaphysics*, 2, 244; *Nicomachean Ethics*, 2, 244, 247

Art: Heidegger on, 96; work of art, 96, 113

Assertion: apophantic, 73–74; and truth, 73–75

Augustine, 200, 267, 272, 288; on love, 212

Austin, J. L., 133, 167

Bacon, Francis, 215

Becker, Oskar, 56

Becoming: and actuality, 33; and Being, 12–13, 16; Hegel on, 19, 34, 111; hermeneutics as philosophy of, 37; and repetition, 59

Being: and being, 173–77, 179–80; Being-in-the-World, 73, 74, 88; Being-toward-Death, 76–77, 199; and becoming, 12–13, 16; of Dasein, 60–92, 96, 106–107, 175, 199; meaning of, 153–54, 158, 171–76, 180, 182, 237–38; as presence, 4–5, 116; and thought, 106; truth of, 153–54, 171–79, 180, 181–82, 203, 236–38, 255, 257

Bernstein, Richard: on science, 216, 218, 253–54; *Beyond Objectivism and Relativism*, 210, 215

Bultmann, Rudolf, 109

Carroll, Lewis, 148

Cartesianism, 95, 244, 255, 261; and ego, 72, 81, 245, 275; and egological metaphysics, 289; and existence of the world, 247; and science, 55; and subject, 98, 223; Husserl's, 55–57, 58–59

Christianity, 13, 14, 15, 25, 35, 242, 245, 265–66

Climacus, Johannes. *See* Kierkegaard

Consciousness, 278; Derrida on, 129–30; its givenness to itself, 27, 133–34, 289; epistemological, 72; fore-structures of, 55; historical 162; intentionality of, 52, 54–57; internal time consciousness, 4, 37, 46, 51, 52, 131, 133–36, 138, 143, 144; and language, 130, 135; object of, 43–44; scientific, 55; and stream of experiences, 37; transcendental,

54, 135; and unity of meaning, 41

Constantinus, Constantin. *See* Kierkegaard

cummings, e. e., 148

Dasein: and anticipation, 76, 77, 84; authenticity of, 77, 89, 90, 199; Being of, 60–92, 96, 106–107, 175, 199; and care, 53–54, 62, 76–77; and concern, 74; and death, 87, 88, 89; existence as its essence, 66; facticity of, 87; fallenness of, 62–63, 73, 77, 84, 86; and heritage, 87, 90; historicity of, 82, 86–89; its possibility to be, 60, 78; resoluteness of, 77, 84, 86, 87; temporality of, 62, 65, 80, 82, 83–84, 86, 175; thrownness of, 87; and understanding, 52, 96, 98, 109–10

Death, 201; Being-toward-Death, 76–77, 199; and Dasein, 87, 88, 89

Deleuze, Gilles, 116

Derrida, Jacques, 1, 3, 7, 17, 18, 35, 36, 39, 41, 49, 57, 85, 86, 113, 222, 241, 243, 254, 255, 263, 264, 269; on *arché*-writing, 138, 169; on circularity, 53, 68; on communication, 132–33; on consciousness, 129–30; on constitution, 130–31, 136; on deconstruction, 65, 95, 97–98, 119, 121, 124, 131, 147, 151–52, 154, 167, 171, 179, 187, 191, 192, 193, 196–98, 206, 213; on *différance*, 123, 129, 130, 131, 138, 139, 141, 142, 144–45, 146, 151, 153, 155, 167, 179, 186, 187, 273; on dissemination, 148, 151–52, 154, 221; on eschatology, 165–67; on geometrical ideality, 124–25; his grammatology, 122–23, 148–49, 191, 193; and GREPH, 193–94; and Heidegger, 65, 83, 104, 107, 116–19, 153–59, 166–72, 177–78, 180, 182, 184–91, 195–96, 201–202, 209; and Husserl, 120–48, 191–92; on internal time consciousness, 135–36, 138; his interpretations of interpretation, 95, 97, 116, 118; on language, 148–49; on logo-centrism, 148, 166; and Marxism, 231; and Nietzsche, 155–57, 159; and onto-hermeneutics, 153–55; on repetition, 121–23, 127, 130, 135–36, 139, 216; on semanticism, 148–51; on semantics, 148–49; on sign, 124, 135–36, 227, 233; on solicitation, 146, 211, 290; on speech, 136–37, 193; on truth, 117–18, 122, 151–52, 192; on writing, 136–37, 193; *La Dissemination*, 139, 147–48; *The Ends of Man*, 193; "The Origins of Geometry," 123–24; *Positions*, 192; *Spurs: Nietzsche's Styles*, 153, 178, 186

Descartes, René, 98; cogito, 72, 245; on ego, 72, 81; and epistemological subject, 263; his ontology, 54, 59; rationalism of, 210; and science, 55. *See also* Cartesianism

315